The Human Tradition in the Atlantic World, 1500–1850

The Human Tradition around the World
Series Editors: William H. Beezley and Colin M. MacLachlan

The Human Tradition in Colonial Latin America
Edited by Kenneth J. Andrien

The Human Tradition in Modern Brazil
Edited by Peter M. Beattie

The Human Tradition in Latin America
Edited by William H. Beezley and Judith Ewell

The Human Tradition in Modern Latin America
Edited by William H. Beezley and Judith Ewell

The Human Tradition in Modern Europe, 1750 to the Present
Edited by Cora Granata and Cheryl A. Koos

The Human Tradition in Premodern China
Edited by Kenneth J. Hammond

The Human Tradition in Modern China
Edited by Kenneth J. Hammond and Kristin Stapleton

The Human Tradition in Modern Russia
Edited by William B. Husband

The Human Tradition in Modern Britain
Edited by Caroline Litzenberger and Eileen Groth Lyon

The Human Tradition in the Black Atlantic, 1500–2000
Edited by Beatriz G. Mamigonian and Karen Racine

The Human Tradition in Mexico
Edited by Jeffrey M. Pilcher

The Human Tradition in Modern France
Edited by K. Steven Vincent and Alison Klairmont-Lingo

The Human Tradition in Modern Japan
By Anne Walthall

The Human Tradition in Imperial Russia
Edited by Christine D. Worobec

The Human Tradition in the Atlantic World, 1500–1850

Edited by
Karen Racine
and
Beatriz G. Mamigonian

ROWMAN & LITTLEFIELD PUBLISHERS, INC.
Lanham • Boulder • New York • Toronto • Plymouth, UK

Published by Rowman & Littlefield Publishers, Inc.
A wholly owned subsidiary of The Rowman & Littlefield Publishing Group, Inc.
4501 Forbes Boulevard, Suite 200, Lanham, Maryland 20706
http://www.rowmanlittlefield.com

Estover Road, Plymouth PL6 7PY, United Kingdom

British Library Cataloguing in Publication Information Available

Library of Congress Cataloging-in-Publication Data
The human tradition in the Atlantic world, 1500–1850 / edited by Karen Racine and
Beatriz G. Mamigonian.
   p. cm. — (The human tradition around the world)
   Includes bibliographical references and index.
   ISBN 978-1-4422-0697-7 (cloth : alk. paper) — ISBN 978-1-4422-0698-4 (pbk. : alk.
paper) — ISBN 978-1-4422-0699-1 (electronic)
   1. History, Modern. 2. Atlantic Ocean Region—Biography. 3. Atlantic Ocean
Region—History. I. Racine, Karen, 1967– II. Mamigonian, Beatriz G. (Beatriz Gallotti),
1969–
   D210.H96 2010
   909'.09821—dc22
                                                                                  2010020805

∞ ™ The paper used in this publication meets the minimum requirements of
American National Standard for Information Sciences—Permanence of Paper
for Printed Library Materials, ANSI/NISO Z39.48-1992.

Printed in the United States of America

Contents

INTRODUCTION

The Human Tradition in the Atlantic World

Karen Racine and Beatriz G. Mamigonian

Roll on, thou deep and dark blue Ocean—roll!
Ten thousand fleets sweep over thee in vain;
Man marks the earth with ruin—his control
Stops with the shore.

—George Gordon, Lord Byron, *Childe' Harolde's Pilgrimage*

Like all other books in the Human Tradition series, this collection of short biographies is intended to put a human face on sweeping historical processes. Whereas today one can jet across the ocean in a matter of hours and can even communicate instantly with unseen and distant people, it is sometimes easy to forget that during the centuries covered here, a journey between continents could take up to three months. Leaving home often meant never seeing or hearing from loved ones again. The Atlantic Ocean thus has meant many things to many people. For some brave or desperate souls, it offered an escape, a source of adventure, and romance. For countless others, it provided a steady source of income and a way of life. For those who voluntarily undertook the voyage, crossing the Atlantic meant hope of a better, happier life; for the millions of less fortunate others who relocated because they had been enslaved, tricked, or banished, the Atlantic was a sea of sorrow and loss. Oceans are complicated spaces—they are not merely empty expanses of water and waves; rather, they are busy zones temporarily inhabited by people coming and going, goods being transported for exchange, and birds, fish, humans, and currents all carrying seeds and germs from one place to another. By emphasizing movement and circulation in its choice of subjects, this volume aims to present the reader with a broad cross section of people whose lives and livelihoods took them across the Atlantic and brought disparate cultures into contact.

Because Atlantic world history encompasses the experiences of Africans, Native Americans, and Europeans, a vigorous debate rages over whether there is enough of a unitary character to render it a meaningful unit for study. For example, is it fair to conceive of the experiences of slave traders and the enslaved as being shared or somehow equivalent? How should we understand the role of religion in the Atlantic world, a region that is overwhelmingly Christian but also with deep sectarian divides and a region that also encompasses both Muslim North Africa and the syncretic religions of Latin America? In a geographic sense, where does the Atlantic world begin and end? In a temporal sense, when does the history of the Atlantic world begin, and when does it cease to have meaning? What sets the essence of the Atlantic world apart from that of the Mediterranean world or the Pacific world or the Indian Ocean? These are not easy questions to answer, and we hope that the biographies contained in this collection will stimulate much thought and reflection as readers look for both patterns and dissimilarities among these Atlantic lives.

As editors, we sought life stories that represented movement across or around the Atlantic Ocean. We intentionally excluded people who merely resided in one region of the Atlantic because we wanted to explore transatlantic connections on a personal level. Each of the lives included here, therefore, tells the tale of a person whose experience took him or her far beyond a local community of origin to a new and unfamiliar place. We wanted to use the lives presented in this volume to emphasize the tremendous creativity and dynamism that resulted from contact between people of different cultures, classes, races, ideas, and systems. At its most fundamental level, the syncretic nature of Atlantic world societies was created and re-created on a daily basis by myriad choices made by hundreds of thousands of individuals.

The collection begins in the early modern period, which was an era dominated by the initial European contact with the New World and a time when expansion, exploration, cross-cultural encounters, colonization, and evangelization were central issues of the day. It moves through the sixteenth and seventeenth centuries when trade networks began to form, African slavery flourished, and European empires jockeyed for power and prestige. Several stories are set in the eighteenth century, sometimes called the Enlightenment or the Age of Revolution, which was a heady and dramatic time during which new scientific methods emerged, ideas of freedom and liberty took hold, and the first rumblings of anticolonial sentiment made themselves felt. The volume ends in 1850 when the advent of steam travel and industrialization dramatically altered the nature and speed of life throughout the Atlantic world, the countries of the American hemisphere had nearly all become independent, and slavery was abolished everywhere except Brazil, the United States, and the Spanish Caribbean islands.

The biographies are arranged in a general chronological order. A few themes, however, become apparent. First, accurate information was one of the most precious commodities in the Atlantic world and, at least for the first three centuries after 1500, a vast amount of information circulated orally. The lack of general knowledge about conditions in distant places both hindered and helped Atlantic people in the pursuit of their own particular goals. For example, both William Lamport and Juan Antonio Olavarrieta fell afoul of the Mexican Inquisition's obsessive desire to control the flow of information and its effects on behavior and tried to resist its reach. The Portuguese Crown hoped scientist João da Silva Feijó would find valuable minerals or resources in their overseas territories, which they could exploit for profit. Museum curator William Bullock made a fortune by tapping into the British public's fascination with Aztec relics and artifacts. James MacQueen sought out information about distant regions of the British Empire (and its rivals) in order to direct investors and to influence government policy. In the past, just as it does in the present, current and accurate knowledge brought power.

Second, residents of Atlantic societies inhabited a mental world that transcended languages, cultures, and even geographic space. Families often had members who resided in at least two of the four Atlantic continents and whose livelihoods depended on commercial contact among the various regions or the industries that facilitated that trade. The most obvious example in this collection would be the biography of the Jewish translator Samuel Cohen, who worked for the Dutch West India Company in the Caribbean, Brazil, and Angola; Cohen moved between languages, cultures, and public expectations of private religious behavior. As a multilingual person from a minority faith, he was able to make one group comprehensible to another. Similarly, both Hendrick and William Johnson had a very clear understanding of the rules of engagement and were able to embrace elements of the other's culture that advanced his own goals or suited his own personal temperament. If some individuals flourished in a dynamic Atlantic environment where different languages and cultures encountered each other on a more immediate and personal level than would have been typical of their more sedentary relatives, others buckled under the strain. The Billington family, for example, squabbled with their neighbors and failed to fulfill their dream of a better life in the New World, and American-born Elizabeth Patterson Bonaparte was not able to turn herself into European royalty no matter how hard she tried.

Third, despite the great distances, a lag in the transmission of news and information, and the concerted efforts of royal administrators who wished to prevent the unauthorized circulation of foreign people, goods, and ideas in their realms, local people nevertheless remained surprisingly aware of what was happening elsewhere and were quick to act on their own behalf. Sailors, soldiers, settlers, and smugglers brought official printed gazettes and private letters from place to place and circulated rumors while on their travels. Sometimes information was woefully out of date or disastrously wrong, and deliberate efforts at spreading misinformation were not uncommon, yet somehow the facts always evaded efforts to stop them at the border. For example, news of the increasingly revolutionary events in France reached colonial Saint-Domingue (today Haiti) and encouraged the freed men of color, such as Julien Raimond, to assert their constitutional rights almost as soon as he and other newly minted citizens learned what they were. Similarly, scientists throughout the Atlantic world paid close attention to their foreign colleagues' discoveries and research that was diffused through printed publication or circulated in manuscript form. German-born governor of New York Jacob Leisler weighed the information coming in from a variety of quarters before daring to break away and effect his own reforms in local governance.

The Human Tradition in the Atlantic World aims to introduce students and general readers to the lived experiences of real people in the past—their loves, their losses, their joys, their suffering. Its companion volume, *The Human Tradition in the Black Atlantic*, contains similar stories drawn from Africa and the African diaspora throughout the Atlantic world. In both cases, the richness and complexity of the emerging Atlantic societies is revealed through the conscious choices and vagaries of fortune met by flawed human beings and their families. The encounter of many different races, classes, languages, cultures, and religions in unfamiliar environments provided a crucible in which to forge something that comprised elements of all its constituent parts but that was at the same time something entirely new.

CHAPTER ONE

Catarina Álvares Paraguaçu (1510s–1582)

Indian Visionary in Brazil and France

Joan Meznar

Not everyone suffered heartbreak and loneliness after crossing the Atlantic. Some marriages overcame tremendous obstacles of language, culture, and religion to become something both real and symbolic. Despite many obvious instances of rape and physical abuse, some unions between European men and indigenous women were genuine and eventually became romanticized as the founding families of hybrid nations in the New World. In one of these remarkable stories, historian Joan Meznar recounts the life of the Brazilian Indian woman Paraguaçu, who married Portuguese adventurer Diogo Álvares in France in 1528. Their life together reveals just how much movement there was around the Atlantic world right from the earliest decades of contact and also reminds us that cultural transmission flowed both ways. Adopting a new persona as Catarina Álvares Paraguaçu, this remarkable woman embraced her husband's Christian religion but was able to domesticate it and blend European ideals with Brazilian possibilities. If the Virgin Mary chose to appear to a poor Mexican Indian named Juan Diego in 1531, she also revealed herself in a vision to the Brazilian Indian Paraguaçu and thereby sanctified the woman's mixed-race family. Brazil likes to call itself the home of racial democracy, and so it should be no surprise that the improbable marriage of Diogo and Paraguaçu remains a popular national romance.

Europeans came slowly to Brazil in the sixteenth century. Fascinated by the people they encountered, they were nonetheless sorely disappointed not

1

to find gold, silver, or spices. For fifty years, a few intrepid tradesmen from Portugal and France profited from shipping brazilwood across the Atlantic. The most successful of these men immersed themselves in their new environ-ment, living with Indian women and fathering many children. Among the Portuguese who thrived in the exotic new land, Diogo Álvares stands out as the most important liaison between Indians and Europeans. The story of his wife Paraguaçu, the daughter of a local Tupinambá chief, illustrates the possibility of significant cultural fusion in Atlantic world cultures. Paraguaçu accompanied her beloved Diogo to Europe, where she was baptized, and they were formally married. On returning home to Brazil, she commissioned the building of the first chapel to honor the Virgin Mary. Her children, sharing both Portuguese and Indian blood, established the most illustrious families of seventeenth-century Bahia. Viewed as Brazil's "founding mother," Catarina Álvares Paraguaçu has come to symbolize the success of racial and cultural blending in Portuguese America. Yet, as her story reveals, that same ideal-ized fusion of very different cultural traditions inevitably favored European norms. Although Paraguaçu embraced the foreign arrivals—first Diogo and then his Christian faith—she has never been portrayed as a traitor to her people. In this regard, she is the opposite of Malinche, the Indian lover of conquistador Hernán Cortés in Mexico, who has become synonymous with cultural and racial betrayal. In contrast, the Brazilian Paraguaçu has been celebrated for her contributions toward a New World society that claims to be built on racial harmony, religious piety, and economic self-improvement.

The world of Paraguaçu's ancestors began a radical transformation in 1500 when the fleet of Portuguese explorer Pedro Álvares Cabral veered off course and landed on the coast of Bahia while making a journey to India. During the second half of the fifteenth century, Portuguese sailors had diligently pursued a sea route to India. As they braved uncharted waters, they dreamed of returning to Portugal in ships loaded with spices, making a sizable profit both for themselves and for their king. The voyages of exploration were not for the faint of heart; they also were not for women. Yet at least one woman always traveled on these ships packed with rugged (and often filthy) men: the Holy Mother. For many decades, sailors had beseeched the Virgin Mary for protection against the known and unknown dangers of the sea. Images of sea monsters, tales of terrible storms, the fear of being stranded at the end of the world for lack of wind and current, the danger of losing one's bearings—all these potential calamities were given over to the Virgin, who was expected to bring her children safely home. Seamen took with them images of Mary, good-luck amulets, as well as rosaries with well-worn beads that they used not only in daily devotion but also to count off prayers when danger loomed.

Priests aboard the caravels held special Saturday services, setting apart with songs and celebration of the mass the day dedicated to the Mother of God.

Faith alone did not strengthen the sailors' resolve; the prospect of great wealth spurred them on as well. The lure of India and its access to the coveted spices of the East caused many young men to face the terrors of the unknown willingly. It was this quest for riches that accidentally brought the first Portuguese caravels to the shores of Brazil in 1500. Well aware that he had stumbled on a new land, Pedro Álvares Cabral instructed his scribe to prepare a report for King Manuel that was taken to Portugal while the rest of the fleet continued its journey to India. In this letter, the first recorded description of what eventually became the country of Brazil (Cabral called it the land of the Holy Cross), Pero Vaz de Caminha praised the land's lushness and tried to convey the lifestyle of its inhabitants. He was struck by their "state of innocence." Both women and men went about their business unhampered by clothing, blissfully unaware that the original sin of Adam and Eve should make them ashamed of their nakedness. The beauty of nude Indian women, in particular, enthralled him. In an often-quoted passage from Vaz de Caminha's letter, he described one of the women he saw: "indeed she was so well built and so well curved, and her privy part (what a one she had!) was so gracious that many women of our country, on seeing such charms, would be ashamed that theirs were not like hers." What clothes the so-called Indians did wear were decorative and very light: headdresses made from colorful feathers, body paint, earrings, and lip plugs. In the hot and humid tropics, just south of the equator, they frequently enjoyed refreshing plunges into rivers and streams. After weeks aboard ship without bathing, the Portuguese marveled at the compulsion toward cleanliness exhibited by these unusual people. The land itself also fascinated them, its long white sandy beaches quickly giving way to forests densely packed with large hardwood trees. Although the Indians seemed not to have domesticated animals, the forests in which they lived housed an extraordinary variety of wildlife, including huge tapirs, vividly plumed birds, and countless reptiles and insects.

At the same time, the Indians' innocence and beauty, not unlike the pristine splendor of their land, masked extreme danger. The European explorers were appalled when they learned that the indigenous people of coastal Brazil practiced cannibalism. In 1501, Amerigo Vespucci described a scene in which Portuguese seamen witnessed the death of one of their own at the hands of "savage cannibals." Even more shockingly, Indian women played a central role in capturing and killing the European man. When the Portuguese came ashore, the Indians brought their women to greet them. A strong and handsome sailor was chosen to go out to meet the women. As Vespucci recounted, they "surrounded him, handling and examining him with evident curiosity and wonder. Presently there came down another woman from the hill, having a stake in her hand, with which she got behind him, and dealt him a blow that brought him to the ground." As the women carried him away from the shore, Indian men fired arrows at the Portuguese boats. The sailors' attempts to frighten the Indians by firing their guns did not prevent their erstwhile companion being dragged up a hill, cut to pieces, broiled over a fire, and devoured. The Portuguese looked on, aghast, from afar. Clearly, there was much about this new place that they did not understand and that would require European care to domesticate and civilize.

Unlike the large urban-based groups of Mesoamerica and western South America, the people of Brazil lived in small communities, moving frequently in search of prey or tracking human enemies. In the early part of the sixteenth century, while thousands of Spaniards flocked to Mexico and Peru to exploit the mines and Indian labor there, few Portuguese bothered to settle in Brazil, where there were no obvious and quick paths to wealth. Some did come in search of brazilwood, the source of a reddish purple dye used to add color to tapestries and cloth that was in high demand in Renaissance Europe. These early traders depended on Indian knowledge and goodwill not only to survive but also to help them fell the large trees and drag them to locations where ships periodically docked to load and transport the logs to Europe. For this reason, they tried to forge alliances with local groups that they cemented through the children they sired with Indian women.

Diogo Álvares was one of the adventurers attracted to Brazil. He was probably born sometime around 1491 in the Portuguese town of Viana do Castelo in the densely populated Minho region. He may have been a younger son of a minor Portuguese nobleman or an outlaw banished to the New World, or he may have been one of those men who simply sought adventure. When the ship in which he was traveling wrecked and he washed up on a Brazilian beach, he and his friends found themselves staring at an even more terrifying danger. Naked Indians attacked, their bodies covered with odd tattoos and war paint, and managed to hit several of the Portuguese with frighteningly sharp arrows. Diogo escaped and, from his precarious hiding place, watched as the Indians prepared, cooked, and ate his friends. Hoping to convince the Indians to spare his own life, he tried to make himself useful by salvaging any remaining items from the wrecked vessel. He was fortunate to find muskets and even some dry gunpowder kegs. The Indians were as taken aback by Diogo's demonstration of musket fire as he had been by their cannibalism. For reasons that remain unclear, they decided to spare his life.

Diogo joined his Indian captors in raids against their enemies and used European firearms to lead them from victory to victory. He earned their respect as a warrior and was given the tribal name "Caramuru," after the whitish, fleshy fish that resembles a moray eel. Once accepted as a valued member of the community, local chiefs began to offer him their daughters. Caramuru gladly accepted his new position, and his family grew. Over time, he convinced his new allies to help him by cutting down brazilwood trees and preparing them for shipment back to Europe. By all accounts, Caramuru developed extraordinarily good relations with the inhabitants of Brazil, especially with the Tupinambá. His local prestige was such that he was often able to keep the Indians from harming other Europeans whose ships ran aground or sank in the area.

At some point between 1526 and 1527, Diogo Álvares Carumuru decided to return to Europe. Some accounts claim that when his besotted consort Paraguaçu learned he had departed, she swam out after the ship until he took pity and brought her aboard. Caramuru's decision to take an American Indian to Europe was not unusual. Amerigo Vespucci's 1501 expedition hauled three Indians back to Lisbon to display at the Portuguese Court. Four years later, Paulmier de Gonneville took a young Brazilian boy to France, where he was raised as a Christian and eventually married the explorer's daughter. Another European-raised Indian returned to Brazil in the mid-1550s to serve as interpreter and intermediary for French Admiral Villegaignon's attempt to establish a permanent colony at Guanabara Bay. Surely the most dramatic presence of Brazilian Indians in Europe was the group who toured France in 1550. That year, an elaborate performance was staged in the city of Rouen to celebrate the visit of King Henry II and his wife Catherine de' Medici and also to encourage French investors to become more active in the Brazil trade. At least fifty Brazilian Indians, along with several hundred nude Frenchmen posing as Indians, recreated a Tupi village on the banks of the Seine and reenacted a battle representing warring Indian groups.

French monarchs were intensely interested in Brazil for more than just economic and anthropological reasons. By the time Caramuru and Paraguaçu arrived on the Continent sometime in 1527, Europe was becoming engulfed in the violence associated with the Protestant Reformation. In fact, one of the greatest leaders of the Protestant Reformation, John Calvin, was a Frenchman. An edict in 1535 banned all heretics from France, and by the 1540s plans to transplant French Calvinists to Brazil started to emerge. The purification of the faith was a matter of intense public discussion. In order to solidify political ties between France and the papacy, in 1533 the future King Henry II married Catherine de' Medici, the niece of a former pope. Catherine was devoted to the defense of the Catholic religion. Thus, the serendipitous arrival of Paraguaçu in France as Christian sects struggled for supremacy there provided the opportunity for an elaborate demonstration of Catholic triumphalism wedded to royal power.

In France, there was no shortage of priests eager to baptize a Brazilian princess. If Indians were becoming Christians in Catholic France, surely this indicated God's favor toward them in their struggle against the Protestants. It also might bolster French claims to Brazilian territory. Paraguaçu was baptized on July 30, 1528, in Saint-Mâlo, France, the hometown of explorer Jacques Cartier. In fact, Cartier's wife Catherine de Granches was her baptismal sponsor. Nevertheless, the legend has persisted that Queen Catherine de' Medici was Paraguaçu's godmother. The story, as romantic as it was politically useful, must be apocryphal because Catherine was only nine years old at the time. When Paraguaçu formally married Diogo shortly after her baptism (in an elaborate wedding ceremony with no less than a bishop presiding), she became Catarina Álvares Paraguaçu. French nobles showered the exotic bride with expensive gowns and sparkling jewels. Paraguaçu had certainly come a long way from the simplicity of Indian maidens who dressed in nothing more substantial than fruit dyes. In the centuries that followed, this improbable couple came to symbolize for Brazilians the union of Europe and America, bound together in love and in faith and solemnized in the Catholic Church.

Diogo had returned to Europe to see his friends and family in Portugal. After a sojourn in France, he requested permission to travel across the Iberian Peninsula. Political tensions between Spain and France, however, prevented the newlyweds from making the journey across the Pyrenees, so they returned to Brazil. As they prepared for their transatlantic voyage, Diogo arranged to ship back to Bahia two vessels filled with European goods to barter with the Indians who he hoped would continue to help him fell brazilwood trees. This seed investment brought rich dividends; in the years that followed, the Álvares family fortune grew much larger as the couple amassed important landholdings and slaves. Certainly, Paraguaçu, now Dona Catarina Álvares, was as homesick for Bahia as Diogo had been for Viana do Castelo. But the time she spent in Europe had changed her; she left as a young Indian girl and returned as a respectable married woman and devout Christian.

It was not only the Portuguese, however, who had their eye on the profits to be made from the brazilwood trade. The French king, in particular, was said to have stated that he doubted that Adam, in his last will and testament, had left the world only to the Iberians. As early as 1504, several years before Diogo Álvares sailed from Europe, French ships had begun to cruise the remote coast of Brazil, and soon Frenchmen were competing with the Portuguese for the valuable wood. When he became involved in the trade, Caramuru showed himself to be a savvy businessman as well as a warrior. He supplied both the French and the Portuguese with the wood his Indian allies provided. This French competition troubled the Portuguese kings, who insisted that Brazil was theirs alone. Yet because of their small numbers, the Portuguese in Brazil found it impossible to protect the territory and its trees from foreign interlopers while at the same time defending themselves from local Indian attacks. Better to collaborate with the French, Diogo decided, than to risk Indians taking advantage of European rivalries to rise up and slaughter them all. Over the course of the years, he became a comfortable part of Tupinambá society. And here the story might have ended, with Caramuru nicely assimilated into Indian society, had the king of Portugal not decided at long last to take steps to assert his claim to the Brazilian territories.

Although the Portuguese Crown remained committed to the India trade in the first half of the sixteenth century, tales spun in Europe of the wealth and splendor of Mexico, bolstered by the phenomenal treasure that Cortés shipped back to Spain, whetted the appetite of other Europeans for New World gold. When the Peruvian Inca Atahualpa's ransom arrived in Europe in the early 1530s, many Europeans became convinced that there must be gold in Brazil as well. Other considerations spurred the Portuguese decision to establish a permanent colony in Brazil. Foreign poachers on the brazilwood trade, they feared, might lead to French settlement on the Atlantic coast of South America, which, in turn, could serve as a base for pirate attacks on vessels returning to Portugal from India. A weak Portuguese presence in Brazil might damage their profitable India trade. Furthermore, some French sailors brought with them the dangerous ideas of the new Lutheran heresy. The Catholic monarchs of Portugal, actively engaged in North African crusades against the Moors as well as inquisitorial efforts to rid their kingdom of Jews, were intent on keeping heretics and infidels out of their domains.

In the early 1530s, in order to ensure Portuguese and Catholic control over Brazil, King João III divided that territory into fourteen grants that he extended to members of the Portuguese elite on the condition that they settle and protect their territory from interlopers. This new arrangement, known as the system of donatary captaincies, had the potential to change relations between Europeans and Indians drastically. In order to sustain their families, the Portuguese settlers would need laborers, and they found it most natural to follow the Spaniards' lead by enlisting the Indians to work for them. Not surprisingly, Indians resisted. For example, for a few years after his arrival in Bahia in 1535, the donatary captain was able to recruit Tupinambá labor to clear the land and help the settlers build sugar mills. Within a short time, however, they rebelled and destroyed both the economic structures and the Europeans' food gardens. The panicked settlers fled Bahia in 1545. Two years later, Diogo Álvares brokered an agreement between the Tupinambá and the donatary captain that permitted the settlers to return. When their ship capsized, however, the unfortunate souls were rounded up, slaughtered, and eaten by the Indians.

Not long after their return, another European ship sank off the coast of Bahia. Learning that a group of Spaniards on their way to Mar del Plata had washed ashore, Diogo organized a rescue expedition to guard them from the elements and also protect them from Indian attacks. He and his Indian wife arranged housing and food for the frightened Europeans, many of them wealthy nobles. Over the years, Diogo had extended Christian aid and hospitality to a number of Portuguese, French, and Spaniards unwillingly stranded in the area. He surely remembered his own experience with shipwreck and the anxious hours in which he feared he would be devoured by hostile Indians. Although he had adopted many native ways, Diogo never relinquished his primary allegiance to Europe. Now Paraguaçu joined in her husband's efforts to rescue the castaways. Following the arrival of this particular group of Europeans in their village, Paraguaçu had a strange dream: a woman came to her, claiming to have been seized by the Indians, begging to be saved. On awakening, Paraguaçu described her vision to her husband, who organized a search party but found nothing. All who had been aboard the shipwrecked vessel were accounted for. Still, the woman would not let Paraguaçu rest. She kept coming to the Christianized Indian in her dreams, pleading for help. After three nights, Diogo organized a search of the Indian homes, where he found a carved image of the Virgin Mary tossed in a dark corner. Paraguaçu immediately recognized the woman from her dreams.

Catarina Álvares Paraguaçu took the Holy Mother's plea for shelter literally. She and her husband quickly erected a temporary building that was later followed by a more carefully constructed chapel to serve as the Virgin's permanent home. Because the wooded statue represented Our Lady of Grace, Diogo and Catarina believed that they had been granted a special grace from God who had chosen them to provide permanent housing for the Virgin. The Spaniards had been taking the image to Buenos Aires in the expectation that Our Lady of Grace would provide protection and patronage for them in their new life. The Virgin, however, seemed to have other plans. Apparently, she preferred to make her permanent home among the Portuguese rather than among the Spaniards, thereby seeming to bestow her approval on their presence in Brazil. More than that, however, the Virgin Mary sought succor not from the best families but rather from an Indian woman. Furthermore, she elected to become part of a mixed community that included Indians, Europeans, and their American offspring. By appearing in a vision to Catarina Álvares Paraguaçu, a new convert, Mary appeared to be granting a special grace to those indigenous people of Brazil who embraced the Roman Catholic faith.

At the same time, Paraguaçu's dream revealed that Mary wished to be housed in an appropriate dwelling. Paraguaçu did not believe that the Holy Virgin had been comfortable tossed in the dark corner of an Indian hut. She required a consecrated chapel, built in European fashion. She should be clothed and adorned in the finest garb Europe had to offer. As prosperous members of their community, Diogo and Catarina also purchased expensive jewels from Europe to adorn her image. The chapel quickly attracted visitors, some merely curious to see this mother and child who visited people in their dreams; others, convinced of her miraculous powers, sought her intercession with God on their behalf. This Virgin of Grace, as interpreted by Paraguaçu, did not symbolize approval of complete cultural miscegenation. Although her favor was granted equally to Indians and Europeans, she remained staunchly European. Our Lady of Grace could not be expected to "go native."

Not long after Mary arrived in Bahia, the Portuguese king decided that the failed donatary captaincies must be replaced with a more centralized government. French incursions into the brazilwood trade had been bad enough. Now, however, increased Spanish presence in the region indicated that Castile might seriously attempt to lay claim to the area despite the boundaries set out in the Treaty of Tordesillas. Furthermore, following the amazing silver strikes in Potosí in 1545, the Portuguese hoped that Brazil might also harbor substantial mineral wealth. In 1549, King João III of Portugal sent the first governor general to Brazil. Six Jesuit fathers sailed with him from Lisbon and were charged with converting the Indians to Christianity. Diogo and Catarina Álvares met the fleet and were instrumental in helping the new government officials and priests become established. They selected a site for the new capital to be located not far from the Álvares home on the Bay of All Saints and named after the Holy Savior: São Salvador da Bahia de Todos os Santos.

Diogo and Catarina threw their support behind the royal government. Diogo's authority among both Europeans and Indians made him an essential ally for any successful government in the region. His wife Catarina also served as a bridge between the New World and the Old. Their children symbolized the hope for a new beginning, with Europeans and Indians forging irrevocable bonds through their common children. Husband and wife had experienced life on both sides of the Atlantic but, in the end, chose the New World over the Old. In Brazil, however, they established a lifestyle that blended elements of both cultures, even though European norms predominated. Their story has been used to show that Brazilian Indians were not conquered and converted to Christianity by force as they had been in Spanish America; Paraguaçu, after all, had actively pursued the new faith of her own accord and, once a Christian, was rewarded with special grace by the Mother of God herself. Yet Paraguaçu and Caramuru were far from typical inhabitants of sixteenth-century Brazil. Few others could experience life in Europe and in America, let alone choose between them. Their children were not typical, either. Several of their daughters, for example, after being baptized by the most illustrious priests available, married Portuguese noblemen who had decided to settle in Brazil. Small wonder, then, that their families formed the Bahian equivalent of European nobility.

Despite the support of the Álvares couple, the Portuguese Christian government of Brazil was threatened on many fronts. The task of bringing Indians to Christ proved daunting. Only a few could be sent to Europe to learn the European languages and practice the European faith. Any hope for converting large numbers of Brazilians meant that European priests must learn Indian languages, preaching to them a message they could understand and taking Indian confessions. Early on, Jesuits enlisted women and children converts to help them in hearing (and understanding) confession. In the era of the Council of Trent, this seemed an extremely dangerous innovation. After all, just as the Church was insisting that priests must serve as intermediaries between God and human beings, priests in Brazil were sharing their duties with women and children. Seeking a solution to the problem, the Jesuits requested that a bishop be sent to instruct them on how to proceed. The tenure of the first bishop of Brazil was disastrous. He disapproved of much the fathers had worked hard to achieve; he was adamant that Indians (and especially Indian women) had no place within the Church hierarchy. Yet, as good Christians, the Jesuits accepted his authority and attempted to change their ways. On a return trip to Portugal, however, the bishop's ship sank off the Brazilian coast, and he shared the fate of so many other Europeans: he was captured and eaten by Indians.

Foreign interlopers also continued to threaten. Not only did the French refuse to give up designs on Brazil, but English corsairs infested Brazil's Atlantic waters in the second half of the sixteenth century. Both the French and the English brought with them dangerous Protestant heresies. In their raids of towns along Brazil's coast, "Lutheran" pirates seemed to take inordinate pleasure in sacking churches and destroying holy images. In 1580, when the Portuguese king died without direct heirs, Philip II of Spain made good his claim to the Crown of Portugal. For sixty years, the Portuguese suffered what some called their "Babylonian captivity" to Spain. In the early seventeenth century, Spanish foreign policy provoked attacks by the Dutch (who were also Calvinists and thus considered heretics), who succeeded in taking and holding for twenty-five years the richest sugar-producing area of northeastern Brazil.

The many reverses suffered by the Portuguese (and Catholic) government of Brazil may help to explain why the story of the Álvares couple became so important as Brazil's "founding myth." It was propagated largely by priests who repeated the story verbally and in print throughout the seventeenth century. Paraguaçu's example demonstrated that Brazilian Indians had a central place in the religious struggle against heresy and in the political battle against other European powers. In recognition of the importance of the Chapel of Our Lady of Grace, the pope endowed it with a number of relics that attracted ever more pilgrims to the site. In 1582, Dona Catarina Álvares Paraguaçu, by then a widow, donated the chapel and its land to the monks of the Order of St. Benedict. It is today the oldest church in Salvador (a city noted for its many old churches) and, of course, was the first sanctuary in Brazil to honor the Virgin Mary. As the Portuguese suffered political reverses, first to Spain and then to the Netherlands, the importance of a Catholic, Portuguese Brazil grew.

Catarina Álvares Paraguaçu, devoted as she became to the Virgin, showed that Indians (aided directly by God and his Mother) were capable of replicating in the New World the religious orthodoxy that was being endangered in the Old. Furthermore, Christian Indian women could be held up as models for Indians and Europeans alike for their devout, chaste, monogamous lifestyles. They could raise daughters worthy of the best European husbands. Although her life story became a tool for Catholic propaganda, the legend surrounding Paraguaçu never shed the image of a beautiful, independent Indian woman who made her own choices and determined her own fate. She has symbolized the positive aspects of race mixture and patriotically chose to return to Brazil rather than settle for a comfortable life in Europe. By the time Portugal achieved independence from Spain in 1640, the place of Paraguaçu in the foundation myths of Brazilian society had been firmly implanted and would continue to capture the imagination and sympathies of Brazilians for the next 350 years. Their story has been retold countless times, from Santa Rita Durão's eighteenth-century poem "Caramuru" to the twenty-first-century feature film *Carumuru: A Invenção do Brasil* (*Carumuru: Brazil Reinvented*), and remains well known to Brazilian schoolchildren today.

Bibliography and Suggested Reading

Amado, Janaína. "Mythic Origins: Caramuru and the Founding of Brazil." *Hispanic American Historical Review* 80, no. 4 (November 2000): 783–811.

Conklin, Beth. "Consuming Images: Representations of Cannibalism on the Amazonian Frontier." *Anthropological Quarterly* 70, no. 2 (April 1997): 68–78.

Dickason, Olive Patricia. "The Brazilian Connection: A Look at the Origin of French Techniques for Trading with the Amerindians." *Review française d'histoire d'outre-mer* 71, no. 264–265 (1984): 129–46.

Forsyth, Donald W. "Three Cheers for Hans Staden: The Case for Brazilian Cannibalism." *Ethnohistory* 32, no. 1 (1985): 17–36.

Goldstein, Donna. "Interracial Sex and Racial Democracy in Brazil: Twin Concepts?" *American Anthropologist* 101, no. 3 (September 1999): 563–78.

Hemming, John. *Red Gold: The Conquest of the Brazilian Indians*. Cambridge, MA: Harvard University Press, 1978.

Léry, Jean de. *History of a Voyage to the Land of Brazil*. Edited by Janet Whatley. Berkeley: University of California Press, 1990.

Monteiro, John M. "The Heathen Castes of Sixteenth-Century Portuguese America: Unity, Diversity, and the Invention of the Brazilian Indians." *Hispanic American Historical Review* 80, no. 4 (November 2000): 697–719.

Nowell, Charles. "The French in Sixteenth-Century Brazil." *Americas* 5, no. 4 (1949): 381–93.

Russell-Wood, A. J. R. "Women and Society in Colonial Brazil." *Journal of Latin American Studies* 9, no. 1 (May 1977): 1–34.

———. "Prestige, Power and Piety in Colonial Brazil: The Third Orders of Salvador." *Hispanic American Historical Review* 69, no. 1 (February 1989): 61–89.

Southey, Robert. *History of Brazil*. 3 vols. London: Longman, 1810–1819.

Volpe, Maria Alice. "Remaking the Brazilian Myth of National Foundation: *Il Guarany*." *Latin American Music Review* 23, no. 2 (Autumn 2002): 179–94.

Whatley, Janet. "Savage Hierarchies: French Catholic Observers of the New World." *Sixteenth Century Journal* 17, no. 3 (Autumn 1986): 319–30.

Whitehead, Neil L. "Native American Cultures along the Atlantic Littoral of South America, 1499–1650." *Proceedings of the British Academy* 81 (1993): 197–231.

———. "Hans Staden and the Cultural Politics of Cannibalism." *Hispanic American Historical Review* 80, no. 4 (November 2000): 721–50.

CHAPTER TWO

John Billington and His Family (c. 1582–1630)

Doomed "Knave" of Plymouth Plantation

John Navin

North American schoolchildren grow up hearing tales of the Mayflower and the Pilgrims and celebrate the early settlers' hardy self-reliance as the very foundation on which the United States was built. Indeed, the entire country observes an annual Thanksgiving Day to express gratitude for the bounty of American soil and to idealize a brief period of cooperation and peaceful coexistence with the region's Indians. Yet, as historian John Navin shows, not all Pilgrims gave thanks for their lot in the New World, nor were all the Mayflower passengers destined to become revered and prosperous founders. Instead, some people like John Billington and his family were constantly at odds with their small community's powerful leaders. Billington epitomizes a certain Atlantic archetype: that of the hardscrabble outsider, the little guy who refused to go along with authority simply and whose life was made more difficult as a consequence. In his case, intransigence and impetuosity ultimately led to the gallows.

In the first half of the seventeenth century, Europeans established numerous settlements along the eastern seaboard of North America, a land fraught with mystery and peril. Ironically, the greatest challenge that confronted many transatlantic pioneers was not the harshness of the American wilderness or resistance shown by its native inhabitants but rather conflicts with their fellow colonists. Members of hardscrabble frontier communities had to "fit in" with their peers; indeed, their very survival often depended on an ability to work together toward common goals. Settlers who proved incompatible or uncooperative endured ostracism, lawful and unlawful retaliation, and even expulsion. Such was the plight of the Billington family who sailed to Plymouth on the *Mayflower* in 1620—strong-willed individuals who found themselves at odds with those in power. The Billingtons' experience reveals that, for European immigrants in the Atlantic world, adversity could spring not only from without but also from within.

John Billington was born in England's northeastern Midlands in the early 1580s, a turbulent period in that nation's history. Queen Elizabeth and her subjects had to contend with political intrigue, military conflict, religious turmoil, overpopulation, and rampant inflation. The 1590s brought mounting infighting, scarcity, economic distress, and war in Ireland. It was about the time that James I succeeded Elizabeth (1603) that Billington married a lovely girl named Elinor Lockwood. By contemporary standards, she was a young bride, just twenty-one or so when she wed. For the next three decades, Elinor's social and material circumstances, not to mention her emotional state, would be linked to a man whom Plymouth's governor, William Bradford, would scornfully describe as a "knave."

About 1604, Elinor gave birth to the couple's first child, whom they named John junior. After delivering a second son, Francis, around 1606, Elinor bore no further children—an oddity during that period unless poor health intervened. Like most of their contemporaries, the Billingtons spent the next decade on the edge of poverty. As circumstances in England grew more difficult, John Billington was one of many men who considered emigration as a solution. It was a dangerous notion: English colonizing ventures to the New World had a dismal record. In the 1580s the settlers on Roanoke Island had mysteriously disappeared, and more recently the Popham Colony in Maine was abandoned after just one winter. Farther south, the Virginia Colony had proven a deathtrap—since 1607 thousands of English subjects, the great majority of them unmarried young servants, had endured the perilous ocean crossing, only to die in America from accident, exposure, starvation, disease, or hostilities with local Native Americans. The relatively few families that migrated there seldom remained intact for long.

In the summer of 1620, a few "well disposed Gentlemen and Merchants of London and other places" hurriedly solicited families and individuals for a colonizing venture to the "northern parts of Virginia"—a vast expanse of land that stretched far above the unwholesome settlements in the Chesapeake. Promoters often described America as a fertile land teeming with wildlife and endless acres of untilled soil. This vision proved irresistible to men like John Billington, whose children faced dim prospects in overpopulated England, so he committed his family to the enterprise. In exchange for their passage, shipboard provisions, and a share of the profits, Billington signed a contract that bound himself, his wife, and their two sons to labor on behalf of the colony until 1627. For the duration of their partnership with the investors, the Billingtons and their fellow colonists would work six days per week for "the Company." All profits from "trade, traffic, trucking, working, fishing, or any other means" would remain in the common stock; even the houses and gardens were to be included in the assets to be divided after seven years. Some people considered the terms "fitter for thieves and bond slaves than honest men," but the prospect of a better life was sufficient inducement for the Billingtons to cast their lot with other hard-pressed families headed for America.

Optimism quickly turned to dismay when the Billingtons boarded ship and encountered their fellow travelers. As it turned out, the main body of Plymouth colonists, including most of the expedition's leaders, was not composed of ordinary English men and women like themselves but rather consisted of religious dissenters in transit from Holland. These pilgrims were caught up in the religious strife that had wracked England for decades. On one side were conforming Anglicans; on the other were Puritans who called for extensive reforms within the established church. Some of the latter became so dissatisfied that they formed their own independent churches. These "Separatists" were often fined or imprisoned and many eventually sought refuge in the Netherlands. There they enjoyed religious liberty but endured great physical hardships.

After a decade in exile, the members of the Separatist church under Pastor John Robinson had concluded that their circumstances in the Dutch city of Leiden were so bleak that removal to North America was the best solution. The decision was not easily reached; many worried openly about "the miseries of the land," which were likely to "consume and to utterly ruinate them"; others feared the "savage and brutish men" who inhabited the American wilderness. In order to finance the enterprise, the Leiden Separatists signed a business agreement with investors in England that called for them to send about 150 members of their church to establish a foothold in the New World. When all was in readiness, their pastor and the remainder of his congregation would join them. Unfortunately, the harsh terms of the investors' seven-year contract, added to the dangers of the ocean crossing and the uncertainty of what lay in store for them in America, meant that the expedition's leaders had trouble finding volunteers. In the summer of 1620 the investors in England undertook a last-minute campaign to recruit additional colonists, regardless of their religious persuasion. Into that breach stepped the hard-pressed Billington family. Years later, William Bradford, governor of Plymouth and ardent Separatist, contemptuously recalled the Billingtons' arrival in these terms: "they came from London, and I know not by what friends shuffled into their [i.e., the Separatists'] company."

The Billingtons were ill suited for a colonizing venture dominated by pious Calvinists. According to Bradford, the Billington clan was "one of the profanest families amongst them." Rather than welcome the newcomers from London, the Separatists regarded people recruited by the investors as "strangers" and viewed them with suspicion. Christopher Martin, the investors' agent aboard the *Mayflower* and himself a Puritan, described the Separatists as "waspish, discontented people." The Billingtons, who remained faithful to the Church of England, had little in common with these dissenters, many of whom had not set foot in their native country for more than a decade. Given their incompatibility with the powerful Separatist contingent, the Billingtons found themselves in an unexpected predicament. Withdrawal was not an option. They had obtained their passage to America by signing a contract and investing what little they had in the enterprise. But fitting in with these dissenters would require a sea change in terms of attitude and religious disposition, and even that was no guarantee of friendship or assimilation. John Billington chafed but could do little to resolve the situation.

Those planning the voyage had envisioned the need for two ships, the 180-ton *Mayflower* and the sixty-ton *Speedwell*, but the latter leaked so badly that both ships, crowded with Separatists and "strangers," were forced to return to port twice. As one delay followed another, the passengers consumed their precious foodstuffs. One predicted that "our victuals will be half eaten up, I think, before we go from the coast of England." Not only had the Billingtons stumbled into the midst of religious radicals, but now they faced the prospect of venturing into a distant wilderness without enough food to survive the coming winter. Separatist Robert Cushman noted the alarm that gripped some of the passengers: "There are others who would lose all they have put in, or make satisfaction for what they have had, that they might depart; but he [the investors' agent] will not hear them, nor suffer them to go ashore, lest they should run away." The colonizing force headed for America was "un-united," and Cushman predicted that "violence will break all." Surely the Billingtons were among those who would have jumped ship and stayed in England had they been given the chance.

Because of the *Speedwell*'s problems, the *Mayflower* ultimately sailed alone and perilously late in the season. In addition to the crew, the ship carried 102 passengers, about half of whom were Separatists. These dissenters enjoyed an intense sense of community; their church covenant and shared mission were sources of strength. In contrast, the Billingtons and other latecomers from London and its environs lacked comparable bonds of kinship, friendship, and spiritual communion. They were strangers not only to their shipmates from Leiden but also to each other. Their isolation meant that life in America would be much more difficult for them.

Although the original destination had been the "northern parts of Virginia," a vast tract that stretched from the upper Chesapeake Bay all the way to the Hudson River, a timely grant made by James I redirected the expedition even farther north. This locale offered ready access to the bountiful waters of Cape Cod and George's Bank, which had attracted European fishermen since the late 1500s. Recognizing the profit to be made from fishing and the northern fur trade, the investors preferred this site for the intended colony. Designated "New England," the new grant was "derived out of the Virginia patent and wholly secluded from their Government." This meant that the Separatists would not have to deal with Anglican rule in Virginia; for members of the Church of England such as the Billingtons, it was a victory for the other side.

The majority of colonists had no part in the decision to plant elsewhere; in fact, most appear to have been left uninformed of the change in plans. Shortly after the *Mayflower* made landfall in early November, when it became clear that the fledgling colony was to be seated north of Virginia, some of the passengers uttered "discontented and mutinous speeches," insisting that "when they came ashore they would use their own liberty; for none had power to command them, the patent they had being for Virginia, and not for New England, which belonged to another government." These protests came from colonists such as the Billingtons who had been hurriedly recruited in England and held virtual prisoners on the *Mayflower*. Having reached America at an unexpected location, some were more than willing to walk away from a contract that required them to labor six days a week for seven years, working on common land and living in company houses, before they could realize any personal profit. They also dreaded the prospect of life in a settlement dominated by overly pious men who rejected Anglicanism and displayed only faltering obedience to the English Crown.

The expedition's Separatist leaders responded to this challenge to their authority by drafting the celebrated Mayflower Compact, a new agreement that was endorsed by all adult males. One powerful incentive for John Billington and other conforming members of the Church of England to sign the compact was that failure to do so would cause him and his family to forfeit any share of the food, gunpowder, and other supplies provided by the investors. In the wintry New England wilderness, that would have been tantamount to a death sentence. Billington and the others also had reason to hope that their inclusion in the newly created Civil Body Politic would enable them to overcome the political sway of the colony's close-knit Separatists. Unfortunately, they miscalculated.

John Jr. and Francis Billington were too young to sign the Mayflower Compact, but their presence hardly went unnoticed. In "Mourt's Relation," Edward Winslow recorded the near catastrophe caused by the youngest Billington in December 1620: "the 5th day, we, through God's mercy, escaped a great danger by the foolishness of a boy, one of Francis [i.e., John] Billington's sons, who, in his father's absence, had got gunpowder . . . and there being a fowling-piece charged in his father's cabin, shot her off in the cabin; there being a little barrel of powder half full, scattered in and about the cabin . . . and many people about the fire, and yet, by God's mercy, no harm done." One month after he nearly blew up the *Mayflower*, thirteen-year-old Francis climbed "to the top of a tree on a high hill" and espied "a great sea as he thought." After a three-mile winter trek, the colonists discovered that "Billington's Sea," as it is still called, was actually two "great lakes . . . full of fish, and fowl." Not to be outdone, his older brother John Billington Jr. caused even greater consternation for Plymouth's leaders the following spring when ten colonists were compelled to undertake a perilous mission on his behalf. In late May 1621, the boy disappeared into the wilderness for five days, living on berries and whatever food he could find. He ended up among Native Americans who had attacked the *Mayflower*'s landing party the previous December. After learning of Billington's location from a friendly Indian, the Plymouth men went heavily armed to the Nauset village. Their fears heightened when "the savages here came very thick amongst us," but "after sunset, Aspinet [the local *sachem* or main chief] came with a great train, and brought the boy with him, one bearing him through the water. He had not less than a hundred with him, the half whereof came to the shallop side unarmed with him, the other stood aloof with their bows and arrows. There he delivered us the boy, behung with beads, and made peace with us." Having to risk life and limb to rescue John Billington Jr. did nothing to endear the colonists to his family.

Despite the problems the boys caused, there is no indication that young John and Francis Billington were publicly chastised. That ignominy would fall to their father. According to Bradford, the first criminal offense committed in Plymouth was the elder John Billington's insolent "contempt of the Captain's lawful commands, with opprobrious speeches." As punishment, the head of the Billington clan was "adjudged to have his neck and heels tied together," but the harsh sentence was commuted "upon humbling himself and craving pardon." The Billingtons were becoming well known in the Plymouth community for their intransigence, their insolence, and the numerous inconveniences they bestowed on their fellow colonists.

Of the 102 colonists who boarded the *Mayflower* in 1620, only fifty survived the first nine months in New England. Families were devastated: six of the twenty-two families were completely wiped out, another six suffered the loss of one parent, and in six others only a lone orphan survived. The Separatists must have pondered the inscrutability of the Divine Will; only four of the fifteen Separatist families could boast more than one survivor, yet somehow the "profane" Billingtons were untouched by the calamity. Plymouth's colonists survived the winter on half rations and, in the spring, resorted to purchasing food from fishing vessels off the Maine coast.

From the investors' perspective, the Plymouth enterprise was producing meager results. The terms of the contract, which imposed a communal lifestyle on the settlers, only aggravated the cleavages in the troubled plantation. Plymouth's youths objected to working "for other men's wives and children" without any recompense, while the older men considered common labor and common property to be a source of "indignity and disrespect." The women, few as they were, deemed it "a kind of slavery" to be commanded to work for other men, dressing their meat and washing their clothes; husbands were also unhappy about sharing their wives' labor. In an effort to increase production, every family in Plymouth was assigned a parcel of land for planting in 1623; this step toward individual ownership "had very good success, for it made all hands very industrious."

If the demise of Plymouth's experiment in frontier socialism had resolved one troublesome issue, another soon followed. Once again, John Billington found himself at the center of the controversy. In 1624, some of the financial backers in England sent an Anglican minister named John Lyford to Plymouth to end the Separatists' stranglehold on the plantation. The ensuing controversy pitted the Leiden emigrants, who rejected Lyford's ministry, against the non-Separatists, who were anxious to eliminate the religious, economic, and political restrictions imposed on them. In a dramatic showdown, Governor William Bradford accused Lyford and his outspoken supporter, John Oldham, of plotting "a reformation in church and commonwealth." During the trial, Oldham identified John Billington as the one who had "informed him of many things and made sundry complaints" against Plymouth's Separatist leaders. For his part, Billington admitted that he was "sometimes drawn to his [Lyford's] meetings" but denied the allegations.

Lyford and Oldham were banished from Plymouth. Their departure provoked an unprecedented exodus as several dozen other colonists, disheartened by the reassertion of Separatist hegemony, abandoned the plantation. Significantly, the Billingtons were not among them. Despite the disfavor, even contempt, in which they were held by their pious neighbors, the family opted to remain in Plymouth. With only three more years before the anticipated division of profits and property, the Billingtons were too deeply invested in the plantation to walk away. Unfortunately, John Billington's complicity in the Lyford affair seems to have intensified his protracted feud with Governor William Bradford and his brethren. The next year Bradford warned Separatist Robert Cushman in London that "Billington still rails against you, and threatens to arrest you." He commented that the family had been "often punished for miscarriages," proof that not all their transgressions are recorded in extant Plymouth Colony records. Yet not everyone shared the Separatists' contempt for the Billingtons. Thomas Morton, a former settler and critic of Plymouth's leaders, later claimed that John Billington was "beloved of many." The decision by two Plymouth defectors to bequeath their garden plots to Billington lends credence to this portrayal, one clearly at odds with Governor Bradford's low opinion of the man. The incident also revealed that, unlike many of his contemporaries, Billington was not cowed by the opposition—even when they held the reigns of power.

In 1626, following a period of negotiation with the disaffected investors—who had seen little profit from the enterprise—Plymouth's settlers assumed full ownership of the plantation. With the long-awaited division of assets, John Billington secured a modest competency for his family, but it was hardly the windfall he had anticipated six years earlier. He received a house in the center of Plymouth, a share in the plantation's livestock, sixty-three acres of land, and rights in future distributions. Billington had reason to be disgruntled. Despite their status as "First Comers," his family received the smallest per capita allotment in the entire colony. Moreover, as a longtime adversary of the governor and his allies, Billington continued to be excluded from all positions of influence in Plymouth. He never held any civil office, was not a member of the church, and lacked the resources to become one of the privileged "Undertakers"—men who assumed financial liability for the colony and controlled its trade with England. The Billingtons were undoubtedly among those persons described by Bradford as "untoward persons . . . which came out of England" who might "endanger to overthrow all, now that other ties and bonds were taken away" when the contract with the investors was terminated in 1626.

John Billington had brought his family to the New World in search of opportunity. Despite many setbacks and complaints, he never wavered in that pursuit. According to Thomas Morton's *New English Canaan*, published in

1637, Billington made a major discovery; apparently he found the "one place . . . in the whole country" where there was a "very useful stone . . . so much commended by Ovid . . . [and he] labored to get a patent of it to himself." Morton's literary reference is a tease: the first book of Ovid's *Metamorphoses* describes gold, silver, bronze, and iron. What type of mineral deposit Billington stumbled on is open to conjecture, but it was probably iron since the Indians called it *cos* and Morton claimed it was useful for the manufacture of edged tools. He suspected that the "Old Woodman" (Billington) wanted to exploit the find for his own benefit, not that of the entire plantation. However, if Billington did attempt to gain exclusive rights to a cache of iron in southeastern New England, his efforts evidently proved futile.

At about the same time, the Billington family suffered a staggering blow. Not long after the division of the plantation's cattle, John Billington Jr. died from an unrecorded cause. The youth had narrowly escaped death in the notorious powder keg episode aboard the *Mayflower*, survived the catastrophic first winter, endured five days of wandering in the forest, and had been graciously entertained by previously hostile Nauset Indians. But just as he entered manhood and came into some property, his luck ran out. Death from disease or accident was common on the early frontier, and it is likely that young Billington fell victim to some such fate. John and Elinor Billington lost not only a beloved son but also a measure of security for their old age.

Not long after that personal tragedy, John Billington learned that Plymouth would soon receive a new wave of impoverished Separatists from Holland. Not only would there be additional competition for arable pasture land and timber, but the established colonists would be expected to support these newcomers for up to eighteen months until they could become self-sufficient. The burden fell heavy on the plantation and exacerbated tensions that simmered just below the surface. Men like Billington were powerless to stem the tide of dissenters from Leiden. His landholdings were modest, his options were limited, his oldest son was dead, and just as he was starting to reap the benefits of his long labors, the colony was saddled with indigent Calvinists who years earlier had shunned the hazards of initial settlement. To add insult to injury, servants began to arrive from England to work for the colony's privileged Undertakers.

After years of strife and frustration, John Billington reached a breaking point. As the decade drew to a close, his frustration and anger got the best of him, and he "waylaid a young man, one John Newcomen, about a former quarrel and shot him." According to one account, "the poor fellow, perceiving the intent of this Billington, his mortal enemy, sheltered himself behind trees as well as he could for a while; but the other not being so ill a marksman as to miss his aim, made a shot at him, and struck him on the shoulder, with which he died soon after." Billington was arraigned by both grand jury and petty jury and was found "guilty of wilful murder, by plain and notorious evidence." Concerned with the possible ramifications of their verdict, Governor Bradford and his peers sought the advice of able gentlemen from neighboring Massachusetts Bay Colony. The Puritan leaders there "concurred with them that [Billington] ought to die, and the land to be purged from blood." After somber deliberations, John Billington was hanged in September 1630. His execution, the first to occur in Plymouth, was considered "a matter of great sadness" but no doubt a relief to the authorities he had annoyed from the settlement's earliest days. Presciently, five years earlier, Bradford had said of Billington that "he is a knave, and so will live and die."

Elinor Billington had lost two members of her small family in less than three years. When her husband was executed, her remaining son Francis was twenty-one years old. The property division of 1626 had provided him with twenty acres of land, and he was eager to find a wife to establish his own household. Faced with the prospect of living alone in hardscrabble circumstances, one might expect that Elinor would follow the example set by previous widows in the plantation and remarry within a year of her husband's death. Instead, the headstrong and independent woman remained unmarried. Although she received at least the traditional "widow's third" of her deceased husband's property, her circumstances must have been difficult, especially given the disdain that the colony's leaders held for anyone with the name Billington. That prejudice resurfaced in June 1636 when the Plymouth court found her guilty of slandering Mr. John Doane, a church deacon and former assistant governor. Although she was an aging widow in her fifties, Elinor was fined £5 and "adjudged to be sett in the stocks & be whipt." It was an indignity that had not befallen any other woman in Plymouth since the *Mayflower*'s arrival sixteen years earlier.

Elinor Billington had fallen on hard times, and her son Francis was not in a position to lend her much support, physically or financially. After his father's execution, Francis labored part-time as a carpenter's assistant for Francis Eaton, a fellow *Mayflower* passenger who had married three times. Eaton died in the winter of 1633, and Francis wed his former employer's widow just eight months later. The quick union brought weighty family responsibilities. Christian Penn Eaton already had three children: Rachel, Benjamin, and an unnamed child described as "an idiot," plus Eaton's son, Samuel, from his first marriage. One year into the marriage, Christian and Francis celebrated the birth of their first child together. By 1652, at least eight other births had followed. Whatever deprivations or discomfort Elinor Billington suffered after the death of her husband, her hardships were fewer than those her son took on himself.

In 1637, the widow Elinor Billington needed money, so she attempted to sell twenty acres in Plymouth Colony's new settlement at Scituate "together wth all houses edifices & buildings thereunto" to a newly arrived colonist. The following March she signed a poignant deed that granted "in consideration of the naturall love that I beare unto ffrancis Billington my naturall sonn" lands north of Plymouth that remained in her possession after her husband's execution. The fact that Elinor expected to have to support herself in her fifties and beyond was evident in the conditions of the grant, which reserved for her use "such a parcel or quantity of lands out of the premises as will make a thousand and a halfe of hills to sett with Indian corne or sowe with English graine." The deed also stipulated that Elinor would retain "a small parcel of ground to make a garden place & erect a house upon." She clearly expected the assistance of her son in these endeavors, since the deed required him to set aside "such a quantitie of land in a new field as the said Ellinor [sic] shall please to be at charge to manure and take in *with the said ffrancis* to be hers to use during her naturall life." Moreover, Francis could not sell his newly acquired lands during Elinor's lifetime unless she gave her consent.

In August 1638, with her property safely transferred to Francis, Elinor married sixty-nine-year-old Gregory Armstrong. She carefully guarded her son's interests, even going so far as to require her second husband to sign a prenuptial agreement. Because Elinor brought to the union "two Cowes," she insisted that if her new spouse "happen to outlive" her, he would give each of her grandchildren, "two heifers of a yeare old." Armstrong apparently brought little other than his person to the match; the prenuptial contract specified that in the case of Elinor's death, he "shall enjoy the house they now liuv in and the lands they occupye during his life"—an indication that he moved into Elinor's quarters and not vice versa. Although she was thirteen years or so his junior, Elinor ultimately did go to the grave before her second husband, who died a widower in 1650 at the age of eighty-one. Just as the date of her birth is unknown, so too the date of Elinor Billington's death remains a mystery. The last reference to her in Plymouth records occurred in May 1643 in conjunction with a minor land transaction.

We can only speculate about Elinor's final years, though it seems certain that the ongoing tribulations of her son and his family caused her much grief. In June 1639, Francis Billington, by then the biological father of three children and stepfather to four others, was sued for debt. Five months later, he and his wife were forced to sell the lands she had inherited from her deceased husband. Shortly thereafter, Christian Billington bore another child, and colony records make it clear that the family was desperately poor. In January 1642, Plymouth's magistrates undertook the "placeing and disposing of ffrancis Billingtons children according to the Act and order of the Court." For the duration of their stay with court-assigned families, the Billington and Eaton children were to be provided with meat, drink, and clothes in return for their labor. Joseph Billington, age six or seven years, was placed with John Cooke Jr., while fourteen-year-old Benjamin Eaton was lodged with John Winslow; both situations were to prevail until the boys reached the age of twenty-one. Five-year-old Martha Billington was placed with Gyles Rickett, and Rachel Eaton was placed with Gabriel Fallowell until the girls reached age twenty. Three months later, six-year old Elizabeth Billington was apprenticed to John and Mary Barnes, the last female to be listed in Plymouth Colony records as entering into the condition of indentured servitude—just one more indignity attached to the Billington surname.

The assignment of five of their children to other homes must have devastated Francis and Christian Billington. Colony records offer some insight into their offspring's distress as well. In July 1643, eighteen months after their family unity was shattered, Francis and Christian were hauled into court to answer for their son's insolent behavior. It seems that young Joseph Billington had run away from his master's service and tried to return home on several occasions. Apparently, the boy had been enticed by his stepbrother, Benjamin Eaton, who had been dismissed from John Winslow's service for similar acts of disobedience. The Billingtons were warned that if they should again receive Joseph into their home, they would be "sett in the stocks every lecture day . . . until the Court shall take a further course w'th them." Benjamin Eaton was warned that he would share "the same punishment w'th his father and mother." The late John Billington's intransigence had passed down through the generations.

Christian Billington gave birth to at least five more children, three of whom lived to adulthood. Within two years, Francis was in court again to answer for unpaid debts and other sundry charges. With nine children and three stepchildren, Francis was stretched beyond his means. His troubles worsened in 1665 when the family house burned down. Taking pity on the most hapless members of their community, the magistrates assigned two men "to see what may be collected for the Reliefe of ffrancis Billington." The next year, Francis had to rescue his daughter-in-law and another woman when an Indian entered a neighboring house and "held up his knife . . . in a threatening way." After relocating to the newly planted town of Middleboro, the Billingtons found themselves on the front lines of King Philip's War in 1675.

Clearly, there was nothing luxurious or patrician about Francis Billington's life in America. The last of the Billingtons who sailed on the *Mayflower*, Francis died in December 1684, fifty-four years after his father's execution.

Almost everything we know about the Billingtons stems from their involvement with Plymouth Plantation. Every Thanksgiving, our nation celebrates the memory of that momentous settlement, taking special note of the harmonious relations its inhabitants maintained with some of their Native American neighbors. We venerate the Mayflower Compact as a paradigm for self-government. But the myth of amity and cooperation that surrounds the Pilgrims masks divisions within their plantation. John Billington and the members of his "profane" family dared to challenge Separatist hegemony in Plymouth Colony, and their lives were made much more difficult as a result.

In 1973, the overseers of Plimoth Plantation determined that an authentic post-in-ground house should be constructed at the site where Bradford's map of Plymouth indicated that the Billingtons lived. Funding for the construction of houses was normally provided by the founders' descendants, but the Billingtons' account contained the paltry sum of just four dollars, so the plantation staff had to build the Billington house themselves rather than hire outside contractors. Three and a half centuries after they first set foot in Plymouth, the obstreperous Billingtons were still personas non grata, neglected by their own descendants and disparaged by those of "better" *Mayflower* families. Time has not erased the unflattering legacy penned for John Billington and his family by Governor William Bradford or recorded in the colony records. Their struggle illuminates the fact that in the seventeenth-century Atlantic world, shared interests were not the same as shared attitudes, and individualism often came at a high price.

Bibliography and Suggested Reading

There is a major online collection of primary sources, known as the Plymouth Colony Archive Project, available at http://etext.lib.virginia.edu/users/deetz.

Beale, David. *The Mayflower Pilgrims*. Greenville, SC: Emerald House Group, 2002.

Bradford, William. *Of Plimoth Plantation 1620–1647*. This work and his personal letter book are available in a facsimile edition at http://www.mayflowerhistory.com and on CD-ROM.

Deetz, James, and Patricia Scott Deetz. *The Times of Their Lives: Life, Love and Death in the Plymouth Colony*. New York: Anchor Books, 2000.

Demos, John. *A Little Commonwealth: Family Life in Plymouth Colony*. Oxford: Oxford University Press, 2000.

Morton, Thomas. "New English Canaan (Amsterdam, 1637)." Reprinted in Nathaniel Morton, *New England's Memorial*. Boston, 1855.

Philbrick, Nathaniel. *Mayflower: A Story of Courage, Community, and War*. New York: Viking: 2006.

Prince, Thomas. "New England Chronology." Reprinted in Nathaniel Morton, *New England's Memorial*. Boston, 1855.

Smith, John. *New England's Trials*. 2nd ed. London, 1622.

Stratton, Eugene Aubrey. *Plymouth Colony, Its History and People 1620–1691*. Salt Lake City: Ancestry Inc., 1986.

Winslow, Edward. *Mourt's Relation: A Journal of the Pilgrims at Plymouth*. London, 1622. Reprint, Bedford MA: Applewood Books, 1963.

CHAPTER THREE

Samuel Cohen (c. 1600–1642)

Jewish Translator in Brazil, Curaçao, and Angola

Mark Meuwese

One of the most underappreciated aspects of the Atlantic encounter is the crucial role played by translators, those nameless functionaries who were present at every negotiation or intercultural conversation and were responsible for making one side comprehensible to the other. Historian Mark Meuwese traces the transatlantic career of Samuel Cohen, a Jewish translator who worked for the Dutch West India Company in several of its ventures. Cohen's experience reveals that individuals with a knowledge of languages and the ability to work across cultures were always in great demand. At the same time, however, Cohen's failure to advance professionally or to build up his own independent personal fortune hints at the ways in which prejudices against racial, religious, and ethnic origins affected all residents of the Atlantic world, not only the more obvious and brutal experiences visited on Africans and Native American peoples.

Samuel Cohen, a Jew in service of the Dutch West India Company was a translator, interpreter and gold seeker in Brazil, Curaçao, and Angola who was treated with much sympathy by his contemporaries. Although anti-Semitic sentiment has been a common thread running throughout Atlantic business history, Company director and major investor Joannes de Laet described Cohen as "a loyal and ingenious man." Twentieth-century biographers have concurred, viewing Cohen as a person who was "versatile and enterprising of spirit." Because he was the first documented Jewish person on

Curaçao, some scholars have erroneously viewed him as the founding father of the oldest continuing Jewish community in the New World. Yet, despite such positive depictions, there is very little that is known about Samuel Cohen's personal life or experiences beyond his connection with the Company and its business activities. Unlike colonial officials, missionaries, or prominent Dutch colonists in Africa or Brazil, Cohen did not leave behind any personal documents that might give insight into his own thoughts or opinions or hopes or dreams. The man is mentioned in several Company letters, and his existence can be traced in Amsterdam notarial records. Nevertheless, the scarcity of documents has not prevented historians from using Samuel Cohen's life and career trajectory to glean insights into the possibilities open to persons of the Jewish faith and to draw some conclusions about the crucial role of translators in the multilingual Atlantic world.

As a Jewish person, Cohen was part of two worlds that overlapped but did not always reconcile easily. He does not seem to have been an especially devout or orthodox Jew, but his name alone would have made his ethnic affiliation obvious to the Christian Europeans who dominated the public institutions of government, business, education, and diplomacy. Cohen was familiar with the beliefs and practices of his coreligionists but also understood the culture and norms of the general European culture in which he was raised and moved comfortably in that world as well. His ability to live his life between different cultures while belonging fully to neither one of them suggests not only that it was Cohen's personality that made him a successful translator but also that it was the essential nature of his life as an assimilated European Jew that habituated him to the practice of helping one group talk to another.

Samuel Cohen's career as a translator was typical of those obscure individuals with language skills and other practical expertise who were in high demand throughout the Atlantic world. Columbus's discovery of the New World in 1492 brought peoples from widely different linguistic backgrounds into sustained commercial and cultural contact across an expansive geographic region that encompassed Europe and the Americas. For this reason, translators and interpreters were indispensable members of any expedition or settlement throughout the Atlantic world. As the Dutch West India Company (West-Indische Compagnie, or WIC) attempted to make inroads into the Spanish and Portuguese empires, its agents required the services of men like Samuel Cohen who were able to translate documents, facilitate discussions during contract negotiations, or communicate with people on ships or in ports. The Dutch trade company was intensely interested in obtaining gold and silver, so Cohen's personal expertise as a miner along with his language facility made him an even more valuable employee. Yet, although he served the WIC loyally for almost thirteen years, Cohen failed to advance through the company ranks as his non-Jewish peers were able to do. When he died in Luanda (Angola) in 1642, Cohen was still working as an interpreter for the WIC just as he had been doing in Brazil and Curaçao over a decade earlier. This clear career stagnation was remarkable for an era in which many less educated colonists enjoyed tremendous social mobility in the colonial societies of the Americas and West Africa. While it is possible that Cohen's Jewish background affected his fortunes in the orthodox Protestant WIC, it is more likely that his linguistic expertise proved so valuable that the company directors resisted his advance because they needed his services. Paradoxically, Cohen's unique and specialized skills actually seem to have prevented him from climbing the social ladder in the emerging Atlantic world.

Samuel Cohen first appears as a historical figure in a formal deposition that was sworn before an Amsterdam notary in June 1629. In this document, Cohen is identified simply as "a Portuguese in Amsterdam." In the seventeenth century, European Christians used the word "Portuguese" as a generic description that referred to all Sephardic Jews from the Iberian Peninsula. This confusing term had its origins in the history of the Jews in Spain and Portugal during the fifteenth and sixteenth centuries. In the face of persecution by Catholic Counter-Reformation militants, most Iberian Jews accepted baptism and became known as "New Christians." Paradoxically, the Jews' conversion to Christianity did not erase the boundaries or ease the tensions between Christians and Jews. Even though many New Christians abandoned Judaic beliefs, they continued to live in special quarters that segregated them from the rest of the population. When the Spanish Crown incorporated Portugal into its dominions in 1580, many of the Portuguese New Christians rightfully feared renewed persecution from the Inquisition. Because international trade was one of the few economic activities in which Iberian Jews had been permitted to engage, the Portuguese New Christians who fled Spanish religious orthodoxy sought refuge in northern European cities that were centers of long-distance commerce and perceived to be more open and tolerant.

In the early 1600s, Amsterdam emerged as the center of international trade in sugar, spices, and tobacco and soon became an attractive place for the people of the so-called Portuguese nation to congregate. Its Jewish community grew rapidly. Although the number of Portuguese residents in Amsterdam was not more than 550 in 1615, by 1639 their ranks had swelled to one thousand, and the city became an influential cultural and religious center for Jews throughout all of northern Europe. Because Dutch Protestant authorities allowed religious minorities to practice their faith as long as it did not threaten the public order, Amsterdam's Portuguese residents were able to reassert their Jewish identity by building synagogues and cemeteries, selecting rabbis, and strengthening family bonds through intermarriage. Moreover, unlike New Christians and Jews elsewhere in Europe, the members of the Portuguese nation in Amsterdam were not confined to a restricted district or ghetto. However, because they shared the same language and culture, almost all Jews resided in the same small neighborhood in Amsterdam. Although the Jewish community of Amsterdam had much more religious and cultural freedom than Jews in other parts of seventeenth-century Europe, Amsterdam magistrates did not grant members of the Portuguese nation the same civil and economic privileges as Protestant residents. For example, Jews were prohibited from serving in the city government, and they were unable to enroll in the influential craft organizations. Moreover, Dutch Calvinist ministers occasionally agitated against the Jews because they were afraid that the latter would seek to convert Christians to Judaism. In general, though, the Jewish community felt very safe in Amsterdam. In contrast to many other parts of Europe, no violent anti-Semitic incidents were ever recorded in seventeenth-century Amsterdam.

Curiously, while practically all members of the early seventeenth-century Jewish community in Amsterdam were Sephardim or Jews from Portugal and Spain, Samuel Cohen was most likely a member of the small Ashkenazi or Eastern European Jewish community in Amsterdam. Although the Sephardic and Ashkenazi Jews obviously shared the same Judaic faith, there were considerable linguistic and cultural differences between both groups. While the Sephardic Jews spoke Spanish and Portuguese, the Ashkenazim spoke Central and Eastern European languages, such as German. Additionally, each group had distinct last names. Since the name "Cohen" is traditionally associated with Ashkenazi Jews, Samuel must have been a member of this group rather than of the Sephardim. Confusingly, the earlier mentioned notary record of 1629 identifies Cohen as a "Portuguese" or Sephardic Jew. While it is possible that the non-Jewish Dutch notary simply did not know the difference between Ashkenazi and Sephardic Jews, it is also likely that Cohen assimilated in the Sephardic community by learning their languages and by adopting their customs.

Since many Jews were extensively involved in trade with the Spanish and Portuguese empires, they became useful informants and mediators for other Dutch merchants who were interested in international commerce. The States-General, the parliament of representatives of the seven United Provinces that made up the Dutch Republic, had granted the WIC in 1621 the exclusive rights to carry out trade and shipping in the Atlantic basin as well as the Pacific Ocean east of New Guinea. The WIC was closely modeled after the Dutch East India Company (VOC), which had received the monopoly rights to trade and shipping in the Indian Ocean and Asia from the States-General in 1602. In addition to their commercial activities, both the VOC and the WIC were intended by the States-General to be military organizations that could extend the Dutch war for independence against Spain outside Europe. When hostilities resumed between Spain and the Dutch in 1621 following a twelve-year truce, the States-General greatly contributed to the financial capital of the WIC in the hope that the company would quickly deal a devastating blow to the Spanish Empire in the Atlantic.

Although the WIC had great interest in capturing the rich silver and gold mines in Mexico and Peru, the company realistically concluded that an assault on these well-defended Spanish mainland colonies was out of the question. A much more attractive and vulnerable target for the WIC proved to be Portuguese Brazil, which had come under Spanish control in 1580. By wresting control of the weakly defended sugar-growing provinces of northeastern Brazil, the WIC hoped to cut off revenues for the Spanish Crown and at the same time take over the profitable Atlantic sugar trade. In 1624, the WIC embarked on an ambitious campaign to capture the Portuguese Empire in the southern Atlantic. While one WIC fleet attacked Salvador de Bahia, the capital of Portuguese Brazil, two other expeditions targeted Portuguese coastal forts in West Africa and Angola from which thousands of enslaved Africans were annually shipped to the sugar plantations of Brazil. Unfortunately, the WIC campaign dismally failed. The two Dutch expeditions were unable to capture the well-defended Portuguese coastal forts in Africa, and the WIC was able to hold Bahia for only one year before a massive Portuguese–Spanish fleet recaptured the city in 1625. Faced with this catastrophe, the WIC switched tactics. From 1625 to 1629, the WIC was primarily a naval power that concentrated on the capturing of as many Spanish and Portuguese ships in the Atlantic as possible. This strategy proved spectacularly successful. In 1628, a WIC fleet captured one of the annual Spanish return fleets loaded with Mexican silver, gold, and other American riches in the Caribbean. Flush with revenues from the capture of the Spanish treasure fleet, the WIC soon planned a second expedition to conquer the sugar-growing regions of northeastern Brazil.

During the preparations for the second invasion of Brazil, the WIC sought out the expertise of Samuel Cohen. In 1629, the WIC hired Samuel Cohen to look for "certain mines of gold, silver, and other minerals" in Brazil. Like many other Jewish merchants in Amsterdam, Cohen may have been involved in the diamond trade and gained his mining experience in that profitable industry. Interestingly, Cohen does not appear to have been associated with the New Christian and Sephardic merchants who played an influential role in the Brazilian sugar trade with the Dutch Republic during the early seventeenth century. Because the Inquisition had no strong presence in Portuguese Brazil, many New Christians from Portugal had settled during the sixteenth century in northeastern Brazil, where they became involved with the export of sugar. After the establishment of the Portuguese Sephardic community in Amsterdam in the early 1600s, New Christian merchants from northeastern Brazil increasingly exported Brazilian sugar to their relatives and associates in the Dutch capital. However, because of his Ashkenazi background, Cohen was not part of this transatlantic network. All evidence indicates that Cohen was hired by the WIC primarily because of his expertise as a miner and not as a person who was connected to the New Christian community in northeastern Brazil. At the same time, Cohen's fluency in the Portuguese language made him also valuable for the WIC as an interpreter and translator. Few Dutch people spoke Iberian languages, so individuals with extensive language skills were in high demand. Translators were crucial components of the European expansion.

Surviving correspondence does not reveal whether the WIC actually used Cohen in their tricky negotiations with the Portuguese administrators when Company troops established a beachhead in the rich sugar province of Pernambuco in 1630. It is certain, however, that Cohen was residing in Brazil in October 1631. The Company's Political Council sent him to accompany an expedition to the northern frontier provinces of Rio Grande do Norte and Ceará. Desperate to advance beyond their stronghold in the coastal town of Olinda in Pernambuco, the Political Council had organized a special mission to forge a military alliance in the northern frontier provinces with the native peoples who were known for their animosity toward the Portuguese colonizers. Acting on intelligence gained from friendly natives and intercepted Portuguese correspondence, the Council was particularly interested in making contact with the Tapuya or Tarairiu Indians who lived in the *sertão* (arid backcountry) of Rio Grande do Norte and actively resisted Portuguese domination. Because the Tapuyas were linguistically distinct from the coastal Tupís, with whom the Dutch were already in close contact, the Political Council needed skilled interpreters who could mediate an alliance. They selected Cohen as the best candidate for his openness, his flexibility, and his quick mind. He joined several Tupí and Tapuya men who went along as mediators. Interestingly, both Cohen and his indigenous colleagues were representatives of marginalized ethnic groups whose lives and livelihoods required them to straddle different cultural norms in order to have their voices heard in the Atlantic colonial system.

The Council's official orders to Commander Elbert Smient of the Company yacht *Nieu Nederlant* instructed him to take aboard his ship "the Portuguese Samuel Cohen who will also be included for this end." The Council clearly valued Cohen's position because they ordered Smient "to allow the same [Cohen] to stay in the cabin and supply him with provisions." Granting Cohen the privilege of staying in the ship's cabin, the comfort of which was traditionally reserved for officers and persons of high social standing, clearly revealed that the Council considered him to be an important person. In a letter to their superiors dated November 1631, Commander Smient, Cohen, merchant J. van Dous, and Captain Adriaen Jorisz Thienpont all testified that they had interrogated some of the recently returned Tarairiu messengers who had attempted to contact their people back in the Rio Grande *sertão* and gained some useful insights about conditions there. The discussions likely took place in Portuguese, meaning that Cohen was the primary translator and cultural mediator. Cohen also spent time translating intercepted Portuguese correspondence and made himself available whenever Portuguese colonists were captured and could offer potentially valuable information. Because the WIC was eager to find gold or silver mines in the interior of Brazil, they charged Cohen with collecting and collating any information about a rich silver mine that was rumored to exist in the northern Ceará region. His work as a translator was at the nexus of information gathering for the Company and, by extension, the larger imperial vision.

Cohen's value as a translator of Portuguese documents became especially clear when he was inadvertently transported back to the Dutch Republic sometime in early 1632. Instead of obeying Smient's orders to wait off the coast of Rio Grande while the commander went to Olinda to gather military reinforcements for a later amphibious attack on Ceará, the *Nieu Nederlant*, with Cohen aboard, unexpectedly faced Portuguese attack; they quickly disembarked their Tupi and Tarairiu allies and sailed away to the relative safety of the Caribbean islands. From there, they returned to the United Provinces in Europe instead of returning to Brazil. The Political Council in Olinda was furious at Captain Thienpont's actions and complained to the Heeren XIX (the WIC Board of Directors, literally the "Lords Nineteen") that mutinous and cowardly fellow had absconded with their irreplaceable employee Samuel Cohen, a man "who was very useful to us in the reading and translation of Portuguese letters." Although Company authorities must have known that Cohen's return to the Dutch Republic had been involuntary, they did not immediately rehire him because he had failed in his quest to find any gold or silver mines in the Brazilian interior.

For his part, Cohen was hesitant to return across the Atlantic because of the unstable situation in Pernambuco, where the WIC forces were waging a ferocious war against Portuguese forces. Furthermore, he was aware that the colony was not always a safe place for Jews. Swearing out a statement before an Amsterdam notary in August 1633, Cohen testified that a Portuguese Jewish merchant from Recife named Symon Drago had been abused by WIC troops. In his deposition, the translator asserted that his friend Drago had been one of the wealthiest merchants in Pernambuco before the Dutch attack on Brazil in February 1630. Under the Dutch occupation, however, Drago had been mistreated by rowdy Company soldiers who injured him, stripped him of his clothes, and left him for dead. WIC officers then broke into Drago's warehouse and confiscated his property, which included almost eighty pipes of wine from the Canary Islands. Although senior Company officials eventually apologized to Drago and agreed to lodge him with one of their officers for more than a month, they never compensated him for his financial or material losses. A humiliated Drago subsequently returned to Amsterdam, where he made a formal complaint about the abuse he had suffered, suspecting anti-Semitism was at its root, and he solicited Cohen's aid in making his case. There were many times in Cohen's life when he was torn between loyalty to friends and coreligionists and his loyalty to his Company and career. He belonged to both worlds and constantly had to negotiate his way between their sometimes competing expectations.

Despite Cohen's damaging testimony about their overseas practices, the Company nonetheless relied on his uncommon linguistic expertise and had little choice but to entice him into their employ again to further their colonial projects throughout the Atlantic world. In April 1634, the Heeren XIX decided to conquer the small Spanish-held Caribbean island of Curaçao off the Venezuelan coast where they hoped to establish a strategic naval base from which to intercept Spanish trade and shipping. In addition to some key territory, in Curaçao the WIC authorities expected to obtain salt and other natural resources that their colonists desperately needed. For this undertaking, the Company needed a reliable interpreter who could speak Spanish and act as a translator for them in the anticipated peace negotiations once the region had been seized successfully. Johannes Van Walbeeck, the expedition's commander, specifically tapped Cohen for the job because of his fluency in Spanish and Portuguese and his reputation for previous excellent service in Brazil. In fact, the two men had been acquainted since the WIC's invasion of Pernambuco in 1630. Furthermore, although the Spanish viewed Curaçao and the neighboring islands of Bonaire and Aruba as *islas inútiles* (useless islands) without valuable minerals to exploit, the Heeren XIX remained naively hopeful that Cohen might succeed in finding a possible gold or silver mine on Curaçao.

In contrast to the costly and difficult invasion of Pernambuco, the WIC's conquest of Curaçao in July 1634 was relatively easy. Since the Spanish were using the dry and rocky island primarily as a large cattle ranch, it was sparsely occupied. In addition to the few Spanish settlers, several hundred Indians called Caquetíos inhabited the island, most whom spoke Spanish, had adopted Spanish names, accepted Catholicism, and worked as cattle herders. When the Spanish garrison was faced with the small WIC fleet consisting of four ships and 250 soldiers, they initially thought that the Dutch intended to land briefly in order to take on fresh food and water, which was a common occurrence. However, after Company soldiers started to build a fort at the entrance to one of the island's bays, Spanish officials belatedly realized that the Dutch had effected an actual invasion and were planning to take possession of Curaçao for themselves. Outnumbered and outgunned by the WIC force, the Spanish colonists has little choice but to surrender to Van Walbeeck on August 21. Samuel Cohen acted as interpreter during the subsequent negotiations.

Once the matter was settled and his linguistic skills were no longer needed, Cohen began to look for gold. According to several Caquetío Indian spies who fled to Caracas to inform Spanish colonial officials about Dutch takeover, "a Portuguese, who the Hollanders call the Jew," had started to dig on a small hill shortly after the Dutch conquest but, they were assured, had not yet found any gold. Cohen did not give up. In October 1635, a Caquetío Indian named Juan Mateo related that "the Portuguese, who they call the gold-digger, was busy making pits all over the island." Mateo added that Cohen "claimed to be looking for gold, but he never found anything." A Flemish observer named Mathias Herman confirmed that by 1636 Cohen still had failed to find gold anywhere, leading the Company to call off all further explorations on the island.

During his time on the tropical Caribbean island, Cohen also became involved with WIC attempts to control its native population. After the Spaniards left Curaçao in August 1634, Van Walbeeck had forced most of the Indians out too because he feared that they would remain sympathetic to their former European administrators. Only some fifteen to twenty Indian families were allowed to remain on the island in order to herd the thousands of cows, goats, and horses that grazed there. Van Walbeeck initially made use of a friendly native headman named Balthazar de Montero as a mediator but quickly discovered that he was not to be trusted. In December 1634, Company officials uncovered an intricate Spanish–Indian plot to drive the Dutch from Curaçao and learned that their erstwhile ally Montero was deeply implicated. Van Walbeeck hurriedly appointed Cohen as overseer of the remaining Curaçao natives. In his position as superintendent of the Indians, Cohen was instructed to make sure that they came to feel a sense of loyalty to the Company. Cohen supplied the Indians with small amounts of trade goods both as a bribe and as a reward for their docility. In addition to linguistic skills that allowed him to communicate with the Spanish-speaking Indians, Cohen's appointment clearly indicated that Van Walbeeck and other senior Company officials on Curaçao viewed him as a loyal individual who could be trusted to deal with such a delicate situation. An Indian informant named Miguel described Cohen as "a great friend of the aforementioned Hollanders."

However, Cohen was not beloved by all the Company personnel on Curaçao. Several captured WIC soldiers testified to the Spanish governor in Caracas in 1636 and 1637 that Cohen was known on the island as "the little Jew." They commented sarcastically that he did not eat pork and lived among the Indians. Cohen's adherence to a special religious diet made him stand out among the Christian population. Spanish authorities were notorious for their anti-Jewish measures, and it seems clear that this denigration of Cohen, a longtime, valuable, and loyal WIC employee, revealed actual views among the Protestant Dutch company sailors and soldiers as well. Anti-Semitic attitudes were common among Christians of all nations in seventeenth-century Europe. Cohen's decision to live among the small population of Curaçao Indians suggests that he deliberately moved away from the colonial community in order to practice his Jewish faith without being insulted by Company employees. In doing so, he aligned himself with a group that was seen as dangerous and untrustworthy by Dutch officials, making the Jew Cohen appear even more suspicious in the eyes of some WIC personnel.

Although it is unknown how long Cohen remained on his post as overseer of the Curaçao Indians, WIC correspondence reveals that he died at the Dutch-controlled port city of Luanda in Angola sometime in the spring of 1642. In the absence of any further documentary records detailing his life, the reconstruction of Cohen's final years remain speculative. Most likely, the WIC called on Cohen's linguistic skills for a third time after the Company government in Dutch Brazil decided to conquer the important Portuguese slave-trading center of Luanda (in today's Angola) in early 1641. The ambitious WIC plan to attack Luanda had its inception in events in both Brazil and Europe. Under the energetic and able command of Governor-General

Johan Maurits, WIC forces had made great progress in their conquest of northeastern Brazil since the mid-1630s. By 1641, the Portuguese were barely holding on to Salvador de Bahia, and the WIC had established effective control over most of the region. At the same time, a revolt broke out against the Spanish Crown in Portugal that quickly led to the independence of Portugal in December 1641. Hoping to exploit the confusion within the Portuguese Atlantic empire, the Heeren XIX in the Dutch Republic encouraged Maurits to capture as much of their territory as possible.

One of the most appealing targets for Maurits was the West African port city of Luanda. From this strategic harbor, the Portuguese supplied the Brazilian sugar-growing province of Bahia with thousands of enslaved African workers. Without Angolan slaves, European sugar planters and mill owners in Brazil would be without workers since Europeans or Indians were not available or willing to do the heavy and dangerous labor. Because the Dutch wanted to increase the export of profitable Brazilian sugar to Europe, Maurits correctly realized that the WIC would need to import additional African labor. By capturing Luanda, the WIC not only would inflict major economic damage on the Portuguese Atlantic empire but also would secure a continuous supply of African slaves for their own Dutch-controlled sugar plantations in Brazil. In May 1641, Maurits dispatched a small Company fleet from Recife to capture Luanda, and they were in control of the lucrative port by August.

It was in the economic and imperial context of an aggressively expanding WIC that Samuel Cohen was sent to Angola to serve interpreter for the Dutch West India Company once again. Cohen's transfer from the Caribbean to Africa demonstrates that the WIC was able to coordinate the postings of their valuable employees throughout a far-flung Atlantic entrepreneurial enterprise. Despite his suspect religious affiliation, Cohen's linguistic skills were difficult to replace, and so the WIC Protestant directors continued to recruit him for their needs. In an era before nation-states coalesced, when private individuals often changed loyalties in order to improve their own fortunes and careers, Samuel Cohen remained loyal and committed to the WIC. He had demonstrated to senior Company officials that he could be trusted to be their interpreter.

On Cohen's arrival in Luanda, he immediately went to work translating communications in the tense negotiations between WIC personnel and the Portuguese colonists who had fled to the hinterland. Company forces repeatedly tried to root out vestiges of the Portuguese resistance, but a small band of hostile colonists continued to hold out against all odds, making it difficult for the WIC to take full control of the Angolan slave trade. Company officials at Luanda tried a strategy of alternating attacks with peace negotiations in order to pressure and persuade the Portuguese to lay down their arms. Cohen was involved in these exchanges and also translated intercepted Portuguese correspondence. In addition to these inter-European communications, Cohen also attempted to mediate and interpret the discussions between the Company and the native African kingdoms. WIC officials in Luanda hoped to establish commercial relations with the powerful African potentates who supplied Europeans with lucrative slaves that they would capture in the interior. Because they had been in extensive contact with European merchants and missionaries since the sixteenth century, a considerable number of Africans in the Angola region had mastered the Portuguese language. The WIC therefore needed skilled and reliable individuals who spoke Portuguese in order to communicate with the West Africans.

Unfortunately, Samuel Cohen fell ill and died in Luanda sometime in the spring of 1642. A letter from Company officials in Angola, addressed to Governor-General Johann Maurits in Dutch-held Brazil, reported in late May 1642 that "Samuel Kocken [Cohen], a Jew who had served us as interpreter in the Portuguese language, has also died." The Luanda authorities asked Maurits to send "us again a skilled person" to replace Cohen, someone who could adequately translate Portuguese letters. Cohen's cause of death was not identified, but he very likely died from a tropical disease like malaria or yellow fever, which felled so many thousands of Europeans in the tropical regions of the Atlantic world. In April 1642, the Company garrison at Luanda had been so ravaged by disease that only 150 out of more than 1,100 men were still fit for service.

Cohen's death occurred at the zenith of the Dutch colonial empire's power throughout the Atlantic World. In the spring of 1642, the WIC had established firm military control over most of northeastern Brazil. By capturing the slave depot of Luanda, the Company was able to supply their Brazilian sugar plantations with thousands of Angolan slaves. Together with other valuable WIC outposts and colonies such as Curaçao in the Caribbean, New Netherland in North America, and Fort Elmina in West Africa, the Company had quickly become one of the most prominent colonial powers in the Atlantic world. However, in 1645, just three years after Cohen's death, a popular rebellion broke out among Portuguese sugar planters in Dutch-controlled Brazil that shook the foundations of that colony. Supported by Portuguese guerrilla forces in Bahia, the Portuguese colonists slowly regained control of northeastern Brazil. At nearly the same time, in August 1648, a Portuguese fleet recaptured Luanda in a surprise attack. Faced with growing challenges of financing their enormously costly operations that spanned the

Atlantic, the WIC eventually surrendered Brazil in January 1654. Barely ten years after Cohen's death, the Company dreams of building a colonial empire on the foundations of the Iberian powers had foundered on the rocky shoals of their own ambition.

Although the WIC failed in its attempt to establish an empire in the southern Atlantic, the Dutch trade company did unintentionally stimulate the development of Sephardic Jewish communities in the Americas. During the twenty-five years of WIC rule of northeastern Brazil, the Pernambuco coastal city of Recife became a magnet for New Christians and Sephardic Jews from Brazil and Europe. At its height in the 1640s, the Sephardic population of Recife numbered more than one thousand people out of an urban population of several thousand. The WIC extensively relied on Sephardic Jews and New Christians as linguistic and financial brokers in Dutch relations with the Catholic Portuguese sugar planters. Many Sephardic merchants loaned money to Catholic planters so that the latter could buy tools and African slaves for their sugar plantations. Taking advantage of the relatively tolerant WIC colonial government, the Sephardic Jews of Recife established a formal synagogue, built schools, and practiced religious rituals that had been formerly prohibited by the Portuguese. Fearing a return of repressive Catholic measures following the expulsion of the Dutch from Brazil in 1654, almost all Sephardic Jews departed from Recife. While some Sephardic Jews migrated to English and French colonies in the Caribbean, most Jews from Recife resettled in Curaçao and Surinam during the 1650s and 1660s where they continued their economic and cultural activities. Finally, a small group of twenty-three Sephardic Jews from Brazil found refuge in the WIC colony of New Netherland in North America in 1654.

By serving the WIC as an interpreter and miner in Brazil, Curaçao, and Angola, Samuel Cohen had played a considerable part in the emergence of the short-lived Dutch Atlantic empire. Cohen's specialized linguistic and mining skills made him a valuable individual for the Company during its expansion throughout the Atlantic world. However, perhaps because of Cohen's Ashkenazi Jewish background, which may have isolated him from the extensive family networks and communities constructed by Sephardic Jews in the seventeenth-century Atlantic world, Cohen failed to benefit personally from his valuable talents. Although Sephardic Jews established thriving communities in Dutch-controlled Brazil and Curacao, Cohen was not part of them. Cohen was never able to locate any gold or silver mines for the WIC that could have brought him a fortune. In addition, Cohen did not obtain significant material or social benefits from his decadelong service as loyal Company interpreter. For all his useful expertise, Cohen remained a marginal character in both the Dutch and the Sephardic Atlantic worlds.

Bibliography and Suggested Reading

Archival material for this chapter has been found in the Notarial Archives of the Amsterdam City Archive and the Archive of the Old West India Company held at the Dutch National Archives in The Hague.

Bernardini, Paolo, and Norman Fiering, eds. *The Jews and the Expansion of Europe to the West, 1450–1800*. New York: Berghahn Books, 2001.

Blom, J. C. H., R. G. Fuks-Mansfeld, and I. Schoffer. *The History of the Jews in the Netherlands*. Translated by Arnold J. and Erica Pomerans. Oxford: Littman Library of Jewish Civilization, 2002.

Bodian, Miriam. *Hebrews of the Portuguese Nation: Conversos and Community in Early Modern Amsterdam*. Bloomington: Indiana University Press, 1997.

Boxer, Charles R. *The Dutch in Brazil, 1624–1654*. Oxford: Clarendon Press, 1957.

den Heijer, Henk. "The Dutch West India Company, 1621–1791." In *Riches from Atlantic Commerce: Dutch Transatlantic Trade and Shipping, 1585–1817*, edited by Johannes Postma and Victor Enthoven, 77–112. Leiden: Brill, 2003.

Emmanuel, Isaac S., and Suzanne A. Emmanuel. *History of the Jews of the Netherlands Antilles*. Cincinnati: American Jewish Archives, 1970.

Gelfand, Noah L. "A Caribbean Wind: An Overview of the Jewish Dispersal from Dutch Brazil." *De Halve Maen: Magazine of the Dutch Colonial Period in America* 78, no. 3 (Fall 2005): 49–56.

Goslinga, Cornelis. *The Dutch in the Caribbean and on the Wild Coast, 1580–1680*. Assen and Gainesville: Van Gorcum Press and University Press of Florida, 1971.

Graizbord, David L. *Souls in Dispute: Converso Identities in Iberia and the Jewish Diaspora 1580–1700*. Philadelphia: University of Pennsylvania Press, 2003.

Israel, Jonathan Irvine. *Diaspora within a Diaspora: Jews, Crypto-Jews and the World of Maritime Empires 1540–1740*. Leiden: Brill, 2002.

Levine, Robert. *Tropical Diaspora: The Jewish Experience in Cuba*. Gainesville: University Press of Florida, 1993.

Pencak, William. *Jews and Gentiles in Early America 1654–1820*. Ann Arbor: University of Michigan Press, 2005.

Ratelband, Klaas. *Nederlanders in West Africa, 1600–1650: Angola, Kongo en São Tomé*, edited by René Baesjou. Zutphen: Walburg Press, 2000.

Reiss, Oscar. *The Jews in Colonial America*. New York: McFarland, 2004.

Ruggiero, Kristin. *Jewish Diaspora in Latin America and the Caribbean: Fragments of Memory*. Sussex: Academic Press, 2005.

Sheinin, David, and Lois Baer Barr, eds. *Jewish Diaspora in Latin America*. New York: Garland, 2006.

Stillman, Yedida, and Norman A. Stillman. *From Iberia to Diaspora: Studies in Sephardic History and Culture*. Leiden: Brill, 1998.

van den Boogaart, Ernst. "Infernal Allies: The Dutch West India Company and the Tarairiu, 1630–1654." In *Johan Maurits van Nassau-Siegen: A Humanist Prince in Europe and Brazil. Essays on the Tercentenary of His Death*, edited by H. R. Hoetink and P. J. P. Whitehead, 519–38. The Hague: Johan Maurits van Nassau Stichting, 1979.

CHAPTER FOUR

William Lamport/Guillén de Lombardo (1611–1659)

Mexico's Irish Would-Be King

Sarah Cline

After the wars of the Reformation, Catholics throughout the Atlantic world shared a complicated and interrelated history. In particular, Catholics in Ireland and Spain viewed themselves as natural allies confronting an aggressive and expansive Protestant England. In this chapter, historian Sarah Cline describes the unlikely tale of Irishman William Lamport, who reinvented himself as a Spanish nobleman named Don Guillén de Lombardo. He was part soldier of fortune, part hardy adventurer, and part lunatic visionary; however, Spanish authorities executed Lamport eventually in November 1659 following his attempt to set himself up as an independent king in Mexico. Lamport's vision for his utopian American kingdom represented quite a departure from conditions in the highly stratified and race-conscious Spanish American colony; he decreed that under his rule, Africans and Indians would be considered equal to whites. His story illuminates not only one typical transnational religious alliance during the era of the Counter-Reformation but also the limits of that same cross-cultural cooperation when one partner became too ambitious.

On November 19, 1659, a fair-skinned, redheaded Irishman was paraded through the thronged streets of Mexico City on the way to his death in an *auto da fé* (public burning). Born William Lamport in Wexford, Ireland, in 1611, he died in a remote land as Don Guillén de Lombardo y Guzmán. His story is both ordinary and unusual in the Atlantic world. Like many Irish Catholics in the seventeenth century, he journeyed to the Continent for his education and fought in the Spanish king's wars against Protestants. He eventually immigrated to the Spanish Indies and became part of the cosmopolitan urban scene of the viceregal capital in Mexico City. Like a few other foreigners who resided there, Lamport came before the Holy Office of the Inquisition, but his real transgression was not the heresy of Protestantism, crypto-Judaism, or unorthodox religious beliefs. His was a political crime: sedition.

In testimony before the Inquisition, the Spaniard who denounced William Lamport/Don Guillén Lombardo said that the Irishman claimed to be the natural son of the late Philip III (r. 1598–1621) and therefore purported to be the half brother of King Philip IV. Just as outrageously, the Irishman had been attempting to organize an uprising to make Mexico independent from Spain, setting himself up as the new nation's king. Don Guillén sought the aid of foreign powers and the local support of Mexican Indians and Africans as well as elite white merchants. To gain allies for his scheme for a politically independent state, he dared to promise equality for the dispossessed racial groups in the new order and freer trade for the rich, American-born merchants. Don Guillén's grandiose plans were aborted in October 1642 when Captain Felipe Méndez Ortiz denounced Don Guillén to the Holy Office. Don Guillén was arrested and taken to the nearby Inquisition prison, from which he emerged only twice, first in an unprecedented one-day escape in 1650 and the last when he was led to the stake in 1659. That year, the inquisitors "relaxed" him to secular authorities; that is, they turned him over to civil officials for execution since only secular authorities were permitted to carry out capital punishment.

Although his spectacular death was unusual, William Lamport's odyssey from Ireland to Spain and from Spain to New Spain (as Mexico was then called) was a fairly typical life story in the seventeenth-century Atlantic world, an era of religious wars with none-too-subtle political overtones. Born the second son to a Catholic merchant family of English origins, William was not able to inherit land and therefore needed to seek his own way in the world. Like many other impoverished Irishmen, he and his brothers traveled to the Continent and then Mexico; his older brother John became a Franciscan friar, and his younger brother Gerald became a mercenary. His younger sister Catherine became a nun. Although the Lamport family was rooted in Ireland, it was rumored that William's father and grandfather had been part of an international network of privateers who preyed on maritime traffic.

Prospects for Catholic families in Ireland started to narrow in the late sixteenth century as the English increased their control over the island and their Protestant monarchs imposed various new restrictions on Catholics in public life. In those circumstances, without available Catholic religious education, Wexford's parish priest oversaw young William's early studies at home. In early adolescence, his mother died, prompting Lamport to leave home and head north to further his studies in Dublin, the largest city in Ireland. As the British Protestant authorities started to extend their control over all areas of Irish life, his Jesuit school was suppressed, and its teachers and the school building were transferred to Trinity College, which was founded for young men's Anglican education. With no educational opportunities left in Ireland, the adventurous youth left Dublin and went to London.

According to his own testimony before the Mexican Inquisition, Lamport claimed that he wrote a pamphlet in which he attacked the English monarch and therefore was forced to flee to the Continent around 1630. One of the frustrating but also intriguing aspects of Lamport's saga is that it is difficult to tell how much of his Inquisition testimony is true, how much was embellished, and how much was outright fabrication. His Inquisition testimony is the closest we will get to an autobiography, and, not surprisingly, he is the hero of his own story, making his adventures larger than life. It is entirely possible that he wrote such an incendiary pamphlet since there is Inquisition testimony by William's older brother John (known in Mexico as Fray Juan) attesting not only to William's brilliance but also to his headstrong nature.

Lamport's version of his flight from England is even more colorful. He claimed to have been captured by pirates in the English Channel while aboard a ship bound for the French port of St. Malo. As he told it, Lamport convinced the French and English pirate captains not only to set him free but also to allow him to join them. For a period of several months, he was a part of this motley crew, but he left them at Bordeaux and made his way to one of Spain's Atlantic ports, La Coruña, in the autumn of 1630. In Spain, Lamport's prospects improved immeasurably when he met the Marqués de Mancera, who arranged for him to attend St. Patrick's College, a school for Catholic Irishmen. In his search for education on the Continent, William was following a well-trod path of young Irishmen to Spain.

Up to this point, the story would have not caused the inquisitors any alarm; Lamport was a Catholic youth, seemingly thumbing his nose at Protestant English authority and seeking refuge in Catholic realms. Since institutions of higher learning were effectively closed to Catholic Irishmen, they sought educational opportunities in Catholic Europe as an alternative. In the early seventeenth century, Irish expatriates founded colleges in France, the Low Countries, Portugal, and Spain in order to train lawyers and priests with the hope that their graduates would return to Ireland and serve their countrymen. Lamport later claimed that he attended the Irish College in Santiago de Compostela, which was founded in 1605 for the sons of Irish nobility following the disastrous Irish–Spanish defeat by the English at Kinsale (Ireland) in 1601. Spain was a popular choice for Catholic Irishmen seeking an education. Not only was Spain the ideological center of the Counter-Reformation, but also the ties between Ireland and Spain were long standing. Irish legend held that Milesius of Spain planned to invade Ireland but died, leaving one of his sons to accomplish it. One sixteenth-century Iberian writer called the Irish *los españoles del norte* (Spaniards of the north). Iberian nobles recognized the Irish nobility on equal grounds, and Irishmen were granted all the rights of Spanish citizens.

At St. Patrick's College for Irish Nobles, Lamport began his transformation to his new Spanish identity as Don Guillén de Lombardo y Guzmán. The title *don* was a marker for noble status in males and considered to be an integral part of a nobleman's name. "Guillén" is a Spanish variant of "Guillermo," which is "William" in English translation; "Lombardo" is a plausible Hispanicization of the name Lamport. The altered name would make him seem less a foreigner in Spain, even if he was the less suspect Irish variety. If Don Guillén ever had aspirations of ordination to the priesthood, these seem to have faded as secular opportunities opened up.

Don Guillén's connection to the Marqués of Mancera permitted him to gain entry to the Spanish Court and access to the patronage of the Count-Duke Olivares, who was the most powerful man in early seventeenth-century Spain. Don Guillén prepared a flattering description of the count-duke for the meeting. His offering, *Laus Comitis Ducis*, apparently had the proper effect since he was hired on as a propagandist for the Crown. Since Don Guillén was a foreigner and apparently without family connections in Spain, his claim of noble birth and literary skills made him a good candidate for such a position since his loyalty would be exclusively to his patron. With court sponsorship, the new Irish Spaniard began studies at the College of San Isidro and then at Lorenzo College at the Escorial, the palace-monastery built by Philip II outside of Madrid.

Much of early seventeenth-century continental history involved warfare with religious implications. Conflicts such as the Thirty Years' War (1618–1648), fought mostly in Germany, and the Eighty Years' War (1548–1648), between Spain and its Low Country provinces in the Low Countries, provided ambitious men with opportunities to distinguish themselves militarily and later petition the Crown for material rewards. As the battlefields beckoned, Don Guillén and his Jesuit teachers ceased their scholarly activities and became active soldiers in service to Philip IV. His mathematics teachers were experts in artillery, the practical application of triangles and arcs.

Don Guillén was part of Philip IV's army that marched on Central Europe through the Alps into Germany. The (Catholic) Spanish army defeated the (Lutheran) Swedish army encamped at Nördlingen in July 1634, a major victory for Spain. During that campaign, Don Guillén apparently came to know Antwerp-born Jesuit mathematician Jean Charles de la Faille, who advised Philip IV on military affairs. In 1638, Don Guillén claimed that he and his brother Gerald joined with Irish mercenaries in the battle of Fuenterrabía, where the French laid siege to a Basque town. For their part, the English encouraged the out-migration of disaffected Irishmen who might cause problems for them at home. Most never returned to Ireland.

After these two military experiences, Don Guillén followed the path of many a warrior and sought compensation commensurate with his services. It was a long-standing practice in Spain for individual acts of bravery or services to the Crown to be rewarded with titles, money, and, during the conquest of the New World, grants of Indian labor. European armies generally were not standing militaries but rather were composed of mercenaries, soldiers of fortune, and conscripts, along with wealthier, ambitious men. The lesser nobility sought military honors through valorous combat, which became an essential way for a noble man to distinguish himself and merit recognition. From Don Guillén's point of view, the honors he was awarded may not have been sufficient, perhaps prompting him to seek his fortune elsewhere.

Around that time, his personal life became complicated. Sometime in the mid-1630s, Don Guillén became romantically involved with a young woman from a good family named Ana de Cano y Leiva. When she became pregnant, the situation was awkward and caused gossip at court, although the situation itself was not entirely unusual. After receiving a man's promise of marriage, Spanish women of noble status often began sexual relations with their future bridegroom. Pregnancy often accelerated the wedding date, but if the man reneged on his proposal, a woman's honor was ruined, and she could file a breach-of-promise lawsuit. Sometimes couples married after the child was born, which legitimized the birth in the eyes of the Church and society. In the case of Don Guillén and Ana, they moved in together, in lodgings near his college that were paid for by her sister, but they did not wed. His oldest brother John, who had also assimilated into Spanish society as the Franciscan monk Fray Juan, appeared in Madrid and urged the couple to marry. Instead, they separated, and Don Guillén moved a few blocks away. Shortly thereafter, perhaps because of the scandal or possibly because of greater opportunities in the New World, he left Europe for Mexico in 1640. There is some evidence that the Crown actually sent Don Guillén across the

Atlantic to gather information on the political ferment in Mexico, especially since he enjoyed the patronage of the powerful Count-Duke Olivares.

Mexico was one of two Spanish viceroyalties in the New World (Peru was the other one). Both regions had dense populations of Indians whose labor could be exploited as well as huge deposits of silver waiting to be mined. Silver was the economic motor of the Spanish Empire and in turn fueled trade and commerce throughout the world. Mexican silver was exported to China in exchange for fine silks and porcelains and was also sent directly to the Spanish king's coffers. For the Spanish monarch, New World silver was manna from heaven since he did not have to tax his Iberian peasants or urban dwelling commoners in order to acquire it. New World laborers, both free and forced, magically brought wealth out of the earth. The maintenance of Spanish control over Mexico and Peru, therefore, was absolutely vital to the Crown's political and economic interests. For that reason, rumors of unrest in Mexico City were of great concern.

In the century or so since the Spanish conquest of the Aztec Empire in 1519, Spaniards turned the former city of Tenochtitlán into the viceregal capital of Mexico City, a place where white Spanish colonists appeared to be firmly in control. The city was also the seat of the archbishopric, and the first university in the New World was established there. It was home to the richest merchants and financiers; the most well-connected clerics, physicians, and lawyers; the finest craftsmen; and the most accomplished artists and musicians. Socially, it was a hierarchical society, with whites at the apex of a complicated pyramid defined by race, wealth, and place of origin. Urban society also included significant numbers of Africans who had been brought to Mexico during the conquest and who, along with the *castas* (mixed race) and Indians, made up the capital's vibrant and volatile scene. The nonwhite population vastly outnumbered the Spanish-born *peninsulares* and American-born *criollos* (creoles), even in the culturally Hispanic cities, but elite European men controlled all positions of power and considered this dominance their birthright.

In 1640, Don Guillén arrived in Mexico on the same ship as two figures of great importance. One was the newly appointed Bishop of Puebla, Don Juan de Palafox, who was to serve as the Crown's inspector-general during the transition from one viceroy's administration to another. The other notable personage was the newly appointed viceroy, the Marqués de Villena, Don Diego López Pacheco y Bobadilla, a relative of King João of the Portuguese house of Braganza. The Spanish Crown had chosen Villena to replace the ineffectual Marqués of Cadereyta, just the second American-born Spaniard ever chosen as viceroy. The Crown traditionally chose viceroys from Spanish noble families of the highest order whose loyalty was unquestioned, although he had some freedom of action to respond to local conditions given Spain's distance from Mexico. Considering the particular voyage on which he sailed, however, Don Guillén de Lombardo may have been sent to Mexico City as a spy for the Crown since the rivalries of high-born officials may have often distorted information that viceroys and archbishops sent back across the Atlantic.

In June 1640, when Don Guillén set out in such illustrious company, the political situation in both Spain and its overseas territories was increasingly unsettled. For the Spanish Crown, these were dangerous times. Portugal, a culturally distinct region of the Iberian Peninsula, was in revolt against Philip IV, who inherited the Crown of Portugal as well as the crowns of Castile and Aragón. In December 1640, France backed the claims of João, Duke of Braganza, who successfully wrested Portugal independence from Hapsburg control after sixty years of Spanish rule.

Once the connection between Portugal and Spain was severed, Portuguese merchants residing in Spanish-controlled territories became deeply suspect. They had already been implicated in anti-Crown agitation in Mexico City as early as 1624, when Viceroy Gelves attempted to break up commercial rackets that kept prices artificially high, benefiting American-born elites and foreign merchants while undermining Crown authority. Gelves's reforms provoked a major riot in Mexico City's *zócalo* (central plaza), a disturbance that forced the viceroy to flee his palace and eventually led to his dismissal. Portuguese merchants were conspicuous in their participation. Ten years later, during Viceroy Cadereyta's administration (1635–1639), rivalries between Mexico City and Puebla elites caused the Crown to perceive a similar "political danger" with the potential for riots. The Crown removed Viceroy Cadereyta and sent the distinguished cleric Palafox to serve as visitor-general as well as to conduct a review of his performance in office (a process known as a *residencia*).

On arrival in New Spain, Bishop Palafox ingratiated himself with American-born elites in his Diocese of Puebla and relatively quickly came into conflict with the new Viceroy Villena. Villena's brother-in-law João was the king of Portugal, and the Spanish Crown was nervous about the possibility for intrigue that emanated from that personal relationship. With a suspect viceroy and a significant Portuguese New Christian merchant community, Palafox sniffed danger for Spanish interests in Mexico and persuaded the Crown to remove Villena to ensure that New Spain would remain loyal. The Crown sought to shore up its control and appear strong, but the rapid turnover of viceroys undoubtedly undermined the central authorities in the minds of the populace.

In this volatile context, Don Guillén Lombardo's own scheme to stir up Mexican Indians and blacks and forge an alliance with white creole merchants to take control of New Spain was not entirely absurd. Since American-born Spaniards were irate that the Crown recently had prohibited direct trade between Mexico and Peru in order to privilege peninsular commercial interests over American ones, there was some potential for elite support of an independent Mexico. More radically, he recognized the potential power of the black and Indian masses, whose participation in riots in 1624 had been the impetus for ousting the viceroy. Don Guillén drew up a document that offered freedom and equality to all slaves, mulattos, *castas*, and Indians and made them eligible for all official honors. He also pledged to restore communal lands taken from the Indians. In his scheme, all those subjugated groups would become personally obligated to him, Don Guillén de Lombardo; the grateful wretches would proclaim him king and support his rule as loyal vassals. As monarch, he would open commerce with France, Holland, England, and Portugal, all enemies of Spain. In this way, he also would satisfy the interests of white merchants whose businesses felt the impact of Spanish mercantilist policies that limited intercolonial commerce and excluded foreign traders. By considering the Netherlands and England as potential trading partners, of course, the Mexican king would have to overlook their status as heretical Protestant countries.

Don Guillén's scheme to gain the support of the racially oppressed majority of New Spain may have recalled his own sense of disenfranchisement as an Irish Catholic forced into exile by his beloved island's Protestant English rulers. Sometime around 1641, he began to organize a popular uprising and invited local elite conspirators to join with him to seize power. Likely realizing that a mass uprising in the capital would not be sufficient to maintain Mexico's independence, he also sought overseas aid from Spain's enemies, the Dutch and the French. The Dutch supported Portugal's bid to regain its independence from Spain, and France supported the province of Cataluña's attempt to win more autonomy from an increasingly centralized Spanish state; both insurgencies benefited the political and economic position of the Netherlands, and there was every reason to suspect that the Dutch would be interested in weakening Spain in its overseas colonial territories as well.

When Don Guillén divulged his plans to a friend named Captain Méndez, he may have been looking for an ally. Instead, Méndez went straight to the Inquisition and denounced the Irishman. Méndez lived nearby and likely observed the comings and goings of Don Guillén's visitors, one of whom was an Indian identified as a "sorcerer." Méndez claimed to have evidence that the two conspirators had taken the hallucinogenic mushroom peyote together. Méndez's denunciation also included accusations that the Irishman practiced astrology and had attempted cures for illnesses that involved pacts with the Devil. In the grand scheme of things, these religious transgressions merited concern but typically did not lead to immediate inquisitorial action. But when Méndez claimed that the foreign-born Don Guillén de Lombardo was conspiring to lead a political uprising against the king, his actions passed out of the realm of religion and heresy and became a serious civil crime. That was a danger that could not be tolerated.

Don Guillén clearly seems to have trusted his neighbor. The too-trusting Irishman was voluble, telling Méndez that he was King Philip IV's natural half brother because his widowed Irish mother had an affair with Philip III and that she had been sent to Ireland to preserve her honor. According to Don Guillén, both Philip IV and the king's minister, Count-Duke Olivares, knew this to be true. Taking Méndez into his rooms, Don Guillén showed him a series of official-looking papers and copies of correspondence that he claimed proved his case. He also had written to the Duke of Braganza, who had become the Portuguese monarch, to French King Louis XIII and even to the pope, seeking their diplomatic and military support for his Mexican scheme. Obviously, Méndez was alarmed by what he saw. Although the nosy neighbor's initial charges were largely religious in nature, the political overtones were serious, and therefore the Inquisition arrested Don Guillén that same Sunday. The urgency of the situation is suggested by the fact that the Inquisition acted so rapidly, even though it was the Christian day of rest.

The Mexican Inquisition had been set up as a separate institution of the Catholic Church in 1571 and had been concerned mainly with prosecutions of crypto-Jews, Protestant foreigners, and heresy. Although the Inquisition in Spain has rightly earned a reputation for large-scale prosecutions, particularly in the sixteenth century, the Mexican Inquisition did not operate on such a grand scale. In 1647, the Suprema (Supreme Council of the Inquisition, based in Madrid) sought to centralize its control by requiring that sentences from each regional Holy Office be reviewed and confirmed by them in Europe as well. In particular, those cases that resulted in the prisoner's "relaxation" to civil authorities for execution always required the Suprema's confirmation. In Don Guillén's case, there were religious grounds for him to be tried by the Inquisition, but the suspicion of conspiracy and sedition against the Crown also put him at risk for a civil trial. The inquisitors wrote directly to the Council of the Indies, the royal administrative body that dealt with Spain's overseas territories, arguing that the Inquisition should retain jurisdiction over this seditious character. They delicately pointed out that a public trial of such a flamboyant and well-connected prisoner who had been arrested while in a compromising position with a high-born lady (rumored to be the viceroy's wife) could cause considerable embarrassment to all involved. A secret trial by the Inquisition would be much better. The arguments must have been convincing because the viceroy upheld the Inquisition's jurisdiction.

The religious charges were not sufficiently severe to merit more than imprisonment, secret trial, reconciliation to orthodox Catholicism, penance, and public humiliation. Most Inquisition trials in Mexico did not result in the prisoner's execution. Relaxation to civil authorities was reserved for recalcitrant "judaizers" and heretics. The Inquisition gathered information from Méndez and other witnesses, while Don Guillén remained incarcerated. Standard operating procedure was for the Inquisition to confiscate a prisoner's property to pay for his or her upkeep during detention. If convicted, the goods remained the property of the Inquisition and were both the institution's major source of revenue and a potential source of corruption. Inquisitors had a financial incentive for convicting the accused. Almost exactly a year after his arrest, Don Guillén was brought before the inquisitors and gave testimony himself. Like most defendants, he knew neither the exact charges he faced nor who had accused him. Although he had alluded to his own royal pedigree and connection to the Spanish monarch when he spoke to Méndez, he made no mention of it in his Inquisition testimony.

Don Guillén could well have expected to get out of the difficulties he found himself in. He had connections to powerful men on both sides of the Atlantic, and such influence was known to affect the outcome of judicial proceedings. In Mexico, Don Guillén appears to have been allied with the Bishop of Puebla, Palafox, who wielded considerable power in both civil and ecclesiastical spheres; in Spain, he had served Count-Duke Olivares. Unfortunately for Don Guillén, both powerful patrons were embroiled in insurmountable troubles of their own, so the Irishman who languished in the jails of Mexico's Inquisition was not helped by his connections. Palafox became involved in a bitter fight between himself, as the leader of the diocesan clergy, and the entrenched forces of the Jesuits and the monastic orders. He also took on the viceroy and the Inquisition, who supported the old power arrangements. Bishop Palafox was forced to return to Spain, where he died in 1659. Olivares was ousted from power in 1643. Meanwhile, Don Guillen languished in prison. In 1649, there was a huge *auto-da-fé* (public pronouncement of an Inquisition sentence, often accompanied by burnings at the stake) in Mexico City where a number of crypto-Jews, most with

Portuguese backgrounds, were burned at the stake. Don Guillén might have been considered for this public display of ecclesiastical and civil power, but his case was deemed too politically sensitive.

Don Guillén had already spent eight years in the Inquisition jails when he escaped briefly on Christmas Eve 1650. He had been assigned a cellmate, Diego Pinto Bravo, an artisan specializing in shoeing horses, whose own crimes were fairly petty. Inquisitors likely placed him with Don Guillén to act as a spy. As if on cue, Don Guillén reiterated his exalted genealogy and spoke of his wealth and bragged about his high connections. If he mistrusted Pinto Bravo, he nonetheless plotted escape from the Inquisition jail with him, itself a daring act that no one had successfully managed. Their plan was to reach a settlement near Veracruz where sympathetic blacks would shelter them. Between Mexico City and the colony's main port of Veracruz, some blacks had successfully established settlements that preyed on travelers and resisted colonial authorities. With no guards on duty during the religious holiday, the pair removed the bars from the stone walls and escaped through the opening.

Once free, Don Guillén made his way to the palace, where he sought to deliver a letter to the viceroy, Don Luis Enríquez de Guzmán, the Conde de Alva de Liste. Although challenged by a palace guard, the audacious escapee claimed to be a messenger from Havana with private letters for the viceroy. Don Guillén then began to plaster the central core of Mexico City with broadsides denouncing the Inquisition as corrupt. How he had managed to get paper and pen to create these letters and broadsides is unclear, but his accusations were political dynamite and quickly became the talk of the town. Subsequent Inquisition testimony indicates that many of the capital's residents were out and about in the middle of the night on Christmas Eve and read the broadsides. The two escapees headed toward a friend's house, but Pinto Bravo separated himself from Don Guillén and fled north to Guanajuato, where he turned himself over to the Inquisition. Once their flight was discovered, priests in Mexico City's churches denounced the men and threatened punishment to any who sheltered them or possessed copies of Don Guillén's subversive accusations against the Inquisition. One researcher sees the rapidity with which the authorities were able to print up two hundred pamphlets denouncing Don Guillén as clear evidence that the authorities allowed him to escape since it would give them grounds to mete out more severe punishment than the original evidence warranted. Shortly thereafter, a man named Alonso de Benavides told Inquisition officials where Don Guillén was hiding, and he was rearrested.

The escape and rearrest of Mexico's Irish would-be king set the stage for yet another Inquisition trial since escape attempts were considered to be the equivalent of an admission of guilt. It also prompted the viceroy to write to Philip IV directly about the events. The viceroy, the Conde de Alva de Liste, told the monarch that he had given the Inquisition the outrageous letters Don Guillén had delivered to him on the night of his escape. The king's reply indicated that he knew the Irishman and viewed him worthy of honors for his services to the Crown. He went on to criticize the viceroy for having acceded to the Inquisition's demand for the evidence, which undermined Crown authority, and rebuked him for not keeping copies of the letters. Once they had the original letters, the Inquisition was able to suppress Don Guillén's accusations of corruption, particularly their financial irregularities and the denial of sacraments to their prisoners.

During the next years of imprisonment, Don Guillén's mental condition deteriorated to the point of madness, but his Inquisition dossier continued to grow. His own brother, the Franciscan Fray Juan, had not yet gone on record and was one of the witnesses called in the new round of investigations; the absence of his testimony may have been a blot on the Inquisition's initial case. Diego Pinto Bravo, who had escaped with Don Guillén, died while incarcerated in the Inquisition's jails. Despite horrific conditions in prison, somehow during the subsequent years of incarceration, Don Guillén managed to compose eight hundred Latin psalms, mostly religious in content, but a few had social themes.

In November 1659, another major *auto-da-fé* was organized for the capital, and this time Don Guillén was eligible for execution. Charges upon charges were piled onto his case, including his illegal flight from prison, his resistance to prison discipline, and his seditious writings. In the end, the catchall charges included Protestant heresy and libel of the Inquisition. In grand ceremony, the *auto-de-fé* created a spectacle for the crowds, reinforcing church and state power. Don Guillén was sentenced to be burned alive since he refused to confess and repent. Had he done so, he would have been garroted, a quick death rather than the protracted agony he now faced. Reports have it that he managed to work himself free of his bindings and strangle himself, giving him a last instant of volition. Nevertheless, Don Guillén's dramatic death had repercussions across the Atlantic. Since the Supreme Council of the Inquisition had not authorized his transfer to secular authorities for execution, the Mexican inquisitors had exceeded their legal authority. Ironically, his death attracted attention to the inquisitors' corruption and abuse of prisoners in ways that his life did not. As a result of a transatlantic investigation, some inquisitors were fined, barred from office, or otherwise penalized for their illegal actions.

William Lamport's death in Mexico City can be seen as the final chapter of a curious transatlantic life filled with adventure. In many significant ways, he was a precursor to Mexican independence, which came much later, in the early nineteenth century. His unusual story has provided inspiration for writers in Mexico and abroad. For example, nineteenth-century historian Vicente Riva Palacio wrote a lengthy romanticized historical novel based on Don Guillén's Inquisition testimony, although the book's title labeled him an "impostor." Another Mexican scholar writing in the late 1990s characterized Don Guillén's life "the labyrinth of deceit." An Italian writer suspects that Don Guillén's biography was the original source for the character of Zorro, which prompted some stories in the popular press about William/ Guillén following the release of the Hollywood movie *The Mask of Zorro*, starring Antonio Banderas.

Irishman William Lamport was a pirate and mercenary soldier who crossed an ocean and transformed himself into Don Guillén de Lombardo, a social and political visionary whose contact with racial and social oppression in Mexico led him to champion the rights of Indians and Africans. It was a long intellectual and cultural journey from his birthplace in the seaport of Wexford, Ireland, to his execution on a fiery stake in Mexico City. William Lamport/Don Guillén de Lombardo's biography is a tale of the seventeenth-century Atlantic world. His career trajectory was influenced by the incessant wars of religion, by a quest for noble status, and by the sense of possibilities that were available in the New World. As Mexico's Irish would-be king, Don Guillén's prescient vision of an independent nation with racial and social equality was far ahead of his time but hinted at the direction that the revolutions for independence throughout the Atlantic eventually would take just over a century later.

Bibliography and Suggested Reading

Bayardi Landeros, Citlalli. "Tres salmos inéditos de Don Guillén de Lampart." Translated by Raúl Falcó. *Literatura Mexicana*, 9, no. 1 (1998): 205–16.

Crewe, Ryan Dominic. "Brave New Spain: An Irishman's Independence Plot in Seventeenth Century Mexico." *Past and Present* 207 (May 2010): 53–87.

Cuevas, Mariano, S.J. *Historia de la Iglesia en México, Tomo III*. Mexico City: Antigua Imprenta de Murquia, 1924. Reprint, Mexico City: Edición Porrúa, 1992.

González Obregón, Luis. *Don Guillén de Lampart: La Inquisición y la Independencia en el siglo XVII*. Paris: Librería de la Viuda de C. Bouret, 1908.

Greenleaf, Richard. *The Mexican Inquisition of the Sixteenth Century*. Albuquerque: University of New Mexico Press, 1969.

Hair, P. E. H. "An Irishman before the Mexican Inquisition: 1574–1575." *Irish Historical Studies* 17, no. 67 (1971): 297–319.

Medina, J. T. *Historia del tribunal del Santo Oficio de la Inquisición en México*. Santiago: Etzeviriana, 1905. Reprint, Mexico City: Fuente Cultural, 1952.

Méndez Plancarte, Gabriel. "Don Guillén de Lámport y su 'Regio Salterio.' Ms. Latino inédito de 1655." *Abside: Revista de Cultura Mexicana* 12, no. 2 (April–June 1948): 123–92; 12, no. 3 (July–September 1948): 285–372.

———. "Memorial de Guillén de Lampart acerca de mal tratamiento que se da a los negros (s. xvii)." In *Historia Documental de México*, edited by Miguel Léon-Portilla et al., 260–61. Mexico City: Universidad Nacional Autónoma de México, 1974.

Meza González, Javier. *El laberinto de la mentira: Guillén de Lamporte y la Inquisición*. Mexico City: Universidad Autónoma Metropolitana, 1997.

Riva Palacio, Vicente. *Memorias de un Impostor: Don Guillén de Lampart, Rey de Mexico*. 2nd ed. 2 vols. Mexico City: Editorial Porrúa, 2000.

Ronan, Gerard. "The 'Zorro' of Wexford." *The Past* 22 (2000): 3–50.

———. *The Irish Zorro: The Extraordinary Adventures of William Lamport*. Dingle, Ireland: Brandon Books, 2006.

Silke, Fr. John J. "The Irish Abroad." In *A New History of Ireland: Vol. 3, Early Modern Ireland 1534–1691*, edited by T. W. Moody, F. X. Martin, and F. J. Byrne, 587–633. New York: Oxford University Press, 2009.

Troncarelli, Fabio. *La Spada e la Croce: Guillén Lombardo e l'Inquisizione in Messico*. Rome: Salerno Editrice, 1999.

Villa-Flores, Javier. *Dangerous Speech: A Social History of Blasphemy in Colonial Mexico*. Tucson: University of Arizona Press, 2006.

~

CHAPTER FIVE

Jacob Leisler (1640–1691)

German-Born Governor of New York

Noah L. Gelfand

Jacob Leisler was both a trader and a traitor. Born in Frankfurt, he joined the Dutch West India Company as a soldier and sailed for the New World. He eventually married, left the service, and embarked on a series of far-flung entrepreneurial trading ventures throughout the North Atlantic. Through a series of fortuitous events, he became governor of New York during the tumultuous era of the Glorious Revolution in England. Inspired by ideals of a citizen's democracy, Governor Leisler implemented a program based on direct popular representation, initiated America's first intercontinental congress, and organized the first independent intercolonial military action. For all these reasons, royalist sympathizers feared the impact of their radical governor's policies and executed him in May 1691. In this fast-paced and rollicking tale, historian Noah Gelfand reminds us that the intersection of religion and politics in American society has existed right from its earliest days and that some Christian doctrines were (and remain) fundamentally democratic, perhaps even subversive.

In the 1760s, a Swiss visitor to America named Pierre du Simitière interviewed the elderly surviving witnesses to one of the most spectacular events in colonial New York history—the May 16, 1691, execution of former governor Jacob Leisler. On that day, the largest public gathering to date in New York City assembled to observe the hanging and beheading of Leisler, who had been convicted of treason for his leading role in the political and social turmoil that plagued New York in the wake of England's Glorious Revolution. According to du Simitière's notes, Leisler's execution, like his tenure in office, divided the colony. At the execution, some cried out in horror and protest, people fainted, and a few women allegedly even went into labor at the shocking spectacle. Others cheered in approval, and reportedly one woman took up Leisler's heart and proclaimed to the crowd, "Here is the heart of a traitor!" Such was the range of New Yorkers' passions and emotions regarding Jacob Leisler.[1]

Leisler's life story intersects with many of the fundamental themes that define the seventeenth-century Atlantic world. He was intimately involved in the transatlantic religious, commercial, and political developments of his era. A rigidly orthodox Calvinist, Leisler found common ground in a shared religious outlook with English Puritans, Dutch Reformed, and French Huguenots on both sides of the Atlantic. As a leading New York City merchant, Leisler participated in a Protestant-based transatlantic trade network that shipped goods between four continents and helped shape the economic development of the Atlantic world. As a politician, Leisler participated actively in a transatlantic debate over the issue of passive obedience to monarchs and was part of a pro-Dutch faction that linked him with radical intellectuals in the Netherlands, England, and New England in the late 1680s. Overall, Leisler was a highly intriguing individual whose life reveals the way in which commerce and politics intersected in the seventeenth century and indicates clearly just how central religion was to one's identity in the colonial Atlantic world.

Jacob Leisler was baptized on Tuesday, March 31, 1640, at the French Reformed church in Bockenheim, just outside of Frankfurt-am-Main, Germany. The son of the Reverend Jacob Victorian Leisler, minister to the refugee French congregation at Frankfurt, and Susanne Adelheid Wissenbach, daughter of a Geneva University regent, Jacob was born during a particularly intense moment in the Protestant–Catholic religious strife. The Leislers, a well-respected gentry family of magistrates, bankers, and Protestant clergy known for their belief in orthodox Calvinist principles, were closely involved in the religious struggles of the era. During the Thirty Years' War (1618–1648), Jacob's father served as minister to congregations in Geneva and the German Palatinate and was forced to flee the latter region when Catholic Spanish troops banished Protestant pastors from the area. These experiences, as recounted by his father, were essential to the formation of Jacob's worldview. As an adult, he would carry on his family's tradition of Calvinist activism while maintaining a lifelong fear and distrust of Roman Catholics.[2]

Wishing to avoid the uncertainties and upheavals of the Thirty Years' War and the Spanish Inquisition, Jacob Victorian Leisler accepted a call to minister to the Protestant community in Frankfurt in 1638, which had emerged as a haven for Calvinists. Frankfurt's authorities recognized the economic benefits that could be accrued from allowing Reformed merchants to conduct business in the city and so encouraged their settlement there. Over time, Frankfurt developed as a substantial mercantile base for one branch of what historians describe as the Protestant International—a widespread cosmopolitan trading community based in kinship ties and a shared Calvinist religious background that transcended national boundaries. Many of Frankfurt's Reformed population became wealthy through their trading activities, and the elder Leisler utilized his connections among this local merchant class and throughout Europe's Huguenot commercial network to obtain resources for the refugee community.

The Leislers' move to Frankfurt ushered in a period of stability and prosperity. While the community in general thrived, the Leisler family in particular lived well and grew in number, eventually totaling six sons and two daughters. As the eldest son of a prosperous family, Jacob enjoyed the benefits of a first-rate primary education, including instruction in Latin, theology, mathematics, and logic. Moreover, because both French and German were spoken at home by his parents, Jacob became fluent in these languages. Later he learned Dutch and English as well. Their happy situation, however, proved to be short lived. In 1651, the Reverend Jacob Victorian Leisler suffered a debilitating stroke and died less than two years later. Although his widow, Susanne Adelheid Wissenbach, was left financially sound, she opted to leave Frankfurt and move to Hanau, Germany. Twelve-year-old Jacob was sent to a Calvinist military academy in Nuremburg, where he learned drill procedures, contemporary military tactics, law, and geography—all of which would eventually be extremely valuable to him in the New World.

After graduating from the military academy, Leisler moved to Amsterdam in the winter of 1658–1659. While the reasons for this move are unknown, historians have speculated that Leisler went to Amsterdam to cultivate his family's connections there among the Protestant International and begin a career in commerce. There he made contact with Cornelis Melyn, a member of the French Reformed community and owner of vast tracts of property on Staten Island in the Dutch colony of New Netherland in America. It was probably due to Melyn's encouragement that Leisler undertook his next move. On April 27, 1660, Jacob Leisler signed on as an *adelborst* (naval cadet) in the service of the Dutch West India Company and set sail aboard the *Gilded Otter* destined for New Amsterdam.[3] At the age of twenty, Leisler arrived in America at a moment when the colonial frontier town was on the verge of being transformed into one of the Atlantic world's most important cities.

Since 1647, Director-General Peter Stuyvesant had instituted a building program to put New Amsterdam in order and make it safe for a large-scale urban population as well as to facilitate an easier flow of commerce. To this end, he had surveyors lay out regular streets and pave lanes with cobblestones. He established five official garbage dumps and made residents sweep the road in front of their dwellings, thus addressing the very real problems of offensive odors and streets being blocked by rubbish that plagued all early modern cities. Stuyvesant also required that all pigs, cows, goats, and horses be fenced in rather than allowed to roam freely. Moreover, to protect people and property alike, a ban was enacted to curtail open fires at night, and a municipal firefighting system was established.[4]

Stuyvesant endeavored to better regulate the colony's exchange of goods and to provide for the population. A municipal market was established on Mondays for the sale of meat, bacon, butter, cheese, and other farm products from the local area. Saturdays were set aside for inhabitants from the rest of New Netherland to come to New Amsterdam and hawk their wares to the townspeople. Thus, Stuyvesant ensured that the people of this developing town would always have a regular source for their food and supplies. Furthermore, Stuyvesant standardized sizes, ingredients, and prices for such things as beer and loaves of bread. Importantly, for the flow of commerce, Stuyvesant also set reliable exchange rates for wampum, an Indian-produced bead that served as the colony's most readily available form of currency.

Peter Stuyvesant's municipal improvements, which also included the granting of a city charter to New Amsterdam in 1653, undoubtedly combined with other factors, such as the Dutch loss of Brazil, to make New Netherland a popular destination for Europeans in the early 1660s. When Leisler arrived in New Amsterdam, the town was in the midst of a rapid population boom, increasing from around five hundred inhabitants to more than 1,500 people in just over a decade. By any measure, this population was an eclectic bunch. As a French visitor during this period observed, at least eighteen languages were spoken on the Island of Manhattan.[5] Among the recent immigrants was a large contingent of Scandinavians, English, French, Germans, and enslaved Africans. The latter group, combined with free blacks, constituted nearly 20 percent of New Amsterdam's total population. Indeed, the New Amsterdam that became Leisler's home may have been the most cosmopolitan urban area in the entire New World.

While Leisler may have arrived in New Amsterdam as a mere soldier in the employ of the Dutch West India Company, it is clear that his class position and family name were well known in the colony. As early as 1662, he appears in Dutch Reformed Church baptismal records as a godfather to a number of children, indicating that people in town considered him a man of honor and substance. Further evidence of Leisler's place within New Amsterdam's developing social hierarchy comes from his marriage in April 1663 to Elsie Tymens, widow of Pieter Cornelisse van der Veen. With his marriage to Elsie, whose mother was married to the wealthy transatlantic merchant Govert Loockermans, Leisler improved his connections within New Netherland's commercial elite significantly.

Shortly after his arrival in New Amsterdam, Leisler had already become involved in trading two of the most valuable commodities in North America—fur and tobacco. The furs came from Iroquois Indian lands up the Hudson River and in Canada, and the tobacco was typically grown in the Chesapeake Bay region of Maryland and Virginia. Leisler entered the trade at a very fortuitous moment. In the 1660s, lower prices, ample supplies, and a strong European demand for the product made tobacco a very profitable commodity for Manhattan merchants. By 1663, Leisler was utilizing commercial contacts, including his brother Frantz, in a transnational Huguenot trade network that stretched from Basel, Amsterdam, and Leiden in Europe to Boston, the Chesapeake, and the West Indies in the New World. Less than two years later, Leisler was the most active Manhattan merchant in the Chesapeake tobacco trade.[6]

In 1664, while Leisler's personal fortunes were rising and New Amsterdam's economy was booming, tensions that had been mounting since the 1650s between the Netherlands and England came to the fore. At the center of the Anglo–Dutch conflict was a rivalry for commercial and maritime supremacy of the Atlantic. For some time, England had been implementing a series of Navigation Acts designed to limit direct Dutch access to English ports and colonial goods. Still, Dutch violations of the Navigation Acts occurred throughout the Atlantic, and the First Anglo-Dutch War (1652–1654) erupted. In the aftermath of this inconclusive war, a number of King Charles II's advisers in England believed that New Netherland's shippers played a large role in the continued Dutch defiance of the Navigation Acts. In March 1664, Charles, acting on previous English claims to the territory, bequeathed the land that made up New Netherland to his brother, James, the Duke of York, as a gift. At the end of August, four English warships arrived in the harbor below Manhattan Island. Outgunned and with a population unwilling to fight a losing battle, Peter Stuyvesant was forced to surrender the colony. On September 8, 1664, New Netherland became New York.

The new English governor Richard Nicolls gave the Dutch very liberal terms for surrender, and most colonists, including Leisler, chose to remain in New York rather than relocate. Leisler and other leading colonists were granted the status of free denizens of New York City, which gave them the privileges of citizenship and allowed them to take advantage of new trade opportunities within the developing English Atlantic empire. In 1664, Leisler expanded the scope of his commercial endeavors, adding wine and beer to the list of products he traded. Later, the array of goods he exported included salt, grain products, fish, whale oil, and horses, while he imported sugar, spices, finished cloth, trade goods, and indentured servants. Leisler also became a leading importer of Africans for the New York slave market, and, like many of his wealthy Manhattan neighbors, he owned several slaves as part of his personal labor force.

By the mid-1670s, Jacob Leisler was well established as one of New York City's most prominent merchants, and in the fall of 1676, he commissioned the construction of a new pinnace to add to his growing commercial fleet. The new ship, named *Susannah* after his mother, was intended for more than just business. Two years earlier, his maternal grandmother, Madame Catherine Aubert Wissenbach, an heiress of the Auberts, a prominent Swiss family, had died and left a substantial inheritance to the Leislers. Jacob planned to sail with his new ship to Europe; visit his mother in Hanau, Germany; claim his share of the Aubert estate; and settle other family matters. In early May 1677, the *Susannah*, with Leisler and a crew of eight men on board, including his two stepsons, set sail from New York City to the Chesapeake, where they picked up 44,000 pounds of tobacco and some cowhides for trade in England. After a six-week Atlantic crossing, the *Susannah* arrived in Dover, England. On July 6, the *Susannah* cleared customs, and the crew readied themselves for the short trip to their next destination, Amsterdam. The ship, however, never arrived. North African Barbary pirates attacked and boarded the *Susannah* in the English Channel, capturing both the ship and its crew. Shackled and with their clothes torn and tattered, Leisler and his crew were sent to Algiers in order to be held for ransom or sold into slavery.[7]

That pirates captured Leisler and the *Susannah* was not unusual. From the sixteenth through the eighteenth centuries, well over a million Europeans and colonial Americans were kidnapped and held for ransom or sold into the slave markets of North Africa by the Barbary pirates. Contemporaries believed that those who fell into the hands of the Barbary pirates were in for a harsh life of hard labor and cruel treatment; it was thought that captured women and young children would be sexually abused and that all captives would experience constant pressures to apostatize and become Muslims. Those Barbary captives whose families or associates were unable to raise ransom funds were turned over to the ruling pasha for work in the galleys and on public projects or sold to private masters. Life in a ship's galley was particularly arduous. Used as rowers, the slaves were chained, subject to beatings, and fed a poor diet that often led to malnutrition. Some galley slaves rowed for decades without ever setting foot onshore, while the majority ended up dying of starvation, disease, or maltreatment.

In the case of the *Susannah*'s crew and perhaps because of Leisler's aristocratic bearing and well-known family name, the Algerian merchants determined to hold them for ransom rather than slavery. The redemption of prisoners was a complex process that involved transatlantic fund-raising, currency exchanges, and international brokers and often took years to complete. In Leisler's case, however, the process moved quickly, and he did not spend too much time in captivity. By the spring of 1678, he was back in England. Documentary evidence suggests that his business associates in Amsterdam and England advanced the unusually high sum of £410 to have him released. In August 1678, Leisler returned to New York City, where the Dutch Reformed Church and New York Governor Sir Edmund Andros had already begun raising funds for the prisoners. New Yorkers from all over the colony—even people who had no personal connection with Leisler or the others—joined in the public effort to help rescue the crew of the *Susannah*, contributing cash and goods totaling over 5,440 guilder. In the end, the captives were returned to Christian territory in April 1680. Sadly, one of Leisler's stepsons, Cornelis van der Veen, had died in Algiers.[8]

Commerce and shipping, however, were not the only investment avenues that Leisler pursued. Leisler, like other successful merchants, sought to invest some of his profits in landed property. On both sides of the Atlantic, landownership was considered to be the highest and most respectable form of wealth during the early modern era. Initially, he bought a lot next to Peter Stuyvesant's on Whitehall Street in lower Manhattan and built one of New York City's finest homes, a three-story brick Renaissance-style townhouse. Over the next two decades Leisler acquired properties throughout the city, which he rented to other colonists. Additionally, he purchased a large farm in Manhattan and extensive tracts on Long Island and in Westchester County, East Jersey, and England and Europe. By 1689, he was one of New York's largest property holders.

Leisler's wealth and social standing placed him in a position to serve his fellow New Yorkers in public office, though he shied away from politics until the dramatic events of 1689. Leisler's prominence, however, did mean that he was selected to participate in the colony's justice system. Over a twenty-five-year period, he served as a juror or arbitrator in many New York civil and criminal court cases and was named a commissioner of the Court of Admiralty in 1683. In addition, during the brief Dutch reconquest of New York in 1673–1674, Leisler assisted the government in an advisory capacity, performing myriad important tasks, including the presentation of a report on the condition of the fort to local authorities. Furthermore, in 1684, Leisler was commissioned as a senior captain of the New York City militia. Significantly, this appointment made Leisler second in command of the militia and placed him in a central position where he was able to act on behalf of the colony during the crisis of 1689.

While his public career was somewhat limited before 1689, Leisler was always very active in church matters. He joined the Dutch Reformed congregation in New Amsterdam shortly after his arrival and was made a deacon and member of the New York consistory by 1670. As an orthodox member of the consistory, Leisler constantly pressed for doctrinal purity and often challenged the practices and beliefs of the colony's ministers. His struggles on behalf of an orthodox Calvinism in New York were, in fact, part of a larger transatlantic theological debate that had repercussions in both the Old and the New World and that was particularly divisive in the Netherlands, England, and New England. Salvation was at the heart of the religious debates that divided these societies. Over the course of the seventeenth century, moderate Calvinists began preaching a doctrine that allowed for the role of human agency in salvation—an idea that would have been odious to sixteenth-century Protestants—while other more orthodox practitioners, Leisler included, were unwavering in their belief in strict predestination. For Leisler and those who shared his religiously conservative outlook, the situation in New York was especially dire as the Duke of York instituted a policy of religious toleration in the colony and English authorities increasingly appointed a liberal, Anglican ministry.

In 1676, with religious tensions rising in New York, a controversy occurred in which Leisler played a leading role. Leisler publicly criticized a Reformed clergyman from Albany, named Nicholas Van Rensselaer, for preaching sermons that he considered heretical. The content of Van Rensselaer's sermons, however, was only a minor part of a much larger issue. The real problem involved the legitimacy of Van Rensselaer's appointment to the Albany congregation. Van Rensselaer was not fully ordained by the Classis of Amsterdam, the religious organization in charge of administration of the Dutch Reformed Church in the New World. Instead, Van Rensselaer received his license from the Anglican bishop of Salisbury and was assigned to the Dutch Church at Albany without the consent of the congregation. This was particularly problematic because the Dutch Reformed system provided each congregation with the right to call and approve or reject its own minister. Hence, Leisler's decision to speak out against Van Rensselaer was in essence both a defense of local Dutch religious rights and a bold challenge to the authority of the English government to determine religious matters in their own colony.

After Van Rensselaer countered the public criticism of his preaching with a lawsuit against Leisler for defamation, and with neither side showing signs of relenting, Governor Andros was forced to get involved. Andros was afraid that the colony was on the verge of a dangerous schism between liberal and orthodox believers. He thus ended matters in Van Rensselaer's favor. Leisler, nevertheless, became something of a hero among Calvinist hard-liners for his refusal to back down in defending against what they considered to be the popish designs of the Duke of York's ministers.[9]

Leisler's reputation as a champion of Protestant causes also grew considerably in the wake of French King Louis XIV's 1685 revocation of the Edict of Nantes, which had given Calvinist Huguenots limited rights to practice their religion and protected them from physical harm in Catholic France for eighty-seven years. Suddenly they were again prohibited from worshipping and subject to severe abuse. Always a friend of the Huguenot community, Leisler's exertions on behalf of French Protestants took on epic proportions. He organized a committee with local wealthy French merchants to find a place for Huguenots to settle in New York. When the other merchants dropped out, Leisler carried on as the endeavor's sole financier. On September 20, 1689, he conveyed to the Huguenot community over two thousand acres of land in Westchester County that he had bought from John and Rachel Pell. The refugees renamed the site New Rochelle.[10]

Leisler's connections with the international Huguenot community were indeed quite profound and multifaceted. As a youngster, his earliest religious experiences had taken place in the French Reformed congregation outside of Frankfurt where his father had been the minister. Later, Leisler noted that the purest Calvinist doctrine could be found in the French confession and after years of struggling with what he considered to be an increasingly lax Dutch Reformed Church, he joined the French congregation in New York. Significantly, many of his initial trade relationships within the Protestant International were with Frenchmen in The Hague, Amsterdam, and the Chesapeake. Overall, in an era in which the concepts of nationality and ethnicity were more fluid and less meaningful than today, the German-born

Leisler, who had been an employee of the Dutch West India Company and was a citizen in an English colony, probably most readily identified himself with French Protestants. Mixed identities, such as Leisler's, were in fact highly characteristic of the seventeenth-century Atlantic world.

In 1685, Charles II died and was succeeded as king of England by his brother the Duke of York, who became known as James II. As a professing Catholic in a Protestant country, the new king's rule was problematic for both his English subjects and the colonists in America. In England, James II appointed Catholic supporters to key positions, formed an alliance with Catholic France, and dissolved Parliament in an effort to reduce its power. In America, James II attempted to rule his colonies more closely by revoking the separate charters of Massachusetts, New Hampshire, Plymouth, Connecticut, Rhode Island, New York, East Jersey, and West Jersey and replacing them with a single administration, to be known as the Dominion of New England. New Yorkers resented the fact that all of their colony's legal records were removed to the dominion's capital located in rival Boston. Among other indignities, this development meant an expensive trip to Boston for any New Yorker involved in legal disputes. On both sides of the English Atlantic, James's policies were met with anger and alarm.

Prince William III of Orange and commander in chief of the Netherlands was married to James II's daughter Mary and had his own designs on the English Crown. On the geopolitical level, becoming king of England made sense to William as a practical way to avoid an Anglo–French alliance against the Dutch and to improve the commercial relationship between Europe's two biggest trading powers. On a more personal and religious level, William, an adherent of Calvinism, could also gain favor with God by saving England for Protestantism. When a son was born to James's wife, ensuring a Catholic heir to the throne, members of the suspended Parliament asked William to be king. On November 6, 1688, the Dutch prince invaded England and found very little resistance. Most of the English nobility and aristocracy remained neutral or actually joined William's march across the country. Eventually, James was forced to flee to France, and in early 1689, William and Mary were crowned as joint sovereigns of England. This event was called the Glorious Revolution because of the relatively bloodless nature of the change in monarchs and the establishment of the tradition of an independent Parliament in England.

The accession of William and Mary to the throne of England had serious ramifications for England's North American colonies. Governors and other royal officials who had been appointed by James II suddenly lost their claims to legitimacy and authority. In Boston, Governor Andros was arrested, while his lieutenant in New York, Francis Nicholson, threatened to burn down the city before later fleeing to England. Amid the chaos of this power vacuum and with rumors abounding of an imminent French invasion from Canada, militia captain Leisler assumed control of Fort James at the foot of Broadway in lower Manhattan on May 31, 1689. With a crowd of civilian supporters joining him, Leisler declared all laws made under the authority of King James to be null and void, renamed the fort after William, and proclaimed his loyalty to the new monarchs, William and Mary.

A ten-member Committee of Safety was set up to govern both the colony and the city. Impressed with Leisler's popularity among the people and his commitment to defending the colony, the committee chose Leisler to be commander in chief of New York. Leisler clearly understood the events of the Glorious Revolution in terms of a struggle between the true Protestant religion and the forces of Catholicism and popery. To Leisler and his followers, who were known as Leislerians, James's officers in New York were obviously part of a popish plot. This meant not only the threat of heresy in the colony but also political tyranny. They saw William of Orange's defeat of James II in the same light as the Protestant Netherlands triumphant revolt against Catholic Spain a hundred years earlier. Moreover, a series of border clashes had occurred along the frontier between New Yorkers and French and Indians from Canada. These skirmishes, combined with King Louis XIV's revocation of the Edict of Nantes and subsequent violence against Protestants in France, gave credence to the idea that a very real transatlantic Protestant–Catholic battle was under way in which the fundamental freedoms and souls of true believers were at stake.

Leisler was joined in this outlook by a number of religious leaders from other colonies, including Cotton and Increase Mather in Massachusetts, and he organized a correspondence between New York and the New England provinces to share intelligence and prepare for a united front against Catholic aggression. After a mixed French and Indian force massacred over sixty residents of Schenectady and similar raids occurred in New England, Leisler arranged English America's first intercolonial congress and planned a joint New York–New England assault by land and by sea on the French at Quebec. While the land expedition failed, the fleet temporarily took Quebec and captured French ships in Canadian waters and on Long Island Sound.[11]

The people of the colony were bitterly divided over Leisler's administration and the legitimacy of his actions. Leisler's followers in New York were a mixed group, not easily categorized. Many were second-generation Dutch colonists born around mid-century, some were wealthy merchants, and others were successful artisans, while shopkeepers, sailors, and laborers of every nationality also supported Leisler. Puritan English villagers on Long Island, who had a long-standing animosity toward Charles II and James II, were also among Leisler's most loyal followers. Additionally, a large share of the colony's women, who believed that Leisler would uphold Dutch law, which afforded them considerably more property rights than under the English system, supported his cause. This diverse group rallied behind the idea that King James had been trying to damn the English nation to popery and slavery. According to their view, James's minions, or grandees, as Leisler referred to them, had already made great strides toward accomplishing that goal in New York.[12]

Not surprisingly, the men whom Leisler considered to be New York's grandees were vehemently opposed to his administration and formed the leadership of the anti-Leislerians. Many were among the top echelon of merchants and men who had served on Lieutenant Governor Francis Nicholson's council, including Nicholas Bayard and the colony's attorney general, William Nicolls. Significantly, a number of these leading men were also related to Leisler through marriage and had been involved in a bitter and protracted lawsuit against Leisler over his wife's inheritance. Several Dutch Reformed Church officials who had managed to accommodate themselves to the English system also joined the opposition to Leisler. Government officials and the leading landowners of Albany refused to accept Leisler's government as well. Overall, it appears that Leisler's opponents were among the wealthiest and most powerful inhabitants of the colony, the very people who stood to lose the most in any challenge to the status quo.

In September 1689, the Committee of Safety called for a general election, and, for the first time, justices of the peace and militia captains were chosen directly by voters. With this unprecedented democratic event, a major shift had clearly occurred in the distribution of political power in New York City. Working-class laborers, who were previously excluded from public office, captured a majority of the seats on the board of aldermen. Leisler's friend, Peter Delanoy, a Huguenot, was elected mayor. To the anti-Leislerian grandees, the new officeholders were an ignorant, drunken rabble. As a result of this redistribution of power, open class conflict took place in New York City. Leislerians attacked the grandees who ventured outside, ransacked their homes and businesses, intercepted mail, and arrested a number of anti-Leislerians, including Nicholas Bayard. In response, saboteurs tried to blow up Fort William, and in June 1690, an angry mob of thirty merchants attacked Leisler himself. He drew his sword and managed to escape.[13]

Leisler's policies managed to alienate nearly everyone in some way. Needing to raise taxes for the defense of the colony, Leisler called for elections to a new Assembly in April 1690. The Assembly went further by breaking up commercial monopolies and ending trade regulations that favored wealthy New York City merchants. Although necessary, the higher taxes alienated many of the colony's poor and the abolition of the trade regulations added further to the group of people disaffected by Leisler's actions. Furthermore, the orthodox Leisler attempted to enforce doctrinal conformity throughout New York, and this proved to be an extremely unpopular move and caused many of his initial followers to abandon their support for his administration.[14]

Meanwhile, Leisler sent word to the Lords of Trade and the Privy Council in London explaining what was happening in New York. But his political opponents did the same and fared much better in influencing English authorities' interpretation of the situation. William and Mary decided to dispatch their own loyal administrator as the new governor, a man named Colonel Henry Sloughter, who left for New York in December 1690. Another shady, ambitious character, however, Major Richard Ingoldsby, was put in charge of the royal troops and managed to arrive in New York before Sloughter and demand that Leisler turn over Fort William to him. Leisler, however, refused since Ingoldsby had no written orders. A tense standoff ensued. Governor Sloughter finally arrived on March 19, 1691. Leisler attempted to negotiate terms for the transfer of power, but anti-Leislerians had already presented their version of what had taken place to Sloughter. Leisler was instead arrested and charged with rebellion.

Governor Sloughter appointed a court to examine the charges against Leisler and his associates. Ingoldsby was among the members of this court, and William Nicolls, who had earlier been imprisoned by Leisler, was made special prosecutor. After a quick hearing in which there was no pretense of impartiality, Leisler, his son-in-law Jacob Milborne, and six others were convicted of a variety of capital offenses. In the end, a total of twenty-six Leislerians were sentenced to death. But in response to public entreaties for clemency and a Huguenot riot on Staten Island, Sloughter paroled all the condemned men except Leisler and Milborne. Leisler and Milborne were hastily executed on May 16, 1691, before any appeals on their behalf could reach William and Mary in England.[15]

On May 3, 1695, King William reversed the New York court's proceedings, posthumously exonerating Leisler and pardoning those of his followers still condemned to death. Most of Leisler's confiscated state was eventually returned to his widow Elsie and their children. In 1698, the bodies of Jacob Leisler and Jacob Milborne were exhumed and brought to the Dutch Reformed Church, where they lay in state for a few weeks before being reburied as heroes on Sunday, October 20, 1698. A crowd of over 1,200 people attended the funeral, attesting to the lasting presence of Leisler in colonial New Yorkers' collective memory. Indeed, the ramifications of Leisler's brief tenure in office continued to be felt for decades afterward as acrimony between Leislerians and anti-Leislerians endured. Today, historians still refer to that period in New York history as "Leisler's Rebellion."[16]

In the end, it was the vast Atlantic Ocean itself that both contributed to the success and prosperity of Jacob Leisler and played a crucial role in his untimely death. Because commercial transactions were carried out across an enormous body of water, religious-based trade networks were essential to the exchange of goods and development of the seventeenth-century Atlantic world. Leisler utilized his connections among the transatlantic Protestant International—and particularly throughout the Huguenot Diaspora—to achieve wealth, prestige, and power in the New World. The great transatlantic distances, which separated communities and made the religious-based trade networks so important, both permitted Leisler's spectacular rise to prominence and authority and ultimately led to his doom. As a barrier to the easy flow of news and information, the vastness of the Atlantic prevented Leisler from getting proper instructions and effectively communicating with England. It simply took too long for word of his arrest and death sentence to cross the Atlantic and reach authorities in England. By the time it did, the time for any appeal had already passed. Jacob Leisler was dead.

Bibliography and Suggested Reading

The Papers of Jacob Leisler Project, located at New York University and directed by Dr. David W. Voorhees, has acquired the most complete archival collection of Leisler-related documents in the world.

Bailyn, Bernard. *From Protestant Peasants to Jewish Intellectuals: Germans in the Peopling of America.* Oxford: Berg, for the German Historical Institute, 1988.

Balmer, Randall. *A Perfect Babel of Confusion: Dutch Religion and English Culture in the Middle Colonies.* New York: Oxford University Press, 1989.

Bosher, J. H. "Huguenot Merchants and the Protestant International in the Seventeenth Century." *William and Mary Quarterly* 52, no. 1 (January 1995): 77–102.

Burrows, Edwin G., and Mike Wallace. *Botham: A History of New York City to 1898.* New York: Oxford University Press, 1999.

Christoph, Peter R., ed. *The Leisler Papers, 1689–1691.* Syracuse, NY: Syracuse University Press, 2002.

Dunn, Richard. *The Age of Religious Wars, 1559–1715.* New York: Norton, 1979.

Goodfriend, Joyce D., ed. *Revisiting New Netherland: Perspectives on Early Dutch America.* Leiden: Brill, 2005.

Greenberg, Douglas. *Crime and Law Enforcement in the Colony of New York, 1691–1776*. Ithaca, NY: Cornell University Press, 1976.

Ingraham, J. H. *Leisler, or, The Rebel and King's Man: A Tale of the Rebellion of 1689*. Charlottesville: University Press of Virginia, 2000.

Jameson, J. Franklin, ed. *Narratives of New Netherland, 1609–1664*. New York: Charles Scribner's Sons, 1909.

Kammen, Michael. *Colonial New York: A History*. Oxford: Oxford University Press, 1996.

Lohr, Otto. *The First Germans in North America and the German Element of New Netherland*. New York: G. E. Stechert & Co., 1912.

Maika, Dennis J. "Jacob Leisler's Chesapeake Trade." *de Halve Maen* 67 (Spring 1994): 9–14.

McCormick, Charles Howard. *Leisler's Rebellion*. New York: Garland, 1989.

Pencak, William, and Conrad Edick Wright, eds. *Authority and Resistance in Early New York*. New York: New York Historical Society, 1988.

Reich, Jerome R. *Leisler's Rebellion: A Study of Democracy in New York, 1664–1720*. Chicago: University of Chicago Press, 1953.

Rink, Oliver A. *Holland on the Hudson: An Economic and Social History of Dutch New York*. New York: New York State Historical Association, 1986.

Voorhees, David William. " 'Hearing . . . What Great Success the Dragonnades in France Had': Jacob Leisler's Huguenot Connections." *de Halve Maen* 67, no. 1 (January 1994): 15–20.

———. "The 'fervent Zeale' of Jacob Leisler." *William and Mary Quarterly* 51, no. 3 (July 1994): 447–72.

———. "Captured: The 'Turkish Slavery' of the Susannah." *Seaport: New York's History Magazine* 31, no. 2 (Fall 1997): 7–12.

CHAPTER SIX

~

Hendrick/Tiyanoga/Theyanoguen (1680–1755)

Iroquois Emissary to England

Troy Bickham

Hendrick was a Native American diplomat who was the most important cultural intermediary between the Indian and British worlds in the eighteenth century. Successful at both making peace and waging war, Hendrick's visits to England were celebrated widely in contemporary ballads and odes; his presence even inspired a London underworld gang to rename itself the "Mohocs." Hendrick's speeches were reprinted on both sides of the Atlantic, and his death in 1755 was widely mourned. Through historian Troy Bickham's colorful retelling of Hendrick's life, students of the Atlantic world can plainly see that American Indians were energetic participants in the construction and maintenance of New World empires. Hendrick's career and personal choices represent the syncretic impulse of the Atlantic world as a region in which natives and newcomers both adopted and adapted elements of each other's cultures. The process of colonial expansion was often violent and one sided, but Hendrick's experiences remind us that other, more complicated scenarios of negotiated race and cultural adaptation also were possible.

Hendrick (also known as Tiyanoga and Theyanoguen) was born around 1680, the son of a Mohegan father and Mohawk mother, probably near what is now Westfield, Massachusetts. While still a young boy, his family moved to the Mohawk valley in present-day New York, where he took his rightful place within his mother's Wolf clan. During his long life, Hendrick rose to a position of prominence, holding the rank of sachem among the Mohawk and becoming a key figure of the Iroquois Confederacy (also called the Five or Six Nations). In the wider British Atlantic world, he achieved a degree of fame that made him a near household name. He featured regularly in histories of America, his speeches were printed and read voraciously, and his death was mourned on both sides of the ocean. Indeed, Hendrick's exploits were so well known that they were even incorporated into absurdly unrelated accounts. Mostyn John Armstrong's history of Norfolk, England, published in 1781, for example, used an anecdote about the famous American Mohawk to illustrate a point about dreams.[1]

Conversant with both the American Indian and British worlds, Hendrick was not only an important character in his own right but also a valuable reminder that North American Indians were confined neither physically nor cosmologically to the North American continent. Like the natives of Europe, Africa, and South America, they were voluntary and involuntary players in the Atlantic world, shaping its direction and expansion. Like most participants in the Atlantic world, exchanges had rapidly altered the Iroquois culture, and Hendrick exemplifies the struggle of negotiated adaptation that so many natives of all four continents experienced. Clearly, Hendrick's life, work, and persona had utility and relevance for writers, politicians, and ethnographers on both sides of the Atlantic, even though historical accuracy sometimes became a secondary concern. In fact, the Hendrick remembered today may have been two distinct people—both Mohawk but living concurrently. Although conventionally treated as one person, which has been the case here, there is growing evidence for a two-Hendricks interpretation.[2]

The Iroquois Confederacy that Hendrick and his generation inherited was a powerful yet declining empire that was caught between the two expanding empires of Britain and France. The confederacy itself consisted of six Indian nations (the Mohawk, Oneida, Onondaga, Cayuga, Seneca, and Tuscarora) that were bound by kinship relations, general cultural practices, and a loose political structure. Life was based around matriarchal villages (or "castles" as the English regularly called them). Ohwachiras (senior matrons) dominated village life; they tended the crops, ran the households, and invested men with political authority. Men hunted in order to provide food as well as skins and furs to trade with Europeans. Through a combination of military prowess, control of trade routes, and savvy diplomacy, the confederacy dominated a region that stretched from present-day Maine to Ohio and claimed authority over numerous subjugated peoples. Adding to the Iroquois longevity was their willingness to assimilate members of other ethnic groups (often taken in raids) and to invest them with all the rights, privileges, and responsibilities of native-born Iroquois. At a time when disease and warfare ravaged American Indian populations, the Iroquois' ability to replenish their population was crucial to their long-term survival. These practices and the matrilineal nature of Iroquois family groups meant that individuals of mixed heritage, such as Hendrick, were fully accepted.

Around the time of Hendrick's birth, the Iroquois Confederacy was establishing its diplomatic stance of armed neutrality toward the European empires. Geographically situated between the French and English (later British) empires, this was a precarious yet effective policy. The Iroquois had watched land-hungry Europeans take advantage of their Indian neighbors' rivalries and had learned firsthand of the destructive potential of going to war against the better-armed European militaries. In 1701, the "Grand Settlement" with France ended years of intermittent warfare for the Iroquois and was shortly followed by a treaty with England. Hendrick was a signatory to this latter document, which conveyed substantial Iroquois lands to England's King William III as part of an effort to solidify goodwill between the two nations. Once in place, these diplomatic moves set a precedent for a policy of armed neutrality that drove the Iroquois' foreign relations until the confederacy's dissolution in the American War of Independence. Under this strategy, those located closer to French settlements would court French interests, while those located closer to English settlements would court English interests. All confederate nations would benefit from the peace and trade rights negotiated by one another. As the easternmost nation, the Mohawk took primary responsibility for handling English relations. In this arena, Hendrick excelled and made his most lasting mark.

Hendrick's political role within the Iroquois Confederacy was multifaceted. By 1710, he held the rank of sachem in the Mohawk village of Canajorharie and represented both his immediate community (and the Mohawk in general) at the Iroquois councils held at Onondaga. There, in meetings that could last weeks, Hendrick honed his skills as a masterful orator, working to win approval for his policies and to advance the position of his community within the confederacy. To a great extent, his status depended on his people's consent, particularly the matriarchs. If they withdrew their support from him, which on at least one brief occasion they did, neither Hendrick nor any other leader could keep his rank.

In 1710, Hendrick made his most celebrated diplomatic mission. He was one of four Mohawk headmen who traveled across the Atlantic to present themselves at the court of Queen Anne in Britain. They had been invited to tour Britain as part of the diplomatic effort led by Francis Nicholson, whose aim was to persuade the queen and her ministers to send substantial naval support for an expedition against New France. The presence of the four "exotic" delegates was intended to emphasize that Nicholson and his comrades had powerful American Indian support for the venture. Despite their relative youth and lack of authority to represent the whole confederacy, the four Mohawk were falsely presented as sovereigns in Britain—Hendrick was described as "emperor," and the others were called "kings." Their novel appearance captured the nation's imagination, and everywhere they went, throngs of Londoners flocked to see them. Queen Anne was quite taken with the visitors, and she commissioned John Verelst to paint their likeness. That their British hosts accepted their Indian visitors as fellow elites is clear both from the important persons the Mohawk met and from the respectful manner in which they were treated. Verelst's portraits, for example, depict the men not as savages or curiosities but rather as country aristocrats. Emulating the standard English aristocratic pose in front of his bucolic estate, the Mohawk were depicted in parallel American wilderness scenes wearing their native finery.

In the popular market, cruder souvenir portraits also appeared to satisfy the public demand. The short pamphlet *The History of the Four Indian Kings* and the chapbook *The Four Indian Kings* both became instant best-sellers, appearing throughout the nation from London to Hull. *The History* depicts the Mohawk's mission to England to seek assistance against the barbarous French. They prostrate themselves before the queen asking for military assistance and instruction in the Protestant religion. As a ballad, *The Four Indian Kings* was conceived more as entertainment, and one version includes a romance in which one of the kings falls in love with an English woman who refuses to marry him until he has converted to Protestantism. He accepts the condition and takes his new religion and wife back to America. The more popular works underscore just how limited British cosmology was at the time. The accompanying illustrations showed the Mohawk kings dressed similar to European kings—illustrations no doubt borrowed from other ballads about fairy-tale princes—and references to America steadily disappeared. In several depictions, publishers equated them with the most well-known exotic traveling kings at the time, the Magi. Despite retaining "four" in the title, one king was dropped from illustration, and images of pyramids and the Star of David became background features. Such blending of East and West was common before the mid-eighteenth century—even the London gang who adopted the name "Mohocs" dressed in turbans and had crescent tattoos, mistaking their "Indian" origins for the Eastern variety—but this confusion was less the consequence of unavailable knowledge than a general lack of concern for such distinctions.[3] For most Britons at that time—and Europeans for that matter—"Indian" was synonymous with "non-European," whatever the geographic origins of the person or object. This tendency to compress all non-European ethnic groups into one generic entity, however, changed dramatically in Hendrick's lifetime.

The primary objective of the diplomatic mission to secure British support for an invasion of New France succeeded, but the attack itself was a failure. In August 1711, after Hendrick and his companions had returned to their homes, 656 Iroquois warriors (an impressive one-third of the total number of warriors in the confederacy) joined Nicholson's colonial force that was gathering in Albany for an attack on New France.[4] Supporting the colonist–American Indian army was an English fleet of over sixty ships. Yet bad weather and poor leadership resulted in a loss of ten ships at the mouth of the St. Lawrence River, followed by panic and withdrawal.

One of the more lasting legacies of Hendrick's diplomatic visit was the establishment of a Church of England mission among the Mohawk. In the context of the imperial struggle for North America, religion was much more than a straightforward issue of conscience. It was simultaneously a weapon of empire and badge of cultural affiliation. French, Spanish, Dutch, and English missionaries poured into the Americas in an effort to bring the natives into the folds of their respective empires. Converts generally made more peaceable neighbors and willing allies in conflicts with European enemies. The advantages to American Indian communities were equally substantial. Having a missionary living among them, a person who was often closely tied to the colonial leadership meant regular diplomatic access to an often-volatile and unpredictable neighbor. Such cultural connections could also cement defensive alliances against other Europeans and hostile American Indian neighbors as well as provide protection from renegade colonists. Regularized interaction translated into stabilized trade, which was essential to the survival of border nations such as the Mohawk, who had become reliant on European goods, particularly firearms, alcohol, knives, and an assortment of luxury goods. The ability of individual American Indian leaders like Hendrick to control the flow of this trade translated into enormous power.

Hendrick's relationship with the Church of England appears to have been a blend of a genuine personal attachment to Christianity and his savvy diplomatic instincts. Hendrick had converted to Christianity in 1690, when he was baptized by the Dutch missionary Godfrey Dellius. The Church of England's missionary wing, the Society for the Propagation of the Gospel in Foreign Parts (hereafter SPG), had as patrons numerous leading officials in Britain and America in its membership including royals, aristocrats, Members of Parliament, government ministers, Indian agents, and colonial governors. As Hendrick accepted the Anglican faith and drew closer to its institutional structure, he raised his own status as a diplomat and gained greater trustworthiness in the eyes of the British. During his 1710 visit to England, Hendrick reiterated his frequent request for Church of England missionaries to be sent to live among his people. In the closing remarks of his formal address to Queen Anne, he cleverly raised the specter of Anglo–French rivalry in order to spur action, warning her that "[we] have often been importuned by the French by Priests and Presents, but ever esteemed them as men of Falsehood, but if Our Great Queen wou'd send some to Instruct us, they shou'd find a most hearty Welcome."[5] The calculated words paid immediate dividends. Queen Anne referred the matter to the SPG, which quickly reaffirmed its primary obligation to the "heathen," declaring,

> That the design of propagating the Gospel in foreign parts does chiefly and principally relate to the conversion of heathens and infidels: and therefore than branch of it ought to be prosecuted preferably to all others. . . . That a stop be put to sending any more Missionaries among Christians, except to such places whose Ministers are or shall be dead, or removed; and unless it may consist with the funds of the Society to prosecute both design.[6]

The SPG interviewed Hendrick and showered him with further promises and gifts of "4 copies of the Bible in quarto with the Prayer book bound handsomely in red Turkey leather."[7] The queen also ordered the construction of Fort Hunter near Albany in the Mohawk territory, which would house a future chapel and the missionaries whose primary duty would be to tend to the Church of England's American Indian flock. She even donated a specially made set of silver Communion plates, which were inscribed to her "Indian Chappel of the Mohawks."[8] To express their gratitude, Hendrick and the Mohawk later sent a letter and wampum belt of friendship to the Archbishop of Canterbury.[9]

The cumulative results of the unique Mohawk–Anglican enterprise were apparent throughout the eighteenth century. Fort Hunter became a focal point of Mohawk–British relations, large portions of the Mohawk nation converted to Christianity, and Hendrick and his Mohawk supporters rose in prominence within the confederacy. The Mohawk leaders kept a close affiliation with the church. Hendrick regularly preached, many of the leaders were regular communicants, and Joseph Brant and others translated gospels and prayers into the Mohawk language. Church positions also became a source of patronage. William Johnson, member of the SPG, trader, and later superintendent of Indian affairs, created and staffed numerous SPG-affiliated churches and schools among the Iroquois that combined with the existing efforts operating out of Fort Hunter. The salaried American Indians who staffed these places were generally Mohawk and/or friends and relatives of Hendrick and his supporters.[10]

Because of their close religious and cultural connections, the British imperial and colonial governments consistently supported the Mohawk above all other native peoples, taking their side in land disputes, recognizing Iroquois claims of authority over other nations, and showering them with gifts. In return, the Mohawk remained steadfastly loyal to Britain, regularly sending warriors into battle alongside the British and working to keep the pro-French factions of the Iroquois at bay. The Mohawk affiliation with the British establishment (which included the Church of England) rather than with the local colonists was most evident at the outbreak of the American War of Independence when the Mohawk, led by Hendrick's heirs and supporters, were among the first American Indians to side with Britain over the colonies.

In the decades that followed Hendrick's 1710 mission to London, his own prominence within the Atlantic world ascended, while that of the Mohawk he represented descended. The fur trade of the Iroquois Confederacy was in decline, and as the easternmost of the component nations, the Mohawk felt the British colonists' encroachment into their territory acutely. As land steadily became the main commodity that the Mohawk could trade, increased dependence on European manufactured goods only exacerbated their problems. Meanwhile, subjugated Indian nations in the Ohio valley were starting to challenge Iroquois authority. Hendrick was present at virtually all land sale negotiations, bargaining for the best deals and complaining about fraudulent practices. In so doing, he became a regular presence in the colonial capitals and even apparently made a second, less celebrated visit to Britain in 1740, when tradition has it that King George II presented his "most faithful Indian" with "a green coat set off with Brussells and gold lace, and a cocked hat."[11]

The eruption of war between Britain and France in 1744 (the War of Austrian Succession, or King George's War) and again in 1755 (the Seven Years' War, or The French and Indian War) translated into opportunities for the Mohawk to regain their prestige, and, as the most seasoned diplomat, Hendrick shouldered the greatest responsibility. Pressure on Hendrick came from three often-conflicting constituencies. First, the Mohawk desired increased prestige, security for their lands, and access to the material gifts that the Europeans gave to their allies. Second, the British leadership expected their long-cultivated relationship with the Mohawk to translate into military support at Iroquois councils. Finally, the majority of the leaders within the Iroquois confederacy viewed the policy of limited neutrality as key to their survival and therefore were not ready to abandon it. Hendrick himself must have been torn. His leadership relied on the consent of his constituent Mohawk, and if he failed them, he would lose his rank and status. At the same time, he had developed close friendships with numerous Britons, including the Church of England missionaries at Fort Hunter and William Johnson, who played a paramount role in Britain's American Indian policy from his arrival in the Mohawk valley in 1738. Nevertheless, Hendrick knew full well that allying himself too closely to the British would threaten the other Iroquois nations, many of whom had comparable associations with the French, and would risk making his people the charity cases of a British government that was hardly celebrated for its generosity toward American Indians.

Within a year, Hendrick attended conferences in Albany, Boston, and Montreal, and in each instance he deftly applied his diplomatic talents. In June 1744, he met with the governor of New York and commissioners from Massachusetts and Connecticut in an effort to resurrect the annual Anglo–American Indian Albany conference. Although the conference had not been held since 1724, Hendrick and his associates learned quickly that the British presumed that the Mohawk would enter the conflict in their favor and that New York in particular presumed a special influence over the Mohawk. He dealt with pressures to join a British military offensive and New York's presumption of a monopoly of British–Iroquois relations by taking the unorthodox step of holding an alternative meeting with Anglo-American representatives, including the governor of Massachusetts, in Boston the following month. In October 1745, Hendrick was once again in Albany. Yet, to again reemphasize Mohawk independence, he also took part in a Franco–American Indian conference in Montreal. Ultimately, Hendrick led a number of Iroquois warriors, mainly Mohawk, against the French but waited until the last possible moment to act and even then did so in a limited capacity. The delay tactic served both Hendrick and his constituents well. It reduced bloodshed, helped to preserve Iroquois neutrality, ultimately placated the British, and ensured the maximum number of gifts for him and his supporters.

Gifts from the European powers were vital to the Mohawk, just as they were to a host of other American Indians, because they provided a steady flow of free needed goods to native peoples who were decreasingly able to trade profitably for them. Under Hendrick's direction, the receipt of gifts became something of a cottage industry for the Mohawk. Although two decades had passed since the last major Albany congress in 1724, Hendrick worked to ensure that after 1744 they were held almost annually until his death over a decade later. These meetings could last weeks and were always conducted at the hosting governor's expense. Hendrick was known for leaving with the lion's share of the gifts on offer—often several wagons full. Moving from meeting to meeting, Hendrick made mention of French overtures for alliances and the growing power of the French supporters among the Iroquois confederacy to milk the colonial and imperial governments for as many gifts as possible. When that failed, he made Mohawk grievances intercolonial issues by treating separately with representatives from the different British colonies, which openly competed with one another for land and trade. By the 1740s, William Johnson emerged as an additional source of potential goods, regularly outspending the colonial and imperial governments. This helped to make him a power in the region and a close ally of the Mohawk. Hendrick was one of the primary beneficiaries of the alliance; indeed, Hendrick's name appears in Johnson's account ledgers far more than any other, and it is clear that the two men had a close working relationship.[12] Their connection was publicly underlined in 1746, when Johnson arrived at the Albany congress riding at the head of a Mohawk delegation dressed in full war paint. But the attachment was not all ceremony and show. When political squabbles caused Johnson to resign his post as New York's Indian agent in 1751, Hendrick placed unceasing pressure on the colony's leaders to reinstate his friend on Johnson's terms. Hendrick's negotiations with other colonies and New France made the issue an international one and placed added pressure on New York. In the end, Johnson was not only restored to his prior position but also made an Indian agent for the British Empire. Furthermore, following a military victory at Lake George in 1755 in which Hendrick supplied most of the American Indian warriors, the king even raised Johnson to the rank of baronet.

By mid-century, the British and their colonists perceived Hendrick as the most important Indian in their North American empire. Yet he did not always feel valued. In 1753, after several years of what Hendrick described as "neglect" by the British, he and sixteen other Mohawk traveled to New York to see Governor Clinton. In a lengthy speech, he scolded Clinton for neglecting the Mohawk and demanded that action be taken to address their concerns over land fraud, making a thinly veiled threat to the safety of any surveyor who came into their lands. Hendrick's frustration and exasperation was evident throughout. "It greives [sic] us to the Heart to know and hear that the Council and Assembly dont take care of Albany but leave it naked and defenceless, and dont care what becomes of our Nation, You sit in Peace

& quietness here whilst we are exposed to the enemy," he declared. "If you dont endeavour to redress our Greivances," he plainly concluded, "the rest of our Brethren the 5 Nations shall know of it and all Paths [across Iroquois territory] will be stopped."[13] In contrast, Clinton's response was evasive, and so Hendrick declared that on returning home he would send a wampum belt to the other Iroquois nations to inform them that the Covenant Chain, the ongoing series of treaties that bound the British and the Iroquois, had been broken. Under Hendrick's direction, the Mohawk blocked communications between New York and the other members of the confederacy—reaffirming to the other Iroquois nations and British colonists alike that the Mohawk alone mediated the relationship.

By the following summer's Albany congress, a looming war with France made both sides eager to return to the negotiating table. As always, colonial governors and their representatives competed for land and fur trade access, but the public tone of the negotiations was changing. Fearful of renewed war in North America, British officials had placed increasing pressure on the colonial governments to unite in common defense and American Indian policies. Hendrick was a major figure both in the private and public realms of the Albany conference. In private negotiations, he was present at many of the land sales between the American Indians and the colonists. He was even involved in the controversial sale of the Susquehanna valley, in which the Iroquois sold the lands of the Delaware people to Pennsylvania. In public, Hendrick took center stage. The other Iroquois deferred to him when speaking, and colonists paid more attention to his speeches than they did to any other. He also benefited materially from the meetings. Able to manipulate his public persona to increase his aura of power, Hendrick arrived fashionably late and took a surprisingly harsh tone. As he explained, "You desire us to speak from the bottom of our hearts, and we shall do it." He first scolded New York for neglecting him and his people since the last war and then turned on Virginia, Pennsylvania, and the French (who were not present) for encroaching illegally on the lands of the Iroquois and their tributary nations. Hendrick left little doubt about the Iroquois' disgruntlement with their British neighbors and the consequences of neglect:

> Brethren. [You have been] neglecting us for these three years past (then taking a stick and throwing it behind his back) you have thus thrown us behind your back, and disregarded us, whereas the French are a subtle and vigilant people, ever using their utmost endeavours to seduce and bring our people over to them. . . . The Govr of Virginia, and the Govr of Canada are both quarrelling about lands which belong to us, and such a quarel as this may

end in our destruction; they fight who shall have the land. The Govrs of Virginia and Pennsylvania have made paths thro' our Country to Trade and built houses without acquainting us with it, they should first have asked our consent to build there.[14]

The speeches ultimately underlined Hendrick's—and the Iroquois'—independence. They were not the tributaries of New York or the British Empire and would (and could) switch allegiances as the situation demanded in order to advance their own goals.

Nevertheless, Hendrick knew that he had tied his success and that of his constituents closely to the British Empire and that mending any rifts would be in everyone's best interest. British power could not be completely undermined since the French were courting the western Iroquois just as heavily, and therefore any collapse of the British association would mean the marginalization of the Mohawk within the confederacy. After making his initial point, Hendrick took a decidedly more conciliatory tone the next day:

> We rejoice that we have opened our hearts to each other, and we return the Govr and all the Commissrs from the several Governts our thanks for the same. . . . We thank the Govr of Virginia for assisting the Indians at Ohio, who are our Brethren & Allies, and we approve of the Govr of Pennsylvania's not having hitherto intermeddled in this affair, he is a wise and prudent Man, and will know his own time. We return the Govr of New York, and all the other Governts our most hearty thanks (here the Speaker made bows to his Honour and all the Commissrs) for the promise of protection given us, of our lands, and the acknowledgement that the right of selling it is in us.[15]

Although the congress failed on a number of levels, Hendrick achieved most of his own goals. He reportedly left the conference with thirty wagons loaded with gifts, a huge chunk of which he had received following his malcontented speech. His complaints of neglect and demands for the reinstatement of William Johnson were heard in Britain, where war-fearing newspaper readers and government officials read his speeches. Even as far as the provincial town of Ipswich, Hendrick's warnings were printed as the nation prepared for war: "Brethren, you were desirous we should open our Minds and Hearts to you; look at the French, they are Men; they are fortifying every where; but, we are ashamed to say it, you are all like Women, bare and open, without Fortifications."[16]

Hendrick's alliance with the British was put to the test almost immediately after it was solidified at Albany. Renewed war with France seemed inevitable as both sides made steady preparations for what would be a climactic end to the imperial powers' centuries-long epic struggle for North America. For the first time, Britain made North America a priority in its war aims and thus sent troops and materials across the Atlantic in unprecedented numbers. The initial plan called for a three-pronged attack against French positions in Canada and the American interior. The center thrust would go directly through Iroquois territory to French-held Crown Point, and therefore Britain's greatest Iroquois friend, Hendrick, was vital to the plan's success. William Johnson, now imperial superintendent for Indian affairs and commissioned a major general by the British commander in America, received orders to rally Indian support for the advance. His alliance with the Mohawk and friendship with Hendrick paid dividends. At a time when few American Indians openly campaigned with the British, Johnson assembled over three hundred warriors, primarily Mohawk under Hendrick's influence.

On September 8, the British force led by Johnson clashed with the French and their American Indian allies at Lake George. Although by now in his seventies and needing Johnson's horse to travel, Hendrick joined in the battle. In the opening skirmish, the British side was ambushed and suffered heavy losses. Hendrick himself was caught in an ambush that left him, thirty other Mohawk, and several dozen colonists dead. According to Hendrick's adopted white son Daniel Klaus, the old warrior met death boldly. When surrounded, he declared, "We are the six confederate Indian nations, the Heads & Superiors of all Indian nations of the Continent of America."[17] Mohawk bravery was noted throughout the British Atlantic. One account that was reprinted widely in British and American newspapers, magazines, and histories praised Hendrick and his comrades and idolized their courageous performance:

> This [the fallen American Indian warrior] was old Hendrick, a sachem, or king, of the Mohawks, and a friend to the general [Johnson]. This valiant Indian, and his followers, fell furiously fighting with their tomahawks, while our men retreated, and are said to have done considerable execution. . . . One of our planters, at the right side of the breast-work, had is piece burst, just as the enemy made their last desperate push on that side; desirous of being farther serviceable, he cried out aloud, What shall I do without a piece? An Indian, that stood next to him, generously said, You made take mine: and without tarrying for an answer, threw it down; then, as if he would show how easy it was to get another, leapt over the barricade, and disarming a French soldier, shot him dead on the spot. He then retreated with the same agility, and took his former station at the breast-work. This way of charging suddenly, from a place of security, and regaining it as dexterously, is what particularizes the Indian method of fighting.

Such exploits made Hendrick and his comrades legends. Despite the initial blunder, the British forces prevailed in the end, dispersing the French force and capturing the French commanding officer, whom Johnson prevented the Mohawk from executing in revenge for Hendrick's death. British casualties, which included a wounded Johnson and much of the Mohawk leadership, were too substantial to allow a continued advance. The American Indians took their dead home to mourn and prepare themselves for winter.

Hendrick's death was felt throughout the British Atlantic world. For his fellow Mohawk, the mourning began immediately; for the British side, the sense of loss was not felt acutely until the following spring, which marked the start of a four-year period in which the British were unable to rally substantial numbers of Iroquois warriors. The circumstances of his death appeared throughout the British press, who were careful to take particular note of the British debt to him during the war.[18] They referred to him reverently as "the brave old Hendrick our fast friend," "this valiant Indian," and "the great Mohawk sachem."[19] His actions and long-standing relationship made him one of the best-remembered American Indians in Britain. Decades later, when Tobias Smollett wrote his *History of England*, he included an admiring account of Hendrick's death, and even the popular *American Gazetteer*—a encyclopedic account of America published in 1798—included Hendrick as a reference point in its contemporary description of the Mohawk valley.[20]

Bibliography and Suggested Reading

Aquila, Richard. *The Iroquois Restoration: Iroquois Diplomacy on the Colonial Frontier, 1701–1754*. Detroit: Wayne State University Press, 1983.

Bickham, Troy. *Savages within the Empire: Representations of American Indians in Eighteenth-Century Britain*. Oxford: Oxford University Press, 2005.

Garratt, J. G. *The Four Indian Kings*. Ottawa: Public Archives: Canadian Govt. Pub. Centre, Supply and Services Canada, 1985.

Hinderaker, Eric. "The 'Four Indian Kings' and the Imaginative Construction of the First British Empire." *William and Mary Quarterly* 53 (1996): 487–527.

———. *Elusive Empires: Constructing Colonialism in the Ohio Valley, 1673–1800*. Cambridge: Cambridge University Press, 1997.

Lydekker, John Wolf. *The Faithful Mohawks*. Cambridge: Cambridge University Press, 1938.

Merrell, James, and Daniel Richter, eds. *Beyond the Covenant Chain: The Iroquois and their Neighbors in Indian North America, 1600–1800*. Syracuse, NY: Syracuse University Press, 1987.

Richter, Daniel K. *The Ordeal of the Longhouse: The Peoples of the Iroquois League in the Era of European Colonization.* Chapel Hill: University of North Carolina Press, 1992.

Shannon, Timothy. *Crossroads of Empire: the Albany Congress of 1754.* Ithaca, NY: Cornell University Press, 2000.

Snow, Dean R. *The Iroquois.* Oxford: Blackwell, 1994.

Vaughan, Alden T. *Transatlantic Encounters: American Indians in Britain, 1500–1776.* Cambridge: Cambridge University Press, 2006.

CHAPTER SEVEN

Sir William Johnson (1715–1774)

English Emissary to the Iroquois

Gail Danvers MacLeitch

In a story that runs parallel to the subject of the previous chapter, cultural historian Gail Danvers MacLeitch recounts the life of Sir William Johnson, an Irish immigrant and resident of the Mohawk valley in New York State who lived at the same time as Hendrick. Johnson became the first British superintendent of Indian affairs when that position was created in 1755; he was responsible for maintaining the political allegiance of the Iroquois, securing their military support, arbitrating land negotiations, supervising Indian trade, and redressing their grievances. For nearly three decades, therefore, Johnson functioned as the principal conduit for British imperial policies among the Iroquois. Through his sustained interactions, Johnson became familiar with Indian customs and sensibilities, married a Mohawk woman, and even was initiated into the Mohawk nation with the adopted name of Warraghiyagey ("he who undertakes great things"). Like Hendrick, Johnson was able to move across cultures with facility and sincerity. At the same time, despite his great sympathy for his Iroquois friends, Johnson was first and foremost an imperial agent whose energies and activities were undertaken in order to advance British goals.

Contemporaries marveled at William Johnson's detailed knowledge of Indian customs and proficiency at securing allies among the powerful Iroquois Confederacy. "By his indefatigable pains among them, and by his compliance with their humours in his dress and conversation with them," one colleague noted, he had "distinguished himself among the Indians." Many believed that he had "so gained their hearts" that he was able to wield an extraordinary influence over them. "When he pleases he can command them," a visitor to the American colonies declared. Still others were titillated by stories of his extravagant sexual liaisons with Iroquois women. In London, rumors circulated over the number of concubines he had, and some claimed that he had as many as seven hundred illegitimate children. For most, however, Sir William Johnson was renowned and revered for his "essential Service" to the British Empire. "He does a great deal of good" in the American colonies a contemporary noted "and is in general much respected."[1]

In the middle decades of the eighteenth century, Sir William Johnson, an Irish immigrant and colonial resident of the Mohawk valley in central New York, dominated British Indian diplomacy in North America. Johnson attained the position of British superintendent of Indian affairs in 1756, an office in which he served until his death in 1774. In this public role, he was responsible for maintaining the political allegiance and military support of the Six Nations of the Iroquois, arbitrating land negotiations, supervising the Indian trade, and redressing Indian grievances. For nearly three decades, he functioned as the principal conduit between the British Empire and the Iroquois Confederacy. Through his efforts to implement imperial policies on the fringes of empire, he forged links between diverse peoples of the Atlantic world.

As his contemporaries rightly observed, Johnson's success at crafting a powerful Anglo–Iroquois alliance had much to do with his aptitude and willingness to adopt Indian practices and values. He appropriated Iroquois dress, ate their food without complaint, followed their forms of diplomatic protocol, and observed their religious rites. Through his careful cultural borrowing and enactment, Johnson appealed to Indian sensibilities and thus won their friendship. Yet, far from being an innocuous cultural broker, Johnson was first and foremost an agent of empire. He utilized his knowledge of Indian customs to serve an imperial agenda. Johnson was employed by the Crown to fashion a British–Iroquois alliance that would promote a cost effective fur trade, facilitate colonial accumulation of Indian lands through legal means, and enlist Indian political and military support against the French. In his private life as well, Johnson embodied the commercial ethos of the eighteenth-century British Empire. Johnson was a merchant capitalist who made his fortune through the Indian trade and land purchases. Thus, both as a Crown official and private entrepreneur, he took a direct interest in Indian lands and resources. Johnson migrated to the Mohawk valley in 1738 under the patronage of his uncle, Peter Warren, who employed him to bring twelve Irish families to settle on his estate along the Mohawk River. Colonial New

York had developed a unique pattern of landholding whereby single own-ers procured large manorial estates and rented out parcels of land to tenant families. Despite its feudalistic overtones, the New York manorial system was oriented toward a protocapitalist economy, as landlords received payment of rent in marketable crops. Johnson quickly adapted to his new surroundings. By 1743, he had settled an additional twenty-six families on his uncle's estate and had purchased his own plantation and home, named Mount Johnson, on the north side of the river. By this time, Johnson had married a local German woman, Catherine Weissenberg, with whom he had three children, Ann, Mary, and John. With a growing family, Johnson explored new opportunities to generate wealth and soon set his sights on the profitable Indian trade. For decades, New York merchants had been procuring animal furs—principally beaver pelts—from Native American hunters. A high demand in Europe for fur clothing made the Indian trade a lucrative enterprise. Albany, in the east, had first dominated the trade, but by the time of Johnson's arrival, Fort Oswego, a British trading post and garrison on the southeastern shore of Lake Ontario, had become a major center of commerce. Johnson soon established a trading post on the banks of the Mohawk River that drew a clientele of traders and hunters passing between Albany and Oswego. He sent agents car-rying his goods to the Indian town of Aughguaga on the Susquehanna River and then gradually broke into the trade at Fort Oswego.

His personal involvement in the trade allowed Johnson to cultivate rela-tions with the local Mohawk, the easternmost nation of the Iroquois Con-federacy.[2] Johnson's fair dealings and readiness to provide goods on credit engendered amicable feelings. Through these early interactions Johnson became seasoned in their cultural practices and beliefs and formed friend-ships with important Mohawk leaders. Whenever he visited the upper Mohawk community at Canajoharie, he stayed in the home of Mohawk *sachem* (member of the ruling council of the Iroquois Confederacy) Brant Canagaraduncka. Similarly, he hosted Indian guests at his home. As a mark of friendship, Johnson was symbolically adopted into the Mohawk nation and given the name Warraghiyagey, "a man who undertakes great things."[3]

Johnson first came to prominence in the Atlantic world during King George's War (1744–1748). At this time, a group of Dutch officials known as the Albany commissioners were employed to oversee Indian affairs. Dissat-isfied with their management, New York Governor George Clinton sought a new agent who could persuade the Six Nations to defend the northern frontier against French assaults. On hearing of William Johnson's close ties with the Iroquois, Clinton appointed him "Colonel of the Forces to be raised out of the Six Nations."[4] Despite this grandiose title, Johnson's influence was confined to the Mohawk. At his first official appearance at Albany in 1746, Johnson led the Mohawk nation to council "dressed and painted after the Manner of an Indian War-Captain."[5] Thereafter, he played a critical role enlisting their warriors to harass the Canadian frontier. All the while, the remainder of the Iroquois maintained a strict policy of neutrality throughout the war. The Mohawks proved the most responsive to Johnson's requests because they were in the greatest need of a colonial ally. Surrounded on all sides by colonial settlement, they saw in Johnson someone who could represent their grievances to the higher powers and who, through his public office and personal involvement in the Indian trade, could provide them with access to the empire's wealth. Hendrick, a chief *sachem* among the Mohawk, went to great lengths to cultivate this relationship. He sponsored Johnson's attendance at village and confederacy councils, reviewed his speeches, and offered advice.

Johnson's public role, however, was short lived. Frustrated by the New York Assembly's unwillingness to settle outstanding payments, Johnson quit his post in 1751. Instead, he concentrated his efforts on developing his mercantile empire in the Mohawk valley. Johnson became an active participant in the Atlantic economy, well attuned to the profits to be made in the transatlantic trade in colonial natural resources and agricultural staples. In the early 1750s, he participated in a booming ginseng trade. Valued for its medicinal properties, this naturally grown root fetched a high price in the China market. Johnson paid entire Indian communities to collect ginseng, which he then sold to New York merchants. He also maintained an active involvement in the fur trade. "The Indian Trade," Johnson asserted, if "wisely & righteously Conducted, will be a Source of Vast Advantages, not only to these Colonies, but to the Commerce & Manufactures of Our Mother Country," especially since Indians were major consumers of British-made goods.[6] Through his endeavors, Johnson emerged as the principal trader in the region. In 1751, one colleague noted that Johnson was "the most considerable trader with the western Indians, & sends more goods to Oswego than any other person does."[7]

Johnson was equally devoted to the profitable land market. In the early 1750s, he continued to enlarge his private landholdings, acquiring a new plantation, called Kingsborough. His growing prosperity enabled him to build a new stone mansion home, named Fort Johnson. While he generally purchased land that had already been patented from Native Americans, he often employed devious means to acquire more land than he was legally entitled to. After clearing the wooded land, he rented out parcels to Irish and German immigrant families. Extremely sensitive to the commercial opportunities flourishing in the colonies, Johnson encouraged tenants on his estate to produce cash crops for foreign export, furnishing them with seeds, tools, and credit. He processed their crops in his own private mill and sold them to New York merchants who exported them to the West Indies.[8]

By 1754, however, peace on the New York frontier was again threatened as a new war between Britain and France loomed. French advances into the Ohio valley in the early 1750s alarmed Whitehall because it threatened to block English traders from the western fur trade and constricted English colonies to the eastern seaboard. For William Johnson, imperial and personal ambitions combined. The economic prosperity of the British Atlantic empire seemed to depend on eradicating the French threat. As war became certain, imperial officials cast their eyes to the Six Nations, which, strategically positioned between the two empires, were recognized at vital allies. With their detailed knowledge of the terrain and experience in forest fighting, they constituted potent military aides. "I am certain they [the Iroquois] might be made a verry usefull Body of men, & the only Barrier against our troublesome Neigbours the French," Johnson contended in 1754.[9] Johnson's success in King George's War had raised his profile among imperial officials in the American colonies and London, and he was duly considered to be the most appropriate individual to manage Indian affairs.

In April 1755, the commander in chief, General Edward Braddock, awarded Johnson a commission as sole manager of Indian affairs. At the same time, he was appointed to lead an army of Indian warriors and colonial militia against the French Fort St. Frédéric at Lake George, known by the English as Crown Point. In July 1755, Johnson held a conference at his home attended by over a thousand Iroquois, at which he appealed to them to support the British war effort and to enlist under his command. By September, Johnson was encamped on the banks of Lake George with militia from New England and New York and around two hundred Indians. Before he was able to lead his army against Crown Point, the French attacked Johnson and his men in ambush. The battle raged for five hours until Johnson's forces finally repelled the French. Poor weather and low supplies deterred Johnson from pushing forward. Instead, the Battle of Lake George marked both the climax and conclusion of the Crown Point campaign.[10] Over forty Mohawk warriors met their death in battle, including Indian leader Hendrick. Johnson himself was shot—a war injury that would plague him for the rest of his years. Yet this minor skirmish with the French, coming as it did after the disastrous defeat of Braddock's forces on the banks of the Monogahela River, was championed as the first British victory of the Seven Years' War. Johnson became an overnight hero, enjoying transatlantic fame. The Battle of Lake George earned him the title of baronet, a gift of £5,000 from the Crown, and, by February 1756, royal confirmation of his appointment as British superintendent of Indian affairs for the northern colonies.

For the remainder of the Seven Years' War, Johnson's primary objective was to secure Iroquois political allegiance. Not prepared to allow the Iroquois to sit on the sidelines despite their formal policy of neutrality, he engaged them in an extensive round of conferences and private meetings at which he begged, bribed, and browbeat them to support the British war effort. His home on the frontier became an open house with a steady stream of Indian delegates, with many permanently encamped on his land. Johnson utilized his knowledge of Iroquois diplomatic tools and procedures to advance his agenda. In particular, he put to work his knowledge of the politics of gift giving. In Iroquois culture, gifts symbolized friendship, hospitality, and reciprocity. Because the recipient of a gift was obliged to reciprocate the kindness shown to them, gifts provided an essential means to forge and maintain alliances. Johnson embraced his role as gift giver with relish. At major conferences, he spent up to £1,000 on gifts ranging from frying pans, teapots, brass kettles, looking glasses, razors, combs, rings, and ribbon. He distributed gifts in a highly political manner, principally granting them to pro-British *sachems*, warriors, and their families, noting as he did that "You may depend upon it I shall never be unmindful of those who are so well attached to His Majesty's Interest."[11]

He created a network of personal alliances by courting powerful *sachems* and installing his own. Once he had distinguished influential headmen, Johnson would endow them with special favors, handsome gifts, and personal attention. Notably, he made extensive use of private councils to flatter *sachems* by feeding their sense of self-importance. He frequently distributed gifts of clothing and cash on such occasions. He used these meetings to exert influence over the Iroquois decision-making process. Instead of waiting for large congresses to consult the Iroquois in one body, Johnson met with leading *sachems* beforehand to present proposed speeches for review and to solicit advice and support. If *sachems* proved obstinate, Johnson exerted pressure "to convince them of their Folly," sometimes causing them to protest his inappropriate conduct.[12] Johnson also created an alliance system through the direct appointment of *sachems*. On the death of a headman, the condolence ritual and requickening ceremony was performed in which a new chief was "raised up" in his place. Johnson gained influence over both of these rites. His involvement in this practice pre-dated the war. In July 1753, he informed Governor Clinton, "It will be verry necessary to make Sachims now when I go up in Everry Nation (as there are severall dead) of those who are most hearty in our Interest. For which purpose I should want at least Eight, or ten Meddalls."[13] The Seven Years' War provided ample opportunity to create new *sachems*. Following a *sachem*'s death, Johnson would "raise up" an appropriate replacement by providing "the proper marks of distinction"—a medal and fine clothing—and then exhort the new *sachem* to "be a firm & zealous Friend to the King of England & his Subjects."[14] Through gift giving, the flattery of private councils, and enactment of the condolence ritual, Johnson established a network of allied leaders. Reflecting on practices, he noted, "I have always made use of a few approved Chiefs of the several Nations, whose fidelity I have had the occasion to put to the test . . . [and] who have never yet deceived me . . . from whom I have obtained timely advices of almost everything of importance in agitation . . . I have made it their interest as much as it is their inclination to be faithful."[15] A second major objective during the war was to enlist Iroquois martial support. The nature of leadership in Iroquois society meant that *sachems* could only advise warriors, not coerce them. Thus, as one *sachem* explained, if their warriors decided to fight "we cant hinder them from going."[16] This meant that following the Battle of Lake George, Johnson and his agents appealed directly to warriors to take up the hatchet against the French. He enjoyed notable success, as warriors from all six nations participated in the war. They engaged principally in scouting expeditions: spying on the French and obtaining captives for intelligence. They escorted provisions to forts and acted as messengers, while some warriors assisted in major campaigns, serving as auxiliaries for the British and provincial armies. Johnson employed a variety of strategies to enlist their labor. In addition to providing political incentives to fight by outlining French treachery, he skillfully drew on their cultural frame of reference, entreating warriors to go on the warpath for the specific purpose of obtaining captives and scalps to replace recently deceased kin. He also appealed to their desire to live up to the warrior ethic. He sought to arouse their martial spirit by leading them in war songs, providing war feasts, and chiding them for behaving more like "silly and fearful women, than brave and honest men" when they refused to fight.[17] Johnson also employed economic gifts to secure their martial manpower. He paid warriors cash and trade goods for their services. As the war dragged on and Iroquois economies faltered, Johnson frequently employed economic coercion to pressure them to lend support. Hence, when a group of "distressed" Oneida Indians appealed for aid in late 1758, Johnson provided minimal assistance, letting them know that he would have been "much readier to relieve" them had their impoverishment "been occasioned by your Mens [sic] being employed in our Service." He noted the possibility of further aid, but only "if you convince me of your deserving it."[18] A third major task Johnson faced during the war was to mediate tensions within the Iroquois–British alliance. Although formerly allies, cultural misunderstandings and prejudices between the Iroquois and British soldiers and settlers led to contentious and sometimes violent exchanges. The Mohawk community leveled a series of complaints against the abusive behavior of British troops garrisoned near their village. Soldiers physically assaulted Indians, stole and damaged crops, and confiscated rum. On one occasion, soldiers pushed an unfortunate Indian to the ground with the butt of a rifle and proceeded to pour the contents of a chamber pot over him. There were also complaints against the dishonest behavior of traders. The killing of settler's livestock by Indian warriors became another source of local tension. Whether this action was motivated out of hunger or through drunkenness made little difference to neighboring Dutch and German farmers who resented this impolite conduct. Repeatedly, Johnson had to diffuse tense situations. He personally arbitrated disputes, counseled Indians, provided gifts to assuage grievances, and represented Indian complaints to higher officials. Johnson was particularly keen to promote harmonious trade relations, as he recognized that "trade is one of the strongest Cements to bind our Indian Connexions."[19] Consequently, he handpicked which traders would be permitted to live among the Iroquois in the early years of the war and sent his agents into Iroquois country to supervise trade. While for the first four years of the war the Iroquois clung to a formal policy of neutrality, in April 1759 they informed Johnson of their decision to join British forces against the French. Although Johnson's skillful mediation and manipulation had won over important allies, he cannot take credit for the switch in Iroquois policy. By the late 1750s, the Iroquois were experiencing significant economic strain and social fragmentation. The British Empire had emerged as the stronger side, so it made political sense to many Iroquois to realign themselves with the winning power. Johnson enlisted just over nine hundred warriors to join himself, General John Prideaux, and their troops for the Niagara campaign in July 1759. The following year, six hundred warriors accompanied Johnson and General Jeffrey Amherst up the St. Lawrence River. Nearly two hundred traveled all the way to Montreal to witness the fall of Canada.

Exhausted but relieved at the close of the war, Johnson expressed a desire to friends to retire from public service and concentrate on private affairs. Matters related to Indians, however, continued to demand his attention. In the summer and fall of 1761, Johnson undertook an extensive trip to Niagara and Detroit to parley with new Indian groups. He faced the tremendous task of incorporating previously French-aligned Indian nations into an alliance with Britain. However many words of peace were exchanged at these meetings, all was not well on the frontier. Distressed by the high cost of trade goods, offended by the British eradication of gifts at posts, and alarmed by the continued British presence of garrisoned forts on their lands, western Indians began to circulate war belts. Tensions mounted, and in May 1763, an Ottawa chief named Pontiac instigated the Anglo-Indian War by leading an assault against Fort Detroit in Michigan. Other Indian groups quickly joined in, including the Seneca—the western nation of the Iroquois—by attacking western British posts. Once again, Johnson found himself at the forefront of Indian affairs. He enlisted the martial support of Iroquois warriors who were sent to destroy enemy Indian towns along the Susquehanna River and to accompany British troops into the Ohio region in the summer of 1764. He was also heavily involved in negotiating the terms of peace, once the embattled Indian warriors surrendered, treating with Pontiac in the summer of 1766.[20]

Although frontier warfare had been quelled, Johnson cautioned his superiors that permanent peace could not be guaranteed until Indian grievances were properly addressed. Abuses in the fur trade were a major cause of unease on the frontier, and Johnson urged Whitehall to establish a regulated system of trade. He advocated that all traders should be licensed, the price of trade goods fixed, and trade itself confined to a limited number of posts where it could be supervised by specially appointed agents. By 1764, the London Board of Trade had incorporated many of Johnson's recommendations into a comprehensive plan that was enacted at key posts.

A second area of contention centered on land. The postwar period was marked by unprecedented efforts by colonists to acquire western lands, particularly in the backcountry of Pennsylvania, Maryland, and Virginia. Although Indians inhabited this region, colonists, made confident by their swelling numbers and by the end of imperial wars, ventured west with boundless determination. As they squatted on Indian lands, cut down forests, and built farms, contact with local Indian groups frequently resulted in violence, especially since accompanying westward migration was a new virulent form of Indian hating. Johnson was alarmed by this pattern of land theft and violence that beset the frontier. He cursed frontier settlers, for they "not only perpetrate Murders whenever opportunity offers, but think themselves at liberty to make settlements where they please."[21] The Proclamation of 1763, issued by the Crown and designed to stem to flow of settlers, had proved ineffectual. By 1765, Johnson began promoting plans to establish a new boundary line.

Although the postwar New York frontier was, by contrast, largely devoid of racially motivated violence, the Mohawk faced enlarged threats to their lands in the form of a series of fraudulent deeds. Genuinely sympathetic but also concerned that loss of their cornfields and hunting grounds would result in the Mohawk being "thrown upon . . . the Government for a subsistence," Johnson championed their cause.[22] But Johnson's sympathies extended only so far. He may have censored the deceitful and grasping behavior of white settlers, but he remained a firm advocate of western settlement as long as it was achieved in a gradual and orderly manner. He believed that native in-habitants could be persuaded to part with their land through legitimate land sales. The natural growth of the colonial population would provide the nec-essary impetus to facilitate this process. To "promote the flourishing state" of the colonies, he deemed, it was essential to treat fairly with the Indians. By so doing, "we may be enabled peaceably & quietly to . . . Settle & Enlarge our Frontier, & in time become an over Match for them in the interior part of the Country."[23] Johnson regarded the white accumulation of Indian lands as inevitable. This perhaps explains why he encouraged the Mohawk to com-promise on land disputes and promoted their involvement in agriculture and husbandry. Johnson in fact operated as an important agent in the transfer of Indian land to colonists. He solicited appropriate buyers and arbitrated land negotiations to ensure that both parties left satisfied.

Johnson also had a very personal stake in land matters. All the while he remained active in Indian affairs, he continued to build his mercantile em-pire. He boasted that during the Seven Years' War, he had settled no fewer than one hundred families on his estate. Following the war, he continued to procure new land. In 1761, Johnson benefited from a "gift" of 40,000 acres from the Canajoharie Mohawk, which became known as the Kingsland patent. Legal wrangling—the land having already been patented by other colonists—meant that Johnson's ownership of this land was not secured for another ten years. Nonetheless, he continued to expand Kingsborough by purchasing more land and settling new families. In the spring of 1763, Johnson built a new manorial home on the frontier. The size and decor of Johnson Hall reflected Johnson's status as a wealthy and genteel landowner and baronet. Johnson filled his home with imported mahogany furniture, oil paintings, crystal glass decanters, and wine glasses and stocked his library full of elite literature and gentlemen's magazines. Although his home housed an array of Indian artifacts, including deerskins, wampum belts, and pipes, their inclusion did not signify Johnson's mutual appreciation of European and Indian material culture. These items were treated as "primitive" and "exotic" curiosities that Johnson both collected and traded with other colonists.[24]

By the early 1760s, Johnson's family had grown substantially. His eldest daughter Ann (or Nancy) married Daniel Claus in 1762, Johnson's aide and then acting deputy for Canada. They moved into Johnson's first home,

Mount Johnson, which had been especially remodeled for them. His younger daughter Mary (or Polly) married Johnson's nephew, Guy Johnson, the following year. Johnson had a new house built for them one mile east of Fort Johnson. His son John, after spending some time in England, moved into Fort Johnson. In addition to his European family, Johnson also had a growing Indian family. Following the death of his first wife sometime in the late 1750s, Johnson had taken a Mohawk woman, named Molly Brant, as his common-law wife. His marriage to Brant cemented his place within the Mohawk kinship network, strengthening his personal relations with this neighboring community. Molly was the stepdaughter of Brant Canagaraduncka and had most likely come to Johnson's attention during his numerous stays at Brant's home. Johnson used his status as a member of an extended Indian family to exert influence. As one contemporary observed, Molly Brant's family connections made her "of great use to Sir William in his Treaties with these people."[25] The status and authority Iroquois culture assigned to women rendered Molly Brant a useful partner regardless of her family ties. Residing in Johnson Hall, Brant played an important role as hostess and housekeeper. She was often responsible for ensuring that Indian and colonial guests were fed, housed, and entertained. Throughout their marriage, Brant assisted Johnson in his diplomatic dealings with Indians, using her influence whenever she could. One acquaintance remarked that she "has always been a faithful and useful friend in Indian affairs, while she resided in Johnston [sic] hall. . . . When treaties or purchases were about to be made . . . she has often persuaded the obstinate chiefs into a compliance with the proposals for peace, or sale of lands."[26]

Johnson had eight children with Brant. In addition, he fathered at least two other illegitimate sons with Indian women, William Tagawirunte later called William of Canajoharie, and "Young Brant," Kaghnaghtago. Johnson was determined to raise his *métis* (mixed-race) children as Anglicized citizens of the British Atlantic empire. He sent Tagawirunte to attend Eleazor Wheelock's missionary school in Connecticut, although "his Pride and the violence of his Temper" caused him to be dismissed in 1766.[27] In his will, Johnson left Young Brant sufficient land, money, and livestock to enable him to become a farmer. His eldest son by Molly Brant, Peter Johnson, was given his father's name and sent to Philadelphia at age thirteen to be apprenticed in the countinghouse of a wholesale business. William Johnson had no intention to allow Peter to become a warrior-hunter, training him instead to assume to role of a New World merchant. His *métis* daughters also received an appropriate education for young European women. In later years, they would marry into the upper echelons of Canadian society.

However much Johnson wished to concentrate on matters related to his family and estate, Indian affairs continued to intrude. Indian complaints against the underhand conduct of traders and settlers persisted throughout the 1760s. By 1768, the trade plan recommended by Johnson was formally rejected by the ministry, who were now more concerned about directing money and troops to deal with rebellious colonists in the east. They stripped Johnson's powers, leaving each colony responsible for regulating its own trade. This was a tremendous blow to Johnson and native peoples who claimed that the absence of regulation had thrown the Indian trade "into utter confusion."[28] Johnson was beset by Indian complaints against trade for the remainder of his days in office. Colonial accumulation of Indian lands also continued at an alarming pace. In an effort to restore peace to the frontier by establishing a permanent boundary line, Johnson negotiated the Fort Stanwix Treaty with the Iroquois in 1768. Although a variety of Indian groups attended—over three thousand Indians in total—Johnson treated only with Iroquois headmen whom he recognized as the true owners of the lands in question. The Six Nations ceded vast areas of land lying south and southwest of Iroquoia. Already disgruntled by British power and now facing new threats to their territory, the Shawnee, Mingo, Delaware, and Western Seneca were incensed by the treaty and began to formulate a militant re-sponse. Johnson spent the last years of his life attempting to undermine this pan-Indian alliance.[29]

The Board of Trade was also disturbed by the content of the treaty. Johnson had acquired much more land for the British than he had been instructed. In response, Johnson reasoned that he wanted to establish a realistic boundary that took into account the degree of white settlement that had already occurred. His actions clearly delighted colonists who had personal interests in the newly ceded lands, and the treaty enriched Johnson himself. Already one of the biggest land barons in the region, following the treaty Johnson patented new lands along the Susquehanna River. As well as acquiring new lands, Johnson was committed to having them settled with "industrious" tenants. Through his efforts, he facilitated the migration and settlement of hundreds of people to colonial New York. In the mid-1760s, Johnson began building a town about one mile away from Johnson Hall, ap-propriately dubbed Johnstown. By the early 1770s, Johnstown housed 120 of Johnson's tenant families. To accommodate their needs, he built a school, a courthouse, an Anglican church, and a jail. When the county of Albany was subdivided in 1772, Johnson employed his political influence to ensure that Johnstown became the county seat of new Tryon County.

As well as prosperity, Johnson's later years were also marked by ill health. Despite recuperating trips to the New England seashore and regular visits to the healing waters of mineral springs, Johnson's wartime wound continued to inflict him. Yet his poor health did not deter him from remaining active in Indian affairs right up until his death. In his dealings with the Mohawk, he continued to arbitrate land deals and assist them against fraudulent claims. Receptive to their requests for Christian missionaries, Johnson helped to organize and fund the building of a church for the Canajoharie Mohawks. In July 1774, Johnson met with the Mohawk and other representatives of the Six Nations for the last time. Exhausted from a trying round of discussions on trade and land abuses, Johnson retired to his residence. He collapsed without warning and died within two hours. Although his nephew and son-in-law Guy Johnson quickly stepped in to assume the mantle Johnson had shouldered for the past three decades, his death left a noticeable gap in Anglo–Indian relations.

William Johnson was a man of his times. He lived and operated as a citizen of the new modern Atlantic world. He was personally keen to take advantage of economic opportunities that flourished in transatlantic trade and commerce but at the same time sought to protect and enlarge the British Empire's presence in North America. Although he made many friends among the Indians, he ultimately always put private and imperial interests first. He used intercultural skills to enrich himself and to strengthen the position of the British Empire. His estate or, rather, estates signified his ascendancy. As his power, wealth, and importance grew, so too did his homes. Yet Johnson was also a remarkable man for his times. In a period when ideas of racial difference were beginning to harden, he demonstrated genuine friendship and respect for his Indian neighbors. They were not permanently different or inferior but important members of the British Atlantic community. Through his public office, Johnson championed their membership by promoting their role as trading partners, consumers of British durables, land sellers, and soldiers. Privately too, by taking a Mohawk woman as his wife, raising *métis* children, and forging close relations with neighboring Indians, he fused Indian and colonial worlds. Even as his actions in the long run served to undermine the integrity of Native Americans, by serving as a nexus between the Iroquois Confederacy and British Empire, Johnson played an important role connecting different peoples of the Atlantic world.

Bibliography and Suggested Reading

Danvers, Gail D. "Gendered Encounters: Warriors, Women and William Johnson." *Journal of American Studies* 35, no. 2 (2001): 87–202.

Fenton, William N. *The Great Law of the Longhouse: A Political History of the Iroquois Confederacy*. Norman: University of Oklahoma Press, 1998.

Flexner, James Thomas. *Mohawk Baronet: A Biography of Sir William Johnson*. New York: Syracuse University Press, 1989.

Green, Gretchen. "Molly Brant, Catherine Brant, and Their Daughters: A Study in Colonial Acculturation." *Ontario History* 81, no. 3 (1989): 235–50.

Hamilton, Milton W. "Sir William Johnson's Wives." *New York History* 38, no. 1 (1957): 18–28.

———. *Sir William Johnson: Colonial American, 1715–1763*. Port Washington, NY: Kennikat Press, 1976.

Huey, Lois M., and Bonnie Pulis. *Molly Brant: A Legacy of Her Own*. Youngstown, NY: Old Fort Niagara Association, 1997.

Jennings, Francis. *Empire of Fortune: Crowns, Colonies, and Tribes in the Seven Years War in America*. New York: Norton, 1988.

Mullin, Michael J. "'Personal Politics': William Johnson and the Mohawks." *American Indian Quarterly* 17, no. 3 (1993): 350–58.

Richter, Daniel K. *The Ordeal of the Longhouse: The Peoples of the Iroquois League in the Era of European Colonization*. Chapel Hill: University of North Carolina Press, 1992.

Shannon, Timothy J. "Dressing for Success on the Mohawk Frontier: Hendrick, William Johnson, and the Indian Fashion." *William and Mary Quarterly* 53, no. 1 (1996): 13–42.

Stone, William L., Jr. *The Life and Times of Sir William Johnson, Bart.* 2 vols. Albany, NY: J. Munsell, 1865.

CHAPTER EIGHT

~

Henry "Harry" Washington (1750s–1790s)

A Founding Father's Slave

Cassandra Pybus

The American Revolution inaugurated an era in which colonists throughout the Americas rejected domination by the European mother countries and fought for independence. The limits of "freedom," however, would remain an issue of contention throughout the next two centuries. For George Washington, "freedom" encompassed the right to self-rule, citizens' individual rights, and free trade. For Harry, an African man who worked as a slave first in Washington's Ferry Plantation, then in his household, "freedom" meant not being enslaved, having a family, and a piece of property for financial autonomy. Historian Cassandra Pybus followed Harry in his quest from British lines during the war and as a black loyalist to Canada and then to West Africa. Neither in Nova Scotia nor in Sierra Leone, recently founded as the "Province of Freedom," were black loyalists recognized as rightful subjects. In fact, the ability and mobilization to claim the rights of the age, seen as natural for whites, would be severely punished when exercised by Africans and African descendants from then on.

As Harry Washington faced a British military tribunal on the west coast of Africa, charged with rebellion against the colonial government of Sierra Leone, he may have seen the irony that fourteen years earlier he had fled his enslavement to the commander in chief of the rebel forces in colonial America to find freedom with the British military and a return to his African homeland. Harry was almost certainly from West Africa and possibly born in the region around the Gambia River around 1740. He was brought to America early in the 1760s on one of the shipments to the South Potomac in 1760 and 1761. Late in 1763, George Washington purchased Harry from the estate of Daniel Tebbs, a plantation owner on the lower Potomac River.

Washington had formed a syndicate called the Dismal Swamp Company with the intention of draining forty thousand acres of a huge swamp in the southeastern corner of Virginia. The Dismal Plantation was managed by his brother John, and Washington's contribution to the enslaved workforce were four people he bought from Tebbs's estate—Harry and Topsom, plus a woman called Nan and a boy named Toney—and two men from Mount Vernon named Jack and Caesar. They worked in appalling humidity, enveloped in clouds of mosquitoes, to cut a canal three feet deep and ten feet wide that would drain into a lake five miles away. In order to get ready cash for the project, they also cut shingles out of the vine-entangled woods of white cedar and cypress. Harry and Nan might have been a couple because two years later they were both taken from the Dismal Swamp to Mount Vernon. If indeed they were a couple, they were not permitted to live together. Harry was employed in or around the house, while Nan labored on one of the outlying farms.

Harry was later described as a very valuable hostler, so his job must have included looking after Washington's horses. He continued to work as a house servant until June 1771, when he appeared in a list of the enslaved laborers on Ferry Plantation, most distant of the Mount Vernon farms. For Harry to be moved from skilled work, which was in some measure self-directed, to grueling plantation labor must have dismayed him sufficiently to precipitate his flight on July 29, 1771. Washington paid one pound and sixteen shilling to advertise for the recovery of his property. The investment paid off when Harry was returned within a matter of weeks and once again put to work back at Ferry Plantation, where he stayed until 1773, when he was redeployed to the house service.

These were turbulent times in Virginia. Late in 1774, Washington had written to a friend that "the crisis is arrived when we must assert our rights, or submit to every imposition that can be heap'd upon us; till custom and use, will make us as tame, and abject slaves, as the blacks we rule over with such arbitrary sway." Sentiments of this nature had been echoed around the dining tables and drawing rooms of Virginian plantations for many months, discreetly absorbed by the footmen and cooks, the valets and maids, and the coachmen and hostlers. Doubtless Harry listened with more than idle interest to this talk about the tyranny of the British masters and the inviolable concept of liberty. Despite having been unsuccessful in his escape in 1771 and having made no further attempt to abscond, he had not abandoned the idea of freedom that now so animated his owner. Even if Washington had been canny enough to send his slave-hostler out of earshot, it would not have been possible to quarantine the ideas that Washington discussed with his friends and neighbors. Snatches of talk overhead were almost instantaneously channeled from plantation to plantation through the complex networks of the enslaved community. The message that Harry would have extracted from the ardent talk swirling around him was that his own attachment to liberty would find no place in the revolutionary ferment sweeping Virginia. As the king was now Washington's enemy, it was to His Majesty that Harry should entrust his aspirations for freedom.

In June 1775, as tension between the colonists and the Crown intensified, the embattled royal governor of Virginia, Lord Dunmore, took refuge on a British warship in the James River and began to assemble a squadron to strike back at the rebellious Virginians, welcoming any fugitive slaves who made their way to his fleet. On November 14, 1775, Dunmore declared martial law and published a proclamation that freed any slaves willing to bear arms for the Crown. Here was every white Virginian's nightmare. Along the length of Chesapeake Bay, alarmed plantation owners and managers did their best to staunch slave defections. At Mount Vernon, the manager, Lund Washington, promoted benevolent paternalism over the precarious dangers of freedom. He was confident that the enslaved community understood that General Washington's care and protection was the best option for them and had "not the least dread" that the slaves might make a bolt for Dunmore's fleet, although he could not vouch for the white indentured servants. Washington was not so sanguine. In his capacity as the commander in chief of the Continental Army, he warned that Dunmore must be crushed, or the momentum of slave defections would increase like a snowball rolling.

Despite savage penalties and increased patrols, a great many runaways still managed to reach Dunmore's fleet in the James River. At the end of November, Dunmore could report, "two and three hundred already come in and these I form into a Corps as fast as they come." Those who got safely to Dunmore came mostly from plantations close to navigable waterways, traveling on small craft, though some came on foot, propelled by sheer willpower, to swim out to Dunmore's ships. Lord Dunmore's Ethiopian Regiment, as the governor styled his new corps, were provided with weapons and taught how to use them. Rumor had it that they were outfitted in a uniform bearing the provocative inscription "Liberty to Slaves," but in reality Dunmore was hard pressed to find any clothing for them. By January 1776, the crowded and inadequate conditions on board Dunmore's fleet had precipitated disaster in the form of epidemic disease.

When smallpox first appeared in Dunmore's overcrowded flotilla, the British were largely immune and the Virginians highly susceptible. The disease hit the black recruits especially hard. They died by the hundreds. In late May, in order to isolate the sick and allow the surgeons to inoculate his recruits, Dunmore moved his base to Gwynn Island, near the mouth of the Rappahanock River, where hundreds of sick men and women endured the awful progress of the disease. Dunmore reported that "there was not a ship in the fleet that did not throw one, two three or more dead overboard every night." On the island, the dead were buried in shallow mass graves. Tragically, Dunmore continued to draw fresh black recruits at the rate of six to eight each day, most of whom succumbed to the disease as soon as they arrived. Moreover, those who recovered from the inoculation fell victim to an outbreak of "fever," almost certainly typhoid fever. In this dreadfully weakened condition, Dunmore's force was easily driven from the island in early July 1776 and took refuge on the fleet once again, having lost up to 70 percent of the black recruits.

In late July, part of the fleet made a foray up the Potomac River to gather fresh water, where they were joined by a small craft that had come down from Fairfax County. The three men on board offering their services to the British were described as three of General Washington's servants. Lund Washington had always suspected that the general's white indentured servants would prove disloyal to him, and perhaps some had seized the opportunity offered by the proximity of Dunmore's fleet. Yet the three "servants" aboard the craft from Mount Vernon must have also included the enslaved hostler, Harry, since he told authorities in New York in July 1783 that he had run away from General Washington seven years before.

Driven out of Virginia, Dunmore went to New York in August 1776, taking three hundred runaways, all that remained of his shattered dream. Harry was among them, and he appears to have been absorbed into a noncombat black army corps called the Black Pioneers, formed in May 1776. Three years later, he was a corporal in the Black Pioneers, part of the seven-thousand-strong force General Clinton took from New York for the invasion of South Carolina. During the siege of Charleston, which began on March 31 and lasted until May 8, the Black Pioneers were employed building the defensive earthworks, making grapeshot and a myriad of support services. Some were armed and engaged in fighting. Once Charleston fell, runaways poured into the British lines, while a fratricidal guerrilla war on the Carolina frontier stimulated a wave of defections to the British outposts in the backcountry.

One prominent patriot claimed to have lost 237 slaves in a mass defection. In May 1780, General Clinton had returned to New York, and few months later General Cornwallis marched north to Virginia, leaving Harry Washington at the British garrison in Charleston.

Early in 1782, news came from England that the British government had granted independence to the American colonies and opened negotiations for peace. Charleston was scheduled for evacuation in June that year. This raised the thorny issue of the British obligations to the black runaways since promises of freedom made by successive British commanders had been contingent on the British winning the war and retaining control of the colonies. No one had a contingency plan for losing the war and leaving America. Confronted with a catastrophic defeat and an unanticipated evacuation of both his army and thousands of loyalist refugees, the British commander, General Leslie, could hardly be expected to concern himself with the runaway slaves, who had, after all, gambled with their future in taking refuge with the king's men. Yet to leave them behind was no easy matter. Every time he looked about, Leslie was exposed to the expectant faces of people who had taken monumental risks in their alliance with the British and who were not prepared to passively submit to reenslavement. By the same token, he had been served an ultimatum by the new governor of South Carolina, that Carolinians would default on debts to British merchants should any slaves be carried off from Charleston. A contest over the fate of runaways presented the humiliated British with the opportunity for a show of moral superiority over the victorious Americans. Weighing up the situation, Leslie concluded that "those who have voluntarily come in under the faith of our protection, cannot in justice be abandoned to the merciless resentment of their former masters." In New York, the commander in chief, General Carleton, was of the same mind.

Throughout November until the final evacuation on December 14, 1782, hundreds of runaways in Charleston queued up to be interviewed by the board established to assess their status. Slave owners, keen to retrieve their property, tried desperately to coax them away, to no good effect. Carolinians bitterly complained that the board had declared obnoxious "almost every Negro, man, woman and child, that was worth carrying away." Leslie stoutly defended his position to Carleton. "I have insisted . . . on the impossibility of delivering up, under any stipulation, a certain description of Negroes, who having claimed our protection and have borne arms in our service, or otherwise rendered themselves more peculiarly obnoxious to the resentment of their former masters," he wrote on October 18. Men and women cleared by the board were allowed to choose their destination, though the availability of transport was a key determinant as to where they went. The largest evacuation fleet took British, German, and provincial troops to New York and also carried several hundred of their black allies. Undoubtedly, Harry Washington was part of this evacuation.

By 1782, there were at least four thousand black men and women living in the British zone in New York. Black artisans worked on rebuilding projects and in the naval yards; black teamsters hauled provisions and collected firewood; black nurses and orderlies staffed the hospitals; black laundresses and needlewomen did the washing and sewing; black pilots guided the ships safely in and out of the port; black musicians provided entertainment at social events; black jockeys rode the horses at the races; and black cooks, servants, and valets ensured the comfort of the elite. Among this teeming black community were people Harry knew from his days of enslavement at Mount Vernon. Eighteen people had run off to the British in April 1781, including two of Lund Washington's slaves. While Washington recovered seven of his chattel, Deborah and Daniel certainly escaped to New York, and possibly Peter, Lewis, Thomas, Stephen, James, and Watty, all young men with skilled trades, found a niche for themselves in New York as free artisans.

Whether they lived in barracks or in the canvas town of the burned-out districts on Manhattan, the black allies of the British formed a community, bound together by the struggle to survive and by forms of cultural expression that reached back to an African past. Central to this community were the black preachers, none more so than the Methodist preacher known as "Daddy Moses," who brought with him a large congregation from Virginia. Blind and lame, probably as a result of smallpox, Daddy Moses was a charismatic preacher who put great store by dreams and visions to reveal the will of God and the sure road to eternal happiness. Harry Washington was among his many converts.

At the time that Charleston was being evacuated, a peace treaty was being hammered out between the British and the Americans in Paris. Hastily included in the treaty was a clause in article 7, to prohibit "carrying away any Negroes or other property of the American Inhabitants." For the black refugees in New York, this was utterly demoralizing. Rumors that the British would be obliged to abandon them in America filled them with anguish and terror. Determined to maintain their freedom, the runaways were kept on constant alert against attempts to spirit them back to slavery. According to a senior Hessian officer, about five thousand people had come to new York to take possession of their former property. His figure may have been exaggerated, but there can be no doubt that a great many slave owners were gaining entry into the British zone, and they were not using sweet reason to reclaim their property. Without warning, runaways could find themselves knocked on the head, bound hand and foot, and kidnapped back to the place they had fled. As most of the runaways behind the British lines had experienced years of freedom, they were horrified at the prospect of reenslavement. Day and night, they pressed their case with the British authorities to make good the promises of freedom and remove them from the reach of their vengeful owners.

The governor of Virginia was furious that the British consistently refused to hand over his absconded chattel. Alarmed by such a flagrant violation of the treaty, he complained to George Washington, who undertook to raise the issue directly with General Carleton. "I have but little expectation that many will be recovered," Washington warned the governor; "several of my own are with the enemy, but I scarce ever bestow a thought on them; they have so many doors through which they can escape from New York." Washington also engaged the army contractor, Daniel Parker, to assist in recovery of the slaves for the governor and asked Parker to also keep an eye out for his property. "If by chance you should come at the knowledge of any of them," he wrote, "I will be much obliged by your securing them so I may obtain them again." Washington's choice of Daniel Parker was strategic. Parker had done personal errands for the general in the past; on this matter, however, he was uniquely positioned to help Washington locate his slaves. He was one of the Americans appointed as commissioners to inspect embarkations to ensure that no American-owned property was taken away.

General Carleton was appalled by the terms of the treaty, but in apparent compliance he allowed the inspection of the departing ships while at the same time making sure that all the runaways who had been with the British for a year were provided with certificates of freedom. He would not permit anyone who met that condition to be claimed as American property. So when Parker inspected the ships in the evacuation fleet that sailed from New York on April 27, 1783, he was impotent to stop the woman named Deborah who had run away from Mount Vernon in 1781 from leaving on the ship *Polly*, bound for Nova Scotia. When Washington protested a violation of the treaty, Carleton told him that the British government would never agree "to reduce themselves to the necessity of violating their faith to the Negroes into the British lines under the proclamation of his predecessors" and further that "delivering up Negroes to their former masters . . . would be a dishonourable violation of the public faith."

Under Parker's impotent gaze, Harry Washington embarked on the ship *L'Abondance* in July 1783, with 405 black men, women, and children going to Nova Scotia. He was said to be forty-three years of age and traveling alone. Despite the protest of Congress and Washington himself, Carleton had facilitated the evacuation of three thousand black refugees whose names were recorded by the commissioners as well another two thousand whose departure from New York was not recorded.

Those on board *L'Abondance* were mostly followers of Daddy Moses, and they settled as a community in Nova Scotia at a place called Birchtown. The muster at Birchtown taken in July 1784 listed Harry Washington, aged forty-four, as a laborer with a wife, Jenny, aged twenty-four. No children were listed. To survive, Harry probably hired himself out to his white neighbors in nearby Shelburne, as most of the black settlers were forced to do. These labor agreements were highly exploitative, with the free blacks regarded as cheap labor by the white loyalist settlers. Sometimes the black workers were never paid at all. Nova Scotia proved hard for both white and black settlers, forced to create a new life in inhospitable weather and faced with innumerable delays in the allocation of the promised land grants. When the grants were made, the lots allocated to the black settlers tended to be smaller than expected and on poor, rocky soil. In many cases, black refugees were still waiting for their land allocation three years after their arrival. In addition to the bitter cold and grinding poverty, tension between the black settlers and their white neighbors ran high. Although the black community persisted, the people at Birchtown were in a pitiful state. A white visitor in 1788 was shocked by "their huts miserable to guard against the inclemency of a Nova Scotia winter and their existence almost depending on what they could lay up in the summer." In the opinion of this witness, "the wretchedness and poverty so strongly perceptible in the garb and continence of . . . these miserable outcasts" was as extreme as he had ever seen. Life was no better at the other black settlements.

Thomas Peters was a runaway from North Carolina who had been a sergeant of the Black Pioneers during the war. He was deputized to voyage to England in 1791 in order to put the grievances of his constituency in Nova Scotia to the British government. In his petition, Peters requested that His Majesty's black subjects in Nova Scotia be resettled or that, should they choose to remain in Nova Scotia, they be given due allotment of the land they had been promised. In response to Peters's acutely embarrassing accusations of bad faith, Pitt's government undertook to pay the necessary expenses to transport as many black settlers as wished to leave Nova Scotia. The Sierra Leone Company, delighted with the prospect of new settlers in their colony on the west coast of Africa, offered free grants of land "subject to certain charges and obligations" to any who wanted to emigrate. New settlers were promised twenty acres for every man, ten for every woman, and five for every child.

John Clarkson, the young naval officer whose brother Thomas was a prime mover in the campaign for the abolition of the slave trade, was the agent appointed by the Sierra Leone Company to oversee the move from Nova Scotia. Harry Washington was among the hundreds of people who attended a meeting in Birchtown, at the church of Daddy Moses, to hear Clarkson explain the offer. Clarkson was adamant that the expression "subject to certain charges and obligations" did not signify that an annual rent would be levied on the land in Sierra Leone; rather, it referred to "a kind of tax for charitable purposes such as for the maintenance their poor, the care of the sick, and the education of their children." Harry and his fellow black settlers accepted Clarkson's explanation. They especially warmed to his assurance that in Sierra Leone, unlike Nova Scotia, where they were barred from voting or serving on juries, there would be no discrimination between white and black settlers. Harry Washington was among a large group from Birchtown who decided to go, even though it meant abandoning his freehold land grants. In the list of settlers relocating from Birchtown, Harry was described as a farmer, born in Africa and aged fifty (although he was probably fifty-three), and traveling with his wife Jenny. He took with him an ax, saw, and pickax, plus three hoes, as well as two muskets and several items of furniture. He left behind two town lots, a house, and forty acres.

As a consequence of Clarkson's assurances, about half of the black refugees in Nova Scotia opted to leave. Nearly 1,200 black settlers were relocated at a cost of 15,500 pounds to the British government. The directors of the Sierra Leone Company were so pleased with the response from Nova Scotia that they shelved plans to encourage white settlers to emigrate from England. Henceforth, the only whites in Sierra Leone would be a handful of company employees. Company director William Wilberforce told Clarkson that he should call the new black settlers Africans, believing that this was "a more respectable way of speaking of them," but this was emphatically not how they conceived of themselves. In their eyes, they were free British subjects, no less than Clarkson. Moreover, Clarkson ruefully conceded, they had "strange notions . . . as to their civil rights."

By the middle of 1792, Clarkson, who had been appointed the first governor of Sierra Leone, was finding that these strange notions were causing no end of grief. Since Clarkson had arrived in Sierra Leone, turbulent discontent he believed to be inspired by Thomas Peters had brought the governor to the end of his tether, yet he maintained a steely determination that he—and only he—would be in charge. Thomas Peters died, profoundly disillusioned, in June, and Clarkson's response was surprisingly rancorous, prompted by fear that Peters believed he should have been the appointed governor of Sierra Leone. Yet everywhere Clarkson cared to look was evidence that Peters was not acting out of personal ambition but rather giving expression to a shared disillusion. As the settlers told him, finding themselves in Sierra Leone with no land, despite all the promises, "makes us very uneasy in our mind that we might be liable to the same cruel treatment as we have before experienced." On the very day Peters died, Clarkson received a petition from the large Methodist congregation in eccentric spelling that betrayed the authors as barely literate. They said they willingly agreed to be governed by the laws of England, but "we do not consent to gave it into your honer hands with out haven aney of our own culler in it," and reminded Clarkson that he had promised them that "whoever came to Saraleon wold be free . . . and all should be equel," so it followed that they had "a wright to chuse men that we think proper for to act for us in a reasnenble manner."

By late July, the settlers were in a fever pitch of indignation because the survey for the farm lots they had been promised had not yet begun. They had only the huts they had built on small town lots carved out of the jungle in Freetown, and the only basis for their subsistence was two-day-a-week work for the company, paid in credit at the company store. Their habit of trusting Clarkson was all that protected the company's handful of haughty, idle, and incompetent white employees from their collective wrath. Clarkson had been forced to persuade the settlers to accept only one-fifth of the land they had been promised, and a bitter grievance had been reignited when he indicated that the company directors would not allow the settlers to take land along the Sierra Leone River. Access to the water was an absolute necessity. There were no carts or horses in Sierra Leone; communication and transport were all by means of water. The settlers reacted with fury to the suggestion, pointing out that this same trick was played on them in Nova Scotia, where white men had occupied the entire waterfront, built wharves along it, and then charged money for access. They had not crossed the ocean to suffer the same discrimination all over again, they said.

In deference to the settlers' fears of further injustice at the hands of self-interested white people, Clarkson hastily rescinded the company instructions concerning the waterfront. He also agreed that the settlers could elect their own representatives as peacekeepers. Clarkson chose not to act on his orders from the company directors to institute a quit rent of two shillings an acre on the settlers' land grants, rationalizing that the company would have to comply with the spirit of his promises. It was a high-risk strategy for a servant of the company who was due to go on extended leave in December 1792.

Clarkson never came back to Sierra Leone. He was dismissed by the company in May 1783 and was replaced as governor by William Dawes, who was in turn succeeded in 1796 by twenty-seven-year-old Zachary Macaulay. By 1796, the settlers were sending anguished appeals to Clarkson to come back as the governor and rescue them from the authoritarian regime of Governor Macaulay, who obliged them to pay the huge quit rent. The Sierra Leone Company was blithely determined to impose a tax that was a hundred times higher than in Nova Scotia, where the colonial government had been forced to abandon the quit rent because settlers, black and white, refused to pay two shillings for every one hundred acres. When Governor Macaulay cut the amount in half, requiring only one shilling an acre, he naively believed that he was being generous to the settlers and fully expected them to be grateful to him.

For more than twenty years, the defining issue for Harry Washington and his fellow black settlers had been to live as free people and not to submit to the indignities and deprivations that had marked their lives as slaves. Owning land—not renting it or working it for somebody else—was critical in their self-definition, as was regulating their own community. It was equally important that men should be responsible for the maintenance of their families and that the women and children should not labor as they had in slavery. For a time after their arrival, Harry had been prepared to endure the indignity of working for credit at the company store rather than monetary wages, even though this was a condition of labor the settlers believed akin to bondage, because he was waiting for the land allocation that would give him the capacity to be independent and self-sustaining. By 1796, land had been granted, and he had already achieved the self-reliance that was now threatened by the quit rent.

On January 5, 1797, the elected representatives met to discuss how to get rid of the quit rent, determined never to submit to an imposition that reduced them to perpetual tenancy. When the demand for the first payment of the quit rent was proclaimed in June 1797, about thirty settlers reluctantly agreed to pay rather than face the governor's wrath, while the great majority held out against it. On August 5, the settlers representatives wrote to the governor reminding him that they had abandoned land in Nova Scotia in the expectation that they would receive land on the same conditions in Sierra Leone and that they were never told that the land belonged to the company for which they must pay quit rent. "Sir if we had been told that, we never could come here," they wrote; "we are astonished why the company could not tell us after three years we was to pay a shilling per acre . . . if the lands is not ours without paying a shilling per acre, the lands will never be ours."

About two weeks later, the governor called a public meeting of heads of households in which he denied that the black settlers had left freehold land in Nova Scotia and insisted that they had always known about the quit rent. The problem with ignorant people, he concluded, was that they were susceptible to "every prating, malicious, designing talebearer" who wished to misrepresent the good intentions of the company. "You have often been made to see the folly of acting thus," he told his stunned audience, "yet you still return like the sow to flounder in the same dirty puddle." For all his sardonic bravado, Macaulay could see that the quit rent could not be imposed without violence. He told the company directors it would be prudent not to collect the rent, at least in the short term.

In November 1798, an edict arrived from the company directors that the quit rent must be paid. Macaulay duly informed the settlers that new titles had been drawn up incorporating the quit rent conditions, for which they must apply by December. This time, about a dozen families accepted the grants, and the rest refused, even though the refusal meant their children were barred from the free company school. A new grants register excluded the names of all those who refused their grants and listed their allotments as unallocated land. Among those whose land was reallocated in this fashion were some of the colony's most successful farmers, including Harry Washington. The governor's action drove nearly every settler into a rebellious coalition against him. In the weeks before Macaulay's departure from the colony in April 1799, he told his fiancée that he felt the need to sleep with loaded muskets in his bedroom.

The moment Macaulay left Sierra Leone for good, the settlers took the matter into their own hands. Without consulting the new governor, a twenty-three-year-old stripling named Thomas Ludlam, they chose a judge and two justices of peace from among themselves. The elected representatives of the black settlers formed into a bicameral parliament, passing resolutions about the day-to-day management of the colony. In September 1799, they resolved that they were the proprietors of the colony since it was to the black settlers that the local African chiefs had ceded the land. The settlers were not to know that in England at the same time, the directors of the Sierra Leone Company had applied to the British Parliament for a royal charter to give the company incontestable jurisdiction over the colony and the power to repress all dissent within the colony. As the directors explained in their subsequent report, "the unwarranted pretensions of the disaffected settlers, their narrow misguided views; their excessive jealousy of Europeans; the crude notions they had formed of their own rights; and the impetuosity of their tempers" made it imperative for the company to have means to "repress the turbulence and assumption of the colonists." There would be no more elections in Sierra Leone.

On September 25, the settlers own code of laws was displayed in Freetown, drawing curious crowds the following day. A witness later reported that "people being on farms, hearing of this news, gathered themselves together to hear and understand" at one of the settlers' houses. The frightened young governor overreacted. He sent to the house a group of loyal black settlers whom he had armed and deputized as marshals with warrants for the arrest of the leaders on charges of treason. The marshals burst into the house just as the meeting was breaking up. In the melee that followed, two were arrested, and others were wounded. Those who had escaped from the meeting fled out of the town and set up camp about two miles away, where they were joined by Harry Washington, whose farm was nearby.

Later the Sierra Leone Company tried to portray these men as armed and dangerous rebels who wished to annihilate the company employees. Significantly, the men labeled as rebels were all past middle age—Harry Washington was sixty—and they were largely without arms. They had some guns but no ammunition, which was almost all stored at Government House. On the third day, they stole a gun and some powder from the governor's farm as well as powder and shot from the farm of a white employee of the company, but this was hardly evidence of preparation for an armed coup; they were as likely to have wanted the arms for hunting game.

On September 30, as if life was imitating fiction, a large British transport ship arrived in the harbor carrying over five hundred Maroons who had been deported from Jamaica after their surrender after the Second Maroon War in 1795. The Sierra Leone Company agreed to take the Maroons from their first place of exile in frigid Nova Scotia in return for additional financial and military support from the British government. Accompanying the Maroons to Freetown was a detachment of forty-seven soldiers of the 24th Regiment. Ludlam could not have prayed for a more timely intervention. The Maroons were extraordinary warriors; for generations, they had been used to repress slave rebellions and hunt runaway slaves. After weeks at sea, they were desperate for some physical activity and so were pleased to be invited to "stretch their legs a little," as one of the company's directors later joked, and hunt the rebels down.

Within a week, Ludlam had thirty-one supposed rebels in his custody, charged with engaging unprovoked rebellion. After a hasty military tribunal, five men were banished to the slave forts of Goree and one to Rio Nunez, a sure sentence of death for men of their age. Two of the leaders were hanged. Harry Washington and twenty-three other men were banished across the Sierra Leone River to the Bullom Shore. The personal tragedy and appalling loss in human resources that resulted from these dubious and draconian decisions—over forty of the colony's most respected settlers dead or banished—were of no consequence to the directors of the company. They believed that Sierra Leone was much better off without these men and "the crude notions they had formed of their own rights." The runaway slaves from America had made "the worst possible subjects," William Wilberforce concluded in disgust, "as thoroughly Jacobin as if they had been trained and educated in Paris." They had, of course, been trained and educated in the American Revolution, and the radical notions about their rights as free men and women were forged in the tortuous negotiations to secure their freedom and to make it a tangible reality in their lives. These were notions that George Washington believed worth dying for. It should be no surprise that a man he once held as property believed the same.

Bibliography and Suggested Reading

Archival sources can be found in the National Archives of the United Kingdom in the series PRO 33/55/100, PRO 30/55/43-60, CO 217/63, CO270/4; the Wray Papers in the Clements Library, University of Michigan; John Clarkson's journal at the New York Historical Society; the Muster Book of Free Black Settlement in the Public Archives of Nova Scotia; the Clarkson Papers in the British Library, London; and the journals of Zachary Macaulay in the Huntington Library, San Marino.

Abbot, W. W., and Dorothy Twohig, eds. *The Papers of George Washington, Colonial Series*. Vols. 7–10. Charlottesville: University Press of Virginia, 1990–1995.

Egerton, Douglas. *Gabriel's Rebellion: The Virginia Slave Conspiracies of 1800 and 1802*. Chapel Hill: University of North Carolina Press, 1993.

Finkelman, Paul. *Slavery and the Founders: Race and Liberty in the Age of Jefferson*. New York: M. E. Sharpe, 2001.

Fitzpatrick, John C. *The Writings of George Washington*. Vol. 26. Washington, DC: Government Printing Office, 1937.

Furstenburg, François. *In the Name of the Father: Washington's Legacy, Slavery and the Making of a Nation*. New York: Penguin Classics, 2007.

Goldstone, Lawrence. *Dark Bargain: Slavery, Profits and the Struggle for the Constitution*. New York: Walker & Company, 2005.

Jackson, Donald, and Dorothy Twohig, eds. *The Diaries of George Washington*. Vol. 3. Charlottesville: University Press of Virginia, 1978.

Kaminski, John. *A Necessary Evil? Slavery and the Debate of the Constitution*. Madison, WI: Madison House Publishers, 1995.

Melish, Joanne Pope. *Disowning Slavery: Gradual Emancipation and Race in New England, 1780–1860*. Ithaca, NY: Cornell University Press, 2000.

CHAPTER NINE

Julien Raimond (1744–1801)

Planter, Revolutionary, and Free Man of Color in Saint-Domingue

John Garrigus

Julien Raimond was a wealthy indigo planter on the island of Saint-Domingue (today Haiti) who owned over one hundred slaves, although he himself was a person of partial African ancestry. Raimond was, perhaps, the most important free man of mixed racial descent in the eighteenth-century Atlantic world. He was the author of over a dozen pamphlets that were published in Paris during the French Revolution, and he lobbied the National Assembly to grant equal rights to men of color. Essentially a social conservative, he remained loyal to France during the tumultuous revolutionary years but, in the end, helped forge the conditions that ultimately led to Haiti's political independence. Historian John Garrigus expertly uses Julien Raimond's life story to reveal the ambiguity of racial categories in the eighteenth-century Caribbean and to show how closely the issues of racial purity and citizenship remained linked in some revolutionary circles who purported to be friends of liberty and democracy.

Julien Raimond was perhaps the most influential free man of African descent in the late eighteenth-century Atlantic world. Born in 1744 to an indigo planter and his free mulatto wife in Saint-Domingue, France's most valuable Caribbean colony, Raimond owned over one hundred slaves by the 1780s. In 1784, he moved to France, where he tried to convince royal administrators to temper the harsh racial laws that restricted every facet of a mulatto's daily life, including dress, occupation, place of residence, deportment in the presence of whites, and access to public office. After 1789, Raimond's speeches and pamphlets awakened revolutionaries in France to the many contradictions between their high-minded ideals and realities of a slave-based colonial society. As legislators started to act to ameliorate the conditions he described, his words provoked a colonial backlash in Saint-Domingue against such "interference" from Europe. Ultimately, this schism among the governing and planter elite destabilized free society in Saint-Domingue and prepared the way for a successful slave uprising in 1791.

In 1793, Parisian revolutionaries jailed Raimond for causing this racial violence, but he managed to get himself exonerated and was sent back to Saint-Domingue as a government commissioner. There, in 1796, he helped to implement a new labor system that was designed to replace plantation slavery, and he eventually became a prominent counselor to the popular black general Toussaint Louverture. Raimond participated in the effort to write an autonomous constitution for Saint-Domingue, but he died in 1801 before the war was over. The man whose words had done so much to inspire his fellow citizens did not live long enough to witness the birth of the new independent nation of Haiti in 1804.

Historians generally have not counted Julien Raimond among the fathers of the Haitian nation. His strong attachment to France, his preference for legal over military action, and his skepticism about making citizens of recently emancipated slaves have all excluded him from the established pantheon of heroes. Yet it was Raimond who convinced French revolutionaries in 1791 and 1792 to extend civil rights to those free men in the colonies who had been scorned for their African ancestry; he urged them to recognize the mulattos' common humanity but curiously enough did not fight actively against the institution of slavery itself, which existed on the island until 1793, when Saint-Domingue's black armies joined forces with the revolution. Nevertheless, Raimond was the first colonist to advance the idea that Caribbean people should be recognized as citizens regardless of their ancestry or racial origins. This was the idea that inspired the establishment of an independent Haiti in 1804.

Raimond emerged from the extraordinary social, economic, and political situation in late colonial Saint-Domingue. By the end of the eighteenth century, enslaved men, women, and children made up nearly 90 percent of the colony's population. French colonists controlled Saint-Domingue's highly profitable plantation system, but their numbers were rivaled by the free population of color, a group that included free blacks but also free mulattos and others of mixed European and African descent.

Table 9.1.   Population of Saint-Domingue according to Royal Censuses

Year	Whites	Free Coloreds	Slaves	Total
1713	5,689	1,189	24,156	31,034
1740	11,540	2,525	108,854	120,394
1754	14,258	4,861	172,548	191,667
1771	18,418	6,180	219,698	244,296
1775	20,438	5,897	261,471	287,806
1786	25,000	15,000	340,000	380,000
1788	30,826	27,548	465,429	523,803

Source: Archives Nationales, Section Outremer, G1509, Nos. 12, 21, 28, 30, 31, 36, 38; data for 1789 comes from Pierre Pluchon, ed., *Histoire des Antilles et de la Guyane* (Toulouse, 1982), 267.

The size of Saint-Domingue's free colored population was due in part to the natural increase of slaves who had been freed in the late 1600s. More important, however, throughout the 1700s French colonists continued to free their favorite slaves, in particular their mistresses and mixed-race children. Many interracial children remained enslaved,[1] but French fathers regularly manumitted, educated, and left property to their favorite mixed-race sons and daughters despite official disapproval. In a number of cases, white men married free black or mulatto women since racial intermarriage had never been outlawed in Saint-Domingue.

Julien Raimond was a product of one such marriage. His father Pierre was born in southern France sometime around 1690. In 1720s, he emigrated to Saint-Domingue's largely unsettled southern peninsula, where he established a plantation to grow and manufacture indigo dye, an enterprise that required a large workforce, distilling vats, expert supervision, and a reliable source of water. By 1726, he solidified his local position and gained some capital investment by marrying the daughter of an established planter; she brought 15,000 livres to the marriage, while he could contribute only 6,000. In 1738, Raimond's mother-in-law sold him land and a valuable well for 10,000 livres, allowing him to pay her gradually from his profits.

It was not until the 1760s that official documents began to identify Raimond's wife, Marie Begasse, as a free *mulâtresse*. An immigrant like Raimond was lucky to marry into a planter family, and many others on the colonial frontier made similar alliances, for there was as yet very little concern for racial "purity." In 1731, an official inspecting the militia in this very parish informed the governor that "there are few whites of pure blood there because all the whites willingly ally themselves by marriage with the blacks, for they, by their thrift, acquire property more easily than the whites."[2] In 1738, Marie's sister Françoise Begasse married another French emigrant, the surgeon Barthelmy Vincent.

By the time Julien Raimond was born in 1744, his parents had achieved a certain respectability, economic success, and public prominence. In 1748, members of the parish chose his father as sexton, responsible for managing church funds. Pierre Raimond ensured that his children were well established as adults, bestowing dowries on his older daughters and oldest son in the late 1750s and early 1760s with 12,000 livres each, roughly twice what other local fathers gave their children. The five children of Barthelmy Vincent and Françoise Begasse received even larger sums. Raimond and Vincent continued another tradition begun by their wives' white father, that of educating their children. In the 1720s, Pierre Raimond was not able to sign his marriage contract, though his wife Marie Begasse did. Her sister Françoise was also literate. But by the 1760s and 1770s, all fifteen of the Raimond and Vincent children were literate, and many of them had been educated in France. At least one of Julien Raimond's cousins and two of his sisters, Elizabeth and Agathe, were in France before their twenty-fifth birthdays. Agathe married a propertied citizen of Bordeaux, while Elizabeth wed a former attorney of the Parlement of Toulouse. A bill among Julien's papers suggests that he was in Toulouse at the age of eighteen.

With the help of his wife's mixed-race family, Pierre Raimond became a wealthy man over the course of nearly fifty years in Saint-Domingue. When he died in 1772, he left a large plantation that included thirty-five slave cabins. Most neighboring planters lived in structures of straw, mud, and logs, but the Raimond house was built of squared timber with masonry and mahogany shingles and was furnished with carved tables, two Russian leather armchairs, and twenty-three silver place settings. Yet the wealth he left his wife and children could not protect them from rising racial tensions.

On the morning of May 15, 1766, Julien Raimond appeared before a colonial notary. At the age of twenty-two, perhaps recently returned from France, the young man could already claim some degree of local respectability because the notary described him using the honorific *Sieur* Raimond. Before affixing his seal to the document, the official noticed that Raimond had omitted something. Following standard procedure, he wrote the racial term *quarteron* (quarter black) in the margin after the young man's name. The emerging practice of describing free wealthy persons by their skin color marked a fundamental change in colonial society. French officials had long been in the habit of categorizing former slaves according to color, but Raimond was a proud slave owner, a man born in freedom. In a petition to colonial administrators that he wrote twenty years later, Raimond still fumed that this new practice was designed specifically to humiliate freeborn men like himself. To be sure, his wealth sheltered him from some of this scorn.

Many other notaries conveniently forgot to describe Raimond as a *quarteron*, and some continued to title him *Sieur*, though the term came to be reserved for white men alone. The racial label deeply offended Raimond's sense that he too was a French citizen, just as much as his white father had been. As the colonial administrators established more overt forms of discrimination in the 1770s and 1780s, Raimond started to mobilize others to challenge the emerging racialized definition of French citizenship.

Six years later, when his father died, Julien Raimond was fast becoming a prominent planter in his own right. In 1770, he bought out his brother Jean's share in a plantation partnership with another brother François, and in 1773 he purchased land adjacent to his father's estate. This was one of the choicest spots in the Aquin plain, although the former owner's house, sheds, and indigo basins had fallen into "total ruin." To reestablish the plantation, Julien, with his brother Guillaume, sold a smaller plot and the indigo works that they had inherited from their father. Along with their brothers François and Jean Baptiste, who also had quadrupled the value of their indigo plantation within six years, Guillaume lent his own slaves and skills to Julien's new venture. Like many eighteenth-century entrepreneurs, the Raimonds worked closely together, yet their family alliances were unconventional, even controversial. For example, in May 1766, Julien's older brother Pierre married their cousin Marie Madeleine Vincent. Only one member of the large Raimond clan, François, witnessed the incestuous nuptials. The groom's parents Pierre and Marie refused to bless the union, although he had sought and received a religious dispensation.

In February 1771, Julien Raimond also married another of the Vincent cousins. Again, the Raimond parents would not give their permission and agree to sign the couple's wedding contract. Marrying without his parents' approval meant that the groom risked disinheritance. Nevertheless, the bride brought 60,000 livres of property, while Julien contributed only 35,000. In his words, the match was "a favorable and advantageous option." The union was not, however, merely a shrewd financial calculation. Increasingly, racial prejudice and colonial regulations barred men of color from taking a white bride. Their options were severely limited; there were few local free women of color like the Vincents, who were born to legitimate marriages and educated in France. Unfortunately, this second Raimond/Vincent union ended after a few years when Julien's wife died suddenly. Because his wife had not yet reached the age of majority, he was forced to return her dowry.

This financial and emotional blow, added to the strain of an increasingly scrutinized social position, caused a rift between Julien and his mother. After the death of her husband Pierre in 1772, Marie Begasse Raimond entrusted her land and slaves to Arnaud Lonné, a French immigrant and wholesale merchant. Julien Raimond, still bitter twenty years later, described Lonné as a predator who set on their family in the way that "all the whites that are not planters make money."[3] With this characterization, Raimond identified the merchant as a *petit blanc*, a notoriously shifty and unreliable category in colonial society. Since the end of the Seven Years' War in 1763, Frenchmen seeking a quick fortune had flooded into Saint-Domingue and been met with some resistance from the locals, who resented the imposition of new ideas and behaviors and the increased competition for the few women who lived there. Raimond and others recalled the "hate [that] these whites without property, education, or morals bear for those of mixed blood."[4] In the 1780s, an anonymous writer described *petits blancs* "competing for the fortunes of widows and orphans, causing quarrels and lawsuits between family members."[5]

Raimond believed that racial jealousy was the reason that Arnaud Lonné appeared before a royal judge in January 1774 to protest against "the insults, threats and acts of violence committed against him by a mulatto from Aquin named Guillaume Raymond [*sic*]." According to Lonné, Guillaume Raimond had tormented his mother and been disagreeable to her in the years since she had become a widow. When Guillaume came to live on Julien's plantation, Lonné claimed, he sent some slaves to ravage the widow's crops and steal her provisions until the white knight Lonné found a peaceful way to end these raids. For this reason, Lonné charged, as he passed the brothers' plantation on his way into town one Saturday morning, a crowd of Guillaume's slaves blocked his way. Guillaume appeared, cursing, and beat Lonné with a club. The white man demanded a settlement of 50,000 livres plus costs, claiming, "The insult is too serious to be described; the color of the one guilty of this crime adds, if that is possible, to its atrocity." The accusation was especially damning for the Raimonds because Lonné had evoked the emerging stereotype of free men of color as impudent thieves with close ties to the vicious slave world from which they had only recently emerged. His description of Guillaume as a mulatto was intended to be another assault on the man's social standing; technically, the Raimond siblings were all quadroons, at least one generation farther removed from their African ancestors.

The day after learning of Lonné's charges, both Guillaume and Julien officially denied that the incident had occurred, identifying themselves in their response as *Sieurs* and "quadroons." Although he had not been named in the complaint, Julien led the counterattack. He claimed that "*Sieur* Lonné does what he can to ruin and disgrace them and to make their mother, the widow Raymond, hate them, though they have never passed the limits of the respect they owe her." Yet this very wording points to strained relations between Marie Begasse and her sons. Julien and Guillaume faced considerable pressure to make their plantation profitable. Rather than wasting time answering Lonné's spurious accusations, the hardworking entrepreneurs protested, they should be supervising the harvest and distillation of their indigo because they could not afford an overseer. It was a difficult situation. While their mother was paying a French immigrant to manage their father's estate, Julien and Guillaume Raimond were so desperate for funds that they sold Lonné 24,000 livres of their inheritance rights for a mere 3,000 livres.

Whether financially or racially motivated, the tension between Marie Begasse Raimond and her sons eventually faded. By the end of 1774, Lonné was no longer living on the widow Raimond's plantation, removing one huge source of contention. In 1781, Julien, François, and Guillaume Raimond appeared with their mother before a royal notary "to testify for the present and for the future their respect and their submission to their mother's wishes." By that time, their own plantation was a success. In 1781, Julien formally dissolved his partnership with Guillaume and paid him 18,370 livres as his share of the increased value of the property.

As Raimond's wealth increased, he adopted the lifestyle of a leading planter, a *grand blanc*, and tried to take on the material and cultural trappings of that station. For example, he paid one of the region's wealthiest men 4,500 livres for a slave who was trained as a pastry chef and confectioner. In 1781, he had an artisan construct an elaborate machine at his well to draw water for his indigo vats, and in 1784 he subscribed 200 livres for the publication of new information about distilling the dye. In four purchases made between 1773 and 1781, Raimond spent over 1,500 livres, the price of a field slave, on music papers, pamphlets, and books, some of them described as histories. He was familiar with Diderot's *Encyclopédie* and cited it in a 1786 memoir. Clearly, Julien Raimond was intent on proving himself to be the intellectual and cultural equal of any white man despite what the changing racial categories of public administration were telling him.

In Saint-Domingue, even destitute ex-slaves sought royal documents to establish their civil status and property rights, but Raimond's legal affairs were more typical of Saint-Domingue's notoriously litigious planters. Between 1772 and 1780, he faced at least ten lawsuits from creditors, including slave merchants who claimed he owed them more than 10,000 livres. He fought one of these claims all the way to an unsuccessful appeal before the Superior Council of Port-au-Prince. This personal loss may have been why, in the 1780s, Raimond maintained that racial prejudice had corrupted the judicial system. He wrote, "If a white man takes and unjustly keeps the property of a person of color, and this person files a legal complaint, he is practically declared guilty for having dared accuse [this white]."

In 1782, with slaves, land and assets worth 202,000 livres, Raimond re-married. His new wife, Françoise Dasmard, was also the free colored child of a successful white planter. Her father, Pierre Dasmard, had been born in the colony in 1700, before the southern peninsula was even open for settlement. He had never married her mother, an ex-slave named Julie. But Dasmard's gifts of land and slaves brought financial security to his mistress and daughter.

Françoise Dasmard had also been married before. In 1760, she had wed a French immigrant named Jacques Challe, contributing to the success of his colonial career, as Françoise brought property worth 71,220 livres, includ-ing a plantation, twenty-two slaves, and livestock into their union. Within ten years, the couple had three children and enough income that Challe was able to return to France alone. He bought a feudal estate in his native province for over 90,000 livres and died there in 1780. Françoise remained in Saint-Domingue, managing their indigo works, which, with its fifty-one enslaved workers, was worth 177,000 livres. It seems likely that she and Raimond, whose plantation was nearby, were close friends before news of Challe's death arrived. In 1777, Françoise's mother Julie drafted a testament leaving half of her estate to her daughter and the other half to Raimond "in order that he remember her in his prayers." When Françoise was widowed, Raimond became her children's legal guardian, keeping this responsibility for two years after the couple married.

Julien Raimond first became involved in public affairs in 1782 when white colonists began to collect money to buy a ship for the Royal Navy. Free men of color proposed to join the donation campaign, and Saint-Domingue's governor appointed Raimond to collect the pledges. In one month, he managed to solicit 9,450 livres from twenty-three families of color in his home parish. For whites, the ship was part of a long-standing debate with royal officials about colonial patriotism. Planters rejected Saint-Domingue's military administration, which wanted to train them as soldiers. Colonists argued that Saint-Domingue's contribution to imperial defense should be financial, not strategic, and in 1779 the colonial news-paper had denounced harshly the Crown's attempt to recruit volunteers to fight in the American Revolution.[6] In contrast, hundreds of free men of color enlisted in the 1779 expedition. Yet poor treatment by their com-manders may have convinced many that military service was not the way to prove their loyalty to France. Raimond's donation campaign, like that of the white colonists, emphasized that free people of color were more valu-able to France as planters than as cannon fodder. Although neither white nor free colored donations ever resulted in a gift to the Crown, Raimond's experience introduced him to the public arena.

In 1783, Raimond wrote to Saint-Domingue's administrators protesting the racial discrimination that people of color suffered, and they recommended that he approach the colonial minister directly. The next year, Raimond and his new wife left Saint-Domingue for France in order to sell Jacques Challe's titled lands. In Bordeaux, Raimond arranged to meet with a former colonial minister, who encouraged him to propose racial reforms. Between 1786 and 1789, he addressed four manuscripts to the French court at Versailles, which constitute his earliest surviving political writings. The petitions aimed narrowly to improve the status of wealthy men like Raimond. He argued that free people of color were whites' natural allies against an enslaved workforce and made the case that legal discrimination against them was a recent development. He blamed white immigrants for the tide of new petty racial restrictions after 1763. Free coloreds were not allowed to ride in coaches, could not dine with whites, and were identified as a separate category in official documents. They could not hold honorable positions and were charged with humiliating duties, like serving two weeks each year on twenty-four-hour-a-day call to the local militia commander.

Perhaps unintentionally, Raimond's petition included examples of restrictions that his family had managed to circumvent, thus undercutting his argument. To prove how free colored travel was regulated, he produced a note from the provincial governor that allowed his mother to use her buggy because of her age and poor health. To underscore the heavy militia duties of free coloreds, he submitted letters addressed to him, as a militia sergeant, ordering him to find men for these extra assignments. Yet Raimond's proposal would not have affected these poorer men. He suggested instead that wealthy, light-skinned free people be exempted from racial discrimination. These privileged "new whites," as he called them, would be chosen among those who were well educated and who were born of a legitimate marriage. In November 1788, he was still awaiting a decision from Louis XVI's cautious bureaucrats.

In mid-July 1789, after a second interview at the colonial ministry, Raimond began to adapt his tactics to the emerging revolutionary situation. On July 29, in the provincial town of Jarnac, he formally transferred his unofficial powers as free colored representative to a sympathetic nobleman who agreed to present Raimond's ideas to France's new National Assembly.[7] Little came of this arrangement, but a month later Raimond himself was among thirty people of color who assembled in the offices of Dejoly, a Parisian barrister, to petition the Nationally Assembly for admission. By November, this colonial lobby group had grown to seventy-nine members, most of them artisans and domestic servants originally from Martinique, Guadeloupe, and France's Indian Ocean colonies as well as from Saint-Domingue. With Raimond playing a secondary role to the French lawyer Dejoly, these "American colonists," as they called themselves, began to work for the extension of civil rights to all free people in the colonies, no matter what their color. Raimond was no abolitionist at this point. He still owned over one hundred slaves in Saint-Domingue and was not looking to upset the entire system. In September 1789, his colonial attorney sold one of Raimond's female slaves to a free colored constable who wanted to marry her. He charged the constable about 4,000 livres, roughly twice the going rate.

By the end of 1789, however, opinions were changing rapidly, and Raimond started to suggest that the revolution might gradually free Saint-Domingue's slaves.[8] Political and ideological pressures in Paris were responsible for this shift. On August 26, three days before meeting with Dejoly's group, he had presented his "whitening" proposal to a group of planters living in Paris. Their cold reception may have pushed him to appeal to the broader ideals of the "Declaration of the Rights of Man and Citizen," which the Revolutionary Assembly adopted that very same day. Raimond may also have been influenced by his developing relationship with the abolitionist club *Les Amis des Noirs* (Friends of the Blacks) at Paris. Dejoly had joined this society in January 1789, and on October 9 the club's founder, Jacques-Pierre Brissot, began to report on free colored political activity in his influential journal *Le Patriote Français* (*The French Patriot*). As Raimond brought abolitionists like Brissot to focus on social and legal issues of race rather than the moral question of slavery itself, he also drew new figures into the abolitionist camp and converted some influential figures to the cause. As a member of the Assembly's Credentials Committee from eastern France, Henri Grégoire had little interest in colonial issues before he met Raimond in October 1789; Grégoire subsequently published influential pamphlets attacking colonial racism, laden with examples from Raimond.[9] From that point until his death in 1831, Grégoire was France's most important abolitionist. Despite the approval of Grégoire's Committee, the National Assembly refused to admit the mulatto Raimond and the other free colored spokesmen.

Pamphlets and speeches by members of the Dejoly/Raimond group and the support of Brissot, Grégoire, and others made free colored civil rights the most pressing colonial issue in the early revolution. In early March 1790, their influence led the National Assembly to name a new committee to study colonial representation, specifically the question of who was qualified to vote. However, planter interests forced the deputies to sidestep the question of free colored suffrage. On March 28, the National Assembly sent vaguely worded electoral instructions that the Saint-Domingue colonists interpreted to exclude free men of color. After this apparent setback, the Dejoly group dissolved, and Raimond began publishing under his own name. In June 1790, Caribbean colonists resident in France wrote to Saint-Domingue about rumors that Raimond and Vincent Ogé, another prominent member of the Dejoly group, were plotting with British abolitionists to invade the colony. They reported that the two had already enlisted fifty experienced whites and had acquired arms, ammunition, and uniforms—"right down to musical instruments for war."

Ogé, a wealthy light-skinned merchant from Saint-Domingue's North province, did in fact return. Landing in the colony in October 1790, he informed the governor that the National Assembly had authorized voting by all financially qualified free men. Yet Ogé could not convince men in the West or Raimond's native South province to join him. He and several hundred supporters clashed with colonial troops outside Cap Français and were eventually captured. On February 25, 1791, Ogé was tortured to death in Cap's public square. When descriptions of his fate arrived in France, they generated more sympathy for the victims of colonial racism.[10]

Raimond, however, denounced Ogé's confrontational tactics. Insisting that men of color would win civil rights in Paris, he and his wife sold their three colonial plantations and over one hundred slaves in August 1790. At the end of that year, he became a member of the Jacobin club. By 1792, the Raimonds were living in the Tuileries section, at the very heart of revolutionary Paris, where he entertained journalists and members of the National Assembly. This political work produced results. On May 15, 1791, one year after the ambiguous ruling that inspired Ogé, the National Assembly voted to allow financially qualified men of color to vote in colonial elections. This decision was a direct consequence of Raimond's campaigns and unintentionally ensured the success of the great slave uprising that launched the Haitian Revolution. Colonial whites categorically refused to accept the decree. Those free men of color who had rebuffed Ogé in late 1790 now took up arms to fight for these limited but unambiguous rights. In the third week of August 1791, therefore, when a well-planned slave uprising broke out in the plain outside Cap Français, whites and free men of color throughout the colony were already fighting each other. Despite the violence of the plantation rebellion, many whites refused to accept free colored citizenship as the price of a strategic alliance against the slaves.

When news of the slave revolt reached Paris, members of the National Assembly accepted colonists' claims that the May 15 decree was somehow to blame. On September 24, 1791, deputies revoked the law, but within weeks French voters chose a new assembly. By early 1792, Jacques-Pierre Brissot, head of Les Amis des Noirs, had become one of the most influential voices in this body. He and others refuted accusations that free men of color had prepared the uprising. Raimond argued convincingly that free colored soldiers were France's best hope for restoring plantation discipline. On April 4, 1792, the National Assembly voted to enfranchise all free men of color. To enforce this controversial measure, the Paris government sent fresh troops to Saint Domingue along with a trio of revolutionary commissioners, led by Légér-Felicité Sonthonax. Yet Sonthonax and his colleagues were unable to defeat the rebels even though they integrated free men of color into their armies. The situation worsened in early 1793, when England and Spain each declared war on France.

Still living in Paris, Raimond came through this period with some difficulty. In September 1793, when Brissot fell from power and was guillotined in the Terror, the Committee of Public Safety arrested Raimond, too, on the advice of colonists who blamed him for the slave revolt. It was true that his political career had stirred up colonial unrest. Yet Raimond was not a radical opponent of slavery. Well after the revolt, he still argued that the extension of civil rights to free colored citizens would reinforce, not destroy, the slave system in the colony. Although he and his wife sold their indigo estates and workers in 1790, they continued to receive payments from this transaction at least until 1795. Furthermore, Raimond's entire family in the colony remained heavily involved in planting. As late as January 9, 1793, his brother and former plantation partner Guillaume paid 90,000 livres for thirty enslaved people, a price consistent with prerevolutionary values.

In a 1793 pamphlet addressed to revolutionary lawmakers, penned after the revolt but before his arrest, Raimond laid forward a plan to save Saint-Domingue.[11] As the most vocal opponent of racism in revolutionary Paris, he had a unique moral authority that was amplified by his background as a colonial planter turned abolitionist. As historian Laurent Dubois notes, Raimond's prescription for extending the revolution to slaves while maintaining the plantation system was hugely influential.[12] Raimond observed that "the insane project of suddenly freeing the slaves . . . would surely bring about the total ruin of the colony." In a part of his pamphlet addressed to the slaves, Raimond explained Saint-Domingue could survive as a plantation colony only if the process of emancipation led workers to adopt a market-based work ethic. He advocated allowing any worker to buy his or her freedom, according to an official price schedule.[13] The government would then require planters to give slaves three free hours a day to work for their own profit. Those who accumulated a certain amount of savings would automatically receive extra time off each week, enabling them to earn more money. Eventually, some would acquire enough to buy their liberty. In Raimond's mind, these ex-slaves would be free, but they would not automatically become citizens. His description of postslavery Saint-Domingue stressed the importance of the rule of law and sexual morality, particularly where women were concerned. It would take time and education before plantation workers would have true civil rights.

In the Caribbean colony, however, time was in short supply. Not long after Raimond's pamphlet was published, Saint-Domingue experienced a different kind of emancipation. In May 1793, counterrevolutionary colonists in Cap. Français rallied around a new governor they hoped would unseat the unpopular French commissioners. Hard pressed to survive this coup, Sonthonax offered to free the rebel slaves who were camped outside the city if they would join his forces. These new soldiers definitively changed the balance of power in the colony. After gradually extending this offer to other colonial provinces, the commissioners issued a general decree of emancipation in September 1793. In early February, the revolutionary government in Paris ratified their actions, voting to end slavery in all French territories. In April 1794, Toussaint Louverture, a former slave and Saint-Domingue's greatest rebel-general, brought his troops to the French side. Over the next four years, as part of the French revolutionary army, he and other former rebel-soldiers defeated British and Spanish invasions of Saint-Domingue and the counterrevolutionaries who supported them.

In May 1795, the Committee of Public Safety cleared Raimond of responsibility for the Saint-Domingue slave revolt and released him. His assertion that ex-slaves had an obligation to work for the good of the republic had already influenced the plantation policies of Victor Hugues, a revolutionary commissioner sent to Guadeloupe in 1794 to implement the end of slavery.[14] Hoping for similar results, in November 1795, France's new government, known as the Directory, made Raimond a civil commissioner and sent him back to Saint-Domingue with four colleagues. Sonthonax had already established a plantation labor system, and Raimond became its new administrator. Faced with hundreds of inactive estates, many of them abandoned by counterrevolutionary planters, he began an aggressive leasing program to return these properties to production. When the number of mulatto and black plantation owners began to increase under his direction, French officials accused Raimond of corruption, noting that he kept the best plantations for himself or his friends. Toussaint Louverture, by then the island's most powerful military figure, defended him. Raimond reciprocated the general's support. As Toussaint began to move toward de facto independence from France, forcing the French civil commissioners to leave the colony one by one, Raimond wrote to the Directors to confirm Toussaint's accusations. In 1798, the Parisian government recalled him amid accusations that he was helping Toussaint work toward independence because he owed French creditors more than he could ever repay.

Nevertheless, in the autumn of 1799, Raimond's knowledge of the colony led Napoleon Bonaparte to appoint him to another civil commission, this time with specific orders to reestablish plantation agriculture in Saint-Domingue. As director of the National Domain in the colony, Raimond continued to confiscate, lease, and administer plantations, but like others he worried about the future of the colony under Bonaparte. In 1800, France's new government adopted a constitution that specified that metropolitan laws would not apply to the colonies, each of which would receive their own separate constitutional regime. A disillusioned Raimond, who had long advised Saint-Domingue's people of color to trust French justice, now joined those who feared a return to the racially restrictive, pre-revolutionary society. In August 1800, he wrote a long letter to Bonaparte, defending himself against the ongoing charges of corruption and asking for assurances that France would never reinstall "bodily slavery." Back in Saint-Domingue, Toussaint's response to the Constitution of 1800 was to ignore the unpleasant turn of events and establish his own constitution. At the beginning of July 1801, he named Raimond to a committee of five men who were charged with drafting this document. Then, unexpectedly, Raimond died in Cap Français.

Julien Raimond did not live to see the massive French expedition of 1802, Napoleon's bid to reestablish control over Saint-Domingue. Nor did he witness the six months of brutal fighting between Toussaint's armies and the French or Toussaint's arrest and deportation. In 1802 and 1803, Saint-Domingue's black and mixed-race soldiers, including many who had landed with the Napoleonic fleet, gradually rallied around Toussaint's leading general Dessalines, defeating those European invaders who had not already succumbed to yellow fever. On January 1, 1804, an uneasy coalition of ex-slaves and the freeborn sons of French colonists joined to proclaim the birth of Haiti, a new American nation. Julien Raimond did not live to see the establishment of racial equality that would accompany the new regime, but his modern notion of citizenship as a birthright independent of racial origins had had a seismic impact on the development of revolution on both sides of the Atlantic.

Bibliography and Suggested Reading

Archival sources used for this essay include the France National Archives in Paris and the Overseas section of the French National Archives in Aix-en-Provence.

Dubois, Laurent. *Avengers of the New World: The Story of the Haitian Revolution.* Cambridge, MA: Harvard University Press, 2004.

Fink, Carolyn. *The Making of Haiti: The Saint Domingue Revolution from Below.* Knoxville: University of Tennessee Press, 1990.

Garrigus, John D. *Before Haiti: Race and Citizenship in French Saint-Domingue.* New York: Palgrave Macmillan, 2006.

———. "Opportunist or Patriot? Julien Raimond (1744–1801) and the Haitian Revolution." *Slavery and Abolition* 48 (2007): 1–27.

CHAPTER TEN

Anne Pépin (1758–1837)

Entrepreneur, Landlady, and Mixed-Race Signare in Senegal

Mark Hinchman

Through the biography of Anne Pépin, an influential woman of mixed-race descent who built a personal fortune as a trader, a landlady, and a consort to European men, architectural historian Mark Hinchman reveals the colorful and vibrant life of the Gorée Island commercial center in West Africa. Through an examination of diverse sources such as archaeological remains, architectural styles, property inventories, contracts, and travelers' accounts, Hinchman is able to reconstruct a social world that was undergoing tremendous changes. He finds that, in contrast to Africans (and African women in particular) under the later nineteenth-century form of European colonization, women like Pépin actually held a great deal of power and autonomy that they maximized by inserting themselves at the nexus of the encounter between European and African traders and government figures.

Anne Pépin was one of the richest and most celebrated women on the West African island of Gorée. The mixed-race companion of a French governor, Pépin was born into the Afro-European class known as *habitants*. Pépin's eventful life, which spanned the eighteen and nineteenth centuries, coincided with the growth of successful maritime economy based in Senegal, a building boom on Gorée Island, the end of the slave trade, and the growing power of the French colonial administration. Her lifetime can rightly be called the golden age of the *habitants*. *Signare* was a prestigious social and economic designation for women, many of them *habitants* who, like Pépin, formed partnerships with European men. In this way, Pépin and women like her stood at the pinnacle of a social structure in which a small number of mixed-race Africans and a few Europeans constituted an elite. Anne Pépin's story is significant because her life activities reveal the degree to which mixed-race women angled for power and position within a system that seemed designed to grant them neither.

Gorée is a diminutive island off the coast of present-day Dakar, Senegal, and lies just south of the westernmost tip of Africa. Gorée was one of several important West African trading centers. From the time of its early incorporation into the Atlantic network, the island was associated with Europeans, Afro-Europeans, and transatlantic trade, including, notoriously, the trade in slaves. The story of Gorée's importance for European explorers and traders begins in 1444, some three centuries before Pépin's birth, when Portuguese explorer Denis Diaz sailed to West Africa and missed the mouth of the Senegal River. As a result of this miscalculation, he landed at N'dar, the island that later became the trading post of Saint-Louis. Farther south, Diaz and his crew arrived at the island that Africans call Ber. He called the island Palma; centuries later, it became important as the Gorée Island slave depot. Gorée derives from its Dutch name, Goede Rede, meaning "good harbor." Thus, in its name, its spoken creole language, as in its architecture, its material culture, and in many syncretic customs, Gorée reveals the island's multiethnic origins and is very typical of Atlantic port societies.

From the fifteenth century on, Gorée became increasingly important in several ways: as a trading post, as a European stronghold on the west coast of Africa, and also as a point of contact for African and European people. In the fifteenth and sixteenth centuries, the island passed several times between Dutch and Portuguese control. In the seventeenth and eighteenth centuries and later in Pépin's lifetime, the English and French fought to control it, and it ended up in French hands. In many ways, the history of Gorée was a microcosm of the history of the European presence in Africa.

A significant population of Luso-Africans, or Afro-Portuguese, developed in West Africa, dating from the early presence of Portuguese explorers and traders. This population of mixed origins frequently functioned as intermediaries who linked inter-African commerce to the wider Atlantic economy. European men who arrived in West Africa in Pépin's lifetime quickly realized that the accomplishment of their economic and political goals depended on their social incorporation into local elites. This consolidation of influence was often accomplished through their association with local African women who provided them with accommodation and food, translated for them, coached them in the local social and commercial practices, did laundry, resolved disputes, tended to their sickness, and provided companionship, including romantic involvements. Some relationships lasted many years and generated officially recognized offspring.

The Afro-Portuguese were Christians, spoke a creole language, and developed a distinct housing type, known as *"maisons à la portugaise,"* or Portuguese houses. These structures resulted from reciprocal influences between Portuguese and local African architecture, dating back to the sixteenth century. Many aspects of Luso-African culture, from the prominent role of women in commerce to two-storied rectilinear houses, were forerunners to the syncretic Franco-African society that developed on Gorée in the eighteenth century.

Anne Pépin was the Senegalese-born daughter of Jean Pépin and the *signare* Catherine Baudet. Baudet had three French husbands: Porquet, the son of a employee of the Compagnie des Indes, with whom she had a daughter; Jean Pépin, a surgeon of the Compagnie des Indes, with whom she had three children, Anne, Jean, and Nicholas; and her last husband, Franciero, with whom she had two sons, Pierre and André. Anne Pépin was born in 1758. Childhood mortality was high, so among her siblings and cousins she no doubt had early experience with the death of loved ones. She was close to her brother, Nicholas, although they were raised differently. He received formal education, but she did not, although she spoke French and Wolof fluently and had some knowledge of several African and European languages. The climate is hot half the year and temperate the other half. On stifling nights, Nicholas and his friends dragged mats to sleep on the beach, but this diversion was likely denied to Anne simply because she was a girl.

As rustic as conditions might have been, there was excitement too. During Anne's childhood, the arrival of any ship in port was an exciting event with which most of the local population was involved either directly or indirectly. Growing up, she encountered countless numbers of foreigners who spoke strange languages and told tales of distant places. The servants and slaves at her mother's home and those of her relatives and friends included African men and women who were Wolof, Lebu, Tukolor, Sereer, Djola, and Mande. She met other Africans and Arabs through their presence in markets set up on the island or who hawked their wares as door-to-door vendors or in private sales. Among European men, she was most familiar with the English and French but had intermittent contact with Americans, Danes, Dutch, Germans, Portuguese, Russians, Spanish, and Swedes. There was no formal church on the island until the nineteenth century. *Marabouts* (religious scholars of the Qu'ran) attended to the majority Muslim population, so she surely had familiarity with Christian, Muslim, and animist religious practices.

By modern standards, Anne's childhood was short. She was, like her mother, extremely beautiful and thus desirable in the marriage market. At the age of fourteen, she had already entered into her first relationship with a European man, Bernard Dupuy, with whom she had her first child a year later. Dupuy was a trader who hailed from Bordeaux and whose father came from Martinique. Together he and Anne had four sons: René Dupuy (1773–1820), two boys who died young, and Jean (1777–?). The island's notary acts officially designated the marriages as "*à la mode du pays*" (according to local custom); their children were baptized, legally recognized, and bore their fathers' names. Marriages between Europeans and Africans, such as the one between Pépin and Dupuy, were entered into according to local Wolof custom. Only infrequently did couples attempt to stage a formal Catholic wedding, although the local mixed-race women generally considered themselves to be Christians. Once the European men left the scene, the African women they left behind were free to remarry.

Significantly, mixed-race children and female companions of European men could inherit their wealth and possessions in the event of the men's death or return to Europe, but the *signares* were never recognized as true and legitimate spouses according to European law. So, on Dupuy's departure in 1779—he fled an outbreak of yellow fever—Anne Pépin became a well-established, independent woman, living in a large house (possibly inherited from her mother), supported by the money she received from her father and her absent common-law husband and by her various commercial activities. Ownership of houses, boats, and slaves were indications of a *signare*'s wealth and provided her with an independent source of income. Nicholas Pépin, Anne's younger brother, was a successful trader to whom documents refer as the island's spokesperson. European norms of written contracts and binding legal decisions were important to Nicholas, who was frequently engaged in court cases as a witness, asked to notarize official documents, and called on to resolve disputes, and there are hundreds of references to his commercial activities. The members of the Pépin family acted as liaisons between mainland African traders and European company agents by providing goods and services and mediating between them.

From the fifteenth century on, European countries conducted their global operations through subsidies to private trading companies. The most famous is the Dutch West India Company, although England and France chartered similar groups, namely, the Royal African Company and the Compagnie des Indes Occidentales (French West India Company). Rapid turnover in personnel characterized the trading companies who enjoyed royal favor. For

European monarchs, this strategy was an effective way of managing a global network with little direct risk or investment, not unlike modern outsourcing. The statute and structure of the trading companies that were granted the royal favor to trade from Gorée varied as time passed. What mattered, however, was that the company held the exclusive right to a portion of the West African trade. For the *habitants*, such as members of the Pépin family, their chief role was to act as liaisons between mainland African traders and European company agents by providing goods and services. The relationship between the *habitants* and the company was fractious and centered on several major points of disagreement: monopoly versus free-trade, official versus contraband trading, and the proportion of export versus locally held slaves. While often in sharp disagreement with the company on these issues, the *habitants* cleverly couched their arguments in terms of their allegiance to France.

It was in the financial interests of the *habitants* to maximize their access to free trade. European men involved with local women often played both sides of the issue, officially promoting legal trade yet engaging in profitable contraband trading through their local connections. The final point of contention concerned slaves. As the demand for slaves in the Americas increased, European traders wanted to increase the number of export slaves and decrease the number of locally owned slaves. The *habitants* were more interested in maintaining their numbers of house slaves as ongoing sources of income rather than selling them to the Atlantic export slave market.

Gorée had few natural resources and scant land to devote to agriculture and animal husbandry. The commercial activities of the *habitants* centered on providing provisions for boats and for local consumption. The goods that originated in the African interior and sold on Gorée included cattle, goats, poultry, salted beef, and smoked fish. High-value provisions included flour, citrus fruits, olives, molasses, and spices. Unfinished luxury items included ivory, ostrich feathers, coral, and gold. The need for large quantities of grain, rice, vegetables, freshwater, and firewood remained constant. Trade dominated by Europeans included guns, gunpowder and ammunition, paper, and a bevy of metal products, including iron bars, jewelry, hardware, rivets and nails, scissors, knives, and padlocks. The sale of slaves in the late eighteenth century and palm oil and gum in the nineteenth century increasingly dominated the island's trade but did try to branch out and tried to enter more lucrative Atlantic commercial markets.

The *habitants*' skilled slaves dominated the local labor market. African seasonal workers included sailors and some agricultural workers. The large number of female slaves on Gorée was related to the services they provided, such as grinding millet, cooking, and washing clothes. The bulk of a slave's wages went to the owner. Although the annual numbers of export slaves increased slightly in response to demand, Gorée and Saint-Louis were never major slave-trading centers. The *habitants* participated in the slave trade mostly by acquiring slaves who served their households. Traders on the island also sold export slaves, but it was never a major slave-trading center; in fact, the trade in slaves was a relatively small proportion of their overall trading activities.

The fusion of Atlantic cultural values and growing wealth of the depot was also made apparent in the region's permanent architecture. Prior to 1750, Gorée was a modest-size town. The European trading companies had few resources to devote to buildings and little interest in establishing a permanent settlement. For centuries, despite the continual presence of Europeans, most buildings were made of straw. Many of the social practices and cultural elements that existed on Gorée were consistent with other West African traditions. While the island today is known for its European-looking architecture, in the precolonial period straw structures stood cheek by jowl with stone and plaster buildings. Scottish travel Mungo Park's description of a modest West African dwelling presents the kind of architecture most people associate with Africa, the type of structure that dominated the Goréen landscape at the time of Pépin's birth:

> A circular mud wall about four feet high, upon which is placed a conical roof, composed of bamboo cane, and thatched with grass, forms alike the palace of the king, and the hovel of a slave. Their household furniture is equally simple. A hurdle of canes placed upon upright stakes, about two feet from the ground, upon which is spread a mat or bullock's hide, answer the purpose of a bed: a water jar, some earthen pots for dressing their food, a few wooden bowls and calabashes, and one or two low stools.

In West African villages, the building block of a single straw dwelling combines with others to create a family's compound the boundary of which is further delineated by a bamboo and straw fence. By Anne's adulthood, the urban fabric of Gorée was a combination of rectangular buildings of hard materials and straw dwellings. Some straw dwellings stood inside the courtyards of larger houses.

French naturalist Michel Adanson noted that the end of the penultimate English occupation of West Africa (1758–1763) resulted in a liberalization of trade that benefited Goréens. By 1764, there were twelve houses made of "hard" materials (in French, *en dur*). Over the course of Pépin's lifetime,

Gorée's inhabitants and foreign visitors witnessed the construction of numerous permanent buildings. A cadastral map prepared in 1776 describes in rich detail the properties, associating each with named owners. At that time, fortifications wrapped around the island's perimeter, dating from the reign of Louis XIV, whose administration required a setback from the water's edge. The political climate had changed by 1779, and areas that had been devoted to fortifications were made available for construction. This resulted in a wave of building on the Goréen littoral, including several prominent houses, one of which was owned by Nicholas Pépin and later inherited by his daughter. It is the most famous structure on Gorée and perhaps in all of Senegal. Known today as the Maison des Esclaves (House of Slaves), in its day it was called the Maison Pépin. It was built between 1780 and 1784. The Maison Pépin was typical of the island's late eighteenth-century houses, which had either one or two stories and galleries that overlooked the courtyard or garden behind the house. In two-storied houses, the residential quarters were upstairs. The hipped roofs were initially made of straw, but later it became fashionable to construct them with tile. Commercial and service areas, including the laundry and kitchen areas, occupied the ground floor. Slaves and servants had rooms on the ground floor that were furnished with their few possessions or items discarded by the house's owners. Anne Pépin owned multiple properties in her lifetime, indicating that she achieved a certain measure of wealth and power although she was a mixed-race woman of African descent. Her principal residence was approximately the same size as her brother's house. However, none of her properties are believed to still exist.

Houses such as Pépin's were the hub of community activity. Chevalier de Boufflers probably first met Anne Pépin when he came to see about securing quarters in her house. Stanislas-Jean de Boufflers was forty-eight when he arrived in Senegal for his first sojourn in Africa in 1786. A nobleman of insufficient means, he was offered the governorship of Senegal, and the post attracted him because of its status and the opportunity it provided to pay off his debts. With dual careers as a writer and as a military commander, Boufflers was a man who chatted as easily with Voltaire at French literary salons, as he had fought in the Seven Years' War. Anne Pépin was twenty-eight when they first met. Their subsequent romantic involvement lasted more than two years and left an indelible imprint on her life. For example, Boufflers moved the capital of Senegal from Saint Louis to Gorée, ostensibly because of the climate but possibly because of his desire to remain close to Anne. This political shift naturally increased the value of her property and consolidated her position as a woman of influence in the region. Yet Boufflers's stay on the island was brief; he left in 1788 and never looked back.

Oddly, he never mentioned Anne in his voluminous writings despite their close relationship. In fact, many of his letters, personal and official, concern his dissatisfaction with the conditions of the government's housing and thus are actually insulting to her. This standard behavior was not as coldhearted as it might initially seem, however. Many of these women consciously chose such a liaison knowing that they could improve their material conditions or gain some advantage through the connection. Anne Pépin certainly was no one's dupe.

After Boufflers's departure, Anne Pépin's enterprises benefited from the boom in Gorée's trade at the turn of the nineteenth century. Although there are no records that Anne or her brother Nicholas were directly involved with the export slave trade, they certainly provided the logistical conditions and material support for European activities. They belonged to the class of mixed-race, slave-owning, Africa-based merchants who benefited from their association with the broader Atlantic economy. As a corpus, Pépin's legal documents present her as a savvy businesswoman, closely attuned to the value of her properties, carefully managing her servants and slaves, and, above all, aware of her responsibilities to her extended family. Scattered documents such as maps, wills, probate inventories, contracts, and concessions open windows into Pépin's activities and her Atlantic connections.

Pépin's life is illustrative of how the *habitants* and specifically the *signares* created successful commercial enterprises that centered on their homes. There were other prominent *signares*, and Pépin knew them all. One of them, Caty Louette, lived in a large house just around the corner from Anne and was the richest woman on Gorée. At one time, Caty had forty-three domestic slaves and twenty-five export slaves. Exceptionally, she signed her own documents, indicating that she was literate. Pépin was on her way to amassing a similar portfolio of slaves and properties. The connection between the private citizen Anne Pépin and the French government was not limited to Boufflers's stay on the island. In 1817, in return for having rented rooms to the government, she was given a property on the northern end of the island. This was a standard development strategy at the time: a concession with obligations. She was obliged to enclose the property with a wall and build on it within five years. Evidently she did, as the will she made on November 29, 1825, referred to her principal residence, the house on the rue Bambara on the southern end of the island, and a house on the northern end of the island. Her official connections resulted in rental income and increased her property holdings.

A typical rental contract, in which a few rooms become the intermediary between a European man and an African woman, was signed on February 5, 1789. It reads, "I the undersigned Marie Guimbaye recognize to have rented to Mr. Jean Peiré a home consisting of a room upstairs, large and small storerooms downstairs, in return for the sum of 48 *livres*, to be paid at the end of each month."[1] This constituted the standard setup of rooms inhabited by European men on Gorée. A room on the upper floor acted as the man's sleeping quarters, receiving room, and dining area. A storeroom (or rooms) on the ground floor held items that the tenant did not want in his main room, and storerooms also held tradable goods. In this scenario, a wealthy African woman was in a position of power in relation to a European man. It is the opposite of how the power dynamic of the precolonial period is normally presented. Properties were proof of wealth, sources of income, and workplaces.

A businessman named Jean Baptiste Levau died at 9:45 A.M. on September 20, 1819.[2] He had a similar housing arrangement with his landlady Anne Pépin. An account taken at the time of death indicated that "the aforementioned Mr. Levau only had in his possession in her house the effects, titles and papers enclosed in two trunks and a dressing case. . . . Mme. Pépin also showed us a storeroom of the house with the following objects: 40 bars of flat iron, a pot made of pinchbeck . . . and two young black servants between 14 and 15 years old, named Bellard and Kekama."[3] The bars of iron attest to Levau's activities as a trader. Pépin likely arranged for and made money from the act of providing him with other necessary operational services, such as board and laundry. She was an efficient entrepreneur, able to function comfortably and profitably within a slave economy despite her own mixed-race status. Her description of Bellard and Kekama as household objects is indicative of their formal legal status and their actual physical locations at the time the inventory was conducted, but it does ignore the more complex social positions they held in the household and in Anne Pépin's broader domestic familial world.

Levau rented just two rooms in Pépin's sprawling house. She kept the best rooms for herself and rented out the extra space to supplement her income. Depending on the respective wealth of both landlord and tenant and the potential for windfall profits, however, the tenant might actually contract for the most desirable part of the house. For example, the *signare* Louison Remy rented to Mr. Jay "a house belonging to her consisting of a room on the upper floor, three small storerooms, the court and outlying buildings . . . Louison Remy keeping only two small rooms for her lodging."[4] Space was at a premium on this island, and frequently a tenant would rent a room for living in one house and a storeroom in another. Because there were no hotels or restaurants on the island, the *signares* were known for their hospitality, or *teranga* as it was known in Wolof culture; of course, for these entrepreneurial women, it was not just a matter of manners but also a good business.

Gorée in the twentieth and twenty-first centuries is most famous for its role in the slave trade. The most significant feature of eighteenth- and nineteenth-century West African slavery was the division between house slaves and export slaves. House slaves (*captives de case*) were an integral part of households, similar to indentured servants. Most export slaves came from the mainland and were destined for the horrors of the Middle Passage and ultimately plantations in the Americas. House slaves formed the largest subpopulation of Gorée, both of which grew consistently during the second half of the eighteenth century. In 1767, when Anne was nine years old, the island had a population of slightly over one thousand people, which is larger than its population today. The island itself is tiny, so during Pépin's lifetime it must have felt crowded, urbane, and lively. In 1785, Bouffler's engineer Golbery estimated the overall population for the island to be 1,840. He broke the number down into the following categories: "116 mulattos & free blacks who owned property, 522 free-blacks without property, 1044 house slaves, 70–80 Europeans, and 200 export slaves."

The extent of the slave trade on Gorée has been a source of controversy, centered mainly around the number of slaves who passed through the depot. While there have been claims of overall figures in the millions, recent scholarship revised these numbers dramatically downward. Gorée was never a principal slave center like Ouidah. The annual number of slaves traded on Gorée during Pépin's lifetime was in the hundreds or thousands. Anne and Nicholas Pépin were definitely slave owners, but there is no evidence that they engaged in large-scale slave trading. What is most significant about Gorée is not its status as a small-scale slave entrepôt but rather that it was a diverse society of slave-owning, Africa-based merchants. In contrast to the American model of plantation slavery, Gorée (like Saint-Louis) presents a dense urban model centered on a large population of professionally trained slaves. Whether weaving cloth, overseeing trade slaves, plastering walls, or making furniture, Goréen "house" slaves were themselves participants in the Atlantic economic sphere.

The largest households featured slaves devoted to professions not practiced in smaller households. When an acquaintance of Pépin, the *signare* Marie-Louise de Saint Jean, died in 1837, she left behind 118 slaves. Even the biggest homes on the island could not have held such a large number of slaves, so most of them were rented out as sailors or general laborers, and some worked as agricultural workers on the mainland. Renting out slaves, besides renting out space, was another one of a *signare*'s sources of income.

In the slaveholding scale, regarding the number of occupants, the *signare* de Saint Jean's household of over one hundred falls on the upper end. Levau and his slaves constituted a small household and demonstrate that modest entrepreneurs like Levau participated in the economic activity of owning and profiting from slaves.

In addition to a cook, a baker named Defène worked in the house of de Saint Jean. Where small houses had only general servants, large houses, such as those of Anne Pépin, her brother, and her niece, might include a valet or personal maid. The largest houses had a tailor in addition to the more common designation of weaver. A slave named Blaise worked as de Saint Jean's personal tailor. Girls and young women were designated attendants, personal maids responsible for helping the *signare* of the house get dressed. Most of Pépin's clothes, in childhood and as an adult, were handmade. The professional lives of multiple people were devoted to ensuring that a *signare* such as Anne Pépin always looked her best.

Anne's domestic slaves, such as Defène and Blaise, did much of their work in the house's courtyard, which was the domain of servants and slaves, particularly during the day. The courtyard was a place for watching children, plucking chickens, cleaning fish, grinding millet, weaving cloth, washing clothes, and cooking food. Slaves socialized here with each other and with slaves from other households. Home to the bustle of daily activities, the courtyard was the communal space of the house. With all the activities that houses slaves carried out in the courtyard of Pépin's house, it functionally operated as an African compound within a context closely associated with the Atlantic trade.

The slaves on Gorée had an international background. Many came from the Bambara states of the Niger River area, the most famous trading centers of which were Jenné and Timbuktu. A neighborhood on the southern part of the island is called the Quartier Bambara, and there is a rue des Bambaras. The word itself is an ethnic signifier, and for Pépin it was virtually synonymous with the word "slave." The Saharan urban centers that traded in Bambara slaves were marvels of synthesis, with traces of indigenous, Islamic, and European cultures. They were quadrate in plan, dated back to the Middle Ages, and had multistoried architecture. Although Goréen houses are often described as European, most of their architectural features are consistent with the buildings of Saharan urban centers.

The documents that record events in the lives of Pépin and Levau can also be read from the perspective of a slave who passed between them. While contemporary documents almost always present slaves as economic entities, they were also social beings. In approximately 1804, a child was born somewhere in the West African interior who came to be called Bellard.⁵ He was either born a slave or became one through capture. When he was fourteen years old, in 1819, he no longer lived with his birth family but arrived on Gorée. A sailor, Bellard was owned by the French businessman Jean Baptiste Levau, who arranged for accommodation in Pépin's house. Bellard and his companion in slavery, Kekama, were roughly the same age. They either were rented out or worked directly for Levau, operating the longboats that plied Senegal's coastal areas and rivers. Bellard's fate and fortune were tied to an unlanded and not particularly wealthy man. Bellard lived in a social and economic system in which his status was tied to his owner and his owner's status was unstable.

When Levau moved into Pépin's house, it was an event that was moderately important to him but that set the course for the rest of Bellard's life. Bellard and Kekama were at first strangers in her house, but over time they became accustomed to its daily rhythm. Whatever work Levau did, he probably did it within the walls of Pépin's house. A domestic environment, which initially seemed strange to Bellard, over time became familiar. Levau's death in 1819 plunged the fifteen-year-old Bellard into uncertainty. The immediate future of a slave whose owner had no obvious heirs or a will was tenuous. Levau may have owed Anne Pépin rent money, as she convinced the Goréen authorities to grant her ownership of Bellard. For at least the next two decades, Bellard's life was connected to Anne Pépin and her family.

During this time Bellard's life acquired a stability it had previously lacked. As a Goréen, he had the status of belonging to one of the most illustrious households on the island. By 1835, Anne Pépin was around seventy-seven years old, and Ballard was in his early thirties, having worked for the Pépin family for nearly twenty years. Unlike Bellard's previous owner, Anne Pépin had a carefully drafted will that stipulated that Bellard was to become the property of her grandson, Nicolas Dupuy. After his ownership transferred to Dupuy, Bellard drops out of the historical record. Bellard's story demonstrates that it is possible to piece together a sketch of a slave's life. Scholars often lament that so little is known about slaves' daily lives, but the information presented here all comes from typical archival documents: a rental contract, a will, and a house inventory.

In 1835, Pépin was near the end of her life, but there must have been moments when her health improved because shortly before her death she gave a party. Samuel Brunner (1790–1844) was a Swiss botanist who published two books on his travel experiences. He is the only author to give a firsthand account of Anne, her house, and a party she hosted: "From a distance, through the narrow streets of the southern quarter, the stately lit house gleamed, adorned with two ascending staircases, of the former lady of the Chevalier Boufflers which he had built for her." Pépin's great-grandson, François Dupuy, acted as Brunner's host during his stay in Senegal in 1837–1838. Brunner did with his text what he did in life. He briefly paid his respects to the septuagenarian hostess of the party and then proceeded to his real interests: flirting with young women and getting drunk.

While he was frustratingly brief in discussing Anne Pépin, his account sheds light on how the balls and entertaining for which the *signares* were known formed an integral part of the Goréen social structure. The *habitants* were an exogenous creole society whose maintenance depended in no small part on a steady supply of foreign males, although the *habitants* also intermarried. This society required a respectable mechanism to promote alliances between two initially separate populations. Balls, like the one Brunner described, hosted by the *signares* and, significantly, celebrating a marriage, were one such venue:

> The main salon with its two side rooms, was decorated as described above, quite spacious and illuminated by a chandelier and numerous wall-sconces. The room was jammed with people, and it was with great difficulty that I made my way to pay my respects to the host. With every fifteen minutes, the crowd grew larger. Sitting in small groups were the yellow-brown *Signares*, a few European women, and even more blacks. Getting closer to the stairs, the curious mob mingled and loitered about, so crowded that only one more accustomed than I could distinguish freeman from slave. The orchestra consisted of a single scratchy violin, played by a watchman from the garrison.[6]

Less than a year after hosting this party attended by Brunner and Dupuy and forty-nine years after she last saw Boufflers, Anne Pépin died in November 1837.

During the eighteenth and nineteenth centuries on Gorée, exceedingly exact inventories were taken of people's possessions on several occasions: when a person made a will, when revisions were made to the will, after the person died, and if the objects were sold at public sale. Within days of Anne Pépin's death, clerks of the court went to her residence and recorded all her possessions. They doggedly worked their way throughout the entire house, room by room, trunk by trunk, drawer by drawer, painstakingly recording everything she owned from gold to green beans. The list of possessions is useful for what it tells us about Pépin and the Atlantic world in which she lived.

The inventory provides a wealth of information about the house itself. The rooms are labeled using an elaborate taxonomy of room names: *chambre*, *cabinet*, *magasin*, *salle*, *galerie*, and so on. Two systems are at play, one that stresses specific function and another that permits a flexibility that can override that designated function. Public was separated from private. Pépin's bedroom, labeled *chambre*, contained her personal possessions, including money, clothes, and jewelry. The *salle* was a public room and contained serving items and multiple chairs. Pépin's house inventory also reveals aspects of her character, for a person's possessions can create a "portrait" of their owner. Probate inventories were so relentlessly thorough that reading them one feels as though one is actually in the house, invading the privacy of someone from centuries past. The rules governing the creation of a probate inventory allowed for little authorial intervention—or so they appear. As we shall see, on closer inspection, probate inventories reveal their own idiosyncrasies. Unlike her prolific companion Boufflers, who literally wrote volumes, there is little information on Anne Pépin. Understanding the character of Anne Pépin through the material objects with which she surrounded herself therefore is quite a different process than reading about the life of her French companion through his own words.

Pépin's possessions make clear that by continental standards she was rich. Inheritances and gifts from her father, mother, and two husbands clearly benefited her, but she expanded her fortune through her own entrepreneurial abilities. She leased properties to the government, she rented out her slaves, and she was actively involved in trade. In her house, she was surrounded by luxurious objects and expensive materials: porcelain, lacquer, silver, gold, pearls, and crystal. It is obvious that Anne cared about and could pay for creature comforts, possessing pillows, cushions, bolsters, mattresses, mosquito netting, and bed warmers. Her properties, her slaves, and her possessions constituted a considerable fortune, partially inherited from others but also multiplied over the course of her lifetime by her shrewd business practices.

Well into her seventies, Pépin's concern about her appearance did not flag. She possessed an extensive wardrobe. Her inventory corroborates the assumption that the *signares* were fastidious about how they dressed. She had seventy-one African wraparound skirts, known as *pagnes*. A small chest held forty-seven colored scarves, which could have been worn around her waist, around her shoulders, or on her head. An explanation given for the elaborate conical headdress, one of the hallmarks of the *signares*, is that it made obvious that its wearer did not do manual labor, such as carrying water on her head. Anne Pépin also owned a considerable quantity of earrings, necklaces, and bracelets. She had achieved a certain position and wanted to ensure that everyone knew it.

Anne Pépin also entertained on a grand scale. She had forty-four plates and forty-four napkins, forty-two painted wooden chairs, and a considerable number of serving pieces. The chairs were used when public sales or balls took place in her house. Hers was a house ready to present a well-orchestrated hospitality. The travel account writers, who were often extremely critical of what they observed, were in agreement about the generous hospitality extended to them by Africans. Pépin's house could accommodate many overnight guests, paying or nonpaying. There were eight beds, fifteen mattresses, and three settees. It is striking how a static list of objects can suggest activity. With bedsheets and mosquito netting in one room and beds in another, there is an implicit request to have beds made and unmade, mosquito netting hung up and taken down, and chairs set up and later stored away. There were always prodigious amounts of clothes and linens to be washed and ironed. Yet these are also the possessions of an old woman. No family members or visitors lived with Anne at the time of her death. It is unusual that a woman approaching eighty lived independently in a household she herself managed.

Pépin's possessions connected her to the global economy, which was the reason why Gorée thrived. Many items traveled long distances to take a place in Pépin's residence. She had American brushes, French money, Dutch blouses, Indian fabrics, clothes made from African textiles, and furniture made from the African wood *cail cedra*, a type of cedarwood. Globalization, a topic that so dominates twenty-first-century popular discourse, has a long history, the antecedents of which can be seen in the inventory of Anne Pépin's possessions. The list also exhibits Pépin's dual African/European background in several ways, such as her dress and her hospitality. She probably wore her *pagnes* with European blouses, which is how artists often depicted the *signares*. The items concerned with the preparation and serving of food also fall into both African and European categories. There are comparatively few cooking items, which suggests that African dishes were prepared; Wolof cooks are skillful at cooking elaborate dishes using one pot and an open-air fire. On the serving side, though, Pépin had an elaborate collection of European housewares with specific functions: teapots, oil vessels, vinegar containers, sugar bowls, soup servers, and coffee spoons.

One way in which Gorée and the other trading centers were remarkable is that, in addition to the intermingling of people from different cultural backgrounds, disparate objects were put together as well. Excavations carried out by Senegalese archaeologist Ibrahima Thiaw included a site on the northern end of the island. It was not conclusively identified as Anne Pépin's house, although conceivably it could be. Buried in the sand for close to two hundred years, quantities of European and African pottery shards emerged. They fall into two categories: imported glazed porcelain and locally made clay pottery.

In the most obvious way, these reflect the racially and ethnically mixed heritage of the *habitants*.

With her possessions, Pépin expresses literacy in neither words nor images. There is no indication that either Dupuy or Boufflers left any books at her home. Or perhaps she herself had no use for them and gave them away or preferred to sell them for cash or trade them for other goods. At the time of her death, she had no books, and all her pictures were locked away, two in a trunk and eight in a storeroom. There is no trace that pictures or printed words played a significant role in her life.

Typically, documents such as wills were signed. Illiterate people marked their documents with a cross (+), around which someone else wrote in a neat circle "*marque ordinaire de* _____" (with the name of the person printed for him or her by proxy). Pépin, exceptionally, never did this; all her documents are unsigned. Her refusal to sign could indicate a range of positions, including embarrassment at her own illiteracy. Or her unusual refusal to mark the documents that carry her name could also hint at a defiant stance against European-imposed standards of literacy. It is also a testament to her status in the community that she alone could defy certain legal obligations.

By the late nineteenth century, the grand age of the *habitants* was over, and Gorée was in decline. The slave trade slowly came to an end just as formal colonialism started to expand. African traders increasingly found work as functionaries in the colonial regime and enjoyed fewer opportunities as autonomous traders. The newer style of colonial system allowed no role at the highest levels for African women in official public business or international commerce, although they continued to be active in local African markets.

The life of Anne Pépin is illustrative of how the *habitants* functioned as an intermediary group that was both African and European, biologically and culturally. They were known for their familiarity with European practices— the clothes they wore, the food they served, and the houses in which they lived—but their world's social and familial structure was firmly embedded in African mainland traditions. Shortly after Boufflers' departure, the capital was transferred back to Saint-Louis, which expanded greatly, as did the nascent city of Dakar. Yet the memory of the *signares* continues. Engravings of them are frequently reproduced. These women are appropriate images of their historical period, for they symbolize the inequities of power; they were, after all, slave owners and traders. Yet they are nostalgically and romantically presented as lovers. Promoting the romance of Anne Pépin and the Chevalier de Boufflers is an informal cottage industry on Gorée, a story that sits uneasily within the context of the island's history of slavery. Their era was one in which some remarkable mixed-race women became rich and exercised real power. They are therefore symbols of achievement and possibility within the urban context of a population most of whose members were slaves.

Bibliography and Suggested Reading

Barry, Boubacar. *Senegambia and the Atlantic Slave Trade*. Cambridge: Cambridge University Press, 1998.

Brooks, George. *Eurafricans in Western Africa: Commerce, Social Status, Gender, and Religious Observance from the Sixteenth to the Eighteenth Century*. Athens: Ohio University Press, 2003.

Camara, Abdoulaye, and Joseph Roger de Benoist. *Histoire de Gorée*. Paris: Maisonneuve & Larose, 2003.

Hinchman, Mark. "House and Household on Gorée, Senegal, 1758–1837." *Journal of the Society of Architectural Historians* 65 (June 2006): 166–87.

Mark, Peter. *"Portuguese" Style and Luso-African Identity: Precolonial Senegambia Sixteenth-Nineteenth Centuries*. Bloomington: Indiana University Press, 2002.

Searing, James. *West African Slavery and Atlantic Commerce: The Senegal River Valley, 1700–1860*. Cambridge: Cambridge University Press, 1993.

CHAPTER ELEVEN

João da Silva Feijó (1760–1824)

Brazilian Scientist in the Portuguese Overseas Empire

Magnus Roberto de Mello Pereira, Translated by Ana Maria Rufino Gillies with assistance from Ian Robert Gillies

João da Silva Feijó was a scientist who tramped all over the Atlantic world in search of knowledge. Sponsored by the Portuguese Crown, Feijó undertook decades of research in the Cape Verde Islands and later traveled to Ceará in Brazil. In both places, he documented the flora and fauna he encountered and searched for potentially profitable commodities. Feijó wrote many scientific treatises, sent plant and animal specimens to his fellow scientists back in Europe, and even helped develop saltpeter mines, which produced an essential component for the manufacture of gunpowder. The scientist's work made a meaningful contribution to the transatlantic community of knowledge during the age of the Enlightenment, but, like many others of a similar inclination, his spirit of enquiry led him beyond the physical world to raise important political and social questions as well. By tracing Feijó's life and activities, historian Magnus Roberto de Mello Pereira highlights the close relationship between scientific expeditions and the quest for economic power that has always motivated European exploration of the Atlantic world.

João da Silva Barbosa was practically a child when he left Brazil in order to start his college education at the famous medieval university of Coimbra. Portugal, the ancient maritime power, had become a decadent country, a land dominated by priests and lawyers that some intellectuals scornfully dismissed as a *Reino cadaveroso* (cadaverous kingdom). The Marquis of Pombal, an enlightened despot who served as the all-powerful minister of King João attempted to remedy this image by ordering a complete institutional reform of Coimbra; he encouraged the teaching of modern experimental sciences by hiring the Italian scholar Domingos Vandelli to assist in the task.

At Coimbra, the study of physics, chemistry, and other natural sciences became mandatory for all students. Additionally, two new courses were created: natural philosophy, which was based in the experimental and observable sciences, and mathematics, which emphasized its practical application, especially as it related to astronomy. Oddly, these new fields did not arouse much interest among the Portuguese students, and almost all the vacancies came to be occupied by enthusiastic young Brazilian students. A curious and ambitious young American, João da Silva Barbosa, traveled across the Atlantic, where he became so animated by Enlightenment science that he changed his name to Feijó, probably to signal his admiration for Spanish naturalist Benito Jerónimo Feijóo, author of the influential treatise *Teatro Crítica Universal* (*Universal Critical Theater*).

João da Silva Feijó was probably born in 1760. The records at the University of Coimbra show that he started to study mathematics at the age of sixteen. He was eighteen when he registered in the Faculty of Philosophy in 1778. That same year, Domingos Vandelli gathered a team of recently graduated naturalists at the Museum of Natural History of Ajuda to begin preparations for a scientific expedition to Brazil, a "philosophical journey" as they were called at the time. The influential Italian professor recruited clever Brazilian Feijó for the team, although he was four or five years younger than the others. He was regularly described as "young," and throughout his life, older men like Martinho de Mello e Castro and Julio Matiazzi took a paternal interest in his career. The Portuguese Crown appointed several other Brazilians to the commission; its commander was a man from Bahia named Alexandre Rodrigues Ferreira, and there were two other young scientists named Joaquim José da Silva and Manuel Galvão da Silva. Nervous about patriotic sentiment that had spread throughout the hemisphere in the wake of American independence, the Portuguese Crown established a policy of co-optation of the educated Brazilian creole elite by incorporating them into the imperial administration. For this reason, there was an increasingly heavy presence of Brazilians in the Portuguese African colonies. Furthermore, the Portuguese Crown believed that Brazilians were hardier people who enjoyed a greater resistance to disease when exposed to the hardships of the African and Asian climates. For Europeans, a post in Africa was often considered to be a death sentence, whereas Brazilians seemed to survive.

European nations were engaged in a race to gather, study, and classify newly discovered mineral, vegetable, and animal species according to the

scientific categories of Linnaeus's taxonomy. Ideally, these new natural resources not only would advance academic study and provide knowledge of
the material world but also would become commercially valuable commodities that would increase national wealth and prestige. Gathering and publishing scientific information about the largest possible number of species had
become a matter of national pride. For this reason, the Portuguese Crown
sent scientific expeditions to all corners of its overseas empire. In 1783, Alexandre Ferreira headed to the Amazon basin, accompanied by two sketch
artists and a gardener in what turned out to be one of the most successful
scientific missions of the eighteenth century. Joaquim José da Silva and
Manuel Galvão da Silva each headed small teams that went to Angola and
Mozambique, where they played dual roles as chief naturalist and secretary
of state of those African colonies. They carried out their missions as best as
they could, given the difficulty in reconciling the positions of naturalists and
bureaucrats. When they had time, they gathered and sent samples of plants
and animals to the museum of natural history in Ajuda, but over time, both
men became distracted and consumed by their governmental responsibilities.

Youthful João da Silva Feijó also received an official appointment as naturalist charged with the exploration of the arid archipelago of Cape Verde but
no additional credentials as governing secretary of state. Although a different man might have considered that to have been a snub, these conditions
suited Feijó just fine. Unlike his friends in Africa, Feijó was able to prioritize
his scientific activities over the few administrative duties required of him.
Nevertheless, the inexperienced young man was entering a hornet's nest
filled with competing interests, conflicts over political and economic power,
and local jealousies that an outsider could never hope to overcome. Cape
Verde was a small place, with an insular elite, military captains, Catholic
Church officials, and imperial administrators, each of whom guarded their
share of power and the benefits to an insane degree. Hoping to weaken its
local rivals, the Portuguese Crown had encouraged the practice of intrigues
and denunciations since the fifteenth century. This sort of "administration
by intrigue" functioned as a governing principle throughout the Portuguese
Atlantic. For example, in a 1782 inquiry related to Brazil, the Overseas
Council expressed clearly that "it was not very convenient to the service of
Your Majesty that between the governors and higher ministers with whom
they serve there would be great friendships, because it would be very useful
that one feared the other."

In fact, such intrigue was so constant in Portuguese colonial administration—particularly in Cape Verde, there was such a strong belligerence—that
for several decades before Feijó's arrival, Portuguese officials were given a

special budget to hire bodyguards. With this money, they created gangs. The local elite complained that, heading these gangs, the officials committed all kinds of violence, corruption, and abuse—especially sexual.

During the first decades of the eighteenth century, the feuds between Cape Verde's governors and hearer, who mutually accused each other of invasion of jurisdiction, were mixed with the high death rate of these officials due to illnesses of "unknown" or very well known causes. On the occasion of Governor Antônio Vieira's death, his widow accused, among others, the hearer Sebastião Bravo Botelho. The succeeding governor was in charge of investigating the event but ducked the task by proclaiming that it was publicly known that Antônio Vieira died because of an "aposthema" caused by a rock thrown at him. But this was no big deal. In 1732, new trouble started when the governor ordered the arrest of the hearer. The latter resisted and ended up being killed, along with two of his supporters. The conflict became so large that the Portuguese Crown sent an investigator, the Brazilian-born Custódio Correia de Matos, who was killed by poison soon after.

The worst moment of the conflicts in Cape Verde was the assassination of yet another general hearer in 1762:

> The Hearer in São Tiago of the Cape Verde Islands being João Vieira de Andrade, and being in that same place to exercise the government of justice in that colony, as determined by Dom José, it so happened that in December 13th, 1762, between 9 and 10 of the evening, his house was surrounded by a large number of armed men, who intended to put his doors down by hitting them with an axe. The said Minister asked who knocked, and was answered that it was the Devil; at the same time, breaking down a window with an axe, some men entered violently in the house at the same time others came through the backyard and killed the Hearer, doing with maces and other weapons many wounds, being the first one with an axe to the head, which immediately sent him to the ground.

Judge José Romão da Silva informed the Crown of this fact, claiming that the instigator was Captain João Freire de Andrade, chief of one of the islands' power struggling factions and Feijó's main future enemy. Despite this unpleasant turn of events, a new judge sent over from Lisbon in 1764 instead blamed the rival party's chieftain, Antônio Barros de Oliveira, who was another powerful Cape Verdean. Tried in Lisbon, his sentence was to be "pulled by the tail of a horse through the streets of the city until the square in the city limits, in which [he was] to die from natural causes forever." His head was to be cut and sent to Cape Verde to be exposed in Praia (the capital city) until it decayed from the elements. Ten other codefendants suffered similar grisly fates, with only one being spared postmortem decapitation. One received the relatively light punishment of whipping before being sent into perpetual exile. Historians who study this era always note that the Portuguese state always handpicked its victims in these cases. With the killing of the Tavora family, Pombal struck fear and terror into hearts of the high nobility and clearly signaled who was in charge. The execution of the heads of the Oporto insurrection was meant to send a message to urban commoners. Unfortunately, they forgot to include these members of the most rebellious colonial urban elites.

In this way, a small trap was set for the unwitting scientist Feijó when he was sent to Cape Verde as a protégé of the archipelago's bishop, D. Francisco de São Simão, who was also governor of Cape Verde. One can speculate that the powerful Overseas Secretary Martinho de Mello e Castro was nervous that scientific inquiry might lead to independent political thought and therefore was anxious to keep a close eye on the young American's activities. It is probable that there was something in the young naturalist's behavior that made him suspicious. He was also very young and impressionable. Mello de Castro told the bishop,

> Your Excellency will be in charge of this young man; who, not having a bad character nor being inert in the profession, the least shadow seems to him a giant and prevents him from doing what he should do, and it will not be pleasant that, there not being anything here related to the natural productions of the islands of Cape Verde, when there's a Naturalist to find them, such arrangement results in nothing or little more than useless words and lists from the said Naturalist.

Feijó, like all his scientific colleagues, had to overcome great resistance in order to be taken seriously in a culture still dominated by the Catholic Church and vestiges of medieval feudalism. On a more prosaic level, he also had to fight to escape the supervisory control of his mentors and the political tutelage that had been imposed on him because of his youth and suspicious talent for natural science.

This double struggle started almost as soon as Feijó disembarked in Cape Verde. As he made preparations to begin for his scientific work, he experienced several small conflicts with Bishop São Simão. Trying to assert himself, the young naturalist accidentally antagonized the bishop by producing a scientific and philosophical text that seemed too irreligious and thus a sort of weapon for the Enlightenment's secularizing goals. Back in Portugal, the more pragmatic government minister Martinho de Mello e Castro was not concerned with Feijó's writing, which he considered to be "useless words" that were "nothing, or little more than nothing." What interested the overseas secretary more was Feijó's regular remittance of well-packed minerals, vegetables, and animals that might prove useful or lucrative for the Portuguese treasury. A strong scientific "collector's spirit" characterized the Enlightenment all throughout the Atlantic world. From the moment the Portuguese government created the Royal Office, it encouraged agents to send specimens back to the museum of natural history. Most specimens were considered to be personal gifts to the minister and therefore were not sent for the disinterested advancement of science. A consignment of exotic birds, a box of rare shells, or a pair of albino or dwarf black children frequently accompanied the request for promotion or a petition to return home from some obsequious high official tired of the inhospitable climate of the overseas colonies. Feijó had little patience for these sorts of bribes and preferred to view his work as part of a shared scientific mission that was building a knowledge base, not merely accumulating curiosities. He sent back notes and recommendations instead.

Feijó was in the vanguard of a new generation of professional scientists. With the establishment of a publication series called *Memórias Econômicas da Academia Real das Ciências de Lisboa* (*Economic Papers of the Royal Academy of Sciences in Lisbon*), the production of scientific treatises started to gain status for their authors. The value of Feijó's literary production slowly became recognized, and his work was published frequently. Nevertheless, his first accounts did little more than irritate his patron the bishop, who thought that all this attention to the natural world somehow diminished God's central role on earth (which, therefore, threatened the Church's primacy in human affairs as well). One could not, it seems, be a scientist without also infringing on politics.

Feijó's initial explorations of Cape Verde were described in *Itinerário filosófico que contém a Relação das Ilhas de Cabo Verde disposto pelo método epistolar* (*Narrative Containing an Account of the Cape Verde Islands in a Series of Letters*). Addressed to Martinho de Mello e Castro, Feijó faithfully and accurately described his activities, starting with his departure from Portugal as well as of his arrival in the archipelago. Already in his first letter, dated June 17, 1783, Feijó hinted that the bishop had already started to interfere with his duties as naturalist. On the island of May, where the bishop had stopped to verify the wreckage of a Danish ship, Feijó took the opportunity to collect shells and skeletons of large sea animals from its beaches. However, the bishop did not authorize this beachcombing, and he jealously ordered his collection to be left behind, much to the young scientist's annoyance.

Feijó arrived at the Brava island on March 20, and the bishop left six days later, freeing him up to start exploring without interference. During eighteen busy days in June, he and a small team covered the island's entire perimeter, taking notes and measurements and gathering specimens of rocks, plants, insects, and small animals.

In a letter dated October 17, 1783, Feijó carefully described Brava, giving prominence to "its climate due to its duration; the fertility of its soil; the endemic illnesses that affect the area; the medicines used by its inhabitants; and finally how its discovery was finally made." He went further and included observations of the island's social customs as well, although his academic, racial and religious prejudices drove him to make some scornful and facetious remarks. "There is nothing that makes me laugh more than watching a wedding in this country," said Feijó, before giving a detailed account of the ceremony and festivities. He left a rich description of Cape Verdean customs that are still practiced in the country today:

> Finally the newlyweds arrive at their houses, and before they enter they stop at the door sided by their respective best men, bridesmaids and godparents to exchange compliments, and then, concluded all this ceremony, they go inside with their entourage, followed by all the foods and drinks. After dinner all the guests leave, to gather again on the bride's house in order to do what they call the bonfire which means leaving that place to go and find the groom, whom they say has run away, and they all go with much feasting to get him, and then bring him to the bride to reconciliate with her, whom, sitting in front of the door much ornamented, waits for him with hugs and kisses exchanged publicly and there giving themselves to each other without respect: how dishonest, Lord, so little respect to the Catholic religion that we profess!

On July 20, 1783, Feijó crossed the sea to the Ilha do Fogo (Island of Fire) "on a wooden craft, openmouthed fifteen-span long, on which the obligation to obey made me risk my life." After resting for eight days, he continued onward, taking down a detailed description of the Ilha do Fogo's physical aspects, particularly the volcano that gave it its name. Feijó categorized the local population according to a rigid racial criteria. Contrary to what he had seen on the islands of Santiago and Brava, where the inhabitants were mostly of African origin, "the majority of inhabitants in the Ilha do Fogo are half-castes, as there are many whites and descendants from whites." As a result, he says that "the natives are more sincere, and extremely obedient lovers of the whites, and hard-working, and fond of finding means of living." The women, in spite of wearing just a cloth on their waists, as on other islands, were described as "more courteous and not so licentious, nor so fond of dancing."

On Fogo, conflict quickly emerged between the scientist Feijó and the local elite. According to his notes, all the men on the island "without exception of widow's sons, old men, the sick, even the very young ones" were susceptible to a draft by the militia "or better said, as slaves of the governor or commander of the provinces." Rather than being employed solely in the islands' defense, however, the garrison's captains instead exploited this free labor to work "on their lands or to spin a pound of cotton, or making deliveries without any other payment but telling them that 'it is for His Majesty's service.'" Feijó also noted that the local elites sometimes charged illegal monetary tributes by offering the poor inhabitants a deal that would substitute a portion of cotton each week in order to release them from labor draft. Realizing that his scientific observations about the social and economic conditions on the island would upset the existing corrupt power structure, Feijó correctly anticipated that his report would cause his local adversaries to launch a defamatory campaign in order to discredit him before his employers in Portugal.

Feijó's expectation was totally justified. The local elite accused Feijó of not having paid for his transportation between the Ilha do Fogo and Santiago and of behaving haughtily toward the "poor inhabitants" by pretending to be someone of great power and authority. Furthermore, they said that he had forced the inhabitants to provide more cotton than was necessary to pack the specimens that he had gathered for shipment. The residents even charged that the lazy young man spent most of his time at home sleeping and actually sent his brother-in-law out to do the collection work. At least some of these complaints may have had a basis in fact. The weaving of cotton cloths for sale in the African continent was one of the main economic activities of Cape Verde. The captain kept for himself a part of that cotton demanded from the residents in the name of the Crown. Feijó, in the name of the service to the Crown, kept part of this cotton for "scientific" use, which was seen as a private cost imposed on the captain. Overseas Secretary Martinho de Mello e Castro sent Feijó an extremely severe letter of warning and instructed the governor to put the young man back on track. Feijó the scientist had entered a snake pit and aggravated centuries-old disputes over land, labor, and power. Government and military positions, rather than being seen as honest opportunities to serve the public good, were considered to be opportunities to enrich oneself and had became an important source of income for the local elite, who guarded them fiercely. The scientist's observations exposed this dirty secret and thus threatened to upset traditional political relations in an era of ambitious central governments animated by Enlightenment theories. Returning from Fogo island, Feijó remained on Santiago for a while to recuperate from *carneirada* (malaria).

The complaints sent to Lisbon that hurt Feijó most referred to his professional behavior on Cape Verde and are related to another fact of his personal life back in Portugal. After leaving Lisbon, it was learned that he had married and had left behind a wife and son, who had become destitute by his inattention. The overseas secretary behaved as an offended father who found out that his son had been very mischievous. He confiscated Feijó's salary, designating part of it to be paid to him in Cape Verde, sending a significant sum to his wife in Portugal, and setting aside a further portion in a kind of compulsory savings account. Feijó tried to get Mello e Castro to change his mind but to no avail. In spite of his protests, Feijó once again was treated as a young man who needed guidance and behavioral correction.

As a result of these conflicts, the central government received the results of Feijó's scientific work coldly, in contrast to enthusiastic response given to the shipments sent by his more pliable colleagues in the African colonies. Feijó's *Itinerário* was dismissed as the empty words of a potentially subversive naturalist. Martinho de Mello e Castro pointedly told Feijó that "with regards to the two shipments that you have sent to the Royal Museum, the first one was very good, but the second was good for nothing." He reprimanded the governor by reminding him that while the bishop was alive, Feijó's reports were of excellent quality and he remained politically inoffensive but that everything had changed following the prelate's death. Of the material from San Nicolau, they were disappointed to have received "nothing of what was expected, consisting mostly of the most ordinary stones and other products of nature that had no singularity enough to be kept." Martinho de Mello e Castro clearly bore ill will toward Feijó. The first shipment sent by the naturalist had not even been sent until December 1783, months after Bishop São Simão's death on August 10.

In many Portuguese colonies throughout the Atlantic, there was marked competition between governors, elites, and the scientific naturalists sent out by the Crown. In Mozambique, for example, Governor Francisco de Mello e Castro had been continuously sending his uncle, Martinho, specimens of natural curiosities, even before Galvão's arrival. Governors in Angola had been sending accounts of the island's events back to Lisbon since the 1750s, during the government of D. Francisco Inocêncio de Souza Coutinho. Once Joaquim José da Silva's mission arrived, there was increased competition for the resources, prestige, and perks that accompanied their discovery. In Cape Verde, however, Governor-Bishop São Simão distrusted the secular world of scientific investigation and obstructed the collection of natural history specimens. A frustrated Feijó recalled that the bishop "had very little taste for these things," which he regarded as unimportant, and that, as a matter of fact, "was an obstacle to his performance."

Mello e Castro, however, did not personally set out to persecute Feijó; he passed the problem to Júlio Mattiazi, who also showed dissatisfaction with the naturalist's performance. Feijó was said to be "ashamed of being admonished by Julio without reason." He was fully aware that his colleagues elsewhere enjoyed significant support teams. Indeed, part of the success achieved by Alexandre Rodrigues Ferreira's philosophical journey is directly related to the enormous quantity of pictures made by the artist who accompanied him. Feijó opined, "If I had a man for the preparation of the birds and fishes, and another who sketched the plants, I assure Your Excellency that I would send very beautiful shipments, but I am alone, and of drawing and painting and preparation I know nothing." The lack of drawings did reduce the effectiveness of Feijó's reports on the Cape Verde expedition.

After his return to the windward islands, Feijó encountered an unexpected ally in Governor Faria e Maia, who managed to shield him from his adversaries for a while. He arrested the hearer and sent him back to Lisbon. He silenced the local military commanders and part of the clergy and personally defended the Brazilian naturalist to Mello e Castro. The governor wrote to the minister saying that Feijó, "for lack of malice, or the knowledge of men, has been doing some *rapaziadas* [mischief], unthinkingly, yes," but arguing that he was not mean or malicious:

> The Naturalist, having arrived to these islands, and having always to be employed under the direction of the Most Reverend Bishop D. Frei São Simão, started his disgrace on the death of this Prelate; not because he could not justify many orders received locally, but because too early did he lack an older person with more knowledge of the world, who would, little by little, let him know what he should really care for and which principles he should embrace. It is true that in the islands of Santo Antão and São Nicolau there were complaints about the mentioned Naturalist because he took a survey of cattle and, suspecting that many residents understated the number that belonged to them, passed these increases on to the Royal Treasury, saying that they did not have owners and that consequently they belonged to the Royal Treasury, which he told the Administrator José Lopes Quaresma. The Naturalist says that he received this orders from the deceased Prelate.

Faria e Maia insisted that Feijó was not guilty of most of the things he had been accused of and reported that he really had been very sick while in Cape Verde. He recalled, "I saw him suffer from very strong seizures which prevented him from returning to his own house for many hours." In this debilitated state, Feijó nevertheless dutifully sailed to the windward islands to continue his work. Once again, he enjoyed the paternal protection of a powerful older man. Mello e Castro ordered that Feijó would be under the tutelage of Colonel José Maria Cardoso. Although this officer previously had sent a shipment of natural curiosities to the Office of the Crown in Ajuda that was considered to be of excellent quality, there is no evidence that there was bigger competition between the two collectors. In fact, Feijó seems to have been happy to be able to use Cardoso as the assistant he so desperately wished to have.

After his return to Santiago, it becomes difficult to trace Feijó's steps since he apparently discontinued taking notes for his *Itinerário Filosófico*, or that part of the manuscript has been lost. He spent the calendar year 1786 revisiting the locales of his first voyages, trying to redeem himself in the eyes of his superiors back in Lisbon. They had complained that he had given enough attention to potentially valuable natural resources like Brava's saltpeter and Fogo's sulfur. Apparently, Feijó had sent insignificant samples without any clear indication whether economically profitable mines existed. Returning to Brava, he and Cardoso realized that there was not enough saltpeter to make its exploitation viable. He then went to Fogo to witness the eruption of the volcano responsible for the island's name and to study the possibility of exploring sulfur. His scientific observations of the phenomenon were recorded in his *Memória sobre a Irrupção do Fogo* (*Memoir on the Eruption of the Fogo Volcano*).

As the years passed, both the governor and Feijó concluded that they had exhausted the range of natural products available to be gathered in the islands. Cape Verde is the most arid of the Atlantic archipelagos and does not have the dramatic biological diversity found in Africa and South America. By 1786, they were expressing regret at not being able to send specimens of quadrupeds and birds. The only exotic mammals that they found were monkeys, but they had received explicit orders not to send any of them to Lisbon. There was only one native species of bird that was not related to "sparrows, crows, ant-thrushes or pigeons," but they could not manage to transport one to Ajuda because it was an insect eater and therefore difficult to feed during the sea voyage. Feijó went as far as Boa Vista island to capture flamingoes and tried to breed them in captivity, but the fragile young ones always ended up dying, and the larger older ones were too intelligent to be caught. He was able to send two barrels of fishes, birds, and lizards to Mello e Castro though. In the revolutionary year 1789, as a direct result of Feijó's success, an enthusiastic Governor Faria e Maia proposed a further expedition to what is today Guinea-Bissau, a territory on the African continent that was administratively annexed to Cape Verde. Feijó would have jumped at the chance to explore further and expand his scientific work, but apparently he never received authorization for the trip.

Following orders from Lisbon, Feijó concentrated on the study of the sea fauna and started to gather material from the windward islands. Beginning in 1789, he started to experiment in the conservation of various species of fish that had the potential to be farmed commercially and compiled his conclusions in an unpublished essay titled *Relação da Factura do Peixe Seco* (*Account of the Manufacture of Dried, Salted Fish*). Faria e Maia then sent him to the island of Santo Antão, where the Crown kept sites for the experimental cultivation of the indigo plant. During this period, the naturalist wrote a *Memória sobre a fábrica de anil da Ilha de Santo Antão* (*Memoir on the Production of Indigo on the Island of Santo Antão*), which was published in the inaugural volume of Memórias Econômicas da Academia in 1789. Even though he was stuck in Cape Verde, Feijó did not give up trying to gain national and international recognition of his work, so the Academy of Science's willingness to publish his observations was an important validation of his efforts. Of the first generation of naturalists sent to the Portuguese overseas colonies, Alexandre Rodrigues Ferreira was the only one to be admitted as a member of the Academy of Science, although Feijó was the only one to have his memoirs published in their main series.

Beginning in the 1790s, Feijó started to be assigned some bureaucratic functions. He appeared in a 1793 document as the government secretary in the district of Cape Verde and as a notary in the War Staff Registration Office. During the same period, he started a campaign to return to Portugal. He requested the intercession of Governor Francisco José Teixeira Carneiro, who wrote to Martinho de Mello e Castro on behalf of "this poor naturalist, who has already been here from ten to eleven years, has behaved with dignity during all the time of my government and deserves that you attend his request and wish him well." At the same time, the governor sent a certificate to the Overseas Council, confirming that Feijó had urgent personal reasons to go to Rio de Janeiro to handle an estate that he had inherited on the death of parents. He also counted on his wife's complicity, who pleaded directly to the Queen D. Maria I to allow her wayward naturalist husband to leave Cape Verde.

The order for Feijó to return to Portugal was signed on June 9, 1795, and left directly from the Palace of Queluz and arrived in Cape Verde in December. At the time, Feijó was a sergeant-major at the fortress of Ribeira Grande and the arbitrator for orphans, which precipitated a very fierce dispute. Both positions were very much coveted by the local elite, principally the latter, which was one of the largest sources of illicit enrichment. Feijó's ascent in the islands' political structure can be credited to the savvy policy he adopted of allying with the various governors. However, Feijó was no longer a carefree youth, and he had started to think seriously of his future, trying to accumulate savings. In spite of his anxiously awaited exit from Cape Verde, he did not hurry back to Portugal when the permission to do so arrived. Instead, he remained a little longer in the archipelago in order to prevent serious losses because he had a lot of possessions of which to dispose and affairs to settle. Nevertheless, his stay was shortened, and he had to hasten home when the government of Cape Verde was given to his sworn enemy, Captain João Freire de Andrade.

In 1796, the year Martinho de Mello e Castro died, Feijó was given a year of unpaid leave to travel to Rio de Janeiro to handle his family business. Later crossing the ocean to settle with his family in Lisbon, Feijó went to work with his old partner Alexandre Rodrigues Ferreira, who had returned from the Amazon to become the deputy director of the natural history museum in Ajuda. Feijó undertook the task of organizing a herbarium with specimens he had sent from the archipelago of Cape Verde and plants that others had sent from various locations around the Atlantic. The German naturalist Johann Heinrich Friedrich Link visited Portugal and the Ajuda gardens. He was impressed by Feijó's work in the same rate that he was not by the work and appearances of Alexandre Rodrigues Ferreira. There were rumors that Ferreira was ill adapted to the sedentary life after his long expedition to the Amazon and was given to drinking too much, something that turns out to have been quite common among eighteenth-century naturalists.

In Lisbon, Feijó participated actively in the Portuguese scientific community and forged links with the Academy of Science. Feijó reorganized some of his texts related to Cape Verde and sent them out for publication, hoping that his work would contribute to the larger international base of knowledge. He wrote *Ensaio econômico sobre as Ilhas de Cape Verde* (*Treatise on the Economy of the Cape Verde Islands*), in which he set out a complete analysis of the archipelago's economic situation for the year 1797. At the same time, he was assigned the task of studying the possibility of discovering saltpeter on the Tejo shoreline. In all these activities, the Brazilian naturalist's interests and work were in accord with new directions in which both the international scientific community's work and the Portuguese imperial policies were heading.

When Melo e Castro died, D. Rodrigo de Souza Coutinho assumed control of imperial affairs and continued his predecessor's policy of gathering specimens for the national botanical garden at Ajuda. However, Souza

Coutinho placed even more emphasis on the identification and exploitation of commercially valuable resources that would offer his government immediate economic results. In his view, the best and richest Crown territory was Brazil and not Portugal. Souza Coutinho wanted to keep the colony loyal and therefore recruited several Brazilians for his projects, using them in scientific expeditions and assigning them to important positions in the civil, military, and judicial government throughout the empire. Among his favorites were Feijó; the astronomer Francisco José de Lacerda e Almeida, who died during an attempt to cross the African continent; and the naturalist and journalist Hipólito José da Costa Pereira, who was sent to Philadelphia on a philosophical journey in order to learn about the progresses of the new American nation, in whose future Hipólito did not put much faith after his journey.

For strategic reasons, Portuguese ministers were anxious to become self-sufficient in the production of saltpeter, which was one of the major components in the manufacture of gunpowder. In February 1799, João da Silva Feijó was appointed sergeant-major for the militia of the Ceará district, which included the duties of official naturalist. Feijó disembarked at Pernambuco and reached his destination on the October 24, 1799, after an overland journey that took thirty-two days. In the region of Canindé, he could not come to any conclusion because it was the rainy season. On the shores of Xoró, he found only sea salt. He went on to Serra dos Cocos, where he had previously examined samples, and came back joyous with positive results.

Between 1799 and 1805, Feijó was responsible for the construction of two laboratories for the extraction of saltpeter. The first one was in Tatajuba, where, according to the naturalist, the mines of the region were quite productive. This laboratory produced small quantities of saltpeter until it became exhausted in 1804, and production was transferred to Pindoba in the Serra da Ibiapaba. A contemporary medical report states that Feijó had almost died. He suffered "an obstruction of the spleen and the liver," which was attributed to the "acid mineral vapors which flow around the atmosphere of the Royal Saltpeter Laboratory." The main symptom was a "large amount of 'Atrabilis' spread throughout his skin," that is to say, it had a yellowish color, allowing us to surmise he had been infected with hepatitis. The enterprise was not particularly successful; according to the governor, Feijó spent more than three times the amount budgeted for the year and obtained no more than a few samples. Apart from the quest for nitrates, the naturalist's attention turned to the evaluation of the economic potential of other mineral resources in the region. In the Serra da Ibiapaba, he reevaluated the copper mines, which had been assumed to hold silver as well. He suspected that copper sulfate ore existed farther afield at Piauí. Feijó also examined the old gold mines of Mangabeira, which appeared to be unproductive.

Running parallel to his work as a mineralogist, Feijó also dedicated himself to the study of the fauna and flora of Ceará as well as to the collection of specimens for shipment across the Atlantic to Portugal. He wrote to the minister Souza Coutinho that he had "particular inclination for the study of Botany." For both of them, Brazil offered "a very vast field for an interesting flora." Therefore, Feijó asked his European patron to send him some updated books on botany and, above all, an artist to accompany his explorations because he had never developed the ability to draw and sketches had to be considered important scientific documentation. In return, Feijó dutifully promised to send extensive shipments back to the Royal Botanic Garden at Ajuda. At the same time, he also sent natural specimens to the Berlin Botanical Gardens, to be studied by a number of German naturalists, including Alexandre von Humboldt. During the years that he remained in Ceará, Feijó strengthened one of his best talents: his composition skills. He did not abandon the preparation of scientific texts, many of which remain the important source of historical information about the various regions he visited. Feijó also embarked on a massive cataloging project that he envisioned would become his master work, a project of major scientific importance that he called the *Flora Cearense* (*Flora of Ceará*).

Even though his stay in Ceará marked Feijó's more mature scientific work, his personal life remained rocky. Having been a young man who caused others to be concerned, he was now in the position of being worried about his own son who had been doing some *rapaziadas* (mischief). When Feijó was sent to Brazil, he left one of his sons in a Lisbon school. The boy was expelled due to misbehavior, and minister Souza Coutinho sent him to Ceará to meet his father. Friction between both of them made life quite difficult. According to the naturalist, "this boy, despite having received repeated warnings, reprehensions and some punishment, does not mend himself, becoming ever more unruly and undignified." Feijó ended up asking D. Rodrigo to punish his son, who was a military cadet, "sending him to serve in Angola, or India, for some time, so that he would mend his ways and be useful to the State and himself." It is not clear when Feijó returned to settle permanently in his birthplace, Rio de Janeiro. He made several trips there, including one taken in 1811 after he had been promoted to lieutenant-colonel of the First Militia Cavalry Regiment of the Ceará district. He visited Rio in 1818 and, in 1822, could be found acting as professor of natural, zoological, and botanic history at the Military Academy in the newly minted capital of the Brazilian Empire. Feijó undertook many scientific and educational enterprises on behalf his country, including a drive to organize natural history textbooks for Brazilian schools. He died in 1824 and was buried in the cloister of Nossa Senhora da Consolação Chapel of the Third Order of São Francisco de Paula.

After his death, Feijó's work was largely forgotten. Napoleon Bonaparte had sent French naturalist Geoffrey de Saint-Hilaire to Lisbon to pillage the herbarium that Feijó had founded with his Cape Verde specimens. A large part of the material the Brazilian naturalists had collected on his various Atlantic "philosophical journeys" was boxed up and sent to the Jardin des Plantes in Paris. Feijó and others had followed Linnaeus's method carefully and had given scientific names to the various plants, but French colleagues redid the classifications and renamed all the species, thus obliterating the Brazilians' work. Nationalism, it seems, overwhelmed the pure scientific enterprise; peripheral countries such as Brazil and Portugal were erased and expelled from their own scientific history. However, when King Dom João VI fled to Brazil with his court in 1808, transferring the imperial capital to Rio de Janeiro, one of his first acts of retaliation against the French was the occupation of Cayenne, capital of French Guiana. There, he ordered the large botanical garden to be pillaged of the tropical specimens that the French kept in the city, spreading the material throughout Brazilian congeners. Emblematic of the forgetfulness and disregard suffered by Feijó and his work was the destiny of his botanical writings. The manuscripts of his *Flora Cearense* were rescued by the naturalist Freire Alemão from a bakery, where they were being used as wrapping paper.

Acknowledgment

Archival research for this chapter was funded by the Fundación Carolina (Spain) and Conselho Nacional de Ciência e Tecnologia (Brazil). Documents related to Feijó can be found in the files of the Overseas Historical Archive in Lisbon, the National Library of Portugal, the Historical Archive of Casa da Moeda in Lisbon, the archive of the Academy of Sciences in Lisbon, the Bocage Museum, the National Library of Brazil at Rio de Janeiro, and José Bonifácio de Andrada e Silva's archive at the Paulista Museum in São Paulo.

Bibliography and Suggested Reading

Feijó published some of his work in the *Memorias Económicas da Academia Real das Sciencias de Lisboa* (1789 and 1815) and in the Brazilian newspaper *O Patriota* (1813 and 1814). The Royal Press at Rio de Janeiro published some of his articles about

Ceará's natural history and economy in 1810, 1811, and 1814. The *Revista do Instituto Histórico do Ceará* has reprinted some of Feijó's texts and extracts from his personal correspondence.

Burns, William E. *Science and Technology in Colonial America*. Santa Barbara, CA: Greenwood Press, 2005.

Carneiro, Ana, Ana Simoes, and Maria Paulo Diogo. "Enlightenment Science in Portugal: The Estrangeirados and Their Communication Networks." *Social Studies of Science* 30, no. 4 (August 2000): 591–619.

Figueiroa, Silvia, and Clarete da Silva. "Enlightened Mineralogists: Mining Knowledge in Colonial Brazil, 1750–1825." *Osiris* 15 (2000): 174–89.

Fishburn, Evelyn, and Eduardo L. Ortiz. *Science and the Creative Imagination in Latin America*. London: Institute for the Study of the Americas, 2005.

Gavrolu, Kostas. *The Sciences in the European Periphery during the Enlightenment*. Dordrecht: Kluwer Academic, 1999.

Goodman, Dena. *Criticism in Action: Enlightenment Experiments in Political Writing*. Ithaca, NY: Cornell University Press, 1989.

Keeney, Elizabeth. *The Botanizers: Amateur Scientists in Nineteenth-Century America*. Chapel Hill: University of North Carolina Press, 1992.

Koerner, Lisbet. *Linnaeus: Nature and Nation*. Cambridge, MA: Harvard University Press, 1999.

Lafuente, Antonio. "Enlightenment in an Imperial Context: Local Science in the Eighteenth-Century Hispanic World." *Osiris* 15 (2000): 155–73.

Miller, David Philip, and Peter Hanns Reill, eds. *Visions of Empire: Voyages, Botany, and Representations of Nature*. Cambridge: Cambridge University Press, 1996.

Muthu, Sankar. *Enlightenment Against Empire*. Princeton, NJ: Princeton University Press, 2003.

Saldaña, Juan José. *Science in Latin America: A History*. Austin: University of Texas Press, 2006.

Schiebinger, Londa L. *Colonial Botany: Science, Commerce and Politics in the Early Modern World*. Philadelphia: University of Pennsylvania Press, 2005.

Simon, William Joel. *Scientific Expeditions in the Portuguese Overseas Territories 1783–1808*. Lisbon: Instituto de Investigação Científica Tropical, 1983.

Stempel, Daniel. "Angels of Reason: Science and Myth in the Enlightenment." *Journal of the History of Ideas* 36, no. 1 (1975): 63–78.

Walker, Timothy D. *Doctors, Folk Medicine and the Inquisition: The Repression of Magical Healing in Portugal during the Enlightenment*. Leiden: Brill, 2005.

CHAPTER TWELVE

Juan Antonio Olavarrieta (1765–1822)

Basque Cleric and Libertine Rebel in Mexico

Andrew B. Fisher

In November 1802, state and ecclesiastical officials raided the home of Father Juan Antonio Olavarrieta in the Indian village of Axochitlan in western Mexico. They suspected that he was the author of a seditious pamphlet titled El hombre y el bruto *(Man and Beast) that had attacked both Catholic beliefs and the Spanish monarchy's political authority. For his extensive work in the poorest and most remote parishes in Mexico, the Basque-born Olavarrieta took ideals gleaned both from his reading of banned Enlightenment books and from his extensive circle of correspondents. Olavarrieta fled his Inquisition trial and turned up in Portugal, where he married and began a family; he later returned to Spain to work as a publisher for members of the Masonic order in Cádiz. Historian Andrew Fisher outlines the process by which Olavarrieta came to identify with the cause of liberty and justice, like the more famous Miguel Hidalgo and countless other good-hearted, hardworking parish priests whose work in poor Indian parishes raised their political consciousness. Yet, at the same time, Olavarrieta's own personal licentiousness and occasional unethical behavior highlights the connection between adherence to the ideals of political liberty and a personal life characterized by unchecked libertinism that so often characterized revolutionaries of that era.*

Under the cover of darkness, on the night of November 24, 1802, a small party arrived in Axochitlan, a rural Indian town tucked away in the isolated *tierra caliente* (hot country) of western Mexico. Led by the district's crown magistrate and a priest, the men acted under secret orders from the viceroy to arrest a suspected heretic and traitor named Father Juan Antonio Olavarrieta. When the intruders confronted him at his house, Olavarrieta's initial reaction was to admonish them and refuse to forfeit his keys. As the men began ransacking his home, Olavarrieta smirked and told his captors that "he had the satisfaction of being a Catholic, and that nothing prohibited would be found among his books." Nevertheless, the party soon discovered not only a manuscript that attacked the tenets of the Catholic faith and monarchical government but also other suspicious papers penned in the priest's hand.[1]

Such a raid was not an uncommon occurrence in Axochitlan (today Ajuchitlán), where secular and religious authorities had clashed throughout the late eighteenth century. One of Olavarrieta's immediate predecessors, a former naval chaplain from Corsica, had been involved in similar actions, sometimes even involving rival gangs of armed supporters. Nevertheless, this arrest was much more serious than previous disputes. Both the colonial government and the Inquisition accused Olavarrieta of embracing radical elements of Enlightenment philosophy, ideas that had become associated with the French Revolution and that threatened to spread like a virus throughout the Atlantic world.

For colonial authorities in Mexico, these were uncertain and dangerous times. Unrest among the Indian and multiethnic masses abounded, while some members of the *gente decente* (decent folk), Spaniards like Father Olavarrieta, flirted with heretical ideas that could lead only to social and political calamity. That an obscure parish priest in a backward corner of the colony could be writing and possibly disseminating pernicious attacks against the twin pillars of colonial rule—the Crown and the Church—alarmed officials in Mexico City. How could it have happened? Like all of us, Juan Antonio Olavarrieta was a complex figure whose life and beliefs cannot be reduced simply to the charges against him. Although he dabbled in the ethereal realm of banned ideas, his practical preoccupations also concerned family, friendship, leisure, and financial security. His intellectual activities led to his arrest in 1802, but all these factors shaped his experience in Spain's transatlantic world. It is to this life that we must now turn.

Juan Antonio Olavarrieta's early years remain obscure. He was probably born in 1765 in Munguía, a *villa* (town) in the Cantabria province in the kingdom of Vizcaya in northern Spain. Of Basque descent, Juan Antonio was the second of four known surviving children (and the only son) born to his parents. In his youth, Olavarrieta entered the Franciscan monastery of Aranzazu, near Oñate, from which he may have eventually fled as an apostate.[2] As the rebellious son later explained to his father, "God did not make me for the cloister nor for the wretched dealings of its inhabitants." Lacking the requisite religious rigor, he blamed his ill-fated decision to join the monastery on "the lack of reflection from my few years, ignorance, and education." The idea that antiquated educational institutions bred religious fanaticism would become an important theme in Olavarrieta's outlook, no doubt because of his miserable monastic apprenticeship. Years later, he still expressed regret to sympathizers that his parents had not provided him a different profession, even one as humble as that of a cobbler.[3]

Wanderlust was the proscribed cure for a squandered youth. Ironically, Olavarrieta often financed his journeys by posing as a cleric, including a probable decadelong stint as a chaplain in the Spanish navy. After one such voyage, in early 1791, he found himself in Lima, Peru, where he discovered a passion for newspaper publishing. He began to offer public commentary on topics ranging from the theater to the ill effects of wet nursing in a newspaper he founded called *El Semanario Crítico* (*The Weekly Critic*). The established press was sensitive to the foreigner's critique of local creole society and went on a counterattack, compelling Olavarrieta to return to Spain in January 1792.[4] He eventually settled in the port city of Cádiz, where he established a press in 1795–1796 and ran afoul of royal officials on at least one occasion. He told his inquisitors that it was there that he embraced the heretical Enlightenment ideals that were espoused by many returning French and Francophile exiles following Spain's brief war with France (1793–1795). Indeed, an acquaintance denounced Olavarrieta to Seville's Holy Office in March 1797 for his anticlerical views and clear infatuation with the French Revolution.

Olavarrieta avoided imprisonment only because he had already left Spain the previous October aboard the frigate *Leocadia* bound for Buenos Aires. He and his friend Jacinto Bejerano made their way to Bejerano's hometown of Guayaquil, a once bustling entrepôt fueled by the export of cacao. As with countless other immigrants, Olavarrieta relied on personal connections to make his way in an unfamiliar place. When Bejerano failed him, however, he curried favor with the port's governor, Colonel Juan de Mata Urbina, and solicited aid from a group of *paisanos* (countrymen), presumably other Basque immigrants. Olavarrieta cultivated the patronage of the Baron de Carondelet (1747–1807), a former governor-general of Spanish Louisiana and incoming president of the Audiencia of Quito, whom he met while they were both lodging at Urbina's house. Olavarrieta boasted in a letter to a friend that, thanks to these connections, "I play more roles in Guayaquil than [Prime Minister] Pitt does in Great Britain and [Napoleon] Bonaparte does in Egypt." He bragged of an ambitious but failed public baths project to erect a "beautiful floating building" that may have lost money but secured the governor's admiration for his bold and creative ideas. Business deals in Panama, facilitated by the friendships he established with maritime captains, may have helped to offset his losses. Olavarrieta relied on his wide social network not only to build his material assets but also to stimulate his burgeoning interest in heretical philosophy. He and Governor Urbina participated in a local *tertulia* (political discussion group), which was a growing fad throughout Spanish America. Often held in salons of well-to-do households, these social gatherings facilitated the discussion of the latest banned Enlightenment treatises trickling into Spain and its American colonies.

Olavarrieta departed Guayaquil for New Spain (today Mexico) in early 1800. He later confessed to the Inquisition that he left because he was unable to secure a parish position in Guayaquil despite the governor's patronage. In letters to his family, Olavarrieta blamed the area's excessive heat and humidity for his transfer, perhaps out of a sense of embarrassment at his failure to procure a post. To his father, Olavarrieta cited his continuing financial difficulties. The prodigal son explained that his "many voyages to America" had been fueled by a desire "to learn about as much of this world that it offers." He also claimed to have finally procured license to serve as a secular clergy— a claim the Mexican Inquisition would later find suspect—and that it was his sole intention to acquire a small savings that would enable him to return to Spain to live comfortably among his books and papers. Although Olavarrieta professed a desire for an appointment in Acapulco—another prominent but also balmy port—his choice of destination was no doubt influenced by the prominent connections that Governor Urbina enjoyed in Mexico City through his wife's family.

At the time of Olavarrieta's arrival, New Spain was experiencing the effects of decades of social, political, and economic upheaval. Mexico was a prosperous colony riddled with endemic poverty, governed efficiently yet strained by widening socioeconomic inequalities and rising ethnic tensions that were in part exacerbated by misguided royal policy. Olavarrieta's relocation further coincided with the Crown's concerted efforts to introduce modern scientific institutions—such as the Royal College of Surgery (1768), the Botanical Garden and Chair (1787), and the School of Mining (1791)—to facilitate a more rational extraction of its natural and financial resources.[5] This energetic and self-interested scientific movement was both a boon and a curse for the Crown. The modernization of scientific knowledge in fields such as agriculture, medicine, and mining offered great potential for social and economic improvement. Nonetheless, royal officials understood that intellectual curiosity could also lead to the dissemination of politically dangerous ideas. From their pulpits, priests launched tirades against the French Revolution, and paranoid colonial officials saw the potential for Jacobin conspiracy around every corner.[6] Olavarrieta likewise cursed Napoleon, but, in contrast to others who opposed Bonaparte's imperial ambitions and domination of the Church, he lamented the betrayal of the radical antiaristocratic ideals of the early revolution. Olavarrieta's intellectual trajectory confirmed official fears that unchecked access to foreign ideas could lead to republican treason.

Olavarrieta wasted little time reaching out to the men involved in Mexico's new scientific projects, mostly through Governor Urbina's mother-in-law. Perhaps the most prominent was Fausto de Elhuyar y de Zubice (1755–1833), an accomplished chemist, administrator of the Mexican mining industry, and the discoverer of tungsten. Olavarrieta could hardly avoid comparing his own life with that of his fellow Spanish-born Basque. While Olavarrieta had languished under the antiquated education of his monastic cell, don Fausto and his equally precocious brother had been funded by the Royal Basque Society of the Friends of the Country to further their studies abroad. After scientific training in France and Central Europe, Elhuyar arrived in New Spain in 1788 as the general director of the Royal Corps of Mining (and later the director of the new College of Mining). Olavarrieta also befriended fellow Spaniards Martín de Sessé y Lacasta (1751–1808), the director of the Royal Botanical Expedition to New Spain; Andrés Manuel del Río (1764–1849), who taught chemistry at Elhuyar's College of Mining; and Vicente Cervantes (1755–1829), who arrived in Mexico in 1787 to introduce Linnaean biology, reform the colony's medical establishment, and serve as the director of the recently established Botanical Garden.[7] These accomplished scientists evidently tolerated the self-taught former monk, but their relationships must have been fairly one sided.

Despite his intellectual inclinations, Olavarrieta's first concern was to obtain employment. The post in Acapulco did not materialize, but his contacts and letters of recommendation did secure an itinerant position in Pénjamo (the birthplace of the insurgent priest Miguel Hidalgo). Rural life was unappealing, and constant travel meant that he lacked a suitable home for himself and his library. Frustrated, Olavarrieta considered his talents unappreciated and neglected. In a letter to Manuel Abad y Queipo (1751–1825), the future bishop-elect of Michoacán, he insisted that he could spearhead numerous public works projects if he were only better situated. Many of his suggestions touched on the very issues that most concerned imperial reformers, including women's education, theater reform, the inability of poorhouses to prevent begging and promote industry, and the improvement and protection of Spain's maritime channels. These useful suggestions may appear to have been an inconsistent position for an accused traitor, but Olavarrieta had a tried-and-true strategy of ingratiating himself to persons of power and influence.

Relief of sorts came relatively quickly. By September 1800, Olavarrieta was assigned to the parish of Axochitlan, a mostly indigenous settlement in the remote and sparsely populated *tierra caliente*. Like so many disillusioned Spanish newcomers before him, Olavarrieta found the region wanting "due to the ignorance and inertia of its dwellers, . . . its excessive heat and . . . piercing mosquitoes . . . and absolutely destitute of all that is Art, Science, Culture, and rational interaction." Furthermore, the libertine cleric considered the local women so deficient that he had "found it convenient to reiterate my solemn vow of chastity, [and] to remain celibate for four or five years."

Olavarrieta appraised the economic potential of his new position and started to imagine how he might accumulate the necessary funds to finance his eventual retirement in Spain. Considering his predecessors' experience, Olavarrieta identified several potential means to this end. Of these, he eliminated several options, particularly the merchandizing of "trinkets and trifles," reporting to an associate that it "does not fit my disposition because I enjoy living with all possible comfort and with the greatest decorum." He determined that the sugarcane business was the best alternative. Olavarrieta began consulting local experts and decided that he would plant cane immediately and construct a small grinding mill the following year. For his project, Olavarrieta located a suitable tract of land with sufficient water and secured a manager to direct the estate's daily operation.

Sugar production, however, required significant capital, which Olavarrieta lacked. As he had done in Guayaquil, the priest sought financial assistance from his network of social and intellectual associates, including Fausto de Elhuyar, who suggested instead that he fatten hogs. Olavarrieta turned eventually to the Count of Contramina, don José Pérez de Soñanes, whose predecessor had been an active investor in the region's mines. In a letter to the count dated February 18, 1801, Olavarrieta estimated that a hacienda could be established for less than 30,000 pesos and would pay its investment within three years. He acknowledged the substantial financial risk of such a venture but reminded his patron of his modest and worthy aspirations to secure nothing more than enough money for a "little country house close to a capital" where he and a "faithful companion" could fawn over their guests. While Soñanes seemed interested, Olavarrieta nonetheless also heeded Elhuyar's advice by quietly forming a partnership to raise hogs with a down-

and-out former taxidermist and surgeon of the royal botanical expedition to Guatemala.

Nearly as compelling as his goal to secure financial security was Olavarrieta's desire for refined society. The Axochitlan post enabled Olavarrieta to establish a stable residence, which he immediately sought to furnish with the appropriate accoutrement of a man of his station: servants, wine, books, and a vegetable garden (for which Elhuyar sent him a watering can as a gift). He regaled the area's wealthy creole ranchers with wine, hot chocolate, and other delicacies—usually with an eye toward improving his economic lot—but, overall, he considered his parishioners to be a rustic and ignorant people. By November 1800, he wrote to his circle of associates in Mexico City entreating them to visit during the initial stages of the dry season, when the area's stifling temperatures briefly abated. He declared his home fit for a viceroy, offered horses for their transportation, and promised them a barrel of wine and fresh vegetables from his garden. Shockingly, Olavarrieta depicted a parish that was bitterly (even violently) divided along class and ethnic lines as an ideal holiday spot, one where his guests would be cheered by the dances of "little Indian girls" and soothed by walks along a nearby river.

Olavarrieta realized that his coveted parish post was turning out to be a mixed blessing. While it provided him with a steady income, he had also returned to a world that he considered tainted by fanaticism and ignorance. Isolation exacerbated his melancholy and desperation. News from home was lacking, causing him to beseech one associate returning to Spain to search out and console his parents, who knew nothing of their son's fate since he left Guayaquil. He read of his Mexico City acquaintances' trips to places like Paris with feelings of envy and loss. Olavarrieta expressed frustration for having been forced into a profession he despised, wasting away in an obscure post just as a brilliant new era of science and modernity was about to dawn. His semiprivate musings depict a solitary figure longing for the company of Governor Urbina and his mother-in-law, Elhuyar, Vicente Cervantes, and their learned compatriots.

The wayward cleric's desire to participate in the birth of an era of modernity and reason helps explain the origins of his manuscript, "El hombre y el bruto" ("Man and Beast"). The brief essay, comprising some twenty-four handwritten pages, was dedicated to his old friend Urbina, with whom he continued to correspond, "as the first fruits of the meditations that I practiced after finding myself established in the absent solitude of my friends." The treatise's fundamental point is that the distinction between man and beast is a false dichotomy. The differentiation is usually justified, Olavarrieta pointed out, because animals are thought to be purely physical beings while humans have been blessed with a soul. Such a hierarchy of existence, however, must be rejected as a "delirium," akin to the hallucinations of a patient on opium. Olavarrieta argued that the myth of human exceptionalism rests entirely on the equally erroneous belief in the existence of supernatural entities like the soul, spirits, and deities. All notions not firmly rooted in the material world are simply products of human imagination, and it is only when these falsehoods are rejected that one is able to discern humanity's true design. The impartial reader must look to nature, therefore, which "tells us that between man and beast there is no other difference than that between the polyp and the monkey."

Observation of nature reveals the similarities between humanity and the animal world. "Man," Olavarrieta declared, "is susceptible to ideas, combines them, deduces them, and for this reason is called . . . a rational entity." The paradox, once the notion of the soul is dismissed, is that animals can master the same operations and yet are considered "irrational." Does not the tiger learn to hunt in the same manner as a "man of industry and talent" learns to subdue the tiger? Nature also yields many examples of intelligent social organization, such as the industrious beehive or the flocks of swallows that migrate in anticipation of inclement weather. Domestic animals demonstrate even further the power of rational thought and the benefits of proper "education": horses anticipate when it is time to eat, canaries learn which notes sound pleasing to their masters, while elephants quickly grasp human concepts and language.

Olavarrieta did not deny differences existed between species, only that human beings had reached a higher degree of "perfection." The apostate blamed organized religion and its educational institutions for propagating the myth of humanity's unique position. Primitive people had rationalized the fearsome aspects of nature by conjuring up supernatural beings. Cults and specialized personnel then developed to satiate these deities, while ambitious "tyrants" used religion to subjugate society, depriving its members of their "natural liberty." Blasphemously, he stated that the Judeo-Christian tradition was no exception. Olavarrieta declared that the revelations of Moses, a man of refinement raised in the Egyptian court, were nothing more than a charlatan's ruse designed to subdue the barbaric, fearful, and superstitious Hebrews. By implication, Olavarrieta denounced the very notion of the Divine Right of Kings to rule over their credulous populations.

Olavarrieta's private musings reached a public audience when he made a brief trip to Mexico City in July 1802. In his absence, a snooping church notary discovered the seditious manuscript and began to circulate it. The essay reached the attention of a priest in the nearby settlement of Cutzamala and the royal district magistrate, both of whom immediately denounced the author to authorities in Mexico City. To their eyes, the essay intended to do nothing less than "to deny the rational soul, destroy sacred scripture, revelation, tradition, authority, and consequently the Catholic religion and monarchical government, treating the latter as pure, tyrannical oppression of the liberty of man." Three state prosecutors concurred, describing the text as "the most monstrous birth of heresies and impiety that hell has vomited." The matter became even more urgent with the discovery of a proposed engraving for the essay that suggested that Olavarrieta intended to circulate the manuscript through a clandestine press. The priest's correspondence also revealed that he had a broad transatlantic network of friends, spanning from Guayaquil to Mexico City to Spain, with whom he had shared his ideas and who had not seen fit to denounce him. State authorities would have to move quickly if they wished to uncover the true extent of this conspiracy.

The wheels of justice moved slowly, however, and Olavarrieta languished under house arrest in Axochitlan until his transfer to Mexico City in February 1803. In the meantime, the prisoner composed a series of petitions to the viceroy in which he fumed that his imprisonment was a scandalous affront to his honor as a Spaniard and a priest. Initially, Olavarrieta feigned ignorance about the discovered manuscript. Nearly a month after his arrest, in a letter dated December 21, 1802, he finally broached the subject with a caveat to the viceroy that if it proved irrelevant to the case, he "should deposit this matter in the recess of your heart with an inviolable seal." What followed was a shrewdly calculated exposition of lies, half-truths, and rationalized excuses. Olavarrieta confessed that he held a treatise for "many years," which he eventually forgot about since it remained filed away in a drawer. The manuscript had surfaced only when two "inconsiderate young men" rifled through his possessions in his absence. Although he considered the subsequent denunciation understandable, his accusers lacked the capacity to understand fully the meaning of the text. Like the planets that appear from a distance to be small globes, the treatise would most assuredly appear in a different light on closer and more careful examination.

Olavarrieta asserted that his treatise was nothing more than a compilation, or extract, of the "most shocking ideas of Mirabeau's system of nature, Rousseau's equality of men, Helvétius's book De l'espirit," and other thoughts derived from "the new philosophers."[8] Distancing himself from authorship, Olavarrieta blamed his misspent youth, the vices of a maritime occupation, and his vain desire to appear intelligent for why he had safeguarded the manuscript. While acting as a naval chaplain, Olavarrieta claimed to have traveled for over a decade throughout the Atlantic, a zone populated by "unbelievers, libertines, and sectarians." And like a torrential rainfall, in each of these ports—"on board the ships, in the cafes and inns"—one must grow accustomed to "dealing with learned people, encountering prohibited books, and discovering curious papers." Although he confessed to possessing an unquenchable curiosity and appetite for prohibited books, he argued that his only ambition had been to perform well in the company of others. For a chaplain to keep silent during the frequent conversations over the nature of religion and its origins, Olavarrieta averred, brought "the greatest ignominy" and the judgment that he was a "vile man capable of betraying the liberty of others." Rather than embracing any heretical or seditious ideas, Olavarrieta claimed that he composed the essay only as a way to master these new concepts so that he could "live with all and all classes of people in friendship and trust." In fact, as a cleric responsible for the souls of those he served, he always read the objectionable tracts in private to avoid the slightest public scandal. He reminded the viceroy that he should not be held accountable for his subordinates' indiscreet exploration of his carefully guarded and locked materials from which they "disinterr[ed] from the tomb of my papers a literary mummy!" Although he should not have had the manuscript in the first place, Olavarrieta countered that one cannot blame the stone for the injury caused by the party who threw it.

When Olavarrieta finally reached Mexico City on February 13, 1803, he was placed in seclusion in a monastery to await his trial. Despite earlier protests that flight was beneath his station, the prisoner escaped on the night of February 25. Inquisition and state agents paid visits to Olavarrieta's associates the next morning and learned that he had visited botanist don José Moziño, whom the Inquisition subsequently suggested the viceroy ought to threaten with arrest "since he will fear bayonets more than excommunication." Friends eventually persuaded Olavarrieta to turn himself in to authorities.[9]

An aborted escape proved to be the rogue cleric's last act of defiance. His Inquisition trial was held between February 28 and March 22, and he was sentenced on May 27, 1803. At a private *auto-da-fé*, he was excommunicated, stripped of his office and all property gained since the time of his heresy, exiled from Spain's overseas empire, and remanded to the Holy Office in Spain for final sentencing. Six other prominent citizens also faced fines ranging from 25 to 500 pesos for sharing and discussing the banned discourse, including Cervantes, del Río, Moziño, and Pérez de Soñanes.

On February 29, 1804, a defeated Olavarrieta appeared for a final time before the inquisitors. He confessed to composing "El hombre y el bruto" in Axochitlan so that Governor Urbina might recall "our old conversations over these matters." He then recanted his treatise as the product of idleness that amounted to nothing more than a work of "nonsense or a youthful prank." He emphasized that he never intended to corrupt anyone, and assured them that Urbina had never received a copy. The governor had expressed an interest in reading it, but the risk of shipping the document was too great. Nonetheless, Olavarrieta recalled that in a later letter Urbina had claimed to "have read the Gospel in triumph," which had removed many of his doubts and transformed him into a "different man." He advised Olavarrieta to read his Bible faithfully and to disregard Mirabeau and "try to become a good priest." The prisoner suggested that he entertained similar doubts, thus explaining why he had never sent Urbina the manuscript.

Authorities seized and auctioned Olavarrieta's property for the modest sum of 1,260 pesos. Unfortunately for the state, the proceeds did not cover the expenses related to his imprisonment, trial, and exile. Several outstanding loans in the priest's name, held by prominent men and others in Axochitlan, Mexico City, and Puebla, fell in arrears and were never recovered. Olavarrieta's efforts to leave the New World with the means to secure a comfortable retirement had vanished. After an inexplicable delay that caused his health to deteriorate and his depression to grow, Juan Antonio Olavarrieta stepped on board the frigate *Anfitrite* on June 9, 1804, to face his fate in Spain. We do not know how the renegade monk dealt with his uncertain future, but one suspects not well. Details are lacking, but by 1806–1807, he somehow made his way to Portugal, where he managed to procure a medical certificate, establish a rural practice, and marry. His exile endured for over thirteen years.

An aging Olavarrieta made his way back to Cádiz in 1820 after the Riego Revolt brought a liberal-minded government to power in Spain. Adopting the pseudonym José Joaquín de Clararrosa and securing the financial support of the city's freemasons, Olavarrieta began to publish a newspaper called the *Diario Gaditano (The Cádiz Daily)* in September 1820. Rumors concerning his past apostasy, travels, romances, and imprisonment only added mystique to the celebrity he soon gained for his attacks on religion and his promotion of free trade and free love. Conservatives were appalled to learn that the name "Clararrosa" might have referred to the fugitive monk's past wives, lovers, or children, but it may have been nothing more than a sentimental touch of bravado that combined the names of two of his sisters. As Clararrosa, Olavarrieta wrote a series of controversial pieces, including an article that supported Spanish American independence, resulting in his brief imprisonment in March 1821. Denouncing his former persecutors, he also published an exposé on the secret jails and procedures of the by-then-moribund Inquisition. Clararrosa alleged that he had received the harrowing account from a certain Father Juan Antonio Olavarrieta, whose tragic story he felt compelled to recount. Even after a rival exposed the journalist's true identity, Clararrosa maintained the fiction by publishing a fabricated obituary of his alter ego Olavarrieta in April 1821.

Antonio Alcalá Galiano, a contemporary liberal writer, reported that Olavarrieta's publications enjoyed the support of Cádiz's baser elements and the provincial authorities' protection. Always a renegade, Clararrosa/Olavarrieta faced the second tribunal of his life in January 1822, this time comprising a hostile group of fellow libertines rather than the enforcers of religious fanaticism. According to Galiano, Olavarrieta performed poorly, unable to present himself as a proper mason fluent with the group's terminology and etiquette. The subsequent rift with the masons spelled his doom. Soon, the city authorities imprisoned him over an offensive article. News spread that from his cell Olavarrieta had denounced some of his former supporters for abandoning him. Released from prison on January 26 for health reasons, he died the following day.

Olavarrieta's final instructions reflected his lifelong ambition and antagonism. He asked to be buried with a book of the Spanish constitution opened to the article that referred to the sovereignty of the people. He also requested that his body be viewed by the public and that no clerics or crosses be present. Rather than having masses offered for his departed soul, patriotic national hymns were to be sung instead. According to an account published in the newspaper La Voz de la Religión (The Voice of Religion) in 1838, Olavarrieta's body was paraded through the streets of Cádiz, with the martyred libertine's weapon of choice, a pen, placed in his hand. An immense crowd bearing olive leaves sang about liberty, transforming the burial into a patriotic display. The corpse was shrouded in white cloth, and various escorts carried branches of myrtle and laurel alongside the coffin. The procession marched to the Plaza de Constitución and stopped pointedly below the balcony of the Masonic leader blamed for Olavarrieta's death. Eulogies were offered at the cemetery as the body was interred.[10] The apostate priest and libertine journalist, one of the Atlantic world's most fascinating and enigmatic wanderers, had finally come home to rest.

Bibliography and Suggested Reading

Anna, Timothy E. *Spain and the Loss of America*. Lincoln: University of Nebraska Press, 1983.

Archer, Christon, ed. *The Birth of Modern Mexico, 1780–1814*. Wilmington, DE: Scholarly Resources, 2003.

Brading, D. A. *The First America: The Spanish Monarchy, Creole Patriots and the Liberal State, 1492–1866*. New York: Cambridge University Press, 1993.

Cañizares-Esguerra, Jorge. *Nature, Empire and Nation: Explorations of the History of Science in the Iberian World*. Stanford, CA: Stanford University Press, 2006.

Chambers, Sarah C. "Letters and Salons: Women Reading and Writing the Nation." In *Beyond Imagined Communities: Reading and Writing the Nation in Nineteenth-Century Latin America*, edited by Sara Castro-Klarén and John Charles Chasteen, 54–83. Baltimore: Johns Hopkins University Press, 2003.

Connaughton, Brian F. *Clerical Ideology in a Revolutionary Age: The Guadalajara Church and the Idea of the Mexican Nation (1788–1853)*. Translated by Mark Alan Healey. Calgary and Boulder: University of Calgary Press and University Press of Colorado, 2003.

Farriss, Nancy M. *Crown and Clergy in Colonial Mexico, 1759–1821: The Crisis of Ecclesiastical Privilege*. London: Athlone Press, 1968.

Hampe-Martínez, Teodoro. "The Diffusion of Books and Ideas in Colonial Peru: A Study of Private Libraries in the Sixteenth and Seventeenth Centuries." *Hispanic American Historical Review* 73, no. 2 (1993): 211–33.

Johnson, Lyman. "The Subversive Nature of Private Acts: Juan Barbarín and the 1795 French Conspiracy in Buenos Aires." In *The Human Tradition in Colonial Latin America*, edited by Kenneth Andrien, 259–77. Wilmington, DE: Scholarly Resources, 2002.

Taylor, William B. *Magistrates of the Sacred: Priests and Parishioners in Eighteenth-Century Mexico*. Stanford, CA: Stanford University Press, 1996.

Viqueira Albán, Juan Pedro. *Propriety and Permissiveness in Bourbon Mexico*. Translated by Sonya Lipsett-Rivera and Sergio Rivera Ayala. Wilmington, DE: SR Books, 1999.

CHAPTER THIRTEEN

Eliza Fenwick (1766–1840)

Feminist Slave Owner in Barbados

Olwyn M. Blouet

Eliza Fenwick was an English writer and intellectual who was a member of the radical literary group that included Mary Wollstonecraft, Mary Hays, William Godwin, and John Fenwick during the 1790s. Women in the circle were early feminists who advocated women's rights and equal education. In their many energetic writings, they drew comparisons between women's place in patriarchal European societies and that of the oppressed African slave. With her family's economic well-being constantly undermined by her spendthrift husband, Fenwick separated from him and tried to earn an independent living as a governess and a writer of children's books. She emigrated to Barbados, where she operated an elite school for white girls and struggled to reconcile her idealization of freedom with life in a Caribbean slave society. Her life reveals the uncomfortable ways in which the notion of freedom and slavery coexisted in the minds and practices of late eighteenth- and early nineteenth-century Atlantic people.

Mary Wollstonecraft, the most famous feminist in eighteenth-century Britain, author of *A Vindication of the Rights of Woman* (1792), died in 1797, eleven days after giving birth to her daughter Mary Godwin, who grew up to marry the romantic poet Percy Bysshe Shelley and write the famous novel *Frankenstein* (1818). As Wollstonecraft lay dying, two close friends, Mary Hays and Eliza Fenwick, were at her side. Hays and Fenwick, like Wollstonecraft, were early feminist writers who favored women's rights and equal education. They held ideas about natural rights and liberty and believed that women were economically and sexually exploited. As feminists, they criticized the dependent nature of women in society. All three authors used images of slavery in their writings to describe the treatment of women in contemporary British society, which they described as the slavery of their sex.

This is the story of Eliza Fenwick, a woman who struggled to earn enough to support herself and two children after her husband John, a political activist and writer, got their family into debt. Few jobs were available to educated, middle-class women, but, like Mary Wollstonecraft before her, Eliza Fenwick gamely tried several occupations. She worked in a bookshop in London, wrote popular children's books, and became a governess in Ireland. But who would have thought that Eliza would move to the slave society of Barbados and open a school? Who would have believed that the feminist author Fenwick eventually would buy slaves, own men, and experience a very different life across the Atlantic Ocean?

Not much is known about Eliza's early years. Born Elizabeth Jago in Cornwall, England, on February 1, 1766, in 1788 she married John Fenwick, who was a friend of Mary Wollstonecraft's husband William Godwin. In the 1790s, the two couples were part of a London intellectual circle that included radical publishers such as Joseph Johnson and Thomas Holcroft (who tutored the family of the abolitionist Granville Sharpe), authors Charles and Mary Lamb and Henry Crabb Robinson, the scientist Joseph Priestley, and the reformer Francis Place. Female writers in this circle included Helena Maria Williams, Elizabeth Inchbald, Anna Laetitia Barbauld, and Amelia Alderson Opie—all of whom were well-educated intellectuals who influenced popular taste. Inspired by the Enlightenment and the ideals of the French Revolution, many in the group questioned the prevailing political and social system by calling for reform of the old order. Mary Wollstonecraft went to Paris in 1792 to experience the French Revolution, as did Eliza's husband, John, who made contact with the revolutionary French government on behalf of British radicals. John Fenwick was an Irish nationalist who edited the republican paper *Albion* before it was closed down by the British government for being too extreme.

Eliza Fenwick herself was involved in London's radical, literary scene and published her well-received, feminist novel *Secresy* [sic]: *or, The Ruin on the Rock*, in 1795. *Secresy*, written in epistolary mode and her only work intended for adults, investigated the nature of women and the role education played in molding their character, a theme popularized by French Enlightenment theorist Jean-Jacques Rousseau. Her heroine, Sibella, was confined to a castle and denied an education by her guardian uncle, fell in love, and entered into a sexual relationship that culminated in a pregnancy and Sibella's untimely death. The work warned against secrecy, excessive sentiment, and the failure to provide women with an education. Central to the novel is the close female bond between Sibella and her friend Caroline. Recently, feminist scholars like Ranita Chatterjee have interpreted *Secresy* as a radical book that challenged contemporary gender narratives and contributed to the nonconformist trends of the 1790s.

Unfortunately, writing and editing did not generate enough income, and the Fenwick family fell further into debt. In 1800, John Fenwick left for Dublin to avoid his creditors. There were two children from the marriage— Eliza Anne, born in 1789, and Orlando, born in 1798. Eliza Fenwick had to earn enough money to support herself plus two children. After 1806, John Fenwick was confined to the area around London's Fleet prison for debt, and Eliza separated from him, preferring to pass herself off as a widow later in life when she went to Barbados.

Left to her own devices, Eliza Fenwick tried several jobs. In 1799, she operated an infant school with six pupils, but the business was unprofitable. She remained in contact with literary friends and began to publish children's books, such as *Mary and her Cat* (1804) and *The Life of Carlo, the Famous Dog of Drury Lane Theatre* (1804), which was modeled on a real dog who had rocketed to public fame the year earlier. In 1805, her antislavery book for children, titled *Visits to the Juvenile Library*, appeared. The story involved five wealthy orphans in the slave society of Jamaica and their black nurse Nora. They arrived in England unlettered and suspicious of reading. Eventually, the children's guardian introduced them to the pleasures and benefits of books. Nora, who had been a slave in Jamaica, learned to read and was converted to the idea that knowledge, not ignorance, led to happiness. In this book, Mrs. Fenwick painted a shocking picture of the children of rich West Indian planters who had been corrupted by life in a slave society. She emphasized that all their wealth had not managed to provide them with either a decent education or a humane character. The idealistic author hoped to convince her readers that education could erase the mental enslavement of both masters and slaves. Her charming little book also served to publicize and legitimize the emerging business of children's literature, an enterprise from which she hoped to profit personally as well.

Two years later, in 1807, Mrs. Fenwick agreed to manage William Godwin's children's bookstore, known as the Juvenile Library, in London. She only remained there for a few months, complaining to her correspondent Mary Hays that she had sold herself into slavery. Eliza continued to write children's books, publishing several successful titles, including *Lessons for*

Children: or Rudiments of Good Manners, Morals and Humanity (1809), *Infantile Stories* (1810), and *Rays from the Rainbow* (1812). Some were published by Godwin, others by Tabart & Company. Her most successful book, *Lessons for Children*, went into many editions and was translated into French. The "Lessons" had a didactic purpose. The story of the "The Bad Family" had characters like Fighting Harry, Idle Richard, and Selfish Sara; in contrast, "The Good Family" included Studious Arthur and Patient Emma. The moral of her stories was that children should be honest, obedient, hardworking, and studious—all the virtues of middle-class, capitalist society. Although some of Fenwick's books sold well (e.g., *Infantile Stories* was already in its fifteenth edition in 1819), she never made much money as a writer. It seems that she was paid a flat fee for her stories rather than continuing royalties. She always felt exploited as a woman writing in a man's world.

In 1808, Eliza Fenwick accompanied her actress daughter, Eliza Anne, to Belfast, where they thought the cost of living would be relatively cheap. Eliza Anne had a role in the theater, and Mrs. Fenwick became a governess with the Mocatta household, a Jewish family that had five children. She was not happy as a governess. In her letters, she complained of overwork and exploitation. Responsible for teaching a wide range of subjects, including English, history, geography, and French, she was also expected to teach piano and singing, which she found exhausting. She later took a position with another Irish family, but, with her son's educational expenses mounting, she found it difficult to survive on her meager salary. The proud feminist hated having to lodge with a family, chronically short of money, and living in a dependent situation.

In 1814, Eliza Fenwick made a dramatic bid for independence. She traveled to Barbados to join her actress daughter, who had gone to the Caribbean island to a well-paying job in Mr. Dyke's drama company in 1811. Mrs. Fenwick was nervous about her daughter working in the theater in Bridgetown, the capital of Barbados. As she hinted in *Visits to the Juvenile Library*, she believed that the West Indian slave society led to ignorance and illiteracy, even among affluent whites. In stereotypical fashion, she felt that all planters were drunkards and sex maniacs and most definitely did not want her daughter to marry one. She also worried about the horrors of slavery. At first, daughter Eliza Anne wrote home describing Barbados as a land of promise; she enjoyed grand dinners and an extravagant lifestyle, her theatrical productions went well, and she attained a measure of success. Even the governor attended her performances. She reported that domestic slaves were lazy and impertinent. There were always three or four slaves to do the work of one person. But soon enough Eliza Anne was informing her mother of the groans and cries of beaten Negroes that kept her awake at night. They dared not strike a white man even in their own defense.

If she had misgivings about living in a slave society, Mrs. Fenwick put them aside in 1814 to be with her daughter, who had married a fellow actor, Mr. Rutherford. She especially wanted to see her new grandson who was born in 1813. Mother and daughter planned to run a girls' school together, and Mrs. Fenwick turned down an invitation to be governess to the grandchildren of the Barbados attorney general, Mr. Beccles. She had always dreamed of being independent and running her own business, and if she had to cross the Atlantic Ocean in order to achieve it, she would.

What was Barbados like when Eliza Fenwick arrived there in 1814? The island had been a part of the British Empire continuously since 1624 and had never fallen into French hands as so many Caribbean islands had during the eighteenth century. The island's economy initially relied on the production of tobacco, cotton, and ginger, worked by indentured laborers from the British Isles until the "Sugar Revolution" of the 1640s changed everything. Sugar cultivation and production were introduced by the Dutch from Brazil, accompanied by the importation of enslaved African laborers and the development of large-scale plantation agriculture. Many of the small landowners and indentured laborers who had served their time soon moved to the American mainland, especially South Carolina. During the seventeenth and eighteenth centuries, many Barbadian planters (if they survived disease) became wealthy and held political power in the island legislature. Some became absentee planters in Britain, where they got involved in the influential West India lobby.

In 1814, Barbados had a total population of almost 100,000. Most were slaves, but approximately 15 percent were resident whites—a large proportion by West Indian standards. White females outnumbered white males. There were a few thousand "free coloreds" (some quite affluent), although a strict color line existed, as Eliza Anne observed when she reported that no coloreds attended her performances at the theater in Bridgetown. The slave trade had been abolished by the British Parliament in 1807, but the Barbadian slave population (unlike that of most Caribbean islands) continued to grow by natural increase. Abolitionists in Britain, such as William Wilberforce, were in favor of freeing slaves throughout the British Empire, an action that finally was legislated by the British Parliament in 1833.

Mrs. Fenwick and her sixteen-year-old son Orlando arrived in Barbados in October 1814, toward the end of the Napoleonic Wars. On the way across the Atlantic, the ship stopped at Cove, Ireland, and the Portuguese island colony of Madeira, where she savored abundant, cheap fruit. On arriving in

Barbados, Mrs. Fenwick complained about tropical insects, extreme heat, and ill health, but she soon settled down to run the school with her daughter. Mrs. Fenwick continued to write to her friend Mary Hays telling her that the school had been successful in attracting the daughters of affluent white families. By the spring of 1815, thirty pupils were enrolled. Although Mrs. Fenwick admitted that the fees were high, ranging from £10 to £40 per year, depending on lessons, her most important consideration was that the school operated profitably. The school offered a range of subjects. Mr. Rutherford taught writing, arithmetic, and geography; Mrs. Fenwick covered English, French, and music; and Eliza Anne had eight pupils in dance. The aim of the school was to prepare young ladies to enter polite society (in Britain, it was hoped) and be polished in the arts of music, dance, and conversation. It was a Barbadian finishing school, designed to provide social graces and prepare females for the marriage market.

The biggest aggravation for Mrs. Fenwick was running the domestic scene and managing the hired workers, who were slaves. She complained to Mary Hays about sticky-fingered house slaves and moaned about how idle and un-grateful they were. Expecting to get a good day's work for a good day's pay, she did not grasp the fact that it was the slave *owner* who received the pay for work performed by slaves. There was no incentive for her hired slaves to excel. Although frustrated, Mrs. Fenwick placed the blame for all the vices in Barbadian society on the masters and the institution of slavery, which she described as horrid and disgraceful. She hated the way female slaves were used as prostitutes because offspring became the property of the owner. Male owners were addicted to their female slaves, she believed.

In the summer of 1815, Eliza Anne had a second baby boy, and Mrs. Fenwick continued to battle the slave domestics. She was annoyed by their disobedience and dishonesty. Unable to order a whipping or to threaten them with reassignment to plantation labor, Eliza felt powerless. Strange as it may seem, she saw herself enslaved in her role as hirer and manager of slaves. She was dependent on slave labor and resented her continuing dependency.

The family-run school prospered and grew. In August 1815, a total of forty-two little scholars attended, including a few boarders who paid extra. The Fenwicks moved to larger premises in Bridgetown, with a fine house and several storehouses, one of which they rented out for additional income. Mrs. Fenwick reported to Mary Hays that everything was going well and that she would soon be able to repay her loans. This moment was the high point of Eliza Fenwick's Atlantic life. It was followed by three common problems associated with living in the Caribbean. First, Barbados experienced a fierce slave revolt that made her ill with fear. Then a hurricane hit the island, causing deaths and severe damage. Finally, and most devastating, she lost her beloved son Orlando to the dreaded disease of yellow fever. All these traumatic events happened between April and November 1816.

In the spring, a large-scale slave revolt rocked Barbados. In the Caribbean islands, where slaves heavily outnumbered whites, slave rebellions were more frequent than on the American mainland. The Barbadian slave uprising, known as Bussa's Rebellion, broke out in April 1816, causing chaos and fear. Several whites were killed, martial law was declared, and many slaves were executed or transported. Mrs. Fenwick became physically sick with terror, and the family expected her to die. The economic impact on Barbados was severe because of property damage and loss of the sugarcane crop, which had been burned by slaves during the revolt. The Fenwicks' business also was badly affected because the school closed for a quarter and some clients could not pay school fees because of their own business losses.

Then, in October, a hurricane bore down on Barbados for several days. Hurricanes form off the African coast and sweep across the Atlantic Ocean annually from June to November. They frequently touch the Caribbean islands, bringing death and destruction with them. In the days before satellite imagery and the weather forecasts on television, hurricane season was unpredictable and frightening. Mrs. Fenwick wrote extensively about the property destruction, the deaths of several acquaintances, and the difficulty of buying food. Although her family managed to buy biscuits and salt fish, her one-year-old grandson needed milk, which was unavailable.

Still, worse was to come. Mrs. Fenwick's son Orlando came down with yellow fever, a deadly disease carried by mosquitoes. After a brief and painful illness, the seventeen-year-old died in November 1816 on the cusp of manhood and full of promise and prospects. Orlando had been working for a Barbadian merchant house, and his career path looked good. Mother Fenwick was devastated by her loss but kept going for her surviving family's sake. Eliza Anne had her third child, a daughter named Elizabeth, in 1817. The new mother became ill and was ordered to take a sea voyage in the spring of 1818. The trip to Demerara (now Guyana) proved refreshing, but on her return to Barbados, she was not well enough to help much with the school.

Mrs. Fenwick hired an English widow to superintend her household's domestic affairs. Widowhood was common in Barbados, and Eliza arranged for the woman, her two daughters, plus several domestic slaves to live with the Fenwick household. In this way, she liberated herself so that she could concentrate on teaching rather than managing slave labor, which she detested. She also hired a male assistant, at a high salary, to cover arithmetic and writing and a little later engaged a French woman to teach the classes in her native language. Several pupils left the school when their families emigrated, but forty still remained. Life was good. The Fenwicks enjoyed a large house and good food. Eliza Anne was acting in the theater twice a week, and her dancing school was full.

In 1819, Eliza Anne's marriage broke down. Mr. Rutherford drank heavily and, like John Fenwick before him, got his family into debt. According to his furious feminist mother-in-law Eliza Fenwick, Rutherford was a disgrace and a burden. He returned to England at about the same time their fourth child, a boy named Orlando, was born. Eliza Anne's poor health, added to the chronic fear of a second slave insurrection, led Mrs. Fenwick to relocate their school business to England. Her plan was to settle in Clifton or somewhere near Bath and to take her pupils from Barbados with her to be educated there. Several families promised to send their daughters, but when the time for departure eventually came, enough of them dropped out so that her relocation plans became unaffordable. Fenwick's plan to escape Barbados failed, and she would not set foot on English soil again.

In 1821, Mrs. Fenwick admitted to her old friend Mary Hays that she had bought her first slave—a male cook. To her annoyance, the man was seized six months later for an outstanding debt owed by the previous female owner. If Mrs. Fenwick wanted to keep the cook, she had to buy him again at auction, which she grudgingly did after securing a loan. In all, she bought five slaves—two men, two boys, and one elderly woman whose job was to care for her youngest grandson, Orlando. She said she would free the old woman when the family left Barbados. Yet Mrs. Fenwick was embarrassed to own slave property. Despite her antislavery inclination, in the end Mrs. Fenwick could not escape the lure of the Caribbean's prevailing economic and social system. She bought slaves because hiring domestic servants was expensive and unsatisfactory. As one who rented slave labor, she had no power and felt that she did not get value for her money.

White women frequently were slave owners, particularly in West Indian urban settings. For example, in 1817, about half of all properties in Bridgetown with fewer than ten slaves were owned by females. If women wanted to run any kind of a business, from a tavern to a school, they had to rely on slaves. Most single women owned female slaves, but for some reason Eliza Fenwick preferred males. Perhaps she wanted to avoid being accused of running a brothel.

White women also owned sugar plantations and estate slaves in rural areas. We know that women received considerable compensation for slaves at emancipation in 1833, when about £20 million was awarded to West Indian slave owners for loss of their human property. Although a full study of white women's roles in the Atlantic slave economies remains to be written, we should remember that they were active participants. Many were entrepreneurs (particularly widows) who were trying to make a living as best they could. If that involved owning slaves, they had little choice but to follow their society's norms.

In 1822, the Fenwicks decided to move their school to the United States, where removal costs were lower and the competition was less stiff than in England. Business was in recession in Barbados, and Mrs. Fenwick was concerned about her family's health. She could not afford to send her grandsons to England for their education, and she was haunted by the possibility of another slave rebellion. Mrs. Fenwick was also keen to get to America to read books again because no public library existed in Barbados. The family decided to move to New Haven, Connecticut, where several West Indian families had already settled and established a small community. The Fenwick household, consisting of Mrs. Fenwick, her daughter and four grandchildren, six pupils, and a servant (who may have been the slave nurse Eliza wanted to free), arrived in New Haven via St. Thomas in September 1822. They settled into a new home and opened the school with fifteen students—all from the West Indies, including Demerara. Before leaving Barbados, Fenwick had sold her slaves for cash at a loss and had left behind over £1,000 in uncollected debts. Although she hired an attorney, she never recovered all that was owed to her.

By August 1823, the New Haven school was operating from a large house, with twenty pupils, nine of them boarders. There were no American students. Mrs. Fenwick had developed a school suited to the cultural and social environment of the British slaveholding Caribbean and found it difficult to attract New Englanders. On a personal level, she liked the cold weather and felt more at home in New Haven than she had ever been in the tropics. In 1825, scandal prompted her to move the school to New York. It seems that the disgruntled family of a former pupil spread rumors about Eliza Anne's morals and raised old charges about Mrs. Fenwick's radical alliances years earlier during her youth in London.

Long in poor health, Eliza Anne died in New York in 1828. Without her assistance, Mrs. Fenwick could no longer manage the school, so she converted it into a boardinghouse that accommodated three families. She was solely responsible for her four orphaned grandchildren; tragedy struck several years later when two of her grandsons drowned. Mrs. Fenwick was living with her granddaughter Elizabeth in Rhode Island when she died in 1840. Elizabeth followed her nontraditional mother and grandmother and struck out on an independent path across the Atlantic. She became a missionary to

West Africa, married the Reverend Thomas Savage in 1844, and later raised six children in the United States.

Eliza Fenwick did not adjust easily to Barbados. The climate, insects, and diseases bothered her. She endured a slave rebellion, a hurricane, and the death of her son from yellow fever. Emotionally, intellectually, and morally, she opposed slavery, which she blamed for West Indian society's faults and debauchery. Eventually, however, after residing in Barbados for some time, the feminist radical succumbed and bought five slaves. She found herself hating slavery but joining the ranks of the slave masters. Eliza Fenwick's Atlantic experiences reveal the wide divide between theory and practice, between emotion and reason, between sensibility and sense. Even a feminist like Eliza Fenwick was co-opted by the system of slavery. She was not alone in her contradictory behavior. Many others, including Thomas Jefferson, claimed moral outrage at the institution of slavery yet remained economically dependent on it. Abandoned by the men in her life, Fenwick always struggled to provide for her family and briefly enjoyed a comfortable standard of living in Barbados, but she could not afford to return home to England. Eliza Fenwick never felt at home in Barbados, where she was ill at ease with slavery and fearful of a slave rebellion. The feminist author never felt independent, and she never felt free.

In a broader sense, what does Eliza Fenwick's life reveal about the Atlantic world? We learn about the difficulties of running a small business—a white girls' school—in the West Indies. Labor was not easy to acquire or control and was expensive. Profits depended on tranquillity and stability, but wars, slave insurrection, and disastrous weather meant that income was unpredictable. We are also reminded that Atlantic citizens moved around a lot. Mrs. Fenwick and her daughter first tried their luck in Ireland before traveling farther out to the colonial island periphery in Barbados. Her daughter's theater troupe performed in Antigua, St. Croix, and St. Bartholomew's. When childbirth left her weakened and unwell, Eliza Anne sailed to Demerara to recover her health. Even young Orlando Fenwick went on a business trip to the islands of Martinique, Dominica, Antigua, and Guadeloupe shortly before his death. The Fenwick family subsequently lived in the mainland United States, and her granddaughter went to West Africa as a missionary. Circulation in the Atlantic world was ubiquitous.

Eliza Fenwick does not fit the stereotype of a typical slave owner in the Atlantic world. First, she was a female owner of slaves in what we have been led to consider a male preserve. But she, like many widows, relied on slave labor for her livelihood. Furthermore, Mrs. Fenwick was an urban slave owner of a small number of domestic laborers in an economic environment overwhelmingly portrayed as rural, agricultural, and dominated by large plantations. Wealthy planters often left records for historians to study, but few small business owners provided materials for their stories to be told. Eliza Fenwick, feminist and slaveholder, was a woman who wanted to be independent and free. Her story provides us with a rare glimpse into the life of a small-scale female entrepreneur whose experiences as a white woman in the Caribbean emphasize the diverse patterns of living and working in the complex, changing environment of the Atlantic world. White women could be slave owners but also endured restricted lives with limited economic potential and no political power. Although she spoke the language of liberation, in the end Eliza Fenwick was more interested in the emancipation of women than the liberty of slaves.

Bibliography and Suggested Reading

Beckles, Hilary. *Black Rebellion in Barbados: The Struggle against Slavery, 1627–1838.* Bridgetown: Caribbean Research and Publications, 1987.

———. *A History of Barbados: From Amerindian Settlement to Nation-State.* New York: Cambridge University Press, 1990.

———. "White Women and Slavery in the Caribbean," *History Workshop Journal* 36 (1993): 66–82.

———. "White Women and a West India Fortune: Gender and Wealth during Slavery." In *The White Minority in the Caribbean,* edited by Howard Johnson and Karl Watson, 1–16. Kingston: Ian Randle Publishers, 1998.

———. *Centering Woman: Gender Discourses in Caribbean Slave Society.* Kingston: Ian Randle, 1999.

Blouet, Olwyn. "Mrs. Fenwick and Her School for Girls in Barbados, 1814–1822." *Journal of Caribbean History* 34, no. 1–2 (2000): 1–20.

Brereton, Bridget. "Texts, Testimony and Gender: An Examination of Some Texts by Women on the English-Speaking Caribbean from the 1770s to the 1920s." In *Engendering History: Caribbean Women in Historical Perspective,* edited by Verene Shepherd, Bridget Brereton, and Barbara Bailey, 63–93. Kingston: Ian Randle Publishers, 1995.

Bush, B. "White 'Ladies,' Coloured 'Favourites' and Black 'Wenches': Some Considerations on Sex, Race and Class Factors in Social Relations in White Creole Society in the British Caribbean." *Slavery and Abolition* 2 (1981): 245–62.

Butler, Kathleen Mary. *The Economics of Emancipation: Jamaica and Barbados, 1823–1843.* Chapel Hill: University of North Carolina Press, 1995.

Chattejee, Ranita. "Sapphic Subjectivity and Gothic Desires in Eliza Fenwick's *Secresy, 1795." Gothic Studies* 6, no. 1 (2004): 45–56.

Coleman, Deirdre. "Conspicuous Consumption: White Abolitionism and English Women's Protest Writing in the 1790s." *English Literary History* 61, no. 2 (1994): 341–62.

Fenwick, Eliza. *Secresy: or, the Ruin on the Rock.* Edited by Isobel Grundy. Peterborough: Broadview Press, 1998.

Ferguson, Moira. *Subject to Others: British Women Writers and Colonial Slavery, 1670–1834.* New York: Routledge, 1992.

Higman, B. W. *Slave Populations of the British Caribbean, 1807–1834.* Baltimore: Johns Hopkins University Press, 1984.

Todd, Janet. *Mary Wollstonecraft: A Revolutionary Life.* London: Weidenfeld & Nicolson, 2000.

Watson, Karl. *The Civilised Island. Barbados: A Social History, 1750–1816.* Bridgetown: Caribbean Graphic Production, 1979.

Wedd, A. F., ed. *The Fate of the Fenwicks: Letters to Mary Hays 1798–1828.* London: Methuen, 1927.

CHAPTER FOURTEEN

Elizabeth Patterson Bonaparte (1785–1879)

Napoleon's American Sister-in-Law

Charlene Boyer Lewis

When the beautiful young American socialite Elizabeth Patterson fell in love with Jerome, youngest brother of Napoleon Bonaparte, their union sparked a transatlantic controversy that had repercussions in both the United States and France. Caving in to his powerful brother's intense pressure, the weak-willed Jerome abandoned his beloved young American wife and their child and slunk back to Europe to marry a more suitable German princess. Elizabeth Patterson Bonaparte never remarried and spent the rest of her life trying to gain recognition for her short-lived royal status. Charlene Boyer Lewis traces the complicated transatlantic identity that Patterson created for herself, carving out a role as one of the most fashionable and influential women in the young American republic by adapting French forms of gentility, dress, behavior, and speech. Her exposure to French monarchy and imperial beliefs increasingly led her to critique American republicanism and democracy as a form of existence that was stagnant and crass. As Elizabeth Patterson Bonaparte's biography reveals, the United States and France have maintained relations that are characterized by an uneasy blend of mutual admiration, suspicion about each other's political motives, and harsh cultural critiques that have persisted into the twenty-first century.

In April 1805, nineteen-year-old Elizabeth Patterson Bonaparte's hopes were high as she looked on the port of Lisbon after a long journey across the Atlantic from her hometown of Baltimore, Maryland. Her courage was undaunted, though the trip had been somewhat difficult because of her pregnancy. She had come to Portugal on her father's ship with her husband Jerome to meet her new brother-in-law—Napoleon Bonaparte, the emperor of France. Having been married for just a little over a year, the newlyweds were excited and anxious. On hearing of his youngest brother's surprising marriage, Napoleon—then first consul—had exploded in anger and ordered Jerome to return immediately to France. Intent on annulling the marriage, Napoleon issued a decree that "prohibited all captains of French vessels from receiving on board the young person to whom Citizen Jerome has connected himself" and proclaimed that Elizabeth would "be not suffered to land" in any French territory.[1] The couple attempted to make the trip three or four different times but always met with stormy weather or enemy British ships eager to capture such an important prize. When the pair finally arrived in Lisbon, an emissary from Napoleon informed Elizabeth and Jerome that "*Miss Patterson*" could not disembark. Elizabeth reportedly responded hotly, "Tell your master that *Madame Bonaparte* is ambitious, and demands her rights as a member of the imperial family."[2] She did manage to get off the boat, and the couple spent three or four days in Lisbon. Shopping and sightseeing, they planned their next move, which Napoleon ultimately made for them. An escort sent by the emperor took Jerome as a virtual prisoner to see his furious brother. When they parted in Lisbon, Jerome assured Elizabeth of his undying love and pledged to her and their unborn child that once he spoke with his brother in person, everything would be all right and they would be reunited. Although he expected to send for her first, he urged her to sail for Amsterdam and have their baby there, if necessary. She never saw him again.

Frightened and worried, Elizabeth heeded Jerome's directions. She soon left Lisbon for Amsterdam with her traveling companions—her brother William, her close friend Eliza Anderson, and Jerome's friend and physician Dr. Garnier as well as several servants. But the port master there had received Napoleon's orders concerning Elizabeth and, fearing his wrath, would not allow the party either to land or to leave. The ship rode at anchor for eight days, surrounded by gunships and guard boats, as the passengers began to run out of food and to grow concerned about Elizabeth and the impending birth. Finally, with the intervention of the American consul, the party left Amsterdam and headed for England, where Napoleon's decrees held no weight. The welcome Elizabeth received must have lifted her spirits considerably. At Dover, "Madame Bonaparte, with her suite, landed amidst a great concourse of spectators." According to the newspapers, "the most conspicuous persons" of the area called on her and "vie[d] in the offer of attentions."[3] With no idea when or if she would see her husband again, Elizabeth delivered their son, Jerome Napoleon Bonaparte, on July 7, 1805. She nicknamed him "Bo." Although Jerome continued to send letters and gifts with assurances of his love and promises of a reunion, a dejected Elizabeth and her baby sailed in September to the only place she had left to go, her hometown of Baltimore.

The marriage, divorce, and later years of Elizabeth Patterson Bonaparte reveal the intriguing confluence of private acts and public events that took place throughout the transatlantic world. Her marriage and divorce were intimate occasions that had international ramifications. Her personal decisions affected two countries—a republic and an empire. During her long life, she crossed the Atlantic Ocean numerous times, making more trips than most women or men of her era. She spent many years living in Europe yet always—if reluctantly—called the United States her home. Her movements across the ocean and between cultures created powerful contradictions in her life as she actively sought to construct a transatlantic life that blended what she thought was the best of both American and European ways. She sought and lived a life very different from most of the women she knew—either American or European.

Elizabeth belonged to one of the wealthiest families in Maryland. Her father William Patterson was an immigrant from Ireland who had accumulated a fortune in Baltimore as a merchant and property owner. Elizabeth, the eldest daughter, helped her mother Dorcas in the house, while the brothers closest to her age, Joseph, Robert, William, and Edward, learned the intricacies of the mercantile trade from their father. Although she assuredly received an education befitting the daughter of an elite family, Elizabeth read and discussed books considered radical for the time that certainly shaped her thinking about the appropriate role for women and their relations with men. Combating the model that her mother provided of a docile and submissive wife were the feminist ideas Elizabeth absorbed from Mary Wollstonecraft's *A Vindication of the Rights of Women* (1792), which advocated equal education for women and marriages based on equality and companionship. Indeed, around Baltimore, Elizabeth was known as "a most extraordinary girl . . . in short, a modern *philosophe*."[4] As she reached marriageable age, she had convinced herself that she was destined for a grander calling than a simple American wife and mother.

By the time Elizabeth Patterson and Jerome Bonaparte met each other in September 1803, she was already renowned for her extraordinary beauty and was one of the most sought-after young women in town. Jerome, a lieutenant in the French navy, had spent the summer traveling between New York City, Philadelphia, and Baltimore with an American ship captain and a number of French friends and servants. Aged nineteen, handsome, dashing, and the youngest brother of the first consul of France, Jerome became the center of attention wherever he went, especially among ambitious young ladies. It is little wonder that the two were immediately attracted to one another. According to legend, Elizabeth and Jerome first saw each other at the Baltimore horse races but did not converse. A few days later, they danced together at a ball and somehow became entangled. Whether it was his watch chain that twisted in her hair or her chain that caught on his gold button, it was love at first sight. Jerome called on her at home soon after the ball. By the end of October, they had decided to marry.[5] But as the appointed day neared, Elizabeth's father received several worrisome warnings. The French consul general in New York made it clear to all the parties involved that it was illegal in France for a man under the age of twenty-one to marry without the consent of his parents and that this marriage would probably outrage Napoleon. Worse yet, an anonymous letter sent to Mr. Patterson apprised him of Jerome's "profligate" character, including tales of several young women that he had "ruined" in France and the West Indies and of a recent proposal to Susan Wheeler (later Mrs. Stephen Decatur), who had had the good sense to refuse him. The correspondent, who must have been someone traveling with Jerome, warned that Jerome would marry Elizabeth "to secure himself a home at your expense" until returning to France as soon as he could and would then "laugh at your credulity."[6] William immediately called off the wedding and sent Elizabeth to stay with relatives in Virginia. There, to her parents' dismay, Elizabeth's feelings for Jerome only intensified. She famously declared that "she would rather be the wife of Jerome Bonaparte for an hour, than the wife of any other man for life."[7] She even let it be known that she was willing to run away with him. Her father, though still very troubled, relented, and the pair married on Christmas Eve. In an effort to make the marriage as legitimate as possible, the highest-ranking Catholic bishop in the United States, John Carroll, officiated, and the French consul in Baltimore, Jerome's secretary, and the mayor signed the marriage certificate.

By marrying the brother of one of the most powerful men in the world, Elizabeth became a national—actually, an international—celebrity. Far from being a modest, respectable wife who, according to American social expectations, would find happiness within her home rather than in the public sphere, Elizabeth relished being in the public eye. The newlyweds captured public attention from New York City to Washington, D.C., and beyond. Newspapers kept track of their every move. Even in private correspondence, Elizabeth's name appeared regularly as writers speculated about the couple's future and Napoleon's response. As they traveled west to Niagara Falls and south to Washington, men and women flocked to get a look at this famous pair and maybe even exchange a word or two. Wherever they went, social leaders gave dinners and balls in their honor. Other than Martha Washington, Abigail Adams, and Dolley Madison, few American women achieved such national renown in this period.

Elizabeth also cultivated her celebrity by wearing fashionable—and scandalous—French dresses to balls and other entertainments. Initially, her clothing was the primary way in which she demonstrated her transatlantic connection. In the early 1800s, dresses inspired by classical Greek design were the height of fashion in France, especially since Empress Josephine wore them. Typically, the gowns were made of lightweight, often white cotton or linen. They were columnar, falling close to the body and clinging to breasts, hips, thighs, and legs. Often lacking sleeves and cut deep in the back and low in the front, the dresses exposed far more flesh than traditional American fashions. It took real courage—or immodesty, depending on the viewpoint—for an American woman to wear them. Elizabeth wore such clothes regularly and with great flair. Her entire wedding outfit, according to one guest, could "have been put in [his] pocket."[8] At a party given for the newlyweds in Washington, she arrived wearing a sleeveless, backless, white crepe dress of French design that Rosalie Stier Calvert described as "so transparent that you could see the color and shape of her thighs, and even more!"[9] A mob of boys swarmed around her as she entered the house of her uncle, Secretary of the Navy Robert Smith. Once inside, according to Margaret Bayard Smith, "her appearance was such that it threw all the company into confusion, and no one dared look at her but by stealth." Outside, crowds gathered to peer through the unshuttered windows at the "extremely beautiful" and "almost naked woman."[10] Several ladies reprimanded her for the sensation that she created, explaining that "if she did not change her manner of dress she would never be asked anywhere again."[11] Elizabeth paid little heed to the warnings, counting on her celebrity—and her daring dresses—to garner her an invitation to almost any society gathering. She calculated correctly. Knowing how important these public occasions were, Elizabeth never shrank from the attention, as well-mannered ladies were supposed to do, and she always carefully dressed for them. Her clothing helped her maintain the celebrity status that she not only loved but also considered a necessary part of her life.

While Elizabeth and Jerome were enjoying their newfound celebrity and marital happiness, her father turned to President Thomas Jefferson, Secretary of State James Madison, and minister to France Robert R. Livingston to help persuade Napoleon to accept the marriage. Because of the husband she chose, Elizabeth's marriage—normally a private event—had an international impact. Like William Patterson and Jerome's advisers, Jefferson, Madison, and Livingston were fairly certain that Napoleon would denounce the marriage since he had already started marrying off his other siblings to European royalty. With the Louisiana Purchase in the final stages and the first consul clearly increasing his power, American policymakers wanted to make sure that the marriage of a young Baltimore woman did not create diplomatic difficulties for the United States. Right before the wedding, Jefferson instructed Livingston to explain that, contrary to what the first consul might believe, the "executive of the United States" was powerless to prevent marriages. He also directed Livingston to assure Napoleon that his brother had married into a family whose station in society was "with the first of the United States."[12] Jerome and Elizabeth, however, were not nearly as worried as the president and his advisers or their own friends and family. All of Napoleon's objections, they believed, would dissipate as soon as he met her and looked on her beauty.

In the summer of 1804, Elizabeth and Jerome learned that Napoleon had proclaimed himself emperor. Their desperation to return to France and share in the imperial honors with other members of the Bonaparte family caused them to risk their lives twice as they attempted to sail from the United States, once in a shipwreck in October and later by British capture in December. In early 1805, their frustration increased as they read reports of Napoleon's grand coronation ceremony. More terrifying was their discovery that Jerome had been left out of the line of succession and that a French civil tribunal had declared their marriage null and void. Deciding not to wait for another French ship, they took one of her father's fastest merchant ships. In March 1805, they set sail hoping to persuade Napoleon to accept Elizabeth and make them an imperial prince and princess, like Jerome's brothers and sisters. But Napoleon dashed their dreams.

Soon after learning of the wedding, Napoleon applied to Pope Pius VII to annul the marriage formally, claiming falsely that the marriage had been hastily performed by a Spanish priest and declaring that, as ruler of Catholic France, he could not have a Protestant among his family. Tired of being controlled by the hot-tempered emperor, Pope Pius carefully reviewed the case and decided that there was no valid reason for an annulment. This decision about the wedding of a mere girl from Baltimore produced a break between the two powerful European men. An enraged Napoleon threatened to remove the pope from his office and make Paris the center of the Church. To his credit, Pope Pius never backed down, and the Catholic Church never annulled the marriage. Meanwhile, Napoleon had ordered Jerome back to France, without his "little girl," even though she carried a possible imperial heir.[13] The couple parted in Lisbon, still believing that Jerome could convince Napoleon to change his mind.

It seems that Jerome underestimated how angry his brother was and how determined Napoleon was to make a dynastic marriage for him. The emperor refused even to meet with Jerome until he wrote a letter of apology for defying his brother and family. Apparently, Jerome had very little courage or character. Even as he continued to write romantic letters to Elizabeth, by June 1805 he had renounced his marriage to her, reconciled with Napoleon, and returned to the navy. A year later, Jerome consented to a divorce in exchange for officially being declared a prince of the empire and an admiral. In 1807, Napoleon arranged a marriage between Jerome and the Princess of Wurtemberg, a Protestant, and gave the couple the Kingdom of Westphalia (now a part of Germany) to rule. Elizabeth had gambled on a happy and exciting future in imperial France and lost. The secretary of the British Legation in the United States, Sir Augustus Foster, remarked in November 1806 that "when Jerome first landed" in Baltimore, Elizabeth "declared she would have him, & that she had rather be Mad[ame] Jer. B. one year tho she was to be nothing afterwards" than marry an American. "She did not know she was so near the real Event."[14] Elizabeth never became a queen, but she insisted on retaining the name Bonaparte for the rest of her life. She never remarried, refusing to let go of this most prestigious symbol of her transatlantic life.

Madame Bonaparte, as most people now called her, returned to Baltimore as the center of a major scandal. Social expectations called for her to retire from public view and live a quiet, modest life. That, however, was not in her character. "Nature never intended me for obscurity," she wrote her father.[15] Elizabeth was determined never to relinquish the public attention that she so craved. Although she had failed in her attempt to join one of the most famous families in the world, she tried to maintain her own fame and popularity. Soon after her return, she ordered a coach with the Bonaparte family crest painted on its doors. She traveled regularly to Washington with her son, always introducing Bo as a prince. One of her closest friends was Dolley Madison, the First Lady from 1809 to 1817, who ensured that Elizabeth received an invitation to all the important gatherings in the capital. Just as she kept her name to remind everyone of her imperial connections, she also continued to flaunt her French fashions to support her cosmopolitan status. Her choice in clothing clearly signaled that she preferred European to American ways and that she would not play the role of the embarrassed divorcée. In November 1811, Catharine Mitchill reported on the sensation that Elizabeth caused at a presidential dinner by wearing a dress that "exposed so much of her bosom" and laid bare her back "nearly half way down to the bottom of her waist." "The state of nudity in which she appeared," Mitchill informed her sister, "attracted the attention of the Gentlemen, for I saw several of them take a look at her bubbies when they were conversing with her."[16] Although nicknamed "Madame Eve" and cautioned that she "must promise to have more clothes on," or she would not receive social invitations, Elizabeth ignored the warnings as usual, certain that the social and political force of her French connections, including her name and clothes, would always gain her an easy admittance into any refined gathering.[17] Although a scandalous woman with scandalous clothes, she rarely spent an evening alone or missed a party. She even received several marriage proposals. Indeed, she was one of the most sought-after women in the capital and elsewhere.

In 1808, Elizabeth was stunned to receive a letter from Jerome, now ruling his own kingdom with his new German wife, requesting that three-year-old Bo be sent to him. She immediately refused. Firmly believing that her son would one day play a major role in the Bonaparte empire, however, she had him baptized in the Catholic Church. Jerome made a second request for his son a few years later and offered to set up Elizabeth in her own castle, slyly adding that she would be near enough for him to visit her regularly. Again, she refused, declaring that she would never relinquish her son and that Jerome's tiny kingdom was "not quite large enough to hold *two queens*."[18] Instead, in 1811, Elizabeth accepted Napoleon's offer of a yearly pension, provided that she could sign the receipts with the name Bonaparte. Napoleon, impressed, agreed. A year later, aware of troubles in the French Empire and eager to protect her assets from her bigamist husband, Elizabeth requested and received an official divorce from the Maryland legislature. She had been right to be so careful. Napoleon abdicated in 1814, and the kingdoms of all his siblings came crashing down along with his.

Napoleon's fall from power meant that Elizabeth could return to Europe with little fear of imperial reprisals, though, for safety's sake, she traveled under the name Mrs. Patterson. That trip confirmed her long-held belief that women with her qualities belonged in elegant European drawing rooms, not in boring American parlors. As she prepared for an exclusive ball in England during her second trip to Europe in 1815, she assured her father,

I get on extremely well, and I assure you that altho' you have always taken me for a fool, it is not my character here. In America I appeared more simple than I am, because I was completely out of my element. It was my misfortune, not my fault, that I was born in a country which was not congenial to my desires. Here I am completely in my sphere . . . and in contact with modes of life for which nature intended me.[19]

Her social success in the most brilliant European circles never astonished Elizabeth. She knew that she had been destined for such environments and expected to move within them easily. The admiration, respect, and friendship she found in Europe, especially France, reinforced her preference for European attitudes. In Baltimore, her talents had rarely been fully appreciated; in fact, they had often been criticized. But in France, England, Switzerland, and Italy, aristocrats, artists, writers, socialites of all kinds, and even members of the exiled Bonaparte family actively sought her company. After she arrived in Paris in the fall of 1815, paying a call on Mrs. Patterson or Madame Bonaparte became all the rage not only for fashionable Parisians but for visiting foreigners as well. The author Washington Irving, the statesman Daniel Webster, the American minister to France Albert Gallatin, and the Marquis de Lafayette all gathered in her drawing room. The Irish novelist Lady Sidney Morgan became her close friend. Even the Duke of Wellington, who had defeated Napoleon at the Battle of Waterloo, became an admirer. An American who returned from Paris in 1816 described Elizabeth's "doors as surrounded. [Her] Stairs thronged with Dukes, Counts, Marquis, [her]self as a little Queen, giving & receiving the most supreme happiness."[20] Elizabeth was finally in her proper sphere.

Of the twenty-five years between the summer of 1815, when she returned to Europe for the second time, and the summer of 1840, Elizabeth spent just eight in the United States. She would return to France two more times before 1861. While many elite Americans managed to visit Europe once or twice in their lifetime, she crossed the Atlantic fourteen times, an uncommon feat for Americans—whether male or female—in that era. Her appropriation of and admiration for French dress, behavior, and ideas increased her antipathy toward parochial American society, politics, and culture over these years. In fact, her anti-Americanism actually intensified with every trip abroad that she made. Although she always called Maryland her home and returned to Baltimore often enough to oversee her American rights and properties, Elizabeth never embraced her homeland; in fact, she felt that being born in America had been the fatal blow to her destiny.

While Americans were energetically building a new republican nation, Elizabeth cultivated a French imperial image and denigrated Americans and American society at every opportunity. She was steadfast in her opinion that a monarchy was better than a republic. She despised the increasing democratization of the United States and longed for the strict social hierarchies of Europe. She found it entirely impossible, as she informed her father, "to be contented in a country where there exists no nobility."[21] And, though never religiously devout, she was convinced that Catholicism was the best religion for rulers and raised Bo in that faith in spite of Americans' general suspicion of Catholics. Her transatlantic experiences and sensibilities led her to find fault with most aspects of her native land. "I can never be satisfied in America," she wrote during her second trip to Europe. "It was always my misfortune to be unfitted for the modes of existence there, nor can I return to them without a sacrifice of all I value on earth."[22] She was happiest in Europe, especially when Bo was with her.

After returning to Baltimore in the fall of 1817, Elizabeth decided it was time for her son to become better acquainted with his Bonaparte relatives. In Elizabeth's opinion, the Pattersons, especially her ardently American father, had too much influence over Bo and were ruining him for the brilliant future that she hoped awaited him in Europe. Joseph Bonaparte, the deposed king of Spain, had escaped to New Jersey when Napoleon was forced into exile. Through a mutual acquaintance, Elizabeth arranged for Bo to meet his uncle, which turned out even better than she had hoped. Joseph recognized Bo as a member of the family and urged Elizabeth to shape his upbringing according to his rank and take him to Europe to meet more of the Bonaparte family. In 1819, she and Bo sailed for the Continent to meet some more Bona partes and to enroll him in a private school in Geneva, Switzerland—a fitting place, Elizabeth believed, for educating a child who would mingle with the rulers of Europe. In Geneva, Elizabeth was again at the center of European society, invited to every party and dinner. Soon after her arrival, the restored Bourbon King Louis XVIII invited her to appear at his court in Paris. The offer must have been tempting—finally a chance to appear on the stage for which she felt destined—but she politely refused, citing her loyalty to Napoleon despite the unhappiness he had caused her. Instead, in 1821, Elizabeth decided that Bo should accept the invitation to visit his father's family in Rome. While she was quite reluctant to interrupt Bo's education, Elizabeth understood the important social and financial advantages that he would reap from a better acquaintance with the Bonapartes. Much to his mother's delight, Bo's Bonaparte grandmother, uncles, aunts, and cousins received him "in the kindest and most hospitable manner possible" and discussed the prospect of him marrying Joseph's daughter Charlotte. Elizabeth was thrilled, but Bo seemed ambivalent about the match. Not wanting to disappoint his mother or his father's family, he seemed to acquiesce, recognizing that the marriage to his New Jersey cousin would mean that he "would return immediately to America to pass the rest of my life among my relations and friends."[23] The planned marriage never occurred for some reason, and Elizabeth was much more devastated than Bo. The young man wanted nothing more than to spend the rest of his life in Baltimore—a dream his mother did everything in her power to prevent. By the spring of 1822, he had returned to Baltimore, headed for Harvard, without ever meeting his father. Elizabeth stayed in Europe for two more years.

Elizabeth was single-minded in her determination to marry Bo to an important European family of noble lineage. "Bo has rank," she wrote her father in 1823; "his name places him in the first society in Europe."[24] No American woman would be suitable for him. In fact, she would have preferred him to remain single than to marry beneath himself. It was with great shock, almost literally, that she received the news in 1829 that Bo had married a Baltimore heiress. "I nearly died when I first heard of it," she assured her father from Florence. She was distraught at Bo's denial of everything that was important to her: "It is unreasonable to expect him to be made happy by the only things which render life at all supportable to me, rank and living in Europe. . . . I tried to give him the ideas suitable to his rank in life; having failed in that, there remains only to let him choose his own course." Having married "the brother of an emperor," Elizabeth had not the "meanness of spirit to descend from such an elevation to the deplorable condition of being the wife of an American." But her son, "not having my pride, my ambition, or my utter abhorrence to vulgar company," had the "right to pursue the course he prefers." She had done "all [she] could to disgust him with America" and had failed.[25]

With neither a husband nor father to control her movements, Elizabeth lived very differently from most women in the early nineteenth century. Although she had desperately wanted to become a princess or queen when she married Jerome, she turned down several proposals from noblemen during her years in Europe. Remarrying, she believed, would damage Bo's future prospects, which she always placed above her own happiness. After her first disaster, she had little admiration for marriage. As a wealthy divorcée, she possessed far more independence than any married woman—and most single women—American or European. She alone had sole charge of her son and her money. She alone determined what was best for Bo and herself. She could live where she liked and spend money on whatever she chose. But with her intense hatred of American society, she was blind to some of the limitations of European society and saw only its opportunities, especially for women. She credited Europeans with knowing how to treat women and giving them a greater role in society. While elite European women may have lacked political power (an issue Elizabeth never questioned), they certainly exerted cultural power in their salons, ballrooms, and dining rooms where they determined the standards of dress, behavior, and conversation for fashionable society.[26] After her second trip to Europe, she formulated a definition of "happiness for a woman": "to be handsome, to be a wit, to have a fortune, to live in Paris, and to have the freedom of the houses of the best circles there."[27]

Elizabeth fully accepted elite European forms of gender roles and relations and was rarely scandalized by behavior that many American visitors, especially women, found sinful in aristocratic circles. In fact, Elizabeth preferred French marriages, in which couples united for the "purpose of enjoying society & spending life agreeably," to American couples who married "from idleness & ennui & call them love matches." Knowing that elite Europeans sometimes permitted adultery and that the fashionable set indulged in other racy behavior, Elizabeth professed, if vice in France "really exist[ed] in a greater degree" than in America (and she was not convinced that it did), it was "less disgusting & more polite." She was never bothered by the infidelities and adulteries of Europe's elite, unlike many of her compatriots who saw them as evidence of the superiority of their simple—and ostensibly more moral—republic. "If [Europeans] commit sins," she decided, "they are more agreeable as sinners than [Americans] are as saints." She generally avoided American travelers in Europe because she "found their whinings so uninteresting [about] the corruption of European morals," and she tired of their hypocritical "growling at my selfishness for engrossing these corrupt people to myself."[28]

Before 1840, whenever Elizabeth returned to Baltimore from Europe, it was only for brief periods and solely to look after her son's interests and her own finances. She always suffered at home and pined for a return to her preferred residence. For example, she visited Baltimore in July 1824 to attend to her financial affairs and spend time with Bo but could not even stand staying a year; the following summer found her back in Paris. Uncertain when she would see Europe again, she arrived in Baltimore in 1834 with her baggage loaded with European finery—dresses, bonnets, jewelry, and even umbrellas. She detested American fashions as much as she detested American society. Her father died soon after her return and used his will to let everyone know exactly what he thought about his headstrong daughter:

> The conduct of my daughter Betsy has through life been so disobedient, that in no instance has she ever consulted my opinion or feelings, indeed she has caused more anxiety & trouble, than all my other children put together, & her folly & misconduct has occasioned me a train of expense that first and last has [cost] me much money, under such circumstances it would not be reasonable, just, or proper that she should at my death inherit & participate in an equal proportion with my other children, in an equal division of my Estate.[29]

Nevertheless, he left her a few properties in the city of Baltimore that provided her principal support for the rest of her life. Her determination to marry Jerome, her anti-American sentiments, and her love of aristocracy had cost her a loving relationship with her father. Learning her lesson, she reconciled with her son and his wife. But she now focused all the energies that she had once devoted to her son on her grandsons. They, she firmly believed, would fulfill their destinies. In time, her eldest grandson Jerome would serve admirably in the French army and be named a personal protector of Empress Eugenie, but that was as much as the American Bonapartes ever achieved in Europe.

Back in Baltimore, Elizabeth monitored closely the deaths of Bonaparte family members and always took pleasure when they remembered Bo in their wills, as several did. The death of Cardinal Fesche, Bo's great uncle, propelled her back to France once more, in early 1839, in order to protect Bo's share in the estate and, furthermore, to enjoy all the pleasures of Paris once again. She reunited with old friends—counts, princesses, and duchesses—and returned to many of her favorite places. But it was a short stay, and she was in Baltimore again by the summer of 1840. She made another brief trip in 1849 while her nephew Louis Napoleon was the president of France's Second Republic. She did not return again until 1860, when she came back fighting. Jerome had died and, true to form, had failed not only to leave a legacy to Bo but even to mention his first son in his will. Elizabeth squared off against the remaining Bonapartes by suing for her son's rights to a portion of Jerome's estate. The case became a real cause célèbre in France; most people sided with the woman whom Napoleon had treated so unfairly so many years ago. While the family recognized Bo as a legitimate Bonaparte, his mother failed to get him named a legal heir. This disappointing trip would be Elizabeth's last.

After 1840, Elizabeth consigned herself to her "Baltimore obscurity." In fact, during her "vegetation in this Baltimore," she "[gave] up all correspondence with [her] friends in Europe." "There is nothing here worth attention or interest," she wrote to her close friend, the famous novelist Lady Sidney Morgan, "save the money market." Her sentiments about the state of American society had not changed in over forty-five years. Even in 1849, she insisted that "society, conversation, friendship, belong to older countries, and are not yet cultivated in any part of the United States." "You ought to thank your stars for your European birth," she assured her friend.[30] She had lived her long life as woman caught between two worlds without ever fully becoming a member of either. After her final trip in 1860, she spent the last years of her life living frugally in a boardinghouse, dressing in her now-antiquated French clothing, and subsisting on memories of her days in Europe. When she died in 1879, she still clung to the hope that her grandsons would fulfill all the imperial aspirations she had possessed when she married Jerome Bonaparte in 1803.

Bibliography and Suggested Reading

Allgor, Catherine. *Parlor Politics: In Which the Ladies of Washington Help Build a City and a Government.* Charlottesville: University Press of Virginia, 2000.

Branson, Susan. *These Fiery Frenchified Dames: Women and Political Culture in Early National Philadelphia.* Philadelphia: University of Pennsylvania Press, 2001.

Jabour, Anya. *Marriage in the Early Republic: Elizabeth and William Wirt and the Companionate Ideal.* Baltimore: Johns Hopkins University Press, 1998.

Kerber, Linda. *Women of the Republic: Intellect and Ideology in Revolutionary America.* Chapel Hill: University of North Carolina Press, 1980.

Levenstein, Harvey. *Seductive Journey: American Tourists in France from Jefferson to the Jazz Age.* Chicago: University of Chicago Press, 1998.

Lewis, Jan. "The Republican Wife: Virtue and Seduction in the Early Republic." *William and Mary Quarterly,* 3rd ser., 44 (October 1987): 689–721.

Stowe, William W. *Going Abroad: European Travel in Nineteenth-Century American Culture.* Princeton, NJ: Princeton University Press, 1994.

Zagarri, Rosemarie. "Morals, Manners, and the Republican Mother." *American Quarterly* 44 (June 1992): 26–43.

≈

CHAPTER FIFTEEN

James MacQueen (1778–1870)

Agent of Imperial Change in the Caribbean and Africa

Jeff Pardue

James MacQueen was a passionate and unabashed imperialist, a Scotsman who actively promoted projects in Africa and the Caribbean to expand the British Empire that also coincided with his own business ventures. Much like João da Silva Feijó's scientific work in Brazil and William Bullock's antiquarian research in Mexico, MacQueen's geographical explorations in Africa reveal the close connection between knowledge, empire, and power in the Atlantic world. Historian Jeff Pardue outlines the high points of MacQueen's long and vocal career as a proslavery planter in Grenada, a pamphleteer in Great Britain during the emancipation debates, an agent for the Colonial Bank, and a self-trained geographer who charted the interior of Africa as part of his plan for expanding the British Empire. MacQueen's life and activities reveal the ways in which the advancing technological abilities of European powers (mail, steamships, and railroads), coupled with more aggressive racial and imperialist attitudes, spurred politicians and capitalists to view Africa as a source of wealth beyond the vestiges of the dying trade in enslaved humans. In this regard, he contributed to the "scramble for Africa" and presaged the more famous career of men like Cecil Rhodes.

In 1805, a young Scotsman named James MacQueen read explorer Mungo Park's travel diary called *Journey into the Interior Districts of Africa in the Years 1795, 1796 and 1797* out loud to the slaves he managed on Westerhall Estate, a large sugar plantation in southern Grenada. He was surprised to discover that some slaves recognized the descriptions of West Africa, especially the area around the Niger River. Park had traveled the region extensively and provided a fascinating account of the peoples and cultures there, but he never managed to answer a centuries-long mystery as to where the river emptied. In the Nile? In Senegal? In the Bight of Biafra? MacQueen, his interest piqued, began interviewing slaves on other estates regarding the Niger's route. His attention to a relatively small geographical question soon broadened into full-fledged dreams of creating a British empire in Africa. Thus began MacQueen's lifelong pursuit.

A plantation manager from Scotland reading to slaves from West Africa in the West Indies: the scene is a perfect metaphor for the British Empire in the Atlantic world. On the one hand, it highlights how the fertile soil of the Americas brought Europeans and Africans (and Amerindians, where they still survived) together in the creation of a truly "New World." On the other, it illustrates how Europeans began looking back across the ocean to Africa in this period. MacQueen's career can help us gain a better understanding of the British Empire, its evolution, and its place in the Atlantic world in the nineteenth century.

The nature of British imperialism changed substantially during MacQueen's lifetime. After the loss of the thirteen colonies in 1783 and for about the next century, the British concentrated more energy on expanding their trade instead of expanding their territorial empire. New economic and political theories undermined the foundations of early modern imperialism. The economic argument stated that trade made money, not colonies, because the administrative and military costs of governing overseas territories offset any significant profits. And the new ideas of liberty and equality challenged not only the hierarchical mother country–dependent colony model but also the slave system that supported it. In light of these changes, it is tempting to label the period from 1783 to 1880 as "antiempire" because of the dampened enthusiasm for large-scale imperialist activities. But this is only if one defines imperialism as conquest and colonization of territory. A more useful definition would include control: control of other peoples or regions by a central authority. MacQueen's career will illustrate that British imperialism was alive and well on both sides of the Atlantic, either through increased commercial control of the West Indies (through regulated banks and mail services) or through government-funded expeditions, naval bases, and anti-slavery squadrons in Africa.

James MacQueen was born June 21, 1778, in Lanarkshire, Scotland, a county about one hundred miles southeast of Glasgow. He came from a family of little means and by all accounts was a competent and tireless worker.

Conservative, humorless, and abrasive, MacQueen made a name for himself first as a defender of slavery and the West Indies, then as an Africa expert. He published dozens of books, pamphlets, and articles in his career, even into his eighties. At one point in the late 1830s (when he was sixty), MacQueen was simultaneously an agent for two companies as well as an adviser to abolitionist T. F. Buxton and the Colonial Office regarding the African slave trade. Meanwhile, he was writing his monumental A Geographical Survey of Africa. MacQueen was also a dreamer. He formulated gigantic schemes to further British interests in both the West Indies and West Africa. One would be hard pressed to find a better example of a person's career more influenced by the Atlantic world than James MacQueen.

In 1796, at the age of eighteen, MacQueen went to the Caribbean island of Grenada to work as a plantation manager, which he did ably for the next fourteen years. It was here that MacQueen came to understand the sugar industry, developed his attachment to the West Indies and their colonial residents, and was introduced to West African people and culture for the first time. During that period, MacQueen also developed his anti-French, proslavery stance, which was hardly unique for his time. In MacQueen's case, however, his attitudes became sharpened because of a nearly successful slave resistance movement. Just prior to his arrival, the island had struggled through Fédon's Rebellion, a French-backed armed rebellion of Grenadian slaves and francophone free coloreds and whites, led by Julien Fédon between March 1795 and July 1796. The rebellion nearly succeeded in removing the British from the island (in January 1796, Fédon's forces held all of Grenada save the capital, St. George's) and was crushed only after a series of bloody engagements. The rebellion had a fatal impact on the island's economy. The extensive damage undermined its sugar production, and the island reverted to small-scale agriculture. More significant, however, was the psychological shock of the rebellion, which convinced many white residents to leave for safer places. The white population sunk to an all-time low of 633 in 1810, the year MacQueen himself left.

MacQueen returned to Scotland and supported himself in Glasgow as a wine and spirits merchant. The Grenada experience affected him deeply. He vented his hatred of the French in his first book, which was titled The Campaigns of 1812, 1813, and 1814; this massive work spanned over one thousand pages and cataloged the destruction resulting from Napoleon's armies in particular and from the subversive ideas of the French Revolution in general. After calculating a staggering £7,119,307,446 damage done to all European nations during the conflict, MacQueen concluded that "such is a faint and but a faint sketch indeed of the system of robbery and oppression exercised in

France during the golden days of Liberty and Equality. . . . From the General on downwards, plunder was the order of the day; and the Liberty and Equality which they carried along with them, entitled them, as they conceived, to make everyone alike, with regard to property." Mediocre in its literary and intellectual qualities, MacQueen's book was forcefully written and had the appearance of authority with his ample use of statistics. In a sense, the work was a sort of personal catharsis and a public rejection of rebellions fought in the name of liberty.

Africa had become MacQueen's real passion. Inspired by his experience with West African slaves and African geographical mysteries, he went to London in 1820 with a grand plan to establish a British empire in West Africa. MacQueen proposed that a government-backed company should explore and exploit those interior regions where the Niger River and its branches reached. By collaborating with native princes, British entrepreneurs could form plantations where they would grow produce using indigenous slave labor. The entire idea hinged on the discovery of the location where the Niger emptied; without this knowledge, there would be no other practical way to penetrate the interior. After consulting a variety of sources, from ancient Greek and medieval Arab to contemporaries such as Mungo Park, MacQueen speculated that the Niger did empty into the Atlantic Ocean at what was called the Oil Rivers delta at the time (today located in southern Nigeria). One potential patron, James, Duke of Montrose, was impressed with MacQueen's research and agreed that his geographical theories "seemed consistent with the facts" but resisted government sponsorship and argued that "Individual Enterprise is the only chance of making these discoveries." Without any significant support from either quarter, MacQueen's plan went nowhere. The experience hardly discouraged him, however; it simply convinced him to change tack. In a letter to his friend, fellow conservative, and publisher William Blackwood, MacQueen swore that from this period forward his "chief object with regards to Africa is publicity." For a visionary like MacQueen, the episode reveals how a person from a relatively low social and economic station could try to realize his plans: first, privately try to secure influential government officials and businessmen; if that fails, "go public." The formula explains MacQueen's extensive publication record.

MacQueen made good on his pronouncement to Blackwood. In 1821, he became the editor and proprietor of the ultraconservative newspaper the *Glasgow Courier* and published a book called *A Geographical and Commercial View of Northern and Central Africa*, which contains a fascinating mix of geography, politics, and self-promotion. On its surface, *A Geographical and Commercial View* is a geographical description of what we would roughly characterize as West Africa today. Most obviously, the maps and the lengthy descriptions of vegetation, resources, and people were all meant to illustrate the economic potential of that region—a promotional strategy that dated back to the earliest European explorers who tried to sell their discoveries back home. MacQueen also expanded on his Niger theory with additional sources and reiterated his call for British bases both at the mouth of the delta and farther upriver in the interior. Of course, any attempt to establish a more consciously exploitative and imperial British base of operations in West Africa would bring the entrepreneur into conflict with the opposing powers who sponsored the only other base in the region: the antislavery colony of Sierra Leone. MacQueen was not ignorant of the implications of his book's argument, and in this way his proslavery politics permeated a work that purported to be geographical in nature.

MacQueen had no intention of overtly alienating antislavery groups at that juncture. Indeed, he attempted to appeal to the widest possible audience not only by promoting the economic potential of West Africa but also by addressing some of the humanitarians' concerns. He altruistically claimed that his scheme would benefit both Britain and Africa: the former by giving it fresh colonies to replace the lost ones and thus reinvigorate the nation and the latter by teaching it to be civilized through legitimate industry. He argued that emancipation would come gradually as these colonies became more prosperous. He then took this logic one step further and argued that European colonial slavery in the New World would end only when slavery ceased in Africa; he wrote, "It is in Africa, therefore, that this evil [slavery] must be rooted out—by African hands and African exertions chiefly that it can be destroyed." Although MacQueen was almost completely ignorant about indigenous forms of African slavery, his statement was particularly self-serving. Nevertheless, his words were prophetic about the necessity of both legitimate trade and African agency in ending slavery.

His book is fascinating for historians today but at the time held limited interest for a very small audience. His own newspaper, the *Glasgow Courier*, was the means by which he aimed to influence the general public. The triweekly publication had been a conservative paper ever since William Reid founded it in 1790, but under MacQueen it became a bastion of high Toryism in the Scottish West. It opposed every major reform of the period, including Catholic emancipation (1829), parliamentary reform (1832), and most (in)famously, the emancipation of slaves (1833). MacQueen's work at the *Glasgow Courier* taught him the skills and methods to fight in a public medium that became immensely important assets for his subsequent career. He put these skills to use almost immediately but not to promote his dreams of Africa. Instead, he found himself aiding a rearguard action on the other side of the Atlantic: the defense of slavery in the West Indies.

"And who is this Mr. MacQueen?" asked the somewhat bewildered London newspaper *The New Times* in September 1824, when a new voice appeared in the debate over slave emancipation. That was the year when James MacQueen came to national prominence either as a powerful and disinterested authority according to those with West Indian interests or as an obnoxious and radical proslavery mercenary according to antislavery proponents. For nearly a decade, until the issue was settled in 1833, Mac-Queen maintained this dual image with a prolific output of material written in a style he had learned in the newspaper business: forceful, personal, and antagonistic. Whatever one's position on the subject, MacQueen undoubtedly had become one of the leading voices throughout the tumultuous debate over British slavery.

The debate over slavery itself was resurrected by an East India merchant, James Cropper, in 1823. Resenting the protectionist duties placed on all non–West Indian sugar, he attacked the economic basis for slavery and West India privilege using the laissez-faire arguments of Adam Smith. Cropper's critique prompted a revival of the Anti-Slavery Society, an organization that attacked slavery on several fronts. The reenergized debate of the 1820s covered a range of issues as old as the antislavery movement itself, including disputes over the relevance of certain biblical passages and comparisons made between slaves and the English working class. Contrary to what we might expect, proslavery advocates in this period such as MacQueen did not defend "absolute and perpetual slavery" (i.e., the idea that African slaves were part of a fixed cosmic hierarchy); that argument had been discredited since the early eighteenth century. Instead, MacQueen and his contemporaries usually prefaced their position with a disclaimer that they opposed slavery in the abstract but that certain economic and cultural imperatives required its continued existence at the present. Of the over 150 proslavery works written between 1823 and emancipation, roughly 25 percent dealt specifically with property rights and compensation. Virtually every defense of slavery followed the same formula: the professed revulsion of slavery as an institution, followed by an appeal to the sanctity of property and British law and the subtle but very important qualifier that if (when?) emancipation should come, remuneration for legally attained property should be forthcoming.

MacQueen's arguments in those years followed this standard pattern; he was one of the most prolific and passionate defenders of slavery and the West Indies generally. He had made enough of a name for himself that by 1823 the West Indian Association in London solicited his polemical services. They paid him one hundred guineas to answer an article on the "sugar question" that had appeared in the influential liberal journal *The Edinburgh Review*. He subsequently published two books, *The West India Colonies* (1824) and *The Colonial Controversy* (1825), which catapulted him into the national debate and won him wider recognition in the Caribbean colonies. The *Barbadian* exclaimed that the former book "ought to be in every man's library" and suggested "that meetings ought to be held in every Colony, to vote an address to Mr. M'Queen, expressive of our grateful sense of his labourious and disinterested exertions . . . calculated, *if any human effort can*, to undeceive the British public on the subject, connected with our future existence as part of the British dominions." On the other side of the issue, he was despised with just as much vehemence. In his hometown of Glasgow, for example, a mocking placard was posted in 1826: "Wanted Immediately: MANUFAC-TURING LABOURERS to go out to the West Indies. 3000 Manufacturing Labourers, who will engage to go out to the West Indies, will receive of course NO wages but all the kind attention, treatment, comfort, indulgences and privileges, etc. etc. . . . with the addition of a LARGE CART WHIP, frequently and powerfully to their bare bones. . . . For particulars, apply to James M'Slavery." MacQueen was hardly deterred by such attacks. Indeed, they only prompted him to redouble his efforts in the debate. Between 1827 and 1833, for example, he published no fewer than fourteen pro–West Indian articles in *Blackwood's Magazine* alone. He was also well rewarded for his efforts: by the time of emancipation, he had received over £6,000.

What distinguished the substance of MacQueen's argument from other writers was his incorporation of continental Africa into the debate. Mac-Queen's two passions came together in a unique moment during the slavery debate. In particular, MacQueen attacked the antislavery colony of Sierra Leone, which had been the refuge of freed slaves ever since 1787. Mac-Queen hoped to undermine the humanitarians' credibility and sense of competence by pointing out the manifold problems with the colony. It was a soft target to hit because the settlement had experienced several difficulties since its foundation. Economically, it struggled along mainly through charitable donations by wealthy sympathizers until 1807 when it became a base for British antislavery operations in West Africa. Since that point, it had survived on government subsidies. It was poorly located for the naval operations that were involved in suppressing the slave trade, and the "court of mixed commission" established there to try illegal slavers became an infamous "European grave" for judges who agreed to serve. MacQueen's devastating offensive in his books and articles helped inspire the appointment of a select committee on the subject to which MacQueen was one of the expert witnesses. The committee concluded that Sierra Leone was, indeed, quite unsuccessful in achieving any of its professed goals, that it was useless for British needs, and that a new base should be formed.

As it became clear that emancipation was coming, MacQueen made a last-ditch effort to rally the colonists by touring the West Indies in 1832 and 1833. Receiving a hero's welcome on every island, he called for unity and conservative defiance that fell short of outright rebellion. His speech in Jamaica was typical. MacQueen shouted, "Colonists! Tell your misguided country that if slavery is a sin, a shame, and a crime, it is she, not you, who is the criminal, because it was she, not you, who created it for the Colonies." His last address in the West Indies is the most interesting because for the first time he appealed to free coloreds to join in the colonial struggle: "Union is strength! Let all classes, but more especially the white and free coloured population, be united, and I am delighted!" It was all too late, however, since the West Indian merchants in London were already negotiating the terms of emancipation and compensation between April and June 1833. MacQueen and his side had failed, but his vociferous defense had gained him credibility for his future schemes in a postslavery world.

It was not long before MacQueen made productive use of this goodwill. If he was bitter, he was also realistic, and urged the West Indians to look ahead. Over the next decade and a half, he helped found two important companies that would aid the West Indies after emancipation: the Colonial Bank and the Royal Mail Steam Packet Company (RMSP). Both were vital in shoring up the ties between the European metropolis and this wilting part of the periphery. The former was formed to cope with the economic revolution of emancipation. Since wages now had to be paid, banking and other financial services were needed to support a free, income-earning society. MacQueen became the Colonial Bank's principal agent in the West Indies, responsible for establishing the company's initial infrastructure there—choosing locations, hiring senior staff, identifying conflicts in the colonial banking laws, and the like. By the end of 1837, there were three principal branches in Jamaica, St. Thomas, and Barbados and thirteen subordinate branches, making the Colonial Bank the largest and most influential institution of its kind in the West Indies.

During his work with the Colonial Bank, MacQueen began planning the RMSP Company, which would offer a regular mail service to the British West Indies. He developed the original plan for the RMSP Company, contributed all the early major modifications for this complex undertaking, single-handedly promoted the plan to the British government, and laid the administrative groundwork on both sides of the Atlantic. Logistics alone hint at the enormity of the project: MacQueen had to locate coal depots (in both Britain and the West Indies), lighthouses, supply stores for vessels, offices, food and uniforms for commanders and crews, and necessary port facilities. He had to promote his plan to government officials in the Admiralty, Treasury, and Post Office as well as to private investors. After four years, his hard work paid off. In 1842, the service became operational with an unprecedented fourteen newly constructed four-hundred-horsepower steam vessels and a £240,000-per-year government subsidy. Despite numerous problems, the company brought speed and regularity to the West Indian mail system for the first time. MacQueen had helped to build another bridge across the Atlantic.

Given his volatile personality, it is perhaps not surprising that MacQueen eventually had a bitter falling out with both companies. More significantly, he began to break with the West Indians more generally over Africa. While his heart was in the West Indies, his head increasingly was immersed in Africa. His differences with the West Indians go back at least to 1821 and the publication of A Geographical and Commercial View when he recognized that the British Caribbean colonies were a dying branch of the empire: "Our West India colonies are . . . on the decline. The system that made them is destroyed; and it is quite certain, that a revolution of internal establishments, violent or gradual, is not far distant, either of which will work such a change as will render these possessions of little value as commercial colonies." Other issues strained his relationship as well. They clashed over the British Antislavery Squadron patrolling the coast of West Africa for illegal slavers: the West Indians saw it as a vital measure to keep illegal slaves from getting into competing foreign colonies; MacQueen saw it as a colossal waste of money that could be much better spent founding new colonies in West Africa itself. At emancipation, MacQueen criticized the larger planters for what he claimed was the unfair distribution of the compensation payments. Subsequently, he continued to attack the policy of African immigration to the West Indies. And, perhaps most disturbing to the West Indian planters, MacQueen had begun to consort with his former enemies, the abolitionists.

In fact, it was the abolitionists who provided the initial opportunity for MacQueen's reentry into African affairs and provided the first major recognition of his work with Africa. With British slave emancipation accomplished, abolitionists turned their attention to the international slave trade. In particular, T. F. Buxton, former leader of the Anti-Slavery Society and one of the most influential men in the country, concluded that the only way to end slavery permanently was to put an end to its roots in Africa; with this object in mind, he helped found the African Civilization Society in 1839.

That MacQueen had been arguing this same point for twenty years perhaps explains why Buxton invited him to Leamington in May 1838 to talk about Africa, specifically the extent of the slave trade and MacQueen's plan to eliminate it. In Buxton's book on the subject, titled *The African Slave Trade and Its Remedy* (1840), he adopted most of the practical components of Mac-Queen's original scheme but none of its political principles. Buxton agreed with the locations of the coastal and interior bases as a way of introducing legitimate commerce and undermining the slave trade. However, he made it clear that he did not intend to erect a new empire in Africa because he believed that Britain had a debt to pay; instead, Buxton urged his readers "to recollect that for centuries we were mainly instrumental in checking the cultivation in Africa: we ransacked the whole continent in order to procure labourers for the West Indies." MacQueen cringed at such statements of moral culpability. Why did these two former enemies meet in the first place? Buxton had been the target of some of MacQueen's most vicious attacks during the emancipation debate. The answer is that at that moment, the two men needed each other: Buxton needed an Africa expert, and MacQueen needed someone of influence who cared about Africa.

Buxton's version of what was essentially MacQueen's plan became a reality in 1839 when the Colonial Office became convinced of its value. MacQueen was again summoned for advice on some of the more specific details. More than this, Colonial Secretary Charles Grant (Lord Glenelg) proposed that MacQueen be appointed as the agent for the upcoming expedition. Because of his age and his work with the RMSP Company at the time, MacQueen did not accompany the expedition, which was just as well for him since the journey ended in disaster. The suggestion, however, confirmed MacQueen's status as one of Britain's foremost authorities on Africa.

After the establishment of the RMSP Company in the early 1840s, Mac-Queen turned his attention exclusively to Africa. In 1840, he published his last major work, *A Geographical Survey of Africa*. Benefiting from the ground-breaking expeditions of the 1820s and 1830s, the book offered a broader and far more accurate picture of the African continent than had existed before. In one respect, the book is a testament to the extraordinary advances that Europeans had made in opening Africa, such as René De Caillié's expedition to Timbuktu in 1827–1829 and Richard Lander's expedition down the last five hundred miles of the Niger River that confirmed that it emptied into the Atlantic. Ultimately, however, this book was part of MacQueen's last attempt to get his plan adopted. In several letters written to government officials in 1844–1845, including Prime Minister Sir Robert Peel, he emphasized the problems of importing free laborers into the West Indies and warned of the dangers arising from Britain's dependence on the United States for almost all its cotton. The government responded with polite apathy, but MacQueen was able to convince a group of private investors to form a company under the directorship of prominent banker Alexander Baring (Lord Ashburton) in 1847. Granted a government charter, the directors drew up a prospectus and held their first meeting. However, the company stalled because of the economic tumult in the wake of the repeal of the Corn Laws and never got back on track.

Repeated failures to colonize Africa increasingly left MacQueen with only his geographical work as a viable legacy. Indeed, MacQueen became a respected geographer. He advised several groups on African affairs, mostly those humanitarian organizations that retained an interest in Africa. He became a fellow of the Royal Geographical Society (RGS) in 1845 and presented half a dozen of his own papers and communicated four others. MacQueen ended his career as a correspondent for the *Morning Advertiser*. By then in his eighties, he managed to jump into the fray of one last public debate, this time over the source of the Nile River, which explorer John Speke claimed to have located in Lake Victoria in 1859. Speke presented his findings to the RGS later that year and then published *Journal of the Discovery of the Source of the Nile* in 1863. His claims were hotly contested by expedition leader Richard Burton, and the dispute split geographers (as well as the reading public) into differing camps. MacQueen threw his weight behind Burton in a manner reminiscent of his earlier days—legitimate questions about the topic at hand obscured by unceasing personal attacks. MacQueen's collected articles on the subject were published in a single volume together with Burton's own views of the Nile's source, which he had previously presented to the RGS. Burton offered an interestingly qualified endorsement of MacQueen in the preface: "To the veteran African geographer, Mr. James Macqueen, my thanks are especially due. . . . His literary labours in the cause of the Dark Peninsula have extended through half a century, and hardly ever before has he shown greater acumen or higher spirit—to say nothing of his inimitable dryness of style—than in those compositions, put forth at a time when the English world was bowing down before it latest idol." Presumably the "latest idol" was Speke's latest theory on the source of the Nile, and thus Burton is praising MacQueen's reviews. Nevertheless, Burton must have been embarrassed by parts of MacQueen's reviews since the book was published just after Speke's shocking "gun accident," which occurred the day before he was to debate Burton at the RGS. On hearing the news, Burton is said to have cried, "By God, he's killed himself."

MacQueen himself died of natural causes on May 14, 1870, aged ninety-two, in his London home at Bury Street, St. James. On his death certificate, his occupation was listed simply as a "gentleman." In almost every sense, this term was inappropriate. MacQueen was never wealthy enough to claim much status. In fact, he died penniless, leaving behind a fifty-nine-year-old spinster daughter named Jean, who was destitute and who subsequently survived on charity collected by RGS fellows. Yet even in his more prosperous days, MacQueen never sought to escape the grind of work or the activity of the city in order to retire to a gentlemanly life in the countryside. Furthermore, he was hardly gentlemanly in his public writings. On the other hand, the term does capture some of the ambiguity of MacQueen's position in British society; he had no professional training or function but was successful as an amateur, enthusiast, and hobbiest of several endeavors.

One can sympathize, then, with those who had to specify MacQueen's occupation. Probably a more accurate term would have been an anachronistic one: "imperialist." The label captures the essence of MacQueen's career and also suggests that he himself was somewhat anachronistic to his age. MacQueen would have been much more comfortable in the mercantilist empire of the seventeenth and eighteenth centuries or in the chauvinistic empire of the late nineteenth and early twentieth centuries. Throughout his life, he seemed to have had one foot in each of these worlds and for the most part seems to have fallen in between them in his own time. His support for the old West Indies culture and economy came too late, while his interest in African potential came too early.

Even MacQueen himself remained a frustrated man because of his inability to connect with government officials or with the British public on his ideas about the British Empire. But it is a mistake to judge his legacy this way, to judge it on the basis of his backward-looking defense of slavery or on his premature plans for an African empire. While MacQueen did not contribute to the direct acquisition of overseas territory—"imperialism" in its classic sense—he did help to turn the eyes of the British government and reading public from the Caribbean toward Africa. His defense of slavery, the establishment of the Colonial Bank and Royal Mail Steam Packet Company, and his efforts to advance the accurate geographical knowledge of Africa are significant examples of his work (even if MacQueen considered them sidelights to his larger goals), and they collectively formed part of the larger developments of British imperialism in this period.

Growing up in a world shaped by mercantilism and war, MacQueen had always fought for strong central authority. His plans for Africa called for state-sponsored protection and, to a lesser extent, administration. Mac-

Queen was part of a more general process of centralizing authority in the metropolis. In MacQueen's experience, this shift took three basic forms: 1) private companies with colonial interests, as with the new multinational banks and stream packet companies, backed by government charters and empirewide government regulations; 2) renewed interest in examining and mapping the wider world, which was encouraged and aided by renewed official support for exploration; and 3) increased government intervention in the form of important policies and regulations that affected the colonies, either directly, as with emancipation, or more indirectly, as with the banking and postal regulations. Many of the developments were outgrowths of larger centralizing trends in Britain, such as the reorganization of the Post Office in the late 1830s and the muscular antislavery policies of the government, represented most clearly by its Antislavery Squadron. MacQueen's long and diverse career allows us the opportunity to see these developments together.

Archival Sources

Blackwood Papers. National Library of Scotland.
Colonial Bank Papers. Barclays Group Archives, Manchester.
Glasgow West Indian Association Papers. Mitchell Library, Glasgow.
Peel Papers. British Library, London.
Royal Geographical Society, General Correspondence. RGS Archives, London.
Royal Mail Steam Packet Company Records. National Maritime Museum, Greenwich.

Bibliography and Suggested Reading

The Barbadian.
Butler, Kathleen Mary. The Economics of Emancipation: Jamaica and Barbados, 1823–1843. Chapel Hill: University of North Carolina Press, 1995.
Cox, Edward. "Fédon's Rebellion 1795–96: Causes and Consequences." Journal of Negro History 67 (1982): 7–20.
———. Free Coloreds in the Slave Societies of St. Kitts and Grenada, 1763–1833. Knoxville: University of Tennessee Press, 1984.
Curtin, Philip D. The Image of Africa: British Ideas and Action, 1780–1850. Madison: University of Wisconsin Press, 1964.
Davis, David Brion. The Problem of Slavery in Western Culture. Ithaca, NY: Cornell University Press, 1966.
Dike, K. Onwuka. Trade and Politics in the Niger Delta 1830–1885. Oxford: Oxford University Press, 1956.
The Glasgow Courier.

Green, William A. *British Slave Emancipation: The Sugar Colonies and the Great Experiment 1830–1865*. Oxford: Oxford University Press, 1976.

Harcourt, Freda. "British Oceanic Mail Contracts in the Age of Steam 1838–1914." *Journal of Transport History* 9 (1988): 1–18.

Hibbert, Christopher. *Africa Explored: Europeans in the Dark Continent, 1769–1889*. Harmondsworth: Penguin Classics, 1985.

Jones, Geoffrey. *British Multinational Banking 1830–1990*. Oxford: Oxford University Press, 1993.

MacQueen, James. *A Geographical & Commercial View of Northern and Central Africa*. Edinburgh, 1821.

———. *The West India Colonies*. London, 1824; 2nd ed. 1829.

———. *A Geographical Survey of Africa*. London, 1840.

Robinson, Ronald, and John Gallagher. *Africa and the Victorians: The Official Mind of Imperialism*. London: Macmillan, 1961.

Stafford, Robert. *Scientist of Empire: Sir Roderick Murchison, Scientific Exploration and Victorian Imperialism*. Cambridge: Cambridge University Press, 1989.

Temperley, Howard. *White Dreams, Black Africa: The Antislavery Expedition to the River Niger 1841–1842*. New Haven, CT: Yale University Press, 1991.

CHAPTER SIXTEEN

William Bullock (1780–1844)

British Museum Curator and Showman in Mexico

Robert D. Aguirre

Antiquities collector and museum curator William Bullock was an important figure in the cross-cultural history of early nineteenth-century Atlantic world. His life and interests reflect a continued interest in Mexican wealth, exoticism, and opportunities that existed centuries earlier when William Lamport hoped to set himself up as its king. A successful museum curator in London, Bullock traveled to Mexico in 1822 and journeyed around the country for six months before returning home with trunks full of strange treasures to display for the voracious crowds. At his Piccadilly Museum, Bullock sponsored the first European exhibit of Aztec antiquities and contemporary Mexican artifacts that had been held in over two hundred years. He also mounted a panorama of Mexico City at the round theater in Leicester Square in 1826 and published a popular memoir of his travels. As cultural historian and literary critic Robert Aguirre shows, Bullock's antiquarian research and display practices capitalized on the British public's fascination with the pre-Columbian past and fed British investors' appetite for access to Mexican mines and markets. The British Museum purchased his collection in the late 1820s, where it now figures prominently in their recently opened Mexican Gallery.

William Bullock is among the most important figures in the early years of Britain's transatlantic relationship with newly independent Mexico. Naturalist, antiquary, traveler, and museum showman, Bullock was the son of William Bullock and Elizabeth, née Smallwood, who were the owners of a traveling waxworks, and he was the brother of George Bullock, a noted Regency sculptor and furniture maker. He had two other brothers, James and Joseph. Although details about Bullock's youth are sketchy, he was probably born in the early 1780s in Birmingham, where his parents are known to have been in business. The shape of Bullock's subsequent transatlantic ventures—the focus of the latter part of this chapter—are suggested by his choice of a career in museum display and his interests in showmanship, rational classification, and ethnography.

Bullock began collecting in the late 1790s while working as a silversmith in Sheffield. By 1801, he had moved to Liverpool, where he opened the Liverpool Museum. He published a series of descriptive catalogs that detailed his rich and extensive holdings: art works, armory, natural history pieces, and curiosities brought by Captain Cook from the South Seas, some of which Bullock had acquired secondhand from Richard Green's Lichfield Museum and Sir Ashton Lever's collections. Bullock took special advantage of Liverpool's rich dockside traffic in exotic wares brought home by overseas explorers, paying special attention to a class of items commonly called "curiosities," a term that is a noun (a curiosity), adjective (it is curious), and a measure of the "knower's intellectual and experiential desire" (one's interest is curious).[1] People like Bullock who valued curiosities were known as *curiosi*. Sir Hans Sloane, whose donated collection of curiosities in 1757 established the British Museum, was England's greatest example of the collector of curiosities, and William Bullock aspired to amass a collection that would rival Sloane's by the 1820s. Bullock's museums, like the British Museum, demonstrated the significance of curiosity as a positive attribute of Enlightenment science; both museums were extensively involved in transatlantic collecting and did much to introduce people and cultures to one another and to display a clear link between commerce, race, and entertainment.

Like other collectors before him, Bullock relied on travelers to supply exotic things for display at home, and he was keen to associate his collections with the exploits of celebrated adventurers. His 1810 museum catalog boasted of "seven thousand natural and foreign curiosities, antiquities, and productions of the fine arts,"[2] which included ethnographic artifacts from Africa and the Americas as well as some "brought from the South Seas during the Voyages of Discovery of Captain Cook," indeed the "*identical* Idols, Weapons, and other domestic and military implements engraved in the History of those Voyages."[3] For Bullock, objects increased in value not only by their rarity and distance from Britain but also by their association with the heroic deeds of explorers such as Cook and his naturalist Joseph Banks. The acquisition and display of these objects, in turn, suggested the appropriative reach of the British Empire and sharpened the distinction, crucial to the cultural justifications for imperial expansion, between primitive peoples, who merely made curiosities, and advanced peoples, who arranged, labeled, and categorized them into rational taxonomies such as the Linnaean order, which Bullock strictly followed. By developing such devices as the habitat group—vivid tableaux that re-created the postures and physical surroundings of creatures in their native surroundings—Bullock made the museum into the image of an orderly world and thus a metaphor for European mastery of the natural world.

In 1809, Bullock moved his museum from Liverpool to London, commissioning the architect Peter F. Robinson (1776–1858) to design an ornate building for his collections in Piccadilly, which was completed in 1812 at a cost of £16,000.[4] The Egyptian Hall, as the building came to be known, featured a facade inspired by the Temple of Hathor at Dendera that played skillfully off the nation's Orientalist fantasies. These fantasies were heightened by the British triumph over Napoleon, whose invasion of Egypt had produced one of the most lavish works of Egyptology, Edme-François Jomard's *Description de l'Égypte* (published 1809–1828) as well as a massive hoard of antiquities that the British appropriated on defeating the French army there. Thus equipped, the Egyptian Hall soon became part of fashionable London, with both its frame and its contents reinforcing an ideology of imperial possession that inspired Bullock's later transatlantic ventures. From rather humble beginnings in the Liverpool dockside trade in curiosities, Bullock rose to an important place in the world of London exhibitionary culture. His showcase extended the Enlightenment concept of possessive individualism to the nation, rivaling (and to some observers besting) the nation's official repository, the British Museum, which, by its recent acquisition of spectacular treasures such as the Rosetta Stone (1802) and the Elgin Marbles (1816), had become a crucial site for expressing Britain's control over the material remains of ancient great civilizations.

The importance of trophies to nationalist sentiment was vividly displayed by Bullock's 1816 exhibition of Napoleon's military carriage, a vehicle that had been captured in the war with France.[5] The carriage was displayed in London for a year before going on an extended tour of the provinces, reaping Bullock a profit of over £25,000. Bullock's exhibition catalog, reprinted by Marie Tussaud when she purchased the carriage in the 1840s, held out the possibility that on seeing the carriage for themselves, viewers would form "an immediate connection" with "the greatest events and persons that the world has ever beheld."[6] In 1819, after the unequivocal success of this display, Bullock auctioned the miscellaneous contents of his London museum—including his thirty-two thousand "remarkable subjects of animated nature"[7]—and mounted a string of single-subject exhibits with strong national themes: Egyptian antiquities collected by the Orientalist adventurer and fellow showman Giovanni Battista Belzoni (1821);[8] a family of Laplanders (1822), which evoked the Polar journeys of James Clark Ross and Edward Parry; and "Ancient and Modern Mexico" (1824). These exhibits functioned as complex, multilayered symbols of Britain's interest in territories at the colonial periphery. They exemplified both a more systematic analysis of "culture"— focused on the material productions of specific groups of peoples—and a closer coordination with the territorial ambitions of the nation. Each staged an exotic region that had recently come—or was in the process of coming— under British domination, and each illustrated the art of dominating from a distance, a principal feature of which was the removal of objects to the centers of calculation in an ever-growing chain of accumulation.[9]

Bullock's six-month tour of Mexico, undertaken in 1823, two years after that country gained its independence, was the most important of his ventures in the Atlantic context. Bullock was fascinated by stories of the ancient glories of the Aztecs and the more recent memories of vast fortunes made in the silver mines. Serving as a template for many subsequent travelers, Bullock's skill in self-promotion and his ability to produce stunning, eye-catching displays made him a celebrity and an assumed authority on indigenous culture. After touring Mexico, surveying its mining industry, and collecting rare artifacts of pre-Columbian antiquity, Bullock returned to Britain full of energy and enthusiasm. He published a best-selling, lavishly illustrated account of his journey called Six Months Travel and Residence in Mexico (1824); exhibited a large panoramic painting of Mexico City in Leicester Square; and mounted an exhibit of ancient and modern Mexican artifacts—the first display to be offered in Europe since the sixteenth century—at the Egyptian Hall in Piccadilly. In 1827, the British Museum acquired Bullock's Mexican antiquities, displaying them first in a gallery of "Artificial Curiosities" and later in the "Ethnographical Room." His collection paved the way for the intense British interest in Mesoamerican art that continued to expand throughout the nineteenth century.[10]

Bullock's Mexican venture, moreover, occurred at a critical moment in the history of the Atlantic world, when British merchants yearned for a trade agreement with the newly independent Spanish American republics and seemingly all of London was astir with news of riches buried in Mexico's silver mines. Bullock's cultural productions fed this frenzy, throwing the bright light of publicity on Mexico's cultural and economic resources and serving as a vivid reminder for the empire's extractive reach. Although self-

described as a "mere searcher after Antiquities" (AMM, iii), Bullock emphasized the economic potential of Mexico by representing it as "one vast field
for the exercise of British capital, machinery, and industry" (MM, 4).[11] The
Times of London, suggesting the link between the scientific and extractive
operations of imperialism, noted that in "ransack[ing] the superb capital of
Mexico" Bullock's only difficulty lay in "how to collect the best and carry off
the most."[12] Like other British travelers to Latin America during this period,
Bullock believed in the "mutually conducive" and "reciprocal advantages" of
laissez-faire trade (AMM, iii–iv). Taking his cue from Adam Smith, he commented that Mexico lacked only the "fostering hand of a free, enlightened
and enterprising" nation and the "knowledge imparted by modern science"
to usher it into a prosperous and technologically sophisticated modernity
(AMM, iv). British overseas capitalism hungered after insider, on-the-spot
knowledge, and Bullock met this need with information designed to be
useful to British road builders, railway engineers, farmers, merchants, and
miners. Driven in part by Bullock's account of a soil "inexhaustible in the
precious metals" (AMM, iv), British investors spent millions on stocks in
Anglo-Mexican mining companies that lost all their value when the market
crashed. Mexicans, of course, also suffered from this cycle of speculation,
which formed an early episode in a century of economic and political en-
tanglement with Britain. Bullock's cultural work played an important role
here; the hunger for Mexican antiquities to display in European museums not
only contributed to the outflow of pre-Columbian art across the Atlantic but
also affirmed, at the level of material culture, an uneven power dynamic in
which modern Mexicans were characterized as technologically undeveloped
and ripe for economic exploitation.

Bullock's Mexican exhibition, which ran from April 1824 to September
1825, represented Mexico at a crucial moment in the transatlantic relationship between the two countries. The *Literary Gazette* observed that his exhibits were "calculated to be very beneficial to [the] country," an opinion shared
by much of the press.[13] The two-part museum exhibition linked commercial
enterprise and cultural knowledge, one part addressing Mexico's indigenous
past and the other showing its potential as a market for Britain's economic
ventures. In a display called "Modern Mexico," Bullock exhibited a carefully
"classed and arranged" array of objects that included models of Mexican
costumes illustrating "persons of all ranks and descriptions"; examples of
Mexican leatherwork, embroidery, and dyed textiles; a collection of minerals "in which the pure ores of gold and silver are seen in their native state";
and exotic vegetables and fruits, including avocados, melons, and mangos
(rich as the "clotted cream of Devonshire"). There were also specimens of

Mexican animals, birds, and fishes, all of which had been carefully preserved by master taxidermist Bullock himself, all intended to "throw a light" over Mexico's "productive industry" (AMM, 8–13). A Mexican native, José Cayetano Ponce de León, emerged from a thatched hut to speak with visitors, suggesting the existence of a "docile," "simple," and "contented" population who could be counted on to work the mines, British steam technology notwithstanding (AMM, 6, 8). The entire exhibit was suffused with economic imagery: Bullock displayed his collection of 170 stuffed hummingbirds in a case painted with a view of a "silver mine of del Bada . . . presented to Mr. Bullock by the Mexican Government"; the birds themselves he compared to the "brightest gems" (AMM, 12, 9). Bullock's miniature wax models of indigenous and Creole Mexicans were also inflected with economic assumptions. Their hierarchical arrangement (from upper to lower classes) mirrored that of the British spectators (AMM, 10, 17), supporting the idea that classificatory schemes underwrite social containment by grouping objects and spectators alike into fixed categories.[14] The lithographs produced for Bullock's travel narrative used traditional ethnographic techniques of visual representation to depict an ordered, settled, and safely postrevolutionary workforce, ready for employment in the service of British industry.

"Ancient Mexico," the other half of the exhibit, was dominated by more impersonal archaeological imagery. The hall was filled with sculptures, painted books (codices), and early postconquest maps that the catalogs described as both grotesque and culturally advanced at the same time. Towering the crowds were massive plaster casts of three Aztec monuments that had been discovered in the 1790s during street repairs in Mexico City: the fearsome nine-foot-high *Coatlicue*, her necklace adorned with severed hands; the *Piedra de Tízoc* (Stone of Tizoc), a giant cylindrical slab bedecked with symbolic carvings; and the *Piedra de Sol* (Stone of the Sun), which measured nine feet in diameter and illustrated the Aztecs' complex grasp of time.[15] It was an impressive show, and the hall was packed with curious audiences for its entire run. The transportation of these objects across the Atlantic illustrated the emergence of a powerful formula in which an initial instance of travel, collection, and exhibition gave birth to a cycle of accumulation that brought ever more objects across the Atlantic to museums and private collections in Britain.

The acquisition and display of archaeological materials constituted a significant advance in museum science and an extension of London's exhibitionary culture across the Atlantic to the Americas. The exhibits meshed closely with Bullock's travel narrative, which narrated key aspects of Mexican history and supplied economically useful ethnographic information about populations, customs, and practices. The show's anthropological dimension—itself oriented toward economic benefit—was embodied not only in the person of Bullock's token Mexican informant, José, but also in the very structure of the exhibit. Partitioned between "Ancient" and "Modern" Mexico, the design reinforced a distinction between the glorious but long-gone past and the present, progressive historical moment of the anthropologist or cultural observer.[16] In the Mexican context, this trope doomed the indigenous and the poor to a temporal no-man's-land outside modernity, separated from their noble past embodied in the pre-Columbian ruins as well as from the technological thrust of a forward-looking modernity typified by Bullock and other Europeans. Furthermore, the accelerating removal of Mexico's cultural treasures to distant museums also hampered the efforts of Mexican creole elites to use the ancient past in writing the new national narratives. The exhibits formed the cultural parallel to the economic designs of British investors, mine operators, and traders who hoped to profit from their transatlantic relationship with Mexico.

Bullock portrayed his Mexican venture as an act of heroic preservation, saving objects endangered by decay or neglect for the enjoyment and edification of future generations. The *Classical Journal* agreed, noting that Bullock had "rescued" many of the "most valuable antiquities," which are now "safely brought over" to England.[17] Yet to be "rescued," the objects had to be severed from their proper contexts, a process that distorted their meaning by placing them into a foreign context. The first clue to that displacement is the design of the galleries in which Bullock housed his collection. He placed "Ancient Mexico" upstairs in the Great Room of the Egyptian Hall, which had been designed in ornate Egyptian style. Bullock's catalog locates the Mexican past within the founding narratives of Western civilization, arguing for "the close and striking resemblance" between the "Antiquities of Mexico and Egypt. The mighty Pyramid, the hieroglyphic writing, the sculptured stone, are almost alike; and their kindred origin can hardly be doubted" (AM, 3). In this way, Mexican artifacts were alienated from their native contexts and enlisted in a display that would justify Britain's role as the rightful keeper and conservator of antiquity and its material remains and thus the possessor of its history.

In "Modern Mexico," Bullock used a panoramic backdrop to frame the exhibit, anticipating the large-scale panorama he later exhibited in Robert Burford's Leicester Square rotunda in 1826. Panoramas were large-scale, circular replicas of exotic locations and scenes (usually cities) that were popular forms of mass entertainment and information exchange in the early nineteenth century. Just as placing ancient Mexico within an Orientalist frame suggested the eventual removal of antiquities to British museums, the visual mapping of contemporary Mexico City laid out the land in ways familiar to the logic of property or mineral surveys, presenting Mexico as a field to be dominated in certain, imperially minded ways. Panoramic imagery invited the viewer to share in a fantasy of possession by looking down through his very eyes at the sweeping scene laid out before him or her. The exhibit's panoramic backdrop allowed a visitor to the London exhibit to recreate Bullock's own experience of seeing Mexico on the spot. The *New Monthly Magazine* praised this effect, noting that the exhibit "renders credible the veriest stories of travelers," and the American historian William Hickling Prescott later remarked that Bullock saw "what has eluded the *optics* of other travelers."[18] The exhibit visually fortified the illusion that Mexico's resources remain unclaimed—its land was unsurveyed and unpopulated and awaited discovery. The panorama thus provides a startling visual example of the ways in which imperial science, intersected with techniques of mass spectatorship, bringing Mexico across the Atlantic for consumption by the British public.

The catalogs that Bullock wrote to guide his viewers through the exhibitions reinforced these subject positions through a carefully constructed vision that contrasted the Spanish model of violent military colonial domination with an idealized British model of gentlemanly, informal, and "reciprocal" engagements (AMM, iii). But Bullock's exhibition catalogs remain ambivalent about the key figure of the sixteenth-century expansion, Hernan Cortés, by alternately admiring and lamenting the success of his "enterprise"—a term that places the conquest under the sign of economics. Although Bullock admired Cortés for his strategic brilliance and stout courage, he also painted him as a ruthless zealot responsible for "ravages and desolation" that "reduced to ruins" a once great culture (AM, 2). The Spanish conquest, he argued, "made but a slight change from the preceding era, when the murderous idolatry of Mexico floated its temples with the blood of human sacrifices" (AM, 4). Nevertheless, the catalogs narrated the conquest from the Spanish perspective, with lengthy excerpts from Cortés's letters to Charles V and the *Historia verdadera de la conquista de Nueva España* of Bernal Díaz del Castillo, Cortés's loyal foot soldier.

Bullock's catalogs contrast competing national imperial models by evoking the "El Dorado of Elizabethan times" (MM, 3) and thus British memories of an older Atlantic conflict with Spain over the Western Hemisphere. The British fascination with Walter Raleigh and the golden age of Elizabethan discovery in the Americas was strong throughout the century but was particularly intense during the 1820s, when the Americas appeared to open up to British penetration once again. In 1826, the same year as Bullock displayed his panorama, the Raleigh Travelers' Club was formed in London and renamed itself the Royal Geographical Society four years later; as one of its first acts, it sponsored Robert Schomburgh's expedition to British Guiana, the legendary site of Raleigh's El Dorado. Raleigh's South American venture was a vivid reminder to British readers of their long, bitter conflict with the Catholic archenemy Spain. Bullock's Mexican productions updated the Black Legend by shifting attention away from the Spanish destruction of indigenous peoples to their contemporary restriction of the activities of scientists, travelers, and other curious observers like the altruistic collector himself. The Spanish Crown, according to the *Classical Journal*, looked with "suspicious eyes" on "those who seemed too curious in their investigations into her possessions in the New World."[19] Bullock summed up the charges by saying, "The Conquerors employed all their means to efface every vestige and recollection of what *had been*, from the minds of the subjugated people; . . . all their valuable books, hieroglyphics, paintings, and historical manuscripts which could be discovered, either by art or force, were indiscriminately committed to the flames" (AMM, 20).

The rhetoric of darkness and Spanish ignorance buttressed Bullock's argument that the British would be the bearers of enlightenment, proven by their interest in antiquarian research, their history of scientific expeditions to far-flung lands, and their great museum collections at home. If under Spanish colonialism "temples were cast down, Idols broken to pieces or buried, and all the memorials of former ages diligently obliterated," the "Catalogue will show that much has been saved" (AM, 2). Where Spain came to plunder and sack, Britain in contrast wanted not only to trade and exchange but also to shed light on the mysteries of the Mexican past, to increase humanity's wealth and knowledge. He explained the trade-off by means of a familiar argument: "intelligent strangers may be induced to visit her, and bring with them the arts and manufactures, the improved machinery and great chymical [*sic*] knowledge of Europe; and in return she can amply repay them by again diffusing through the world her immense mineral wealth" (SMR, 130). Britain will bring enlightenment and the colonies will return wealth. These stereotypical representations—Mexico was backward and ignorant, Britain was technologically advanced and enlightened, and Spain was cruel, superstitious, and unscientific—reinforced a progressive narrative of history that assumes Mexico's need for a benevolent tutor from outside to achieve its fullest potential.

The greater Atlantic context of Bullock's Mexican journey, however, would be incomplete without attention to American events that occurred as a direct result of the curator's visit. Although Bullock justified Britain's claim to ownership of monuments and thus control over the past, his acquisitions sparked a vigorous Mexican debate over the ownership of their cultural patrimony. If the control of foreign antiquities—and, by extension, domination of world historical representation itself—was crucial to an emerging Victorian identity, it was no less central an issue to the Mexicans themselves. As independent leaders of a new yet paradoxically ancient country, Mexican politicians sought to preserve their own past and incorporate sacred objects into the national mythology. The government officials who Bullock claimed assisted him in removing precious artifacts, Lucas Alamán and Carlos María de Bustamante, later used their writings and legislative acts to protest against the cultural robbery visited on Mexico by British travelers and antiquarians. In 1823, Secretary of State Alamán delivered a speech to the Mexican Congress that covered topics such as public works and services for the poor, but he also made pointed reference to Mexico's libraries, archives, and museums, reminding the Congress that they were filled with "highly valuable monuments of Mexican antiquity." He observed sadly that many precious items had disappeared, thus undermining Mexico's efforts to establish a museum where ancient codices and painted books—their culture's written memory— could be read by learned and studious persons. Alamán's speech reflected the importance of museums and archives in the construction of Atlantic national identities. And even with its passive linguistic constructions—"the monuments have disappeared [*han desaparecido*]"—it suggests a critique of imperial plunder that would grow over the next several years as the scale of looting came to light.[20]

Alamán's speech was immediately translated into English. Joel Poinsett, the first American ambassador to Mexico and himself a passionate collector of Mexican antiquities, printed a translation as an appendix to his *Notes on Mexico*, which was published and widely read on both sides of the Atlantic in Philadelphia (1824) and in London (1825). Future Prime Minister Benjamin Disraeli, his head swimming with speculative schemes, reprinted the speech in its entirety in *The Present State of Mexico* (1825), a tract designed to elicit British investment in Mexican mining schemes. Bullock wrote a letter to the British Museum Trustees in July 1825 in which he advised their prompt action on his offer to sell them his collection: "as the government of Mexico has since issued an edict prohibiting any more [antiquities] from leaving the country; in consequence of it being their immediate intention to establish a national museum in the city of Mexico, it may be fairly inferred that these are the only specimens that will find their way to Europe."[21] The editors of *Gentleman's Magazine* also pressed the British Museum to purchase the collection, echoing a warning that the Mexican law forbidding exports of antiquities was a preliminary step to "forming a National Museum of their own upon a very extended scale."[22] Thus, while Mexican elites sought to conserve their nation's antiquities in the service of patriotism, their announced intention to form their own museum was being used by transatlantic competitors to speed up the pace of their plunder, to hinder the repatriation of already-acquired treasures, and to fuel imperial rivalries between European nations.

A few years later, after more collections of antiquities were spirited out of Mexico to foreign museums, Bustamante wrote more directly of the assault on Mexico's national heritage. In his *Mañanas de la alameda de México* (1835), a set of dialogues on native history, Bustamante laid the blame for the outflow of the nation's cultural heritage squarely on foreign capitalists and travelers. From the moment we "opened our doors to free European commerce," Bustamante wrote, travelers arrived seeking to study "our history," to inquire after "our origins," and to copy the few remaining antiquities "left to us." Driven by their "*curiosidad*," these travelers bought up the scarcest productions and took them away across the ocean to be housed in European museums and cabinets. Most grievous, Bustamante wrote, was the removal of the ancient maps executed on maguey paper that preserved "*la verdadera Historia Antigua*" (the true ancient history of the Mexican people).[23] He may have been referring to Bullock specifically, who carried away and exhibited the so-called *Plan de Maguey* and many other rare codices—some later returned to Mexico and others sold at auction and thereby vanishing forever from the historical record. Of these lost treasures, Bustamante could not speak without feeling "profound grief." Although he introduced legislation in 1829 that explicitly forbade the export of antiquities, he noted ruefully that "the gold that purchases artifacts is stronger than any law."[24] In 1846, Isidro Gondra, the first director of the Museo Nacional, registered his disgust at Bullock's acquisition of the precious codices and explained how, through the persistent efforts of patriotic Mexican officials, they were eventually returned to their native land.[25]

Creole reverence for the glorious Aztec past, however, did not translate into efforts to improve the miserable conditions in which contemporary indigenous Mexicans lived. Independent Mexico was sharply divided along racial and cultural lines, with the indigenous people trapped at the bottom of the economic and social hierarchy. When rebellions periodically occurred, authorities used brutal force to put them down. Even the most liberal Mexican antiquarians and historians combined "valorization of pre-Hispanic Indians, compassion for colonial Indians, and embarrassment for contemporary Indians."[26] As we have seen, when British travelers commented on the disinterest that indigenous Mexicans had in their own monuments, they rhetorically divided them from history and thus from progress. Nineteenth-century creoles absorbed that rhetoric, imposing an internal version to control and manipulate the indigenous past for their own political ends. Creole historiography, whether in museum or academic form, perpetuated the "exclusion [of the indigenous] from the national project."[27] The transatlantic attitude of condescension and condemnation that the British observers directed toward the Mexicans was replicated internally by urban creole Mexicans toward the indigenous rural inhabitants.

Despite these exclusions, however, the creole emphasis on the nation's written memory rebutted the presumed cultural authority of British travelers and collectors and asserted the need for citizens of the Atlantic world to interpret their own cultures for themselves. Mexicans were well aware of the steep financial and cultural price they had paid for assistance from abroad. The arrival of foreign travelers such as Bullock, who removed and controlled the founding documents of Mexican antiquity, imperiled the nation's cultural memory and thereby undermined the culture from within. Indeed, for Bustamante, the theft of the maps and codices had left his countrymen in the dark as to how to interpret the few remaining texts left in Mexican archives. As European interest in pre-Columbian antiquity increased over the next several decades, oblivious tourists and greedy speculators continued to steal irreplaceable objects of antiquity, depositing them in distant museums and private collections where they served other purposes, other people, and other national narratives. In 1859, the Mexican Society of Geography and Statistics, a leading scientific body, published the report of a special commission again calling for stronger laws to protect cultural heritage, urging that the government claim that Mexico's archaeological monuments were state property. Darkly, it commented on the formula of desire and appropriation noted previously: "In proportion to the increased European cult for the study and possession of antiquity, so will the danger increase to those few monuments that now remain."[28] The roots of this massive transatlantic relocation of museum property lay in Bullock's venture, whose example of travel, collection, and exhibition remained in inspiration for many others to follow.

It is ironic that Bullock himself did not enjoy as much private personal success as did his public collections. When the Mexican mining boom ended in financial disaster in the mid-1820s, some angry investors like Henry George Ward blamed the immoderate enthusiasm of early Mexico promoters like William Bullock. Indeed, after the Mexican displays, Bullock largely disappeared from the London scene. He sold his Mexico collections to the British Museum and returned to Mexico in 1827. From there, he journeyed northward, describing his travels in a book called *Sketch of a Journey through the Western States of North America* (1827). He fell in love with Cincinnati and purchased a large estate just outside the city in Ludlow, Kentucky. There, he commissioned his old friend John B. Papworth to design a plan for a town called Hygeia, after the Greek goddess of health. Similar to his compatriot Robert Owen in New Harmony, Indiana, Bullock had high ambitions for his utopian town, which he vigorously promoted in his book. Hygeia would have areas set aside for agriculture and horticulture, housing suitable for all social classes, and a large establishment for Bullock himself, who retired there with his wife in 1828. Bullock's scheme came to naught, however, and in 1830 he was forced to sell most of his property and take up residence in a small cottage on his only remaining land; he finally conceded defeat and sold this last bit in 1836 before his return to Britain. The last years of his life, like the first, are shrouded in historical doubt, though he is known to have been in London in 1843. No full-length biography of this curious Atlantic traveler and curator has ever been published, but his Mexican monuments are still on display in the British Museum.

Notes

Chapter 5: Jacob Leisler (1640–1691)

1. Pierre du Simitiere, "Notes on Jacob Leisler's Execution," Pierre du Simitiere Collection, yi 1412 Q 56, 1769 (Philadelphia: Historical Society of Pennsylvania); David William Voorhees, "The 'fervent Zeale' of Jacob Leisler," *William and Mary Quarterly*, 3rd ser., 51 (July 1994): 467; Edwin G. Burrows and Mike Wallace, *Gotham: A History of New York City to 1898* (New York: Oxford University Press, 1999), 102. In all likelihood, the story of the woman holding up Leisler's heart before the crowd is apocryphal. There is no evidence that Leisler's heart was actually cut out. Still, that such a story circulated in the recorded memories of those who attended the execution points to the extreme fervor that the event inspired.

2. Peter R. Christoph, *The Leisler Papers, 1689–1691: Files of the Provincial Secretary of New York Relating to the Administration of Lieutenant-Governor Jacob Leisler* (Syracuse, NY: Syracuse University Press, 2002), xiv; Voorhees, "The fervent zeale," 452.

3. "Roll of Soldiers to Sail to New Netherland, April 24, 1660," *New York Colonial Manuscripts* 13, no. 106, New York State Archives, Albany.

4. Burrows and Wallace, *Gotham*, 43.

5. Father Isaac Jogues, "Novum Belgium," in *Narratives of New Netherland, 1609–1664*, ed. J. Franklin Jameson (New York: Charles Scribner's Sons, 1909), 259.

6. Dennis J. Maika, "Jacob Leisler's Chesapeake Trade," *de Halve Maen* 67 (Spring 1994): 9.

7. David William Voorhees, "Captured: The 'Turkish Slavery' of the *Susannah*," *Seaport: New York's History Magazine* 31, no. 2 (Fall 1997): 7.

8. Robert Davis, "British Slaves on the Barbary Coast," http://www.bbc.co.uk/history, 2, September 23, 2003; Ellen G. Friedman, "Christian Captives at 'Hard Labor' in Algiers, 16th–18th Centuries," *International Journal of African Historical Studies* 13, no. 4 (1980): 617; Voorhees, "Captured," 8, 11.

9. Randall H. Balmer, *A Perfect Babel of Confusion: Dutch Religion and English Culture in the Middle Colonies* (New York: Oxford University Press, 1989), 17; Voorhees, "The fervent zeale," 464.

10. Voorhees, "'Hearing . . .What Great Success the Dragonnades in France Had': Jacob Leisler's Huguenot Connections," *de Halve Maen* 67 (Spring 1994): 17–18.

11. Voorhees, "Jacob Leisler's Huguenot Connections," 19; Christoph, *The Leisler Papers1689–1691*, xxi.

12. Burrows and Wallace, *Gotham*, 98.

13. Burrows and Wallace, *Gotham*, 99–100.

14. Voorhees, "The fervent zeale," 472.

15. Christoph, *The Leisler Papers 1689–1691*, xxii; Burrows and Wallace, *Gotham*, 102.

16. Balmer, *A Perfect Babel of Confusion*, 46; Christoph, *The Leisler Papers 1689–1691*, xxii.

Chapter 6: Hendrick/Tiyanoga/Theyanoguen (1680–1755)

1. Mostyn John Armstrong, *History and Antiquities of the County of Norfolk*, 10 vols. (Norwich, 1781), vol. 6, 137–38.

2. For details of the lineage of a single Hendrick, see especially Richard Aquila, "Hendrick," *American National Biography* (New York: Oxford University Press, 1999); John Wolf Lydekker, *The Faithful Mohawks* (Cambridge: Cambridge University Press, 1938), appendix B, "Pedigree of 'King' Hendrick and Joseph Brant"; and Dean R. Snow, *The Iroquois* (Oxford: Blackwell, 1994), 136–37. Timothy Shannon has raised the possibility that there were two Hendricks who have been merged in the historical record in *Crossroads of Empire: The Albany Congress of 1754* (Ithaca, NY: Cornell University Press, 2000), 30–31; Alden Vaughan has made a more detailed case in "American Indians Abroad: The Mythical Travels of Mrs. Penobscot and King Hendrick," *New England Quarterly* 80 (2007): 299–316.

3. *Spectator*, No. 324, March 12, 1712. The account was again raised and confirmed by readers in the *London Chronicle*'s discussion on clubs and societies, March 21, 1758. The gang, however, had by then disappeared according to the paper.

4. Richard Aquila, *The Iroquois Restoration: Iroquois Diplomacy on the Colonial Frontier, 1701–1754* (Detroit: Wayne State University Press, 1983), 88–90.

5. The full address is reprinted in Lydekker, *The Faithful Mohawks*, 27–28.

6. Cited in C. F. Pascoe, *Classified Digest of the Records of the Society for the Propagation of the Gospel in Foreign Parts, 1701–1892*, 3rd ed. (London, 1893), 69.

7. Pascoe, *Classified Digest of the Records of the Society for the Propagation of the Gospel in Foreign Parts, 1701–1892*, 69.

8. Lydekker, *The Faithful Mohawks*, 31.

9. *Documents Relative to the Colonial History of the State of New York*, ed. E. B. O'Callaghan (Albany, NY: n.p., 1853–1858) (*NYCD*), vol. 5: 1707–33, 279.

10. For examples, see Society of the Propagation of the Gospel Papers, Lambeth Palace Library, London, vol. 5: Minutes, 1745–1750, fols. 263–68, 285–92, and 293–97; Lydekker, *Faithful Mohawks*, 68–74; and Frank J. Klinberg, *Anglican Humanitarianism in Colonial New York* (Philadelphia: The Church Historical Society, 1940), 87–121.

11. Lydekker, *The Faithful Mohawks*, 26.

12. Shannon, *Crossroads of Empire*, 37–43.

13. *Documents Relating to the Colonial History of New York*, vol. 6: 1734–55, 783.

14. *NYCD*, vol. 6, 869–70.

15. *NYCD*, vol. 6, 876.

16. *Ipswich Journal*, June 7, 1755.

17. Quoted in Milton W. Hamilton, *Sir William Johnson: Colonial American 1715–1763* (Port Washington, NY: Kennikat Press, 1976), p. 160.

18. See, for example, the *Gentleman's Magazine*, which was the most widely distributed magazine in Britain, November 1755, 519.

19. For examples, see John Entick, *The General History of the Late War: Containing Its Rise, Progress, and Events, in Europe, Asia, Africa, and America* (London, 1763–1764), vol. 1, 159; *An Impartial History of the Late Glorious War, from Its Commencement to Its Conclusion* (Manchester, 1764), 15, and Richard Rolt. *The History of the Late War; from the Commencement of Hostilities after the Peace of Aix-la-Chapelle, 1748* (London, 1766), 234.

20. Tobias Smollett, *The History of England, from the Revolution to the Death of George the Second. (Designed as a continuation of Mr. Hume's History . . .)*, 5 vols. (London, 1791), vol. 3, 455; Jebidiah Morse, *The American Gazetteer, Exhibiting, in Alphabetical Order, a Much More Full and Accurate Account Than Has Been Given, of the States, Provinces . . .* , 2nd ed. (London, 1798), 76.

Chapter 7: Sir William Johnson (1715–1774)

1. *Documents Relative to the Colonial History of the State of New York*, 15 vols., ed. E. B. O'Callaghan and Bethold Fernow (Albany, NY: Weed, Parsons and Company, 1856–1887) (hereafter, *DRCHNY*), 6:738; *Journals of the Hon. William Hervey, 1755–1814* (Bury St. Edmonds: Paul & Mathew, Butler Market, 1906), 5; *The Papers of Sir William Johnson*, 14 vols., ed. James Sullivan et al. (Albany: University of the State of New York, 1921–1965) (hereafter *Johnson Papers*), 9:386; John Lees, *Journal of J. L. of Quebec, Merchant* (Detroit: Society of Colonial Wars for the State of Michigan, 1911), 16.

2. The Six Nations include the Mohawk, Oneida, Tuscarora, Cayuga, Onondaga, and Seneca. The Tuscarora did not become the sixth tribe until 1722, when the Iroquois Confederacy formally adopted them.

3. "Journal of Warren Johnson, 1760–1761" in *In Mohawk Country: Early Narratives about a Native People*, ed. Dean R. Snow et al. (New York: Syracuse University Press, 1996), 258.

4. *Johnson Papers*, 1:60.

5. Cadwallader Colden, *The History of the Five Indian Nations of Canada*, 2 vols. (1747; New York: AMS Press, 1973), 2:220.

6. *Johnson Papers*, 3:29.

7. DRCHNY, 6:738.

8. On Johnson's land speculation, see John C. Guzzardo, "Sir William Johnson's Official Family: Patrons and Clients in an Anglo-American Empire, 1742–1777," PhD diss., Syracuse University, 1975.

9. *Johnson Papers*, 1:430.

10. For a detailed account of this battle, see Ian K. Steele, *Betrayals: Fort William Henry and the "Massacre"* (New York: Oxford University Press, 1990), chap. 2.

11. *Johnson Papers*, 9:589. On Johnson's role as a gift giver, see Wilbur R. Jacobs, *Wilderness Politics and Indian Gifts: The Northern Colonial Frontier, 1748–1763* (Lincoln: University of Nebraska Press, 1966), chap. 5.

12. *Johnson Papers*, 10:76.

13. *Johnson Papers*, 9:108–9.

14. *An Account of Conferences Held and Treaties Made between Sir William Johnson, Bart., and the Chief Sachems and Warriors of the . . . Indian Nations . . . at Fort Johnson . . . in the Years 1755 and 1756* (London, 1756), 59–60; *Johnson Papers*, 9:963.

15. *Johnson Papers*, 9:119.

16. *Johnson Papers*, 9:935.

17. DRCHNY, 7:235.

18. *Johnson Papers*, 10:68–69, 72–73.

19. *Johnson Papers*, 10:102.

20. For an account of this war, see Gregory Dowd, *War under Heaven: Pontiac, the Indian Nations, and the British Empire* (Baltimore: Johns Hopkins University Press, 2002).

21. DRCHNY, 7:836.

22. *Johnson Papers*, 11:923–26. On Mohawk land grievances, see Georgiana C. Nammack, *Fraud, Politics and the Dispossession of the Indians: The Iroquois Land Frontier in the Colonial Period* (Norman: University of Oklahoma Press, 1969).

23. *Johnson Papers*, 10:462, 464.

24. Wanda Burch, "Sir William Johnson's Cabinet of Curiosities," *New York History* 71, no. 3 (July 1990): 261–82.

25. Tench Tilghman Papers, 1775–1786, 9, Library of Congress Manuscript Division, Washington, DC.

26. Quoted in Lois M. Feister and Bonnie Pulis, "Molly Brant: Her Domestic and Political Roles in Eighteenth-Century New York," in *Northeastern Indian Lives, 1632–1816*, ed. Robert S. Grumet (Amherst: University of Massachusetts Press, 1996), 302.

27. *Documentary History of the State of New York*, 4 vols., ed. E. B. O'Callaghan (Albany, NY: Weed, Parsons and Company, 1849–1851), 4:231.

28. DRCHNY, 8:475.

29. On works on this treaty, see Ray A. Billington, "The Fort Stanwix Treaty of 1768," *New York History* 25 (1944): 182–94; Peter Marshall, "Sir William Johnson and the Treaty of Fort Stanwix, 1768," *Journal of American Studies* 1 (1967): 149–79.

Chapter 9: Julien Raimond (1744–1801)

1. David Geggus finds that about 5 percent of all island-born plantation slave children were of part-European ancestry. See, for example, his article "Les esclaves de la Plaine du Nord à la veille de la révolution française: Les équipes de travail sur une vingtaine de sucreries. Partie IV," *Revue de la société d'histoire de géographie d'Haïti* 42, no. 144 (1984): 20.

2. AN Colonie F3 91, 96–97.

3. Julien Raymond [*sic*], *Observations sur l'origine et les progrès du prejugé des colons blancs contre les hommes de couleur* (Paris, 1791), 41.

4. Raimond, *Observations sur l'origine . . .* , 11–12.

5. AN Col. F3 192, ms. "Réflexions sur la position actuelle de St Domingue."

6. John D. Garrigus, "Catalyst or Catastrophe? Saint-Domingue's Free Men of Color and the Battle of Savannah, 1779–1782," *Revista/Review Interamericana* 22, no. 1–2 (1992): 109–25.

7. André Maystre du Chambon, "Acte notarié relatif aux doléances des 'gens de couleur,'" *Mémoires de la société archéologique et historique de la Charente* 1931: 5–11.

8. Julien Raimond, *Observations adressées à l'Assemblée Nationale par un deputé des colons américains* (S.l., 1789), 14–15.

9. See Abbé Grégoire, *Lettre aux philantropes, sur les malheurs . . . des gens de couleur de Saint-Domingue* (Paris, 1790); Jacques Godechot, "DeJoly et les gens de couleur libres," *Annales historiques de la révolution française* 23 (1951): 52.

10. David P. Geggus, "Racial Equality, Slavery, and Colonial Secession during the Constituent Assembly," *American Historical Review* 94, no. 5 (December 1989): 1302.

11. Julien Raymond [*sic*], *Réflexions sur les véritables causes des troubles et désastres de nos colonies* (Paris, 1793).

12. Laurent Dubois, "'The Price of Liberty': Victor Hugues and the Administration of Freedom in Guadeloupe, 1794–1798," *William and Mary Quarterly* 56, no. 2 (April 1999): 372.

13. Raymond, *Réflexions . . .* , 18, 24.

14. Dubois, "'The Price of Liberty,'" 372.

Chapter 10: Anne Pépin (1758–1837)

1. Archives du Sénégal, hereafter AS, Z, February 5, 1789.

2. AS, 1 Z 21, September 20, 1819.

3. AS, 1 Z 21, September 20, 1819.

4. AS, Z, SL-1822, July 22, 1822.

5. AS, 1 Z 21, September 20, 1819.

6. Samuel Brunner, *Reise Nach Senegambien und den Inseln des Grünen Vorgebürges im Jahre 1838* (Bern: J. Körper, 1840), 164–65.

Chapter 12: Juan Antonio Olavarrieta (1765–1822)

1. I have located evidence of Olavarrieta's life and career in archives and libraries in Mexico, Spain, and the United States. For this biographical sketch, I have relied most heavily on documents found in the Criminal (vols. 582 and 676), Inquisición (vols. 1410 and 1454), and Real Fisco de la Inquisición (vol. 136) sections of the Mexican National Archives in Mexico City. Unless otherwise noted, the chapter's quotations are drawn from this material. The translations are my own.

2. Manuel Ravina Martín, "El entierro de un masón: José Joaquín de Clararrosa (1822)," *Revista de historia contemporánea* 1 (1981): 77–78; Pío Baroja, *Siluetas románticas y otras historias de pillos y de extravagantes* (Madrid: Espasa-Calpe, 1934), 82–83.

3. Daniel Muñoz Sempere and Beatriz Sánchez Hita, eds., *Viaje al mundo subterráneo y secretos de la Inquisición revelados a los Españoles. Seguido de El Hombre y el Bruto y otros escritos* (Salamanca: Universidad de Salamanca, 2003), 194. Academic opinion is divided over how to reconstruct Olavarrieta's life given its many gaps and ambiguities. I have relied most heavily on this recent study (not without its errors) to supplement my own research, particularly for the years he spent in Spain and Portugal. Space constraints prevent further citation.

4. Raúl Zamalloa Armejo, "La polémica entre el *Mercurio Peruano* y el *Semanario Crítico* (1791)," *Histórica* 17, no. 1 (1993): 109–18.

5. Roberto Moreno de los Arcos, "La ciencia de la Ilustración Mexicana," *Anuario de Estudios Americanos* 32 (1975): 39.

6. Carlos Herrejón Peredo, "La revolución francesa en sermones y otros testimonios de México, 1791–1823," in *La revolución francesa en México*, ed. Solange Alberro, Alicia Hernández Chávez, and Elías Trabulse (Mexico City: El Colegio de México, Centro de Estudios Mexicanos y Centroamericanos, 1992), 97–110; Marta Terán, "La Virgen de Guadalupe contra Napoleón Bonaparte: La defense de la religión en el obispado de Michoacán entre 1793 y 1814," *Estudios de Historia Novohispana* 19 (1999): 91–129.

7. Samuel Ramos, "El Movimiento Científico en la Nueva España," *Filosofía y Letras* 3, no. 6 (1942): 169–78; Arturo Arnaiz y Freg, "D. Fausto de Elhuyar y de Zubice," *Revista de América* 6 (1939): 75–96; José Luis Peset, *Ciencia y libertad. El papel de científico en la independencia Americana* (Madrid: Consejo Superior de Investigaciones Científicas, Centro de Estudios Históricos, 1987), 143–267; Carlos Prieto et al., *Andrés Manuel del Río y su obra científica. Segundo Centenario de su Natalicio (1764–1964)* (Mexico City: Compañía Fundidora de Fierro y Acero de Monterrey, 1966); J. Luis Maldonado Polo, "La Expedición Botánica a Nueva España, 1786–1803: El Jardín Botánico y la Cátedra de Botánica," *Historia Mexicana* 50, no. 1 (2000): 5–56.

8. Elías Trabulse has noted that, ironically, neither Olavarrieta nor his inquisitors realized that he mistakenly attributed his inspiration to Mirabeau rather than Jean Baptiste de Mirabaud (also known as Paul Henry de Thiry, Baron D'Holbach); Elías Trabulse, "Aspectos de la difusión del materialismo científico de la ilustración francesa en México a principios del siglo XIX," in Peredo, *La revolución francesa en México*, 89.

9. Trabulse, "Aspectos de la difusión del materialismo . . . ," 86–87.

10. Antonio Alcalá Galiano, *Memorias de D. Antonio Alcalá Galiano. Publicados por su hijo*, vol. 2 (Madrid: Enrique Rubiños, 1886), 191, 208–9, 226, 232–3; Baroja, *Siluetas románticas . . .* , 85; Marcelino Ménendez-Pelayo, *Historia de los heterodoxos españoles, vol. 6 (Heterodoxía en el siglo XIX)* (Madrid: Santander, Aldus, 1946–1948), 123, fn. 1.

Chapter 14: Elizabeth Patterson Bonaparte (1785–1879)

1. M. Dacres to L. A. Pichon, April 20, 1804, translation, in *The Bonaparte-Patterson Marriage in 1803, and the Secret Correspondence on the Subject*, ed. W. T. R. Saffell (Philadelphia, 1873), 67.

2. As quoted in Eugene L. Didier, *The Life and Letters of Madame Bonaparte* (New York: Charles Scribner's Sons, 1879), 25.

3. "Latest European Intelligence," *Scioto Gazette*, July 29, 1805.

4. Rosalie Stier Calvert to Madame H. J. Stier, November 1803, in *Mistress of Riversdale: The Plantation Letters of Rosalie Stier Calvert, 1795–1821*, ed. Margaret Law Callcott (Baltimore: Johns Hopkins University Press, 1991), 62.

5. Most accounts of their meeting and marriage are overly romanticized and unsupported or simply fictional. See, for example, Geraldine Brooks, *Dames and Daughters of the Young Republic* (New York: Thomas Y. Crowell, 1901); Alice Curtis Desmond, *Bewitching Betsy Bonaparte* (New York: Nelson Doubleday, 1958); Susan Ertz, *No Hearts to Break* (New York: D. Appleton-Century, 1937); and Daniel Henderson, *The Golden Bees: The Story of Betsy Patterson and the Bonapartes* (New York: Frederick A. Stokes, 1928). Neither Elizabeth nor Jerome left an account of how they met.

6. Anonymous to William Patterson, [c. November 5, 1803], in Saffell, *The Bonaparte-Patterson Marriage . . .* , 29–30.

7. As quoted in Didier, *The Life and Letters of Madame Bonaparte*, 7–8.

8. As quoted in Didier, *The Life and Letters of Madame Bonaparte*, 8.

9. Rosalie Stier Calvert to Madame H. J. Stier, March 2, 1804, in Callcott, *Mistress of Riversdale*, 78.

10. Margaret Bayard Smith to Mrs. Kirkpatrick, January 23, 1804, in *First Forty Years of Washington Society*, ed. Gaillard Hunt (New York, 1906), 46–47.

11. Rosalie Stier Calvert to Madame H. J. Stier, March 2, 1804, in Callcott, *Mistress of Riversdale*, 78.

12. Thomas Jefferson to Robert R. Livingston, November 4, 1803, in *The Writings of Thomas Jefferson* (definitive ed.), ed. Andrew A. Lipscomb and Albert Ellery Bergh (Washington, DC: Jefferson Memorial Association, 1905–1907), 10:424–25.

13. Captain Bentalou to Robert Patterson, October 17, 1805, in Saffell, *The Bonaparte-Patterson Marriage . . .* , 218. Napoleon also implied that he considered Elizabeth nothing more than Jerome's mistress.

14. Sir Augustus John Foster to Lady Elizabeth Foster, November 27, 1806, Augustus John Foster Papers, Library of Congress, Washington, DC.

15. EPB to William Patterson, September 2, 1815, in Didier, *The Life and Letters of Madame Bonaparte*, 45.

16. Catharine Mitchill to Margaret Akerly Miller, November 21, 1811, in Carolyn Hoover Sung, "Catharine Mitchill's Letters from Washington, 1806–1812," *Quarterly Journal of the Library of Congress*, July 1977, 184.

17. Mary Caton Smith to EPB, as quoted in Desmond, *Bewitching Betsy Bonaparte*, 243.

18. Didier, *The Life and Letters of Madame Bonaparte*, 197.

19. EPB to William Patterson, September 2, 1815, in Didier, *The Life and Letters of Madame Bonaparte*, 44.

20. [Nancy] Ann Spear to EPB, May 30, 1816, Elizabeth Patterson Bonaparte Papers, MS 142, Maryland Historical Society (hereafter referred to as MdHS).

21. EPB to William Patterson, December 4, 1829, in Didier, *The Life and Letters of Madame Bonaparte*, 218.

22. EPB to William Patterson, February 22, 1816, in Didier, *The Life and Letters of Madame Bonaparte*, 52–53.

23. Jerome Napoleon Bonaparte to William Patterson, January 7, 1822, in Didier, *The Life and Letters of Madame Bonaparte*, 86.

24. EPB to William Patterson, May 6, 1823, in Didier, *The Life and Letters of Madame Bonaparte*, 136.

25. EPB to William Patterson, December 21, 1829, in Didier, *The Life and Letters of Madame Bonaparte*, 220–22.

26. European women's historians support the same conclusions. See, for example, Dena Goodman, *The Republic of Letters: A Cultural History of the French Enlightenment* (Ithaca, NY: Cornell University Press, 1994); Amanda Foreman, *Georgiana: Duchess of Devonshire* (New York: HarperCollins, 1998); and Amanda Vickery, *The Gentleman's Daughter: Women's Lives in Georgian England* (New Haven, CT: Yale University Press, 1998).

27. Horace Holley to Mary Austin Holley, March 20, 1818, Holley Papers, Clements Library, University of Michigan.

28. EPB to John Spear Smith, August 22, 1816, EPB Papers, MS 142, MdHS.

29. Will of William Patterson, February 6, 1835, Patterson Papers, MdHS.

30. EPB to Lady Sidney Morgan, March 14, 1849, in Didier, *The Life and Letters of Madame Bonaparte*, 253.

Chapter 16: William Bullock (1780–1844)

1. Nicholas Thomas, "Licensed Curiosity: Cook's Pacific Voyages," in *The Cultures of Collecting*, ed. John Elsner and Roger Cardinal (Cambridge, MA: Harvard University Press, 1994), 122.

2. William Bullock, *A Companion to Mr. Bullock's Museum* . . . , 8th ed. (London, 1810).

3. William Bullock, *A Treatise on the Art of Preserving Objects of Natural History, Intended for the Use of Sportsmen, Travellers, and Others* (London, 1818), 34, emphasis added.

4. For a compact history of the Egyptian Hall, see volume 29 of the *Survey of London. The Parish of St. James Westminster. Part One: South of Piccadilly*, ed. F. H. W. Sheppard (London: University of London, 1960), 266–70.

5. W. Bullock and Marie Tussaud, *The Military Carriage of Napoleon Buonaparte* (London, 1843); Jean Hornn and W. Bullock, *The Narrative of Jean Hornn, Military Coachman to Napoleon Bonaparte*, 2nd ed. (London, 1816).

6. Bullock, *The Military Carriage of Napoleon Buonaparte*, 10–11.

7. Bullock, *A Treatise on the Art of Preserving Objects of Natural History* . . . , 34.

8. See Susan M. Pearce, "Giovanni Battista Belzoni's Exhibition of the Reconstructed Tomb of Pharoah Seti I in 1821," *Journal of the History of Collections* 12, no. 1 (2000): 109–25.

9. Bruno Latour, *Science in Action: How to Follow Scientists and Engineers through Society* (Cambridge, MA: Harvard University Press, 1987), 220.

10. See Robert Aguirre, *Informal Empire: Mexico and Central America in Victorian Culture* (Minneapolis: University of Minnesota Press, 2005), and Michael P. Costeloe, "William Bullock and the Mexican Connection," *Estudios Mexicanos/ Mexican Studies* 22, no. 2 (Summer 2006): 275–309.

11. Quotations from Bullock's Mexican works are cited in the text as follows: SMR: *Six Months' Residence and Travels in Mexico* (London, 1824); MM: *Catalogue of the Exhibition, Called Modern Mexico* (London, 1824); AM: *A Description of the Unique Exhibition, called Ancient Mexico* (London, n.d.); MM: *A Descriptive Catalogue of the Exhibition, Entitled Ancient and Modern Mexico* (London, n.d.)

12. "Travels and Acquisitions in Mexico [by Mr. Bullock]," *Times* (London), January 12, 1824, 3b.

13. "Six Months in Mexico," *The Literary Gazette*, June 19, 1824, 390.

14. Roland Barthes, "The World as Object," in *A Barthes Reader*, ed. Susan Sontag (New York: Hill and Wang, 1982), 67.

15. The originals of these monuments are in the Museo Nacional in Mexico City.

16. Johannes Fabian, *Time and the Other: How Anthropology Makes Its Object* (New York: Columbia University Press, 1983), 31–32.

17. "Some Observations Caused by the Recent Introduction by Mr. Bullock into England of Various Rare and Curious Specimens of Mexican Antiquity . . . ," *The Classical Journal* 29 (1824): 186.

18. "Mexican Curiosities," *New Monthly Magazine* 12 (1824): 163; William H. Prescott, *History of the Conquest of Mexico*, 3 vols. (Philadelphia, 1863), 2:390, emphasis added.

19. "Some Observations Caused by the Recent Introduction . . . ," 177.

20. [Lucas Alamán], *Memoria que el Secretario de Estado y del Despacho de Relaciones Esteriores é Interiores presenta al Soberano Congreso Constituyente sobre los negocios de la secretaria de su cargo. Leida en la sesión de 8 Noviembre de 1823* (México, 1823), 23.

21. William Bullock to British Museum Trustees, July 8, 1825, Original Papers, Central Archives, British Museum.

22. "Mexican Curiosities," 168.

23. Carlos María de Bustamante, *Mañanas de la alameda de México* (Mexico City: Instituto de Bellas Artes, 1986), xii.

24. Bustamante, *Mañanas de la alameda de México*, xiii.

25. Isidro R. Gondra, "Esplicación de las láminas pertenecientes a la historia antigua de México . . . ," in W. H. Prescott, *Historia de la conquista de México, por W.H. Prescott*, 3 vols. (México: Ignacio Cumplido, 1844–1846), 3:10.

26. Catalina Rodríguez Lazcano, "La interpretación nacional (1821–1854)," in *La antropología en México: Panorama histórico*, ed. Carlos García Mora and Arturo España Caballero (Mexico City: INAH, 1987), 288.

27. Anthony Alan Shelton, "Dispossessed Histories: Mexican Museums and the Institutionalization of the Past," *Cultural Dynamics* 7, no. 1 (1995): 79.

28. H[ilarion] Romero Gil, "Dictamen presentado á la Sociedad de Geografía y Estadística por la comision especial que suscribe con objeto de pedir al Supremo Gobierno que declare propiedad nacional los monumentos arqueológicos de la República," *Boletín de la Sociedad Mexicana de Geografía y Estadística* 8, no. 9 (1862): 440.

Recommended Reading

Theoretical Works and the Idea of Atlantic History

Armitage, David. "Three Concepts of Atlantic History." In *The British Atlantic World 1500–1800*, edited by David Armitage and Michael J. Braddick, 11–27. New York: Palgrave Macmillan, 2002.

Bailyn, Bernard. "The Idea of Atlantic History." *Itinerario* 20, no. 1 (1996): 19–44.

Bentley, Jerry. "Seas and Ocean Basins as Frameworks of Historical Analysis." *Geographical Review* 89, no. 2 (1999): 215–24.

———. *Atlantic History: Concepts and Contours*. Cambridge, MA: Harvard University Press, 2005.

Cañizares-Esguerra, Jorge. "Some Caveats about the Atlantic Paradigm." *History Compass* (2003). http://www.history-compass.com.

———. "Entangled Histories: Borderlands Historiographies in New Clothes?" *American Historical Review* 112, no. 3 (June 2007): 787–99.

Eltis, David. "Atlantic History in Global Perspective." *Itinerario* 23, no. 2 (1999): 141–61.

Gabaccia, Donna. "A Long Atlantic in a Wider World." *Atlantic Studies* 1 (2004): 1–27.

Games, Alison. "Atlantic History: Definitions, Challenges, and Opportunities." *American Historical Review* 111, no. 3 (2006): 741–758.

Greene, Jack D., and Philip D. Morgan, eds. *Atlantic History: A Critical Appraisal*. Oxford: Oxford University Press, 2008.

Laing, Annette. "Exploring the Atlantic World: An Experiment in Teaching in an Emerging Paradigm." *Teaching History: A Journal of Methods* 8, no. 1 (2003): 3–13.

Lewis, Martin W., and Karen E. Wigen. *The Myth of Continents: A Critique of Metageography.* Berkeley: University of California Press, 1997.

Mann, Kristin. "Shifting Paradigms in the Study of the African Diaspora and of Atlantic History and Culture." *Slavery and Abolition* 22, no. 1 (2001): 3–21.

O'Reilly, William. "Genealogies of Atlantic History." *Atlantic Studies* 1 (2004): 66–84.

"Round Table Conference: The Nature of Atlantic History." *Itinerario* 23, no. 2 (1999): 48–173.

White, Deborah Gray. "Yes, There Is a Black Atlantic." *Itinerario* 23, no. 2 (1999): 127–40.

General Works on Atlantic History

Adelman, Jeremy. "An Age of Imperial Revolutions." *American Historical Review* 113, no. 2 (April 2008): 319–40.

Amory, Hugh, and David Hall, eds. *A History of the Book in the Americas: Vol. 1—The Colonial Book in the Atlantic World.* Chapel Hill: University of North Carolina Press, 2007.

Back, Rebecca Ann. *Colonial Transformations: The Cultural Production of the New Atlantic World 1580–1640.* New York: Palgrave, 2000.

Bailyn, Bernard, and Pat Denault, eds. *Soundings in Atlantic History: Latent Structures and Intellectual Currents, 1500–1830.* Cambridge, MA: Harvard University Press, 2009.

Benjamin, Thomas. *The Atlantic World: Europeans, Africans, Indians and their Shared History 1400–1900.* Cambridge: Cambridge University Press, 2009.

Benjamin, Thomas, Timothy Hall, and David Rutherford, eds. *The Atlantic World in the Age of Empire.* Boston: Houghton Mifflin, 2001.

Bolster, W. Jeffrey. "Putting the Ocean in Atlantic History: Maritime Communities and Marine Ecology in the Northwest Atlantic, 1500–1800." *American Historical Review* 113, no. 1 (February 2008): 19–47.

Breslaw, Elaine. *Witches of the Atlantic World: An Historical Reader and Primary Sourcebook.* New York: New York University Press, 2000.

Butel, Paul. *The Atlantic.* New York: Routledge, 1999.

Cañizares-Esguerra, Jorge. *How to Write the History of the New World: Histories, Epistemiologies and Identities in the 18th Century Atlantic World.* Stanford, CA: Stanford University Press, 2001.

Cañizares-Esguerra, Jorge, and Erik R. Seeman. *The Atlantic in Global History, 1500–2000.* Upper Saddle River, NJ: Pearson Prentice Hall, 2007.

Canny, Nicholas, and Anthony Pagden, eds. *Colonial Identity in the Atlantic World 1500–1800.* Princeton, NJ: Princeton University Press, 1987.

Cormack, Margaret, ed. *Saints and Their Cults in the Atlantic World*. Columbia: University of South Carolina Press, 2007.

Crosby, Alfred. *Ecological Imperialism: The Biological Expansion of Europe 900–1900*. Cambridge: Cambridge University Press, 1986.

Delbourgo, James, and Nicholas Dew, eds. *Science and Empire in the Atlantic World*. New York: Routledge, 2007.

Egerton, Douglas, Alison Games, Jane G. Landers, and Kris Lane. *The Atlantic World: A History, 1400–1888*. Wheeling, IL: Harlan Davidson, 2007.

Eltis, David. "Atlantic History in Global Perspective." *Itinerario* 23, no. 2 (1999): 70–83.

Engerman, Stanley L. "The Atlantic Economy of the Eighteenth Century: Some Speculations on Economic Development in Britain, America, Africa, and Elsewhere." *Journal of European Economic History* 24, no. 1 (1995): 145–75.

Falola, Toyin, and Kevin D. Robert, eds. *The Atlantic World, 1450–2000*. Bloomington: Indiana University Press, 2008.

Games, Alison, and Adam Rothman, eds. *Major Problems in Atlantic History: Documents and Essays*. London: Wadsworth, 2007.

Gould, Eliga. "Entangled Histories, Entangled Worlds: The English-Speaking Atlantic as a Spanish Periphery." *American Historical Review* 112, no. 3 (June 2007): 764–86.

———. "Entangled Atlantic Histories: A Response from the Anglo-American Periphery." *American Historical Review* 112, no. 5 (December 2007): 1415–22.

Kidd, Colin. *The Forging of Races: Race and Scripture in the Protestant Atlantic World, 1600–2000*. Cambridge: Cambridge University Press, 2006.

Klooster, Wim. *Revolutions in the Atlantic World: A Comparative History*. New York: New York University Press, 2009.

Klooster, Wim, and Alfred Padula, eds. *The Atlantic World: Essays on Slavery, Migration, and Imagination*. Upper Saddle River, NJ: Pearson Prentice Hall, 2005.

Langley, Lester. *The Americas in the Age of Revolution 1750–1850*. New Haven, CT: Yale University Press, 1996.

Mancall, Peter C. "Atlantic Colonies." *New England Quarterly* 75, no. 3 (2002): 477–87.

McNeill, William H., ed. *Transatlantic History*. College Station: Texas A&M University Press, 2006.

Morrison, Michael A., and Melinda Zook, eds. *Revolutionary Currents: Nation Building in the Transatlantic World*. Lanham, MD: Rowman & Littlefield, 2004.

Pietschmann, Horst, ed. *Atlantic History: A History of the Atlantic System, 1580–1830*. Göttingen: University of Göttingen Press, 2002.

Quilley, Geoff, and Kay Dian Kriz, eds. *An Economy of Colour: Visual Culture and the Atlantic World, 1660–1830*. New York: Manchester University Press, 2003.

Safier, Neil. *Measuring the New World: Enlightenment Science and South America*. Chicago: University of Chicago Press, 2008.

Schiebinger, Londa. *Plants and Empire: Colonial Bioprospecting in the Atlantic World.* Cambridge, MA: Harvard University Press, 2007.

Williams, Eric E. *Capitalism and Slavery.* New York: Russell and Russell, 1961.

Williams, Gwyndwr. "'Savages Noble and Ignoble': European Attitudes towards the Wider World before 1800." *Journal of Imperial and Commonwealth History* 6, no. 3 (1978): 303–13.

Anglo-American Atlantic

Aguirre, Robert. *Informal Empire: Mexico and Central America in Victorian Culture.* Minneapolis: University of Minnesota Press, 2005.

Appelbaum, Robert, and John Wood Sweet. *Envisioning an Empire: Jamestown and the Making of the North Atlantic.* Philadelphia: University of Pennsylvania Press, 2005.

Armitage, David, and Michael J. Braddick, eds. *The British Atlantic World, 1500–1800.* London: Palgrave Macmillan, 2002.

Bailyn, Bernard. *The Peopling of British North America.* New York: Vintage Books, 1988.

Bailyn, Bernard, and Philip Morgan, eds. *Strangers within the Realm: Cultural Margins of the First British Empire.* Chapel Hill: University of North Carolina Press, 1991.

Baker, Frank. "The Trans-Atlantic Triangle: Relations between British, Canadian and American Methodism during Wesley's Lifetime." *Bulletin of the Committee on Archives and History of the United Church of Canada* 28 (1975): 5–21.

Boelhower, William. *New Orleans in the Atlantic World: Between Land and Sea.* New York: Routledge, 2005.

Byrd, Alexander. *Captives and Voyagers: Black Migrants across the Eighteenth Century British Atlantic World.* Baton Rouge: Louisiana State University Press, 2008.

Coclanis, Peter, ed. *The Atlantic Economy during the Seventeenth and Eighteenth Centuries: Organization, Operation, Practice, and Personnel.* Columbia: University of South Carolina Press, 2005.

Conway, Stephen. *The British Isles and the War of American Independence.* Oxford: Oxford University Press, 2000.

Fitzmaurice, Andrew. *Humanism and America: An Intellectual History of English Colonisation 1500–1625.* Cambridge: Cambridge University Press, 2003.

Fischer, David Hackett. *Albion's Seed: Four British Folkways in America.* New York: Oxford University Press, 1989.

Gould, Eliga, and Peter S. Onuf, eds. *Empire and Nation: The American Revolution in the Atlantic World.* Baltimore: Johns Hopkins University Press, 2005.

Hall, Timothy, and Tim Breen. *Colonial America in an Atlantic World.* London: Longman, 2003.

Harland-Jacobs, Jessica. "'Hands across the Sea': The Masonic Network, British Imperialism, and the North Atlantic World." *Geographical Review* 89, no. 2 (1999): 237–53.

Hatfield, April Lee. *Atlantic Virginia: Intercolonial Relations in the Seventeenth Century.* Philadelphia: University of Pennsylvania Press, 2004.

Hornsby, Steven J. *British Atlantic, American Frontier: Spaces of Power in Early Modern British America*. Lebanon, NH: University Press of New England, 2004.

Karras, Alan L., and J. R. McNeill, eds. *Atlantic American Societies: From Columbus through Abolition 1492–1888*. New York: Routledge, 1992.

Mancall, Peter C., ed. *The Atlantic World and Virginia, 1550–1624*. Chapel Hill: University of North Carolina Press, 2007.

O'Shaughnessy, Andrew Jackson. *An Empire Divided: The American Revolution and the British Caribbean*. Philadelphia: University of Pennsylvania Press, 2000.

Parrish, Susan Scott. *American Curiosity: Cultures of Natural History in the Colonial British Atlantic World*. Chapel Hill: University of North Carolina Press, 2007.

Pestana, Carla Gardina. *The English Atlantic in an Age of Revolution, 1640–1661*. Cambridge, MA: Harvard University Press, 2007.

Raven, James. *London Booksellers and Their American Customers: Transatlantic Literary Community and the Charleston Library Society, 1748–1811*. Columbia: University of South Carolina Press, 2001.

Rhoden, Nancy L., ed. *English Atlantics Revisited: Essays Honoring Ian K. Steele*. Montreal: McGill-Queen's University Press, 2007.

Rushforth, Brett, Paul Mapp, and Alan Taylor, eds. *Colonial North America and the Atlantic World: A History in Documents*. New York: Prentice Hall, 2008.

Shannon, Timothy. *Atlantic Lives: A Comparative Approach to Early America*. New York: Pearson Longman, 2004.

Siminoff, Faren, ed. *Crossing the Sound: The Rise of Atlantic American Communities in Seventeenth Century Eastern Long Island*. New York: New York University Press, 2004.

Steele, Ian Kenneth. *The English Atlantic, 1675–1740: An Exploration of Communication and Community*. New York: Oxford University Press, 1986.

Vigne, Randolph, and Charles Littleton, eds. *From Strangers to Citizens: The Integration of Immigrant Communities in Britain, Ireland and Colonial America 1550–1750*. Brighton: Sussex Academic Press, 2001.

Ward, Lee. *The Politics of Liberty in England and Revolutionary America*. Cambridge: Cambridge University Press, 2004.

Irish, Scottish, and Welsh Atlantic

Canny, Nicholas. *Kingdom and Colony: Ireland in the Atlantic World 1500–1800*. Baltimore: Johns Hopkins University Press, 1988.

———. *Making Ireland British 1580–1650*. New York: Oxford University Press, 2001.

Gleeson, David T. *The Irish in the South 1815–1877*. Chapel Hill: University of North Carolina Press, 2001.

Griffin, Patrick. "America's Changing Image in Ireland's Looking-Glass: Provincial Construction of an Eighteenth-Century British Atlantic World." *Journal of Imperial and Commonwealth History* 26, no. 2 (1998): 28–49.

Hamilton, Douglas. *Scotland, the Caribbean, and the Atlantic World, 1750–1820*. New York: Palgrave, 2005.

Miller, Kerby A., Arnold Schrier, Bruce Boling, and David Doyle, eds. *Irish Immigrants in the Land of Canaan: Letters and Memoirs from the Colonial and Revolutionary America 1675–1815*. New York: Oxford University Press, 2003.

Simonson, Harold P. "Jonathan Edwards and his Scottish Connections." *Journal of American Studies* 21, no. 3 (1987): 353–76.

Szasz, Margaret. *Scottish Highlanders and Native Americans: Indigenous Education in the Eighteenth Century Atlantic World*. Norman: University of Oklahoma Press, 2007.

Williams, Gwyn A. "Frontier of Illusion: The Welsh and the Atlantic Revolution." *History Today* 30, no. 1 (1980): 39–45.

Wilson, David A., and Mark G. Spencer, eds. *Ulster Presbyterians in the Atlantic World: Religion, Politics, and Identity*. Dublin: Four Courts Press, 2006.

Dutch Atlantic

Emmer, Pieter. *The Dutch in the Atlantic Economy, 1580–1880: Trade, Slavery, and Emancipation*. Aldershot: Ashgate, 1998.

Emmer, Pieter, and Wim Klooster. "The Dutch Atlantic, 1600–1800: Expansion without Empire." *Itinerario* 23, no. 2 (1999): 48–69.

Frijhoff, Willem. *Fulfilling God's Mission: The Two Worlds of Dominie Everardus Bogardus, 1607–1647*. Leiden: Brill, 2007.

Goodfriend, Joyce, ed. *Revisiting New Netherland: Perspectives on Early Dutch America*. Leiden: Brill, 2005.

Jacobs, Jaap. *New Netherland: A Dutch Colony in Seventeenth Century America*. Leiden: Brill, 2005.

Klooster, Wim. *The Dutch in the Americas, 1600–1800*. Providence, RI: John Carter Brown Library, 1997.

———, ed. *Power and the City in the Netherlandic World*. Leiden: Brill, 2006.

Page, Willie F. *The Dutch Triangle: The Netherlands and the Atlantic Slave Trade, 1621–1664*. New York: Garland, 1997.

Postma, Johannes M. *The Dutch in the Atlantic Slave Trade, 1600–1815*. Cambridge: Cambridge University Press, 1990.

Postma, Johannes M., and Victor Enthoven, eds. *Riches from Atlantic Commerce: Dutch Transatlantic Trade and Shipping, 1585–1817*. Leiden: Brill, 2003.

Schmidt, Benjamin. *Innocence Abroad: The Dutch Imagination and the New World 1570–1670*. Cambridge: Cambridge University Press, 2001.

VandenBogaart, Annette M. "The Life of Teuntje Straatmans: A Dutch Woman's Travels in the Seventeenth Century Atlantic." *Long Island Historical Journal* 15, no. 1–2 (2002–2003): 35–53.

French Atlantic

Banks, Kenneth J. *Chasing Empire across the Sea: Communications and the State in the French Atlantic 1713–1763*. Montreal: McGill-Queen's University Press, 2002.

Blaufarb, Rafe. *Bonapartists in the Borderlands: French Exiles and Refugees on the Gulf Coast, 1815–1835*. Tuscaloosa: University of Alabama Press, 2005.

Bond, Bradley, ed. *French Colonial Louisiana and the Atlantic World*. Baton Rouge: Louisiana State University Press, 2005.

Drayton, Richard. "The Globalization of France: Provincial Cities and French Expansion, c.1500–1800." *History of European Ideas* 34, no. 4 (December 2008): 424–30.

Dubois, Laurent. *Avengers of the New World: The Story of the Haitian Revolution*. Boston: Belknap Press, 2005.

Kramer, Lloyd. *Lafayette in Two Worlds: Public Cultures and Personal Identities in an Age of Revolutions*. Chapel Hill: University of North Carolina Press, 1999.

Mandelblatt, Bertie. "Beans from Rochel and Manioc from Prince's Island: West Africa, French Atlantic Commodity Circuits, and the Provisioning of the French Middle Passage." *History of European Ideas* 34, no. 4 (December 2008): 411–23.

Marzagalli, Silvia. "The French Atlantic." *Itinerario* 23, no. 2 (1999): 70–83.

Meadows, R. Darrell. "Engineering Exile: Social Networks and the French Atlantic Community, 1789–1809." *French Historical Studies* 23, no. 1 (Winter 2000): 67–102.

Pritchard, James. *In Search of Empire: The French in the Americas, 1670–1730*. Cambridge: Cambridge University Press, 2004.

Robbins, Kevin C. *City on the Ocean Sea: La Rochelle 1530–1650, Urban Society, Religion, and Politics on the French Atlantic Frontier*. Leiden: Brill, 1997.

Van Ruymbeke, Bertrand, and Randy J. Sparks, eds. *Memory and Identity: The Huguenots in France and the Atlantic Diaspora*. Columbia: University of South Carolina Press, 2003.

Luso-Iberian Atlantic

Adelman, Jeremy. *Sovereignty and Revolution in the Iberian Atlantic*. Princeton, NJ: Princeton University Press, 2006.

Bleichmar, Daniela, Paula de Vos, Kristin Huffine, and Kevin Sheehan. *Science in the Spanish and Portuguese Empires, 1500–1800*. Stanford, CA: Stanford University Press, 2008.

Cañizares-Esguerra, Jorge. *Nature, Empire, and Nation: Explorations of the History of Science in the Iberian World*. Stanford, CA: Stanford University Press, 2006.

———. *Puritan Conquistadors: Iberianizing the Atlantic, 1550–1700*. Stanford, CA: Stanford University Press, 2006.

Chávez, Thomas. *Spain and the Independence of the United States*. Albuquerque: University of New Mexico Press, 2002.

Costigan, Lucia Helena. *Through Cracks in the Wall: Modern Inquisitions and New Christian Letrados in the Iberian Atlantic*. Leiden: Brill, 2010.

Curto, José C. *Enslaving Spirits: The Portuguese-Brazilian Alcohol Trade at Luanda and Its Hinterland, c 1550–1830*. Boston: Brill, 2004.

Elliott, J. H. *Empires of the Atlantic World: Britain and Spain in America, 1492–1830.* New Haven, CT: Yale University Press, 2006.

Fuente, Alejandro de la. *Havana and the Atlantic World in the Sixteenth Century.* Chapel Hill: University of North Carolina Press, 2008.

Newson, Linda, and Susie Minchin. *From Capture to Sale: The Portuguese Slave Trade to Spanish South America in the Early Seventeenth Century.* Leiden: Brill, 2007.

Pescador, Juan Javier. *The New World inside a Basque Village: The Oiartzun Valley and Its Atlantic Emigrants, 1550–1800.* Reno: University of Nevada Press, 2004.

Pieper, Renate, and Peer Schmidt, eds. *Latin America in the Atlantic World.* Köln: Böhlau, 2005.

Racine, Karen. *Francisco de Miranda: A Transatlantic Life in the Age of Revolution.* Wilmington, DE: Scholarly Resources, 2002.

Russell, P. E. *Portugal, Spain and the African Atlantic, 1343–1490: Chivalry and Crusade from John of Gaunt to Henry the Navigator.* Aldershot: Variorum, 2005.

Schultz, Kristin. *Tropical Versailles: Empire, Monarchy and the Portuguese Royal Court in Rio de Janeiro, 1808–1821.* New York: Routledge, 2001.

Schwartz, Stuart B. *The Iberian Mediterranean and Atlantic Traditions in the Formation of Columbus as Colonizer.* Minneapolis: University of Minnesota, Associates of the James Ford Bell Library, 1986.

———. *All Can Be Saved: Religious Tolerance and Salvation in the Iberian Atlantic.* New Haven, CT: Yale University Press, 2009.

Studnicki-Gizbert, Daviken. *A Nation upon the Ocean Sea: Portugal's Atlantic Diaspora and the Crisis of the Spanish Empire.* Oxford: Oxford University Press, 2007.

Subrahmanyam, Sanjay. "Holding the World in Balance: The Connected Histories of the Iberian Overseas Empires, 1500–1640." *American Historical Review* 112, no. 5 (December 2007): 1359–85.

Wilcken, Patricia. *Empire Adrift: The Portuguese Court in Rio de Janeiro 1808–1821.* London: Bloomsbury, 2005.

African Atlantic

Andrews, George Reid. *Afro-Latin America 1800–2000.* Oxford: Oxford University Press, 2004.

Brown, Vincent. *The Reaper's Garden: Death and Power in the World of Atlantic Slavery.* Cambridge, MA: Harvard University Press, 2008.

Byrd, Alexander. *Captives and Voyagers: Black Migrants across the Eighteenth-Century British Atlantic.* Baton Rouge: Louisiana State University Press, 2008.

Carney, Judith. *In the Shadow of Slavery: Africa's Botanical Legacy in the Atlantic World.* Berkeley: University of California Press, 2010.

Curtin, Philip D. *The Atlantic Slave Trade: A Census.* Madison: University of Wisconsin Press, 1969.

Curto, José, and Renée Soulodre-LaFrance, eds. *Africa and the Americas: Interconnections during the Slave Trade.* Trenton, NJ: Africa World Press, 2004.

Eltis, David, Philip Morgan, and David Richardson. "Agency and Diaspora in Atlantic History: Reassessing the African Contribution to Rice Cultivation in the Americas." *American Historical Review* 112, no. 5 (December 2007): 1329–58.

Fabre, Geneviève, and Klaus Benesch, eds. *African Diasporas in the Old and New Worlds: Consciousness and Imagination.* Amsterdam: Rodopi, 2004.

Falola, Toyin, and Matt Childs, eds. *The Yoruba Diaspora in the Atlantic World.* Bloomington: Indiana University Press, 2005.

Geggus, David P., ed. *The Impact of the Haitian Revolution in the Atlantic World.* Columbia: University of South Carolina Press, 2001.

Gilroy, Paul. *The Black Atlantic: Modernity and Double Consciousness.* Cambridge, MA: Harvard University Press, 1995.

Heywood, Linda M., and John Thornton. *Central Africans, Atlantic Creoles, and the Foundation of the Americas, 1585–1660.* Cambridge: Cambridge University Press, 2007.

Inikori, Joseph, and Stanley Engerman, eds. *The Atlantic Slave Trade: Effects on Economies, Societies and Peoples in Africa, the Americas and Europe.* Durham, NC: Duke University Press, 1992.

Kerr-Ritchie, J. R. *Rites of August First: Emancipation Day in the Black Atlantic.* Baton Rouge: Louisiana State University Press, 2007.

Linebaugh, Peter, and Marcus Rediker. "The Many-Headed Hydra: Sailors, Slaves, and the Atlantic Working Class in the Eighteenth Century." *Journal of Historical Sociology* 3, no. 3 (1990): 225–52.

Lovejoy, Paul, Naana Opoku-Agyemang, and David V. Trotman. *Africa and Trans-Atlantic Memories: Literary and Aesthetic Manifestations of Diaspora and History.* Lawrenceville, NJ: Africa World Press, 2008.

Mamigonian, Beatriz G., and Karen Racine, eds. *The Human Tradition in the Black Atlantic 1500–2000.* Boulder, CO: Rowman & Littlefield, 2009.

Mann, Kristin. "Shifting Paradigms in the Study of the African Diaspora and of Atlantic History and Culture." *Slavery and Abolition* 22, no. 1 (2001): 3–21.

Matory, J. Lorand. *Black Atlantic Religion: Tradition, Transnationalism and Matriarchy in Afro-Brazilian Candomblé.* Princeton, NJ: Princeton University Press, 2005.

Mitchell, Mary Niall. "A Good and Delicious Country: Free Children of Color and How They Learned to Imagine the Atlantic World in Nineteenth-Century Louisiana." *History of Education Quarterly* 40, no. 2 (2000): 123–44.

Morgan, Philip. *African American Life in the Georgia Lowcountry: The Atlantic World and the Gullah Geechee.* Athens: University of Georgia Press, 2010.

Northup, David, ed. *The Atlantic Slave Trade.* Boston: Houghton Mifflin, 2002.

———. *Crosscurrents in the Black Atlantic, 1770–1965.* New York: Bedford/St. Martin's, 2007.

Ogundiran, Akinwumi, and Toyin Falola, eds. *Archaeology of Atlantic Africa and the African Diaspora.* Bloomington: Indiana University Press, 2007.

Okpewho, Isidore, Carole Boyce Davies, and Ali Mazrui, eds. *The African Diaspora: African Origins and New World Identities.* Bloomington: Indiana University Press, 1999.

Potkay, Adam, and Sandra Burr, eds. *Black Atlantic Writers of the Eighteenth Century.* New York: Palgrave Macmillan, 1995.

Scott, Rebecca. *Degrees of Freedom: Louisiana and Cuba after Slavery.* Boston: Belknap Press, 2005.

Scully, Pamela, and Diana Paton, eds. *Gender and Slave Emancipation in the Atlantic World.* Durham, NC: Duke University Press, 2005.

Sensbach, Jon. *Rebecca's Revival: Creating Black Christianity in the Atlantic World.* Cambridge, MA: Harvard University Press, 2006.

Shepherd, Verene A., and Hilary McD. Beckles, eds. *Caribbean Slavery in the Atlantic World: A Student Reader.* Kingston: Ian Randle, 2000.

Smallwood, Stephanie. *Saltwater Slavery: A Middle Passage from Africa to American Diaspora.* Cambridge, MA: Harvard University Press, 2007.

Solow, Barbara, ed. *Slavery and the Rise of the Atlantic System.* Cambridge: Cambridge University Press, 1991.

Thornton, John. *Africa and Africans in the Making of the Atlantic World 1400–1680.* Cambridge: Cambridge University Press, 1992.

———. *The Kongolese St. Anthony: Dona Beatriz Kimpa Vita and the Antonian Movement, 1684–1706.* Cambridge: Cambridge University Press, 1998.

———. *Warfare in Atlantic Africa.* London: University College London Press, 1999.

Walvin, James. *Making the Black Atlantic: Britain and the African Diaspora.* London: Cassell, 2000.

Indigenous Atlantic

Axtell, James. *Natives and Newcomers: The Cultural Origins of North America.* New York: Oxford University Press, 2001.

Bickham, Troy. *Savages within the Empire: Representations of American Indians in Eighteenth Century Britain.* Oxford: Oxford University Press, 2005.

Blanton, Dennis B., and Julia A. King, eds. *Indian and European Contact in Context: The Mid-Atlantic Region.* Gainesville: University Press of Florida, 2004.

Boucher, Philip P. *Cannibal Encounters: Europeans and Island Caribs, 1492–1763.* Baltimore: Johns Hopkins University Press, 1992.

Bourne, Russell. *Gods of War, Gods of Peace: How the Meeting of Native and Colonial Religions Shaped Early America.* New York: Harcourt, 2002.

Calloway, Colin G. *New Worlds for All: Indians, Europeans and the Remaking of Early America.* Baltimore: Johns Hopkins University Press, 1997.

Cohen, Paul. "Was There an Amerindian Atlantic? Reflections on the Limits of a Historiographical Concept." *History of European Ideas* 34, no. 4 (December 2008): 388–410.

Forbes, Jack D. *The American Discovery of Europe.* Urbana: University of Illinois Press, 2007.

Hall, John W. *Uncommon Defense: Indian Allies in the Black Hawk War.* Cambridge, MA: Harvard University Press, 2009.

Hindebaker, Eric. *The Two Hendricks: Unraveling a Mohawk Mystery*. Cambridge, MA: Harvard University Press, 2010.

Mallios, Seth. *The Deadly Politics of Giving: Exchange and Violence at Ajacan, Roanoke, and Jamestown*. Tuscaloosa: University of Alabama Press, 2006.

Merritt, Jane T. *At the Crossroads: Indians and Empires on a Mid-Atlantic Frontier, 1700–1763*. Chapel Hill: University of North Carolina Press, 2003.

Roeber, A. G., ed. *Ethnographies and Exchanges: Native Americans, Moravians, and Catholics in Early North America*. University Park: Pennsylvania State University Press, 2008.

Silver, Timothy. *A New Face in the Countryside: Indians, Colonists and Slaves in South Atlantic Forests, 1500–1800*. Cambridge: Cambridge University Press, 1990.

Stevens, Laura M. *The Poor Indians: British Missionaries, Native Americans, and Colonial Sensibility*. Philadelphia: University of Pennsylvania Press, 2004.

Vaughn, Alden. *Transatlantic Encounters: American Indians in Britain 1500–1776*. Cambridge: Cambridge University Press, 2006.

Mercantile Atlantic

Birmingham, David. *Trade and Empire in the Atlantic 1400–1600*. London: Routledge, 2000.

Bruyn Kops, Henriette de. *A Spirited Exchange: The Wine and Brandy Trade between France and the Dutch Republic in Its Atlantic Framework, 1600–1650*. Leiden: Brill, 2007.

Cesarani, David, ed. *Port Jews: Jewish Communities in Cosmopolitan Maritime Trading Centres, 1550–1950*. London: Frank Cass, 2002.

Coclanis, Peter, ed. *The Atlantic Economy during the Seventeenth and Eighteenth Centuries: Organization, Operation, Practice and Personnel*. Columbia: University of South Carolina Press, 2005.

Davis, Ralph. *The Rise of Atlantic Economies*. Ithaca, NY: Cornell University Press, 1987.

Evans, Chris. *Baltic Iron in the Atlantic World in the Eighteenth Century*. Leiden: Brill, 2007.

Farley, James. "The Ill-Fated Voyage of the Providentia: Richard Vaux, Loyalist Merchant, and the Trans-Atlantic Mercantile World in the Late Eighteenth Century." *Pennsylvania History* 62, no. 3 (1995): 364–75.

Finn, Janet L. *Tracing the Veins of Copper, Culture and Community from Butte to Chuquimata*. Berkeley: University of California Press, 1998.

Gervais, Pierre. "Neither Imperial, nor Atlantic: A Merchant Perspective on International Trade in the Eighteenth Century." *History of European Ideas* 34, no. 4 (December 2008): 465–73.

Haggerty, Sheryllynne. *The British Atlantic Trading Community, 1760–1810: Men, Women, and the Distribution of Goods*. Leiden: Boston, 2006.

Hancock, David. *Citizens of the World: London Merchants and the Integration of the British Atlantic Community, 1735–1785*. Cambridge: Cambridge University Press, 1995.

————. "The British Atlantic World: Co-ordination, Complexity, and the Emergence of an Atlantic Market Economy, 1651–1815." *Itinerario* 23, no. 2 (1999): 107–26.

Hunter, Phyllis Whitman. *Purchasing Identity in the Atlantic World: Massachusetts Merchants, 1670–1780*. Ithaca, NY: Cornell University Press, 2001.

Janzen, Olaf Uwe. *Merchant Organization and Maritime Trade in the North Atlantic, 1660–1815*. St. John's: International Maritime Economic History Association, 1998.

Kagan, Richard, and Philip D. Morgan, eds. *Atlantic Diasporas: Jews, Conversos and Crypto-Jews in the Age of Mercantilism, 1500–1800*. Baltimore: Johns Hopkins University Press, 2008.

Klooster, Wim. "Winds of Change: Colonization, Commerce and Consolidation in the Seventeenth-Century Atlantic World." *Halve Maen* 70, no. 3 (1997): 53–58.

Liss, Peggy. *Atlantic Empires: The Network of Trade and Revolution, 1713–1826*. Baltimore: Johns Hopkins University Press, 1983.

Liss, Peggy, and Franklin Knight, eds. *Atlantic Port Cities, 1650–1850*. Knoxville: University of Tennessee Press, 1991.

Moya Pons, Frank. *History of the Caribbean: Plantations, Trade, and War in the Atlantic World*. Princeton, NJ: Markus Wiener Publications, 2007.

O'Hearn, Denis. *The Atlantic Economy: Britain, the US and Ireland*. Manchester and New York: Manchester University Press and Palgrave, 2001.

Ormrod, David. *The Rise of Commercial Empires: England and the Netherlands in the Age of Mercantilism*. Cambridge: Cambridge University Press, 2003.

Rediker, Marcus. *Between the Devil and the Deep Blue Sea: Merchant Seamen, Pirates, and the Anglo-American Maritime World, 1700–1750*. Cambridge: Cambridge University Press, 1993.

————. *Villains of All Nations: Atlantic Pirates in the Golden Age*. Boston: Beacon Press, 2004.

Rediker, Marcus, and Peter Linebaugh. *The Many-Headed Hydra: Sailors, Slaves, Commoners and the Hidden History of the Revolutionary Atlantic*. Boston: Beacon Press, 2000.

Roper, L. H., and B. van Ruymbeke, eds. *Constructing Early Modern Empires: Proprietary Ventures in the Atlantic World, 1500–1750*. Leiden: Brill, 2007.

Schwartz, Stuart B., ed. *Tropical Babylons: Sugar and the Making of the Atlantic World 1570–1670*. Chapel Hill: University of North Carolina Press, 2004.

Townsend, Camilla. *A Tale of Two Cities: Race, Gender and Economic Culture in Early Republican North and South America (Guayaquil and Baltimore)*. Austin: University of Texas Press, 2000.

Tracy, James, ed. *The Rise of Merchant Empires: Long-Distance Trade in the Early Modern World, 1350–1750*. Cambridge: Cambridge University Press, 1990.

Vicente, Marta. *Clothing the Spanish Empire: Families and the Calico Trade in the Early Modern Atlantic World*. New York: Palgrave Macmillan, 2006.

Filmography

1492: Conquest of Paradise (director: Ridley Scott, 1992) 154 mins. Dramatic and highly inaccurate retelling of Columbus's voyages to the New World, in which he is depicted as a hero and savior of the Taino people he encountered.

1776 (director: Peter H. Hunt, 1972). This film grew out of a successful Broadway musical and reflects the contentious political atmosphere of the 1970s and consciously invokes the Founding Fathers' vision of freedom in the midst of war. Authors and scriptwriters have incorporated dialogue drawn from actual historical documents produced by Washington, Franklin, John Adams, and John Hancock, among others.

Adanggaman (director: Roger Gnoan M'Bala, 2000) 90 mins. Set in West Africa in the seventeenth century, this fictionalized account of enslavement and the slave trade opposes the actions of King Adanggaman, who orders his forces to raid villages of other kingdoms and sell residents into slavery, and Ossei, whose family is affected by these acts.

Aguirre, Wrath of God / Aguirre, der Zorn Gottes (director: Werner Herzog, 1972) 93 mins. A stylized and embellished artistic representation of the life of Basque explorer Lope de Aguirre, who joined the expedition of Pedro de Ursúa to seek out the mythical kingdom of El Dorado along the Amazon River in 1560. During the voyage, in circumstances that still remain murky, Aguirre led a mutiny, killed Ursúa, and ultimately was captured and executed by agents of the Spanish king at Barquisimeto.

Amazing Grace (director: Michael Apted, 2006) 111 mins. British abolitionist William Wilberforce spent decades lobbying his fellow members of Parliament to end their country's transatlantic slave trade and used the Christian hymn "Amazing Grace" to help make an emotional, religious, and moral case against slavery. The Slave Trade Act finally passed in 1807, at great personal cost to Wilberforce.

Amistad (director: Steven Spielberg, 1997) 152 mins. Based on the true story of a mutiny aboard the slave ship *Amistad* in 1839 led by a former African tribal leader named Cinque. When the ship landed on U.S. territory, the rebels were seized as runaway slaves. The film focuses on the trial of their case before the U.S. Supreme Court, where they were defended by the abolitionist, former president John Quincy Adams.

Atlantic Ferry (director: Walter Forde, 1941) 98 mins. Set in 1840, the film tells a fictionalized story of two rival companies who were in an energetic competition to create the fastest steamship cargo line between the United States and Great Britain (although real historical figures like Samuel Cunard are incorporated into the narrative). The film's topic carried particular contemporary relevance because it was made during World War II, a time when U.S. and British naval cooperation in the Atlantic theater was gaining strategic significance.

Battle of the Brave / New France / Nouvelle France (director: Jean Boudin, 2005) 143 mins. Set in Montreal and New France (today Québec) in the tumultuous 1760s as England and France battled for control of Canada, this epic film tells the fictional love story of a trapper and a impoverished widow.

Beaumarchais, The Scoundrel / Beaumarchais, l'Insolent (director: Eduard Molinaro, 1996) 116 mins. This French film depicts the dashing life of Pierre-Augustin Caron de Beaumarchais, author of *The Barber of Seville*, an Enlightenment libertine who was a playwright, a spy for the French king, a notorious lover, and a gun smuggler during the American Revolution.

Belizaire the Cajun (director: Glen Pitre, 1986) 103 mins. Drama set in mid-nineteenth-century Louisiana in which the title character attempted to defend his brethren from persecution by English-speaking state officials and local landowners who viewed the French- and Creole-speaking Cajuns as uncivilized obstacles to economic progress.

Black Robe (director: Bruce Beresford, 1991) 101 mins. Recounts the challenges faced by two idealistic young Jesuit priests venturing through the forests of New France (today Québec) to join a mission dedicated to the conversion of the Algonquin and Huron Indians. Based on a historical novel by Brian Moore, the film emphasizes the priest's spiritual journey in an unforgiving environment and makes an argument for the mutual incomprehension of the European and Amerindian cultures.

Blackbeard the Pirate (director: Raoul Walsh, 1952) 99 mins. A treatment of the life and activities of the Caribbean pirates Henry Morgan and Edward "Blackbeard" Teach as seen through the eyes of a bounty hunter masquerading as a ship's captain.

Bonnie Prince Charlie (director: Anthony Kimmins, 1948) 136 mins. A dramatized take on the life of Charles Edward Stuart (also known as the "Young Pretender"), the exiled Jacobite claimant to the British throne who was defeated by the Duke of Northumberland at the momentous Battle of Culloden in 1746.

The Buccaneer (director: Anthony Quinn, 1958) 119 mins. Inaccurate but entertaining film based on the life of Louisiana pirate-bootlegger Jean Lafitte, who agreed to help U.S. General Andrew Jackson and his vastly outnumbered forces defeat the British during the War of 1812.

Cabeza de Vaca (director: Nicolás Echevarría, 1991) 111 mins. An innovative Mexican production that retells the life of Álvar Núñez Cabeza de Vaca, whose ship ran aground off the Florida coast in 1528 and who then spent eight years wandering around the Rio Grande territories, living among indigenous people and learning their languages and shamanic traditions before returning to Spain to publish an account of his experiences and advocate more humane policies.

Captain from Castile (director: Henry King, 1948) 140 mins. Purports to tell the dramatic story of Hernán Cortés's conquest of Mexico-Tenochtitlán in 1518 through the eyes of a fictional young foot soldier named Pedro de Vargas.

Captain John Smith and Pocahontas (director: Lew Landers, 1953) 75 mins. Picks up the often-told tale of the relationship between the English settler Captain John Smith at Jamestown and his Powhatan love Pocahontas at the point where Smith had returned to England to plead his case before the court of James I.

Carlota Joaquina, Princess of Brazil / Carlota Joaquina, Princesa do Brazil (director: Carla Camurati, 1995) 100 mins. A dramatized retelling of the life of a Spanish princess who married the future King João VI of Portugal. When the Iberian Peninsula was threatened by Napoleon in 1808, she relocated to Brazil, where she immediately started plotting to take control of the Banda Oriental (today Uruguay) and Buenos Aires.

Catherine of England / Catalina de Inglaterra (director: Arturo Ruiz Castillo, 1951) 110 mins. A Spanish film that recounts the ill-fated marriage of Spanish Princess Catherine of Aragón and English King Henry VIII.

Cutthroat Island (director: Renny Harlin, 1995) 119 mins. Widely panned campy flick that capitalizes on the memory of famous female pirates Anny Bonny and Mary Read. Geena Davis stars as a slave-owning female pirate who set out in search of hidden treasure on a Caribbean island.

Danton (director: Andrzej Wajda, 1983) 136 mins. A French-Polish collaboration made on the two-hundredth anniversary of the year in which Robespierre and the Committee of Public Safety seized power during the early, violent stage of the revolution. Danton, played by Gérard Depardieu, is celebrated as a moderate man of reason and law.

Dawn of America / Alba de América (director: Juan de Orduña, 1951, 1952) 112 mins. A mid-century, Francoist-era retelling of Columbus's voyages to America that praised his efforts as an attempt to spread the benefits of Spanish civilization and the Catholic religion to the savage indigenous inhabitants of the New World.

Elizabeth (director: Shekhar Kapur, 1998) 124 mins. Starring Cate Blanchett, this film focuses on the formative years of the future Queen Elizabeth I, including her introduction to government, gender roles, social expectations, betrayal, and romantic love.

Elizabeth: The Golden Age (director: Shekhar Kapur, 2007) 114 mins. Another based-on-a-true-story film about Queen Elizabeth I of England, this one focusing on her complicated relationship with the explorer-settler Sir Walter Raleigh. There are many historical inaccuracies.

The Fighting Prince of Donegal (director: Michael O'Herlihy, 1966) 110 mins. Based on the life story of Hugh O'Donnell, Prince of Tyrconnell, who was kidnapped by the English Viceroy Sir John Perrot and used as a hostage to extract promises of obedience from the Irish clans and sow division among them. O'Donnell escaped and went on to lead the Nine Years' War from 1595 to 1603, which had as its goal the desire to drive English settlers out of Ireland.

Francisco de Miranda (director: Diego Rísquez, 2006). Venezuelan film that tells the adventurous life of the great Precursor, who fought in the American and French revolutions, knew Catherine the Great, and spent decades lobbying for British support for Spanish American independence before dying in a Cádiz prison in 1816.

How Tasty Was My Little Frenchman / Como Era Gostoso o Meu Francês (director: Nelson Pereira dos Santos, 1971) 84 mins. Tells the story of a French sailor who was captured, tried, and enslaved by the Tupinamba Indians of Brazil who mistook him for one of their enemy Portuguese. He integrated himself into Tupinamba society, formed a relationship with one of their women, and trained them in the use of gunpowder to defeat their indigenous enemies, the Tupiniquins, but ironically this led to him being eaten in a postvictory ritual.

Hudson's Bay (director: Irving Pichel, 1941) 95 mins. Recounts the story of Pierre Radisson, a French explorer who convinced King Charles II to sponsor his voyage to Canada, where he dreamed of establishing an empire based around Hudson's Bay in 1668. Highly fictionalized account of his relationships with the Iroquois, his activities along the St. Lawrence River, and the founding of the Hudson's Bay Company.

I, the Worst of All / Yo, la peor de todas (director: María Luisa Bemberg, 1990) 105 mins. Argentine film made during the transition from dictatorship to democracy, tells the life and sacrifice of seventeenth-century Mexican poet-nun Sor Juan Inés de la Cruz, who struggled between personal fulfillment and institutional censorship and labored under restrictive gender roles.

The Knight of the Sword / El Santo de la Espada (director: Leopoldo Torre Nilsson, 1970) 120 mins. Argentine film recounts the life of independence-era patriot General José de San Martín, who led the victorious Army of the Andes to victory in Chile and Peru.

Let Joy Reign Supreme / Que la fête commence . . . (director: Bertrand Tavernier, 1975) 114 mins. Set in France in 1719 during the regency of Philippe, the Duc d'Orleans, the film plays up the royal court's intrigues, the ecclesiastical power's venality, and the elites' dissolute behavior that preceded the French Revolution.

The Libertine (director: Laurence Dunmore, 2004) 114 mins. Johnny Depp stars in this version of the life of John Wilmot, the notorious second Earl of Rochester, who was a scandalous literary and court figure in Restoration England. Rochester was a poet, playwright, and libertine whose sexual excesses were legendary.

The Madness of King George (director: Nicholas Hytner, 1994) 107 mins. Based on a play by Alan Bennett, this film uses the story of King George III's bouts with dementia to serve as a metaphor for power, the loss of the American colonies, the importance of family, and the continuity of transatlantic affinities.

Mary, Queen of Scots (director: Charles Jarrott, 1972) 128 mins. Vanessa Redgrave stars as Mary Stuart, Queen of Scotland, who was imprisoned and eventually executed by her cousin and imperial rival Elizabeth Tudor (later Elizabeth I).

Master and Commander (director: Peter Weir, 2003) 138 mins. A fictionalized account of British and French naval rivalry during the Napoleonic Wars. Based on the novels of Patrick O'Brian.

Mayflower: The Pilgrims' Adventure (director: George Schaefer, 1979) 97 mins. A film version of the *Mayflower* Pilgrims emigration to the New World in 1620, this one idealizing the values of adventure, self-improvement, self-help, individualism, and freedom from persecution. A small hardy band of settlers struggle with each other and achieve reconciliation on the high seas.

Miranda Returns / Miranda regresa (director: Luis Alberto Lamata, 2007). Produced by President Hugo Chavez's state film studio to mark the two-hundredth anniversary of Miranda's effort to ignite a revolution for independence, this film sets up a heroic version of the Venezuelan-born precursor to Spanish American independence and emphasizes his commitment to the lower classes and slaves.

The Mission (director: Roland Joffé, 1986) 126 mins. Set in the 1740s as Spain and Portugal struggle for control of the disputed territory along the Paraguayan–Brazilian frontier, the film attempts to evoke an idyllic image of the colonial Spanish American *reducciones* (missions) as a haven for arts and culture and safe refuge for the Guaraní Indians who are hunted by slave traders.

The Monroe Doctrine (director: Crane Wilbur, 1939) 22 mins. A short, dramatized version of President Monroe's efforts to assert control over the Western Hemisphere by challenging Spain's claim to its rebellious American colonies.

Mrs. Fitzherbert (director: Montgomerty Tully, 1947) 99 mins. A dramatization of the life of Maria Anne Smythe Fitzherbert, a beautiful Catholic widow who married the Prince of Wales (the future George IV) in a secret ceremony in 1785. Despite true affection between the couple, the wedding was declared illegal under English civil law because of her religion.

The New World (director: Terrence Malick, 2005) 150 mins. Powhatan princess Pocahontas fell in love with seventeenth-century explorer-colonist John Smith but was tricked into believing that he died in a shipwreck and thus married another man, John Rolfe. On discovering the truth, she had to choose between her two English men.

No, or the Vain Glory of Command / 'Non,' ou A Vã Glória de Mandar (director: Manoel de Oliveira, 1990) 110 mins. Portuguese film that utilizes a narrator—a soldier marching through an African colony in 1972—to introduce episodes

in Portuguese military history, ranging over several centuries, including Roman
Lusitania, Vasco da Gama's discoveries, and colonial events in Africa and Brazil.

Old Ironsides (director: James Cruze, 1926) 111 mins. The USS *Constitution* headed
to the Mediterranean sea to help battle Barbary pirates in the early nineteenth
century.

Old Louisiana (director: Irvin Willat, 1937) 60 mins. Set in 1803 as the U.S. government was negotiating the Louisiana Purchase from France, this film dramatizes the
various plots and swirled around the bayou at that time. Settler John Colfax tried
to convince his neighbors to employ peaceful means to have their taxes and duties
removed, while a local fur company entrepreneur Luke Gilmore set himself up as
governor of the new territory backed by smuggled weapons and mercenary troops.
Tagline was "a stirring drama of the first historic conflict between an American
President and the Supreme Court."

One Man's Hero (director: Lance Hool, 1999) 121 mins. Tells the story of the San
Patricios, a famous brigade of Irish soldiers who experienced religious persecution
in the U.S. army, escaped to Mexico, and then fought on its behalf during the
Mexican-American War in 1846–1848.

Plymouth Adventure (director: Clarence Brown, 1952) 105 mins. Based on a novel by
Ernest Gebler and starring Spencer Tracy, this is a dramatized version of the 1620
Mayflower voyage that speculates that Captain Christopher Jones attempted to
seduce William Bradford's wife, resulting in a tragic love triangle.

Pocahontas (directors: Mike Gabriel and Eric Goldberg, 1995) 81 mins. The Disney
cartoon version of the legendary life of Princess Pocahontas, the daughter of a
Powhatan chief who fell in love with John Smith, a settler in seventeenth-century
Jamestown Colony.

The Pride and the Passion (director: Stanley Kramer, 1957). A historical drama starring Frank Sinatra, Cary Grant, and Sophia Loren that tells the story of a British officer who commanded a ragtag group of Spanish guerrillas fighting to clear
Napoleon's forces from Ávila by hauling a huge cannon to the battle. Based on a
novel by C. S. Forester, author of the Horatio Hornblower series set on the seas
during the Napoleonic era.

Princess Caraboo (director: Michael Austin, 1994) 97 mins. The story of a strange,
tattooed woman who turned up in Bristol in 1817, speaking an unknown language
and claiming to be a foreign princess. Her story quickly caught the imagination of
the British public, and she was housed by an aristocratic family who flaunted their
guest to their neighbors, academics, and journalists alike. The publicity backfired
when someone recognized the woman and identified her as an unemployed house
servant named Mary Wilcocks Baker.

The Private Lives of Elizabeth and Essex (director: Michael Curtiz, 1939) 106 mins. A
film adaptation of the notorious, highly speculative, and ill-starred relationship between the future Queen Elizabeth I and Robert Devereux, the Earl of Essex. Made
in the aftermath of another royal scandal caused by the 1936 abdication crisis

in which King Edward VIII gave up the throne to marry the divorced American Wallis Simpson.

Samuel Lount (director: Laurence Keane, 1985) 97 mins. Canadian film recounts the life of Samuel Lount, a blacksmith in Hollis Landing, Ontario, who was a dedicated pacifist, a Member of Parliament, and leader of the 1837 Upper Canada Rebellion against the slow pace of British government reforms.

The Sea Hawk (director: Michael Curtiz, 1940) 109 mins. A romanticized film about an Englishman who fled the comfortable life and joined the pirate forces that harassed the Spanish Armada as it advanced toward England in 1588.

Seven Cities of Gold (director: Robert D. Webb, 1955) 103 mins. Based on the expedition of Gaspar de Portolá in 1769 to seek out the fabled Seven Cities of Cíbola in the California territories and to settle the region to stave off the threat of Russian occupation. The film also includes the efforts of Franciscan friar Junípero Serra to evangelize and domesticate the indigenous people they encountered.

That Night in Varennes / La Nuit de Varennes (director: Ettore Scola, 1982) 135 mins. Set in 1791 as King Louis XVI and Marie Antoinette flee Paris with the intention of joining their monarchist supporters in exile before they are discovered and arrested in Varennes. This film, a joint production between France and Italy, imagines the attitudes and conversations of other contemporary travelers had they been journeying in a stagecoach at the same time, including Thomas Paine, Casanova, and one of the Queen's ladies-in-waiting.

The Virgin Queen (director: Henry Koster, 1955) 92 mins. Bette Davis stars as Queen Elizabeth in this film, which focuses on the monarch's relationship with Sir Walter Raleigh.

Waterloo (director: Sergei Bondarchuk, 1970) 123 mins. Recounts the dramatic battle of Waterloo, which put a decisive end to the Napoleonic Wars in June 1815. Picks up the story at the time of Napoleon's last great attempt to subdue the European continent on his escape from the island of Elba in February and the determination of the British general, the Duke of Wellington, to defeat him.

Young Bess (director: George Sidney, 1953) 112 mins. A fictionalized account of the future Queen Elizabeth I's youth and coming of age.

Index

About the Editors and Contributors

Editors

Beatriz G. Mamigonian earned a PhD from the University of Waterloo in Canada. She is a professor of history at the Universidade Federal de Santa Catarina in Brazil and also spent a semester as a visiting professor of history at Michigan State University. Her fields of study are comparative slavery and the African diaspora, and her research interests focus on the impact of British abolitionism on the Brazilian slave system throughout the nineteenth century and its human consequences. She is the coeditor (with Karen Racine) of *The Human Tradition in the Black Atlantic 1500–2000* (2009) and has also published a number of chapters in edited collections and journal articles in English and in Portuguese, including one in slavery and abolition. She is completing a book manuscript on the fate of the Africans who were emancipated in the course of the suppression activities in Brazil.

Karen Racine received her PhD from Tulane University and is associate professor of Latin American history at the University of Guelph in Canada. She is the author of *Francisco de Miranda: A Transatlantic Life in the Age of Revolution* (2003) and coeditor of *Strange Pilgrimages: Travel, Exile and National Identity in Latin America 1800–2000* (2000). Her current research focuses on cultural connections between Britain and Latin America in the late eighteenth and early nineteenth centuries and on patriotic civic culture in Spanish American independence. She is completing two book manuscripts, one on Latin American independence leaders in London and the other on British poet laureate Robert Southey's work on the Luso-Hispanic world.

Contributors

Robert D. Aguirre received his PhD in English and American literature and language and is associate professor of English at Wayne State University. He is the author of *Informal Empire: Mexico and Central America in Victorian Culture* (2005) and coeditor of *Connecting Continents: Britain and Latin America 1780–1900* (forthcoming) and has had articles appear in the journals *Victorian Studies*, *Victorian Review*, *Biography*, and *Genre*.

Troy Bickham received his DPhil from Oxford University and is assistant professor of history at Texas A&M University. He is the author of *Savages within the Empire: Representing the American Indians in the Eighteenth Century* (2005) and has had scholarly articles appear in *Eighteenth-Century Studies*, *Past and Present*, *Journal of Eighteenth-Century Studies*, and the *William and Mary Quarterly*.

Olwyn M. Blouet earned her PhD from the University of Nebraska and is professor of history at Virginia State University. She is the author of *The Contemporary Caribbean: History, Life, and Culture since 1945* (2007) and coauthor (with Brian Blouet) of the popular geography textbook *Latin America and the Caribbean: A Systematic Regional Survey* (5th ed., 2005) and has written several articles on education in the British Caribbean.

Sarah Cline has a PhD in history from the University of California, Los Angeles, and is professor of Latin American history at the University of California, Santa Barbara. She has published several books, including *The Book of Tributes: Early Sixteenth Century Nahuatl Censuses from Morelos* (2000), *Colonial Culhuacan 1580–1600: A Social History of an Aztec Town* (1986), and a critical edition of Bernardino Sahagún's *The Conquest of New Spain, 1585* (1989). Her current research focuses on the visual history of race and gender in colonial and mid-nineteenth-century Mexico.

Andrew B. Fisher earned a PhD from the University of California, San Diego, and is assistant professor at Carleton College. He was a faculty fellow at the Center for U.S.-Mexican Studies at the University of California, San Diego, for the 2006–2007 academic year. He is revising a book manuscript on the colonial history of the indigenous communities in the "tierra caliente" of the Mexican state of Guerrero and is coeditor (with Matthew O'Hara) of a collection of essays called *Imperial Subjects: Race and Identity in Colonial Latin America* (2009).

John Garrigus received a PhD from Johns Hopkins University and is associate professor of history at the University of Texas at Arlington. He was a Fulbright Professor at the École Normale Supérieure et Faculté d'Ethnologie at the State University of Haiti and has published widely on issues of race in colonial St. Domingue. His important recent books are *Slave Revolts in the Caribbean, 1789–1804: A Brief History with Documents* (with Laurent Dubois, 2006) and *Before Haiti: Race and Citizenship in French Saint-Domingue* (2006), and he is the editor of the *Encyclopedia of the Caribbean* (forthcoming). His current research focuses on the Haitian revolutionary leader Vicente Ogé.

Noah L. Gelfand is an assistant professor in the Humanities and Social Sciences at the Cooper Union in New York. He received his PhD in Atlantic and American history at New York University in 2008 with a dissertation that explored the commercial and communal activities of Jewish merchants in the Dutch Atlantic in the seventeenth and eighteenth centuries. He worked as an assistant editor and researcher for the Papers of Jacob Leisler Project and has been a research fellow at the John Carter Brown Library and the McNeil Center for Early American Studies. He is working on a book on the Jewish Atlantic.

Mark Hinchman is an associate professor of interior design at the University of Nebraska at Lincoln. He earned his master's in architecture from Cornell and his MA and PhD from the University of Chicago. He is a licensed architect in the state of Illinois and has worked for design firms in both the United States and Germany. He is a member of the Society of Architectural Historians, the College Art Association, the American Society of Eighteenth-Century Studies, and the West African Research Association.

Charlene Boyer Lewis received her PhD from the University of Virginia and is associate professor of history and director of American studies at Kalamazoo College. She is the author of *Ladies and Gentlemen on Display: Planter Society at the Virginia Springs 1790–1860* (2001) and has published an article on Elizabeth Patterson Bonaparte in the *Journal of Women's History*.

Gail Danvers MacLeitch earned a DPhil in at the University of Sussex and currently is a lecturer in American studies at King's College, London. She has received several research grants and is the author of two articles on Native American women in early American history. Her book *Imperial Entanglements: Iroquois Change and Persistence on the Frontiers of Empire* is (2010).

Mark Meuwese received his PhD from the University of Notre Dame and is assistant professor of history at the University of Winnipeg. His dissertation undertook a comparative history of the contacts between the Dutch and indigenous groups in Brazil and North America. He is the author of an article in the *Portuguese Studies Review* and several others in edited collections, all of which treat the subject of European contact with indigenous people in colonial Brazil.

Joan Meznar received a PhD from the University of Texas at Austin and is professor of history at Eastern Connecticut State University. She is a Brazilian specialist and has published articles on gender, religion, and religion. She is completing a book on faith and politics in Brazil's Old Republic.

John Navin has a PhD in American history from Brandeis University and is associate dean and associate professor of history at Coastal Carolina University. He has published several articles and delivered many conference presentations. His research interests lie in the colonial history of New England.

Jeff Pardue earned a PhD from the University of Waterloo and is associate professor of history at Gainesville State College in South Carolina. His research focuses on James MacQueen and the changing nature of British imperialism in the nineteenth century.

Magnus Roberto de Mello Pereira received his doctorate from the Universidade Federal do Paraná, where he is currently professor of history. One of his major publications is *Semeando iras rumo ao progresso: Ordenamento jurídico e econômico da sociedade paranaense, 1829–1889* (1996).

Cassandra Pybus received her PhD in history from the University of Sydney, where she currently teaches and also holds a prestigious Australian Research Council Research Chair. She is the author of eleven books, most recently *Epic Journeys of Freedom: Runaway Slaves of the American Revolution and Their Global Quest for Liberty* (2006), and is coeditor (with Marcus Rediker and Emma Christopher) of *Other Middle Passages: Forced Migration and the Making of the Modern World* (2007).